Ernst Wolff
Between Daily Routine and Violent Protest

Ernst Wolff

Between Daily Routine and Violent Protest

Interpreting the Technicity of Action

DE GRUYTER

 The publication of both paper and OA versions of this book was made possible by Internal Funds from the KU Leuven.

ISBN 978-3-11-126722-7
e-ISBN (PDF) 978-3-11-072504-9
e-ISBN (EPUB) 978-3-11-072514-8
DOI https://doi.org/10.1515/9783110724974

This work is licensed under the Creative Commons Attribution-NonCommercial-NoDerivatives 4.0 International License. For details go to http://creativecommons.org/licenses/by-nc-nd/4.0/.

Library of Congress Control Number: 2021905145

Bibliographic information published by the Deutsche Nationalbibliothek
The Deutsche Nationalbibliothek lists this publication in the Deutsche Nationalbibliografie; detailed bibliographic data are available on the Internet at http://dnb.dnb.de.

© 2023 Ernst Wolff, published by Walter de Gruyter GmbH, Berlin/Boston
This volume is text- and page-identical with the hardback published in 2021.
The book is published open access at www.degruyter.com.

Printing and binding: CPI books GmbH, Leck

www.degruyter.com

Preface

Most human action has a technical dimension. This book is a first consolidation of my research into this simple fact. On the one hand it required an examination of the two constituents of the technicity of action: acquired capabilities and the means of action. On the other, I had to examine the interrelation between the technicity of action and how it is activated, given its tension with normative considerations. I have followed the intuition that the technicity of action stretches as far as human action itself, including spheres of interaction where there are good reasons to fear a technicist reduction of action, namely ethics and politics. Consequently, my study covers the entire gamut of human action between the extremes of daily routine and violent protest.

Although it is clearly impossible to discuss every kind of human action, the chapters of this book cover a substantial and representative selection of major forms of action. Moreover, the interdisciplinary cast of the book is aimed at rendering what can be considered core features of action in all human beings, while giving us the means by which to remain attentive to the socio-historical particularities of action as it plays out in different contexts. Hermeneutics (understood as the philosophical inquiry into the human phenomena of meaning, understanding and interpretation) and social science (as the study of all human affairs) represent the two main disciplinary orientations of this book. There are many books of philosophy and of social theory in which hermeneutics is simply understood as synonymous with the name of Hans-Georg Gadamer. In the Introduction I explain why I have instead chosen Paul Ricœur as my principal hermeneutic interlocutor for the purposes of this book.

Previous versions of some of the chapters have been published elsewhere. I thank the journals and publishers for permission to include translated, reworked and expanded versions of these texts here: "Transmettre et interpreter," *Médium* 6 (January-March 2006): 30–47 / "Mediologie en hermeneutiek," *Tydskrif vir Geesteswetenskappe* 47, no. 1 (March 2007): 81–94; "Habitus – means – worldliness. Technics and the formation of 'civilisations'," in Oliver Kozlarek, Jörn Rüsen and Ernst Wolff, eds., *Shaping a Humane World – Civilizations, Axial Times, Modernities, Humanisms* (Bielefeld: Transcript, 2012), 25–53; "Compétences et moyens de l'homme capable à la lumière de l'incapacité," *Études Ricœuriennes / Ricœur Studies* 4, no. 2 (2013), 50–63; "Ricœur et Giddens: l'herméneutique de l'homme capable et la théorie de structuration," *Études Ricœuriennes /Ricœur Studies* 5, no. 2 (2014), 105–127; "Of what is 'Ricœur' the name? Or, philosophising at the edge," *Leuven Philosophy Newsletter* 26 (2018–2019), 7–22; and "Justice despite institutions. Struggling for a good life from the destitute edge of society," in Geoffrey Dierckxsens, ed., *The Ambiguity of Justice. New Perspectives on Paul Ricœur's Approach to Justice* (Leiden: Brill, 2020), 97–127.

Over many years of ruminating on this project, I have had the benefit of hospitality and funding for which I would like to express my gratitude. I was generously received by Jörn Rüsen (Kulturwissenschaftliches Institut in Essen), a visit partially funded by the Mercator Stiftung, Axel Honneth (Goethe University in Frankfurt), supported by the Alexander von Humboldt Stiftung, and Olivier Abel and Laurent Thévenot (in the framework of the Fonds Ricœur and the EHESS, Paris), where two research visits were partially funded by the National Research Foundation of South Africa at a time when I was still employed at the University of Pretoria.

I would like to thank Idette Noomé very warmly for her indefatigable work in editing the final manuscript. Rachel Mahlangu and her colleagues at the library of the University of Pretoria, and Stefan Derouck and his colleagues at the library of the KU Leuven deserve my grateful recognition for their services to me in this project. Christoph Schirmer, Mara Weber, Florian Ruppenstein and their colleagues at De Gruyter have accompanied me through the publication phase of this book in a most professional way. Finally, I would like to express my deepest gratitude to my wife and children for their patience and support.

Ernst Wolff
KU Leuven, May 2020

Contents

Introduction

The Technical Dimension of Action —— 3
1. Basic Orientation: Approaching the Composition of Action —— 3
2. Ricœur and Social Theory —— 5
3. Ethics and Means in Ricœur. A Preliminary Exploration —— 9
   3.1 Efficacy, without Abandoning Ethics —— 9
   3.2 An Ethics of Limited Violence —— 12
   3.3 With and Against Ricœur —— 15
4. A Contribution to Interpretive Social Theory —— 15
   4.1 Part 1: The Technicity of Action: Capabilities and Means —— 17
5. The Heat of Action —— 21
   5.1 Part 2: Finding Compromises in Practice —— 24
6. Intermediary Reflexion and Conclusion: Towards an Integrated Theory of the Technicity of Action —— 27

Part 1: **The Technicity of Action: Capabilities and Means**

Chapter 1: The Effectiveness of Symbols: Mediology and Hermeneutics —— 33
1. Introduction —— 33
2. Enter Mediology —— 34
3. The Technical *Milieu* and the *World* of Technology —— 36
   3.1 Transmission and Communication —— 37
   3.2 Transmission in the Mnemosphere —— 38
   3.3 Clothes: Transmission and Understanding —— 41
   3.4 No Mediology without Hermeneutics. No Milieu without a World —— 42
4. Autonomy and Appropriation —— 45
   4.1 Discourse as Action —— 46
   4.2 Autonomy and the Effectiveness of Symbols —— 47
   4.3 On Reception: Reading Texts and Artefacts —— 50
5. Vigilance and Politics —— 53
6. Conclusion —— 55

Chapter 2: Habitus – Means – Worldliness —— 58
1 Introduction: "Civilizing Processes" as Processes of Hominization —— 58
2 Human Technicity and the Civilizing Processes —— 63
3 *Technics* and *Narrativity* —— 66
   3.1 Prefiguration —— 67
   3.2 Configuration —— 70
   3.3 Refiguration —— 74
4 Conclusions —— 77

Chapter 3: Human Capabilities in the Light of Incapabilities —— 83
1 Introduction: A Hypothesis on the Technicity of Capabilities —— 83
2 The Capable Human is the Incapable Human —— 86
   2.1 Five Figures of Incapability —— 87
   2.2 Incapability as a Practical Horizon of Action. (In)capability as a Mark of Uncertainty —— 91
   2.3 The Capable Human is the Finite Human —— 93
3 The Capable-Incapable Human Discloses the Technical Human —— 94
   3.1 Misrecognition of Incapability, Practical Horizon and Primary Technicity —— 95
   3.2 Reflection, Level of Competence and Secondary Technicity —— 95
4 Social Theoretical Horizon —— 97
5 Conclusion: The Technical Paradox and its Political Relevance —— 100

Chapter 4: Organized Action: Agency, (In)capabilities and Means —— 103
1 Organized Action as Part of the Technicity of Action —— 103
2 Organized Action and the Agency of Organizations —— 105
   2.1 Entities of Participatory Belonging and Institutions —— 106
   2.2 Practices and the Example of Advisory Bodies —— 112
   2.3 Social Capabilities —— 114
   2.4 Scales of Organized Action, its Capabilities and Means —— 116
3 Capabilities and Incapabilities of Organizations —— 119
4 Conclusion. Paradoxes, Risks, and Political Implications of Organized Action —— 124
   4.1 The Paradox of Organized Action —— 125
   4.2 Organized Action in the Social Sciences —— 126

Chapter 5: The Hermeneutics of Human Capabilities and the Theory of Structuration —— 128
1 Introduction —— 128

2 Ricœur: Individuals and Society in the Hermeneutics of the Capable Human —— 131
  2.1 First Approach: Ricœur on Institutions —— 132
  2.2 Second Approach: Practices Between "Basic Actions" (Danto) and "Narrative Unity of Human Life" (MacIntyre) —— 140
3 Giddens: Individual and Society in Structuration Theory —— 144
  3.1 Giddens: Action, the Original Sociological Problem —— 144
  3.2 Giddens: Action and Duality of Structure – Some Specifications —— 147
4 Conclusion: Contributions of Structuration Theory to the Hermeneutics of the Capable Human —— 154

Intermediate Reflection: Tools for Critique —— 159
1 Something Is at Stake —— 159
2 On Critique —— 160
3 Towards the Intricate Relations between Technicity and Ethics —— 162
4 Working in Anticipation —— 163

Part 2: Finding Compromises in Practice

Chapter 6: Of What Is "Ricœur" the Name? Or, Philosophising at the Edge —— 167
1 What's in a Name? —— 167
3 "The Colonial Question" —— 168
4 Ricœur's Anticipation of Global Politics after Independence —— 171
5 Ricœur's View on the Philosophical and Cultural Critical Consequences of Decolonization —— 173
  5.1 Interim Conclusion: Disillusioned Modernity and the Task of Hermeneutics —— 177
6 Okolo – "Praxis Triggers the Hermeneutical Process and Gives it an Orientation" —— 180
  6.1 Taking Stock: Engagement without Promises —— 186
7 Conclusion: Philosophising at the Edge —— 188

Chapter 7: Acts of Violence as Political Competence? From Ricœur to Mandela and Back —— 191
1 Introduction —— 191
2 Three Categories of Competence in Socio-political Action —— 192
  2.1 Ricœur with and against Honneth —— 193

    2.2   A Missed Opportunity. Boltanski's Two Forms of Non-equivalence —— 196
3   Mandela on Sabotage and the Gradient of Violent Strategies —— 200
4   Elaboration: Mutual Implication of Strategy and Value —— 206
    4.1   Entanglement with Ethics —— 207
    4.2   Combining Strategy and Value —— 208
    4.3   Maintaining the Perplexity —— 210
    4.4   Responsibility in Politics and Science —— 212

Chapter 8: Justice Despite Institutions. Struggling for a Good Life from the Destitute Edge of Society —— 214
1   Conflict and Violence in View of Justice —— 217
2   Violent Democracy and the Violence of the Vulnerable —— 223
    2.1   Violent Democracy – Von Holdt's Challenge —— 226
    2.2   Violence close to the Centres of Privilege and Violence at the "Edge" —— 228
3   Two Ambiguous Strategies to Further the Good Life in Violent Democracies —— 229
    3.1   The Ambiguities of Violence at the "Edge" —— 230
    3.2   The Ambiguities of Refraining from Violence at the "Edge" —— 234
4   Conclusion: Attestation of Prudence at the "Edge" —— 238
    4.1   Conflictual Ethics: Composing Action as Prudent "Relative to us" —— 238
    4.2   Attestation, Action, Self-confidence —— 240
    4.3   Justice despite Institutions —— 242
    4.4   Epilogue —— 244

Conclusion

An Integrated View of the Technicity of Action and the Question of Responsibility —— 247
1   The Technicity of Action – a Short Synthesis —— 248
2   Ambiguity —— 255
3   Responsibility – On the Technicity of Ethico-political Action —— 259
    3.1   Technicity of Ethico-political Action and the Need for Normative Orientation —— 261
    3.2   Responsibility as a Key to Thinking Action in an Era of Uncertainty —— 263
    3.3   The Fragility of Responsibility —— 267

Bibliography —— 272

Author Index —— 288

Subject Index —— 292

Introduction

The Technical Dimension of Action

1 Basic Orientation: Approaching the Composition of Action

One of the remarkable features of our contemporary international scene is the number of intense social movements. From Caracas to Bagdad, from Hong Kong to Paris, the instances are legion. Protesters adopt strategies that range from peaceful protest to acts of violence, justifying their action with an array of arguments, communicating their grievances through different channels and attempting to bind isolated individuals into reliable groups supporting their cause. All of them act within existing social and political contexts: more or less firmly established institutions, varying economic conditions, more or less ruthless states, available forms of justification for police or military intervention, etc. In short, in each case, a dense and complex cocktail of disparate and mutating elements plays out in a rich diversity of events.

Impressive (and sometimes frightening) as the spread and intensity of these diverse events may be, at their core, there are a number of persistent features of social upheavals and, indeed, of human action in general. Four of these features are the object studied in this book. First, in each case, different individual, organizational or institutional agents combine actional *capabilities* with tools, institutions, infrastructure, etc. by *means* of which they act. In this volume, I refer to this combination of capabilities and means as the "technical dimension of action" or simply as the "technicity of action". Second, the deployment of capabilities and means is consistently permeated by *ethical* aspirations and hesitancies. Third, the myriad of strategies and forms of protest events vividly illustrates this task of combining capabilities with means and its impregnation by ethics; yet, one finds it in *all domains* of human action: in the workplace, in different forms of education, in commerce, and even in religious practices and in domestic interaction. Fourth, the current global spread of these events provides sufficient material to convince us that the need to combine capabilities with means, and these together with ethics, is typical of human life in *general*, and not just a regional or culturally specific phenomenon.[1]

In this book I attempt to think through these four basic components of social interaction. How is this to be done? First, careful attention is paid to the fact that action has meaning for agents. Let us call this the interpretative or *hermeneutic concern* of this study. Second, equally careful attention is given to the complex-

---

[1] The point is precisely the generality of this feature, not defining what human is, nor excluding the possibility that this remark may also be valid in respect of animals.

ities of action as interaction in social contexts. Let us call this the *social theoretic*[2] *concern* of this study. These two orienting concerns should already make it plain that this study aims neither at a philosophy of technology, nor at an exploration of the material background of action or a theory of culture – although the insights developed here should be relevant to these fields too. *The aim of the study is to develop in outline an interpretative theory of technicity as an aspect of human action.* I know of no equivalent endeavour in the scholarly literature to date.[3]

This initial indication of the orientation of the book calls for three clarifications, which is the task of this Introduction.

My primary strategy is to integrate the hermeneutic and social theoretic concerns by drawing the maximum of insights from an author in whose work they are coordinated: Paul Ricœur. It is this fine coordination, buttressed by the strength of his broader philosophy, that justifies the central attention to him in this book. The best way to clarify my choice of Ricœur as my main ally in hermeneutics is by providing a brief survey of the relation of his hermeneutics to

---

2 I use the term "social theory" simply to designate all the different contributions, independent of the disciplinary specificity of their authors. The point is not a polemic opposing philosophy to theory.

3 To be precise, there is a wide array of literature with which I can find a meaningful connection and from which I can draw insights for my project. After all, the technical dimension of action is a basic given of human existence. Moreover, drawing from such exchanges is a structuring feature of this book as a whole. Still, I do not know of any work that is dedicated to the technicity of action across the entire breadth of human action and interaction, and that is written from an interpretive or hermeneutic point of view. A review of recent overviews of social theory confirm this, see Philippe Corcuff, *Théories sociologiques contemporaines: France, 1980–2020* (Malakoff: Armand Colin, 2019), Claudio E. Benzecry, Monika Krause, and Isaac Reed, eds., *Social Theory Now* (Chicago, IL, and London: University of Chicago Press, 2017), Seth Abrutyn, ed., *Handbook of Contemporary Sociological Theory* (Cham: Springer, 2016), Patrick Baert and Filipe Carreira Da Silva, *Social Theory in the Twentieth Century and Beyond*, 2nd ed. (Cambridge: Polity Press, 2010), Georg Kneer and Markus Schroer, eds., *Handbuch Soziologische Theorien* (Wiesbaden: Springer VS, 2009), Gerard Delanty, *Handbook of Contemporary European Social Theory* (London: Routledge, 2006).

There are also a number of works which I recognize as displaying some proximity to my project – e.g. Johannes Robeck, *Technologische Urteilskraft. Zu einer Ethik technischen Handelns* (Frankfurt am Main: Suhrkamp, 1993), Christoph Hubig, *Die Kunst des Möglichen* (Bielefeld: Transcript, three volumes, 2006, 2007 and 2015) and Werner Rammert, *Technik – Handeln – Wissen: Zu einer pragmatistischen Technik- und Sozialtheorie*, 2nd ed. (Wiesbaden: Springer VS, 2016). However, since these volumes are not concerned with the hermeneutic approach that I set out to develop, and since they are aimed more specifically at application in various fields of technology (in contrast to the more ethical and political orientation of my last Chapters), discussing them falls beyond the scope of this book.

social theory (§2) and the presence of the problematic of the technicity of action in his (early) philosophy (§3). However, I do not accord Ricœur dogmatic authority, nor is this a purely exegetical study. This is avoided by the specific design of the chapters – which is my next point.

In each chapter insights are gathered from Ricœur's work and submitted to critique through dialogue with other theorists and intellectuals from a host of different social scientific backgrounds and disciplines: Régis Debray, Norbert Elias, Anthony Giddens, Luc Boltanski, Nelson Mandela, Okolo Okonda, Karl von Holdt and others – each chosen for the specific questions addressed in that chapter. My own theoretical developments emerge from these confrontations. The best way to clarify what this entails is by an overview of the chapters and the relations between them. This is done in two steps, for Part 1 (§4) and Part 2 (§5) of the book, respectively.

Finally, I comment on the "Intermediary reflexion" (which links the two parts of the book) and on the Conclusion, both of which serve to qualify the nature and ambition of this project (§6).

2 Ricœur and Social Theory

One of the most formative readings of my academic life thus far has been Joas and Knöbl's *Social Theory: Twenty Introductory Lectures*. Their masterly panorama of post-World War II social theory covers a wide variety of authors and movements of Western social theory in a compelling argumentative and historical presentation. Chapter XVI is dedicated to three French authors, collectively typified as "non-structuralist": Castoriadis, Touraine and Ricœur.[4] The significant position accorded to Paul Ricœur (1913–2005) by these two erudite sociologists may have come as a surprise to readers who were acquainted with the reception of Ricœur's philosophy during most of his lifetime. For a long time, his name was mostly associated with a kind of phenomenology, a philosophy that was then somewhat out of sync with mainstream "French theory", and concentrated instead on a hermeneutic turn to symbols, metaphors, narratives and perhaps the capable human. However, what Joas and Knöbl correctly recorded was, on the one hand, the tremendous wealth of social theoretic thought of this French

---

[4] Hans Joas and Wolfgang Knöbl, Lecture XVI: "French anti-structuralists (Cornelius Castoriadis, Alain Touraine and Paul Ricœur)," in *Social Theory: Twenty Introductory Lectures* (Cambridge: Cambridge University Press, 2009), 401–31.

philosopher, and on the other, the strongly welcoming reception from theorists in various social sciences that he began to enjoy later in life.

This shift needs some clarification. It is worth recalling that even before his reception in French sociology, Ricœur had cultivated a keen interest in a variety of social sciences throughout his career. Whether in political science, sociology, anthropology, or historiography, one has no difficulty finding the traces of reflection and concentrated discussions with contemporary authors in his work, such as Lévi-Strauss, Weber, Elias, Boltanski and Thévenot, Mannheim, and Geertz. This is no artificial addition, as his entire work can be described as a reflection on human action,[5] from which the well-known works of hermeneutics are but a long detour. To get an impression of his sustained contribution to social theory, one can enumerate the themes to which Ricœur devotes substantial study: action and fallibility, practical reason and ideology, interpersonal action and institutions, historicity and modernity, justice and recognition – the list is far from exhaustive.[6] All this work is infused with insights from his hermeneutics, the significance of which for post-World War II philosophy is commonly recognized.

Next, stepping from the philosopher to his social scientific reception, one could indicate several social scientists who made some use of his work in devel-

---

5 Cf. Paul Ricœur, "Préface," in Maurizio Chiodi, *Il cammino della libertà. Fenomenologia, ermeneutica, ontologia della libertà nella ricerca filosofica di Paul Ricœur* (Brescia: Morcelliana, 1990), ix-xix, and Paul Ricœur, "Proménade au fil d'un chemin," in Fabrizio Turoldo, *Verità del metodo. Indagini su Paul Ricœur* (Padua: Il Poligrafo, 2000), 13–20. The anglophone public has been sensitised to this dimension of his work by a volume edited by Cambridge sociologist John Thompson, namely Paul Ricœur, *Hermeneutics and the Human Sciences: Essays on Language, Action and Interpretation* (Cambridge: Cambridge University Press, 1995).
6 The bulk of this work is contained in Paul Ricœur, *L'idéologie et l'utopie* (Paris: Seuil, [1986] 1997) / *Lectures on Ideology and Utopia* (New York, NY: Columbia University Press, 1986), Paul Ricœur, *Du texte à l'action. Essais d'herméneutique II* (Paris: Seuil, 1986) / *From Text to Action: Essays in Hermeneutics II*, trans. Kathleen Blamey and John Thompson (London: Athlone, 1991), Paul Ricœur, *Soi-même comme un autre* (Paris: Seuil, 1990) / *Oneself as Another*, trans. Kathleen Blamey (Chicago, IL: University of Chicago Press, 1992), Paul Ricœur, *Le juste 1* (Paris: Esprit, 1995) / *The Just*, (Chicago, IL: University of Chicago Press, 2000), Paul Ricœur, *Le juste 2* (Paris: Esprit, 2001) / *Reflections on the Just*, trans. David Pellauer (Chicago, IL: University of Chicago Press, 2007), and finally, Paul Ricœur, *Parcours de la reconnaissance* (Paris: Gallimard, 2004) / *The Course of Recognition*, trans. David Pellauer (Cambridge, MA: Harvard University Press, 2005). Parts of the book of interviews, Paul Ricœur, *La critique et la conviction. Entretien avec François Azouvi et Marc De Launay* (Paris: Calmann-Lévy, 1995) / *Critique and Conviction: Conversations with François Azouvi and Marc De Launay. European Perspectives* (New York, NY: Columbia University Press, 1998) and to a lesser degree the tome on the philosophy of history, Paul Ricœur, *La mémoire, l'histoire, l'oubli* (Paris: Seuil, 2000) / *Memory, History, Forgetting* (Chicago, IL: University of Chicago Press, 2004), should likewise be taken into account here.

oping their own views – to cite but two random examples: V. Y. Mudimbe in his understanding of the invention of Africa or Clifford Geertz's symbolic anthropology.[7] Much more significant is the "Ricœur effect" in French social science, already recorded by François Dosse in 1995.[8] The most significant names to mention in this regard are Luc Boltanski and Laurent Thévenot, the originators of "French pragmatism."[9]

A third layer of the relation between Ricœur and social theory is presented by recent scholarship.[10] Over the last two decades, this scholarship has over-

---

[7] Valentin Yves Mudimbe, *The Invention of Africa: Gnosis, Philosophy, and the Order of Knowledge*. African Systems of Thought (Bloomington, IN: Indiana University Press, 1988); Arun Micheelsen, "'I Don't Do Systems': An Interview with Clifford Geertz," *Method and Theory in the Study of Religion* 14, no. 1 (2002): 2–20.

[8] François Dosse, *L'empire du sens. L'humanisation des sciences humaines* (Paris: La Découverte, 1995), see Chapter 14, "Une philosophie de l'agir: Paul Ricœur," 170–79.

[9] Luc Boltanski and Laurent Thévenot. *On Justification: Economies of Worth* (Princeton, NJ: Princeton University Press, [1991] 2006). Laurent Thévenot's major publication, *L'action au pluriel. Sociologie des régimes d'engagement* (Paris: La Découverte, 2006) is dedicated to Ricœur.

[10] In recent years the number of *thematic volumes of journals* dedicated to Ricœur have shown an increasing interest in the social and political philosophical aspect of his work, cf. the *Journal Phänomenologie* 21 (2004), the *Journal of French Philosophy* 16, nos. 1–2 (2006), the *Revue de Metaphysique et de Morale* 2 (2006), *Cités* 1, no. 33 (2008), *Philosophiques* 41, no. 2 (2014), the *Revue des Sciences Philosophiques et Théologiques* 99, no. 4 (2015), *Chiasmi International* 17 (2016). Among the volumes of the *Ricœur Studies/Études Ricœuriennes*, see for example, 2, no. 1 (2011) (on recognition), 3, no. 1 (2012) (on the social sciences), 4, no. 1 (2013) (on feminism), 6, no. 2 (2015) (on justice), 9, no. 1 (2018) (on ideology and utopia), 9, no. 2 (2018) (on vulnerability), 10, no. 2 (2019) (on practical wisdom).

A similar trend can be seen in *collected volumes:* cf. some of the essays in Christian Delacroix, François Dosse and Partick Garcia, eds., *Paul Ricœur et les sciences humaines* (Paris: La Découverte, 2007), David Kaplan, ed., *Reading Ricœur* (New York, NY: State University of New York Press, 2008), Scott A. Davidson, ed., *Ricœur Across the Disciplines* (New York, NY: Continuum, 2010) (some chapters in this volume, with its accent on textual disciplines), and almost all of the contributions in Farhang Erfani and Lorenzo Altieri, eds. *Paul Ricœur: Honoring and Continuing the Work* (Lanham, MD: Lexington Books, 2011). The titles of two new publications are telling: David Lewin and Todd S. Mei, eds., *From Ricœur to Action: The Socio-Political Significance of Ricœur's Thinking* (London, and New York, NY: Continuum, 2012) and Marcelino Agis Villaverde, *Knowledge and Practical Reason: Paul Ricœur's Way of Thinking* (Berlin and Zurich: Lit Verlag, 2012). Other relevant texts are Roger Savage, *Paul Ricœur in the Age of Hermeneutical Reason: Poetics, Praxis, and Critique*. Studies in the Thought of Paul Ricœur (Lanham, MD: Lexington Books, 2015), Annemie Halsema and Fernanda Henriques, eds., *Feminist Explorations of Paul Ricœur's Philosophy* (Lanham, MD: Lexington Books, 2016), Suzi Adams, ed., *Ricœur and Castoriadis in Discussion: On Human Creation, Historical Novelty, and the Social Imaginary*. Social Imaginaries (Lanham, MD: Rowman and Littlefield International, 2017), and Stephanie N. Arel

whelmingly confirmed the significance of the socio-political dimension of his work, which justifies discarding the outdated idea that Ricœur was only interested in matters of textual interpretation which bears no relevance to practical philosophy.

My book is situated in the extension of these three layers of connection between philosophy and social theory. From this perspective, this book aims at making a contribution to both the interpretation of Ricœur's socio-political thought and the development of significant features of it. We will explore why human action is not merely an instrumental concatenation of sub-actions aimed at a preestablished goal, but is rather a much more complex exercise of practical or conscious interpretation and adaptation of courses of action. How action is always informed – that is, guided or impaired – by normative or ethical concerns, hesitations and dispositions, is a second question. At the same time, we will see that the practical situations in which people act do not always allow them simply to realize their normative motives, and in fact, the very means by which they hope to realize them often negatively affect other concerns. A central contention of this book is that we can only gain a proper grasp of the difficult composition of efficiency and normativity in action from a coordination of hermeneutic and social theoretic inputs.

But I must pre-empt the sceptic. As significant as these questions may be, are they not marginal to Ricœur's thought? Surely this is not a theme by

---

and Dan R. Stiver, eds., *Ideology and Utopia in the Twenty-First Century: The Surplus of Meaning in Ricœur's Dialectical Concept* (London, and New York, NY: Lexington Books, 2019).

Likewise, one could consider a number of *monographs*: Bernard Dauenhauer, *Paul Ricœur: The Promise and Risk of Politics* (Lanham, MD: Rowman and Littlefield, 1998), David Kaplan, *Ricœur's Critical Theory* (Albany, NY: State University of New York Press, 2003), Johann Michel, *Paul Ricœur. Une philosophie de l'agir* (Paris: Cerf, 2006), Peter Kemp, *Sagesse pratique de Paul Ricœur: Huit études* (Paris: Editions du Sandre, 2010), Molly Mann, *Ricœur, Rawls and Capability Justice: Civic Phronesis and Equality* (London, and New York, NY: Continuum, 2012), Pierre-Olivier Monteil, *Ricœur politique* (Rennes: Presses Universitaires de Rennes, 2013), Inge Künle, *Das Selbst und der Andere bei Paul Ricœur und Amartya Sen* (Berlin: Lit Verlag, 2014), Michael Sohn, *The Good of Recognition: Phenomenology, Ethics, and Religion in the Thought of Levinas and Ricœur* (Waco, TX: Baylor University Press, 2014), Maureen Junker-Kenny, *Religion and Public Reason: A Comparison of the Positions of John Rawls, Jürgen Habermas and Paul Ricœur* (Berlin: De Gruyter, 2014), Jean Greisch, *L'herméneutique comme sagesse de l'incertitude* (Paris: Le cercle herméneutique éditeur, 2015), Timo Helenius, *Ricœur, Culture and Recognition: Hermeneutics of Cultural Subjectivity* (Lanham, MD: Lexington Books, 2016), Dries Deweer, *Ricœur's Personalist Republicanism. On Personhood and Citizenship* (Lanham, MD: Lexington Books, 2017), Geoffrey Dierckxsens, *Paul Ricœur's Moral Anthropology: Singularity, Responsibility, and Justice* (Lanham, MD: Lexington Books, 2018).

which to present the reader with a substantial view on Ricœur's social theory? To both objections I would respond: Not at all!

3 Ethics and Means in Ricœur. A Preliminary Exploration

Once made aware of it, one cannot help but notice how often and how thoroughly Ricœur grappled with the question of the need *and* the ambiguity of the *means* of action as encountered in the heat of the action.[11] This is a question of efficacy, but the urgency of the "heat" of action is equally informed by agents' ethical investment in what they do. In this book, I explore this dimension of Ricœur's thought by focusing on his later work (roughly from the 1970s to 2005, although the exact demarcation is not important). However, one can introduce the issue with reference to much earlier texts to get an impression of how this dimension of his thinking emerged.[12] In this way, the contemporary relevance of the question will also become apparent.

3.1 Efficacy, without Abandoning Ethics

At the end of the 1940s, Ricœur engaged Merleau-Ponty in a debate about the possible sources for positive change in society. On the one hand, he seemed reluctant unreservedly to accept Merleau-Ponty's version of the recourse to "progressive" violence found in *Humanism and Terror*. On the other hand, he had had five years in a prisoner-of-war camp to ruminate on the inadequacies of his pre-war pacifism. His response, published as "Non-violent Man and His Presence to History" in 1949, can be schematized in a number of steps.[13]

---

11 For an encompassing study of Ricœur's views on technology throughout his work, see Ernst Wolff, "Ricœur's Polysemy of Technology and its Reception," in *Interpreting Technology*, eds. Mark Coeckelbergh, Wessel Reijers and Alberto Romele (Lanham: Rowman and Littlefield, forthcoming 2021).
12 The interpretation of Ricœur's earlier philosophy is itself a major topic. I have dealt with it on its own in a separate monograph, entitled *Lire Ricœur depuis la périphérie. Décolonisation, modernité, herméneutique* (forthcoming). Harvesting the insights of Ricœur's earlier work, especially *Freedom and nature. The voluntary and the involuntary* and *Fallible Man*, would certainly add valuable material to the argument of the present book, but this will have to be dealt with in a separate study.
13 Paul Ricœur, "L'homme non-violent et sa présence à l'histoire" [1949], *Histoire et vérité* (Paris: Seuil, 1964), 265–77 / "Non-violent Man and his Presence to History," in *History and Truth*, trans. Charles A. Kelbley (Evanston, IL: Northwestern University Press, 1965), 223–33.

As a first step, he sketches a vast anatomy of violence in society: military, political, religious, or economic violence, but also the "violence of law and order",[14] of poverty, and of exploitation. It is a philosopher's social diagnostic, but it stands for a thorough, realistic study of social complexities and his avoidance of a simplistic view on society as a family, a club or contract-based cooperation. This is essential to Ricœur's lifelong indebtedness to the social sciences: instead of constructing ideal theory in abstraction of social reality, he aspires to philosophise from the thick of it.

The product of this realist approach is his insistence on the problem of efficacy, which forms the next step. Ricœur seeks to understand efficacy, which is bound up with an ethical sensitivity (a *"prise de conscience"*) to the harm of violence. In terms both he and Merleau-Ponty adopt from Koestler, efficacious (and not just theoretical) improvement of society has to be sought by avoiding the extremes of moralist detachment and brutal realism, positions designated by the ideal-typical role of the "yogi" and the "commissar" respectively. Between these extremes, Merleau-Ponty situates the uncertain, but progressive, violence of the "proletarian". Ricœur concurs, writing that "there is a political task and this task is in the thick of history [*en pleine pâte dans l'histoire*]".[15] Still, he is worried that, in practice, nothing would prevent the "proletarian" from eventually sliding into the role of the "commissar".

The third step is Ricœur's argument that there is something in human societies that may put a brake on this degeneration of the "proletarian". This social role is named the "prophet", which is distinct from the yogi.[16] This role stands for the human possibility to produce signs, markers or pointers – reminders – of that which the "proletarian" is fighting for. This is by no means a simple fantasy. Ricœur's prime example is that of Gandhi, although not as an idealized Indian mystic, as Ricœur had his reservations regarding some aspects of the Gandhian doctrine. His point is *not* that the Gandhi-like "prophet" has to replace his political partner, the "proletarian", but rather that "prophets" can guide "proletarians" by singular, occasional demonstrations critiquing the *status quo*.

The fourth step – the significant issue I want to highlight – has to do with the exact characterisation of this social role. There can be a real "dialectic of prophetic non-violence and progressivist violence,"[17] but only if non-violence can be efficient[18]. *This* is what qualifies Gandhi as a "prophet": "far from the non-vio-

---

14 Ricœur, *Histoire et vérité*, 269 / *History and Truth*, 226.
15 Ricœur, *Histoire et vérité*, 276 / *History and Truth*, 232 (translation modified).
16 Ricœur, *Histoire et vérité*, 271, 273 / *History and Truth*, 228, 230.
17 Ricœur, *Histoire et vérité*, 276 / *History and Truth*, 232.
18 Cf. Ricœur, *Histoire et vérité*, 271 / *History and Truth*, 228.

lent person banishing these goals from history and deserting the scheme of means, leaving them to their impurity, the non-violent attempts to bring them together in an action which is at one and the same time a *spirituality* and a *technique* [une *spiritualité* et une *technique*]".[19] It is, as Ricœur emphatically repeats, a strategy which combines the generating symbols expressive of an ethical *prise de conscience* of difficult situations on the one hand and, on the other, a technology ("technique") of resistance and of disobedience.[20] Moreover, the "prophet" is never to go it alone: this role needs its dialectical counterpart in the continuous, political action of the "proletarian".

For our current purposes, the issue is not whether we accept Ricœur's mobilisation of four ideal typical social roles or his enthusiasm for Gandhi. The point is rather that Ricœur's whole effort consists of thinking through the coordination of major, conflicting dimensions of action – violence, withdrawal, collaboration, ethical aims, strategy – in the course of action. We can measure the significance of Ricœur's insistence on the problematic coordination of ethics (or symbols) and technics (or efficacy) by glancing back at the text by Merleau-Ponty to which he responds. Merleau-Ponty describes exactly this difficult coordination as insurmountably part of the human condition.[21] One person who understood this dilemma, Merleau-Ponty claimed, was Max Weber, notably in his opposition of an ethics of conviction centred on pursuing pre-established principles, and an ethics of responsibility, which, in full knowledge of the unforeseeable circumstances of actions, engages with the means at one's disposal. Those who operate under an ethics of conviction are the naïve idealists, those who operate under an ethics of responsibility are the realists.[22] Ricœur's article on violence and non-violence is an attempt to acknowledge the full significance of the uncertainty involved in action, while recognizing the unavoidability of using means, even powerful and lethal ones, in pursuit of efficient interventions in reality. At the same time, he is willing neither to abdicate ethical considerations, nor to abandon

---

19 Ricœur, *Histoire et vérité*, 273 / *History and Truth*, 230 (translation modified).
20 Cf. Ricœur, *Histoire et vérité*, 274 / *History and Truth*, 231.
21 Maurice Merleau-Ponty, *Humanisme et terreur: Essai sur le problème communiste* (Paris: Gallimard, 1947), 30 / Maurice Merleau-Ponty, *Humanism and Terror: The Communist Problem*, trans. John O'Neill (New Brunswick, NJ: Transaction, 2000), xxxviii.
22 This is Merleau-Ponty's reading. I differ somewhat from this reading, cf. Ernst Wolff, *Political Responsibility for a Globalised World. After Levinas' Humanism* (Bielefeld: Transcript Verlag, 2011), 189–203, summarised in Ernst Wolff, "Responsibility to Struggle – Responsibility for Peace: Course of Recognition and a Recurrent Pattern in Ricœur's Political Thought," *Philosophy & Social Criticism* 41, no. 8 (2015): 771–90, here 773–75, 189–203. See also the contemporary analysis and appraisal in Etienne de Villiers, *Revisiting Max Weber's Ethic of Responsibility* (Tübingen: Mohr Siebeck, 2018).

them to moralists. The question of coordinating a "spirituality" and a "technology" is the question of coordinating human capabilities and means with normative considerations. In the decades that followed, Ricœur worked on coordinating the *affirmation* of an uncertain human context, and the quest for efficient interventions in it, with the critical *negation* of mere acceptance of the *status quo*.

3.2 An Ethics of Limited Violence

This position can be seen again in a quite different argumentative context: Ricœur's seminal essay on political philosophy, "The Political Paradox".[23] The article is written as a reflection on a particular historical event, namely, the Russian suppression of the Hungarian uprising in 1956. The argument, however, is established from a purely philosophical basis with a view on what Ricœur considers the most lasting general features of politics. We are only able to understand the violence of Budapest, or any other political brutality, he claims, if we understand what is specific about politics or, as he says, the political (*le politique*). He attempts to grasp this specificity with the help of the history of political philosophy. Everything depends on how one understands the relation between a number of basic views.

To begin with, one must acknowledge the truth of a tradition stretching from Aristotle to Rousseau and Hegel, which sees an essential component of our humanization in political life, that is, life as a citizen of a state. This is a peculiar truth; it is not simply a given, but rather a valid aspiration (aim or *"visée"*[24]). Each critique of an abuse of political power silently presupposes the "reality of this ideality".[25]

However, it is not very helpful merely to affirm this point without examining how to realize this virtuous work. Therefore, one also has to grant the validity of two quite different views on the state. First, Ricœur affirms with Eric Weil that the state is the expression of the will of the people. This is not meant to be a categorical approval of what states do, rather, it simply means that the state is necessary to bind the plurality of citizens together in order to enact what it is they want to do. States allow people to achieve things that are unimaginable in a condition of statelessness. However, following this line of thought, Ricœur encounters the validity of Weber's instrumentalist view of the State, namely as the entity

---

[23] Paul Ricœur, "Le paradoxe politique" [1957], *Histoire et vérité*, 294–321 / "The Political Paradox," *History and Truth*, 247–70.
[24] Cf. Ricœur, *Histoire et vérité*, 297 / *History and Truth*, 249.
[25] Ricœur, *Histoire et vérité*, 300 / *History and Truth*, 252.

that successfully lays claim to a monopoly on the legitimate use of violence within a given territory. For Weber, it is nonsense to speak about the aim of a State. All we know is that it is a powerful tool, and that having a vocation for politics implies a willingness to take the powerful tools of the State into one's hands.

In this combination, Weil theorizes the relay from popular will to the powers of the State, while Weber contributes the dimension of the state as an instrument under conditions of uncertainty. Together, this accounts for political action as "rational organization"[26] and for its ability to take and execute decisions. The junction of Weil-Weber with the aforementioned tradition of flourishing through political life gives us an affirmative view on political matters, in the sense that it emphasises what can or should be realized.

But there are also a host of negative discourses on politics and the state. Authors expose the abuses of power, the hypocrisy of the state, rulers that parade as champions of the people while facilitating their exploitation, etc. This is the invaluable contribution of thinkers such as Marx or Lenin. Whatever the myriad of dissenting arguments may be, they all draw their force from presupposing the validity of people's aspiration toward a better life through political coexistence (on which the argument is premised from the beginning).

Far from a position of non-committal or a random conflation, Ricœur attempts to coordinate these positions into something like a lasting grammar of political power. This grammar of political power drives politics again and again into a series of interrelated paradoxes. I identify three in this text:[27]
- The means and power to give effect (and efficacy) to the collective will is a power which can turn against the citizenry.
- Hence, a specifically political evil emerges from the possibility of a specifically political good. Political evil is a perversion of political rationality itself.
- For the sake of avoiding political evil, the same liberty of the citizenry that founds states as powerful entities for the realization of liberty has to limit that same power of States.

With these three paradoxes, we are already at the heart of the point I wish to make about this key text of Ricœur's. For Ricœur, a paradox[28] is an opposition or contradiction that cannot be solved in *theory*, but that must instead be

---

26 "[O]rganisation raisonnable," Ricœur, *Histoire et vérité*, 303 / *History and Truth*, 255.
27 For a detailed discussion of the "political paradox" throughout Ricœur's work, see Monteil, *Ricœur politique*, 27–68.
28 Ricœur's own definition, albeit from a much later essay, is that a paradox is "a situation in which two contrary theses equally oppose being refuted and, as a result, require being preserved or abandoned together," Ricœur, *Le juste 2*, 27, 86 / *Reflections on the Just*, 19, 73.

dealt with in *practice*. This is of cardinal importance, as it shows how his initial political-historical argument drives us directly into the arms of the problems of action. The paradox arises from both an insistence on the difficulty and uncertainty of action and an affirmation of the urgency to deal with it (because something is at stake in it). Ricœur comments on these complexities in the frame of his reflection on politics. If the exposition above is correct, then, Ricœur argues, the central problem of democracy is that of the people controlling the State. Or, as he says explicitly, "to devise institutional *techniques* especially designed to render possible the exercise of power and render its abuse impossible."[29] His point is neither technocratic nor instrumentalist. Rather, it is that abstract moralization is worth nothing: if we are serious about action, we must consider the means by which to give effect to our concerns. Among these institutional "techniques of controlling the State",[30] what Ricœur has in mind are the free activity of trade-unions, the independence of the judiciary, the availability of education, free circulation of information, and generally submitting the State to control through democratic debate. It would be missing the point to see here only the advocacy of political liberties. Ricœur does not dream of a minimal State, since, in the very specific sense described above, he views the State as something good. People need an efficient State. But there is no escaping the political paradox, and hence, Ricœur advocates an "ethic of limited violence",[31] that is, striving to let normative considerations weigh in on the means chosen for action, in full knowledge of how dangerous they may be. Nor does he dream of reducing the State to an apparatus for distributing goods and tasks – the State is devoid of meaning without the aspiration of people to which it is to give effect.

In short, prompted by dramatic political events, the philosopher passes in review insights gathered from the history of his discipline, only to return again through this detour to the very complexity of action. At the heart of his problem are the questions that concern this book: the tension between individual and collective action, the technical dimension of action, the coordination of ethical considerations and the desire for efficacy, and realism about the difficulty of finding an appropriate course of action in a given context.

---

29 My emphasis, Ricœur, *Histoire et vérité*, 311, similarly 314–15 / *History and Truth*, 261–2, similarly 264–65.
30 Ricœur, *Histoire et vérité*, 321 / *History and Truth*, 270.
31 Ricœur, *Histoire et vérité*, 312 / *History and Truth*, 262.

3.3 With and Against Ricœur

It is this problem complex (which, as I have just demonstrated, emerges from the heart of Ricœur's early socio-political thought) that I do not see explored in the scholarship,[32] and that is precisely the lacuna that I hope to fill. Since Ricœur's early work on the phenomenology of the will, it is evident that he was bent on understanding action. The two early texts we have considered briefly, "Non-violent Man…" and "The Political Paradox" add a number of details to this well-known fact. They give us a view on the kind of problems which continuously nourished Ricœur's abiding fascination with action. No matter how far the historical or philosophical detour may go, this reflection aims at the difficulties of action in a context. Furthermore, they also confirm my claim that the coordination of capabilities and means (the "technicity" of action) and the difficult coordination of these dimensions of action with ethical concerns have, from early on, formed part of Ricœur's socio-political thought. Finally, the place of ethics in action is demarcated and the difficult adjustments between ethics and the context which allows agents to realize it are thought through. However, the question of the ultimate foundation, or at least justification, of ethics is not addressed in these texts. For this reason, these studies point rather to an action theoretical reflection than to a fundamental "moral philosophy".

Seen from this perspective, Ricœur will be my ally throughout this book. However, my aim still remains to make an independent contribution. For this reason, I have not hesitated to express my disagreement with Ricœur (as I do with other scholars) and to develop additions or improvements where I considered them necessary. Since this is an equally important part of the project, let us look at it more closely.

4 A Contribution to Interpretive Social Theory

Although I do not claim to give an exhaustive survey of Ricœur's contribution to social theory, by working on the questions outlined above, it is possible to offer a more systematic exploration of the central tenets of this aspect of his work than, for instance, Joas and Knöbl could do in *Social Theory: Twenty Introductory Lec-*

---

[32] Of course, texts abound in which the question of the difficult compromise between ethics and morality is thematized, following Ricœur's own examination of prudence in action. But even there, the question of actional efficiency is largely neglected.

tures to which I referred above.[33] In order to keep the scope of the study manageable, I do not discuss his earlier philosophy of the will,[34] but focus instead on his later practical philosophy and the hermeneutics of human capabilities. Furthermore, I diverge quite sharply from Joas and Knöbl by incorporating authors from outside of the West as essential conversational partners in this book.[35] In a book where universal anthropological claims are being made, such openness is indispensable, and, regardless of this point, the reader will see that this is done in service of answering my central questions (more about this below). Furthermore, while I gratefully draw from Ricœur's hermeneutics and strive to do justice to his work, this study also aims to do more than add to Ricœur scholarship in three respects.

First, each chapter contains expositions of his work, but proceeds by extending his arguments, filling in lacunae, exploring unexamined possibilities or contradicting his views.[36] This is done both by critically commenting on his work and by engaging with social scientific theories. The latter interlocutors have been chosen in each chapter specifically to help me advance in one or another problem, relative to the broader project of understanding the technicity of action. A short overview of what this entails is given in the chapter summaries below. The outcome is a study that has definite Ricœurian traits, but is also clearly an independent contribution.

Second, although I have demonstrated above that the overall theme of this book is not foreign to Ricœur, it would have been a vain endeavour to look for a developed hermeneutics of the technicity of action in his work. This thematic de-

---

[33] Johann Michel, *Paul Ricœur. Une philosophie de l'agir* (Paris: Cerf, 2006) gives an interpretation of Ricœur's major works as they relate to action.

[34] On this work, see Scott A. Davidson, ed., *A Companion to Ricœur's Freedom and Nature* (Lanham, MD: Lexington Books, 2018) and Jean Greisch, *L'herméneutique comme sagesse de l'incertitude* (Paris: Le cercle herméneutique éditeur, 2015), 59–116.

[35] However, both of them have taken these questions seriously in other publications. See, for instance, Wolfgang Knöbl, *Die Kontingenz der Moderne. Wege in Europa, Asien und Amerika* (Frankfurt am Main: Campus Verlag, 2007) and Hans Joas, *Sind die Menschenrechte westlich?* (Munich: Kössel Verlag, 2015).

[36] In successive chapters, I draw from Ricœur's general textual hermeneutics, his narrative hermeneutics, his hermeneutics of human capabilities and aspects of his social philosophy. Then I draw from his early texts on decolonization, the question of symbolics in *Course of Recognition* and finally again the more political side of human capabilities. In each case, I critique him and develop my own views on the technical dimension of language utterances, the hermeneutics of human-technology relations, incapabilities, organizationized action and the broader social theoretic framework. Finally, unlike in Western philosophy, violent action and the difficulties of protest strategies are thematized.

velopment is my own. A synthetic view of this development is given in the Conclusion.

Third, in the "Intermediary reflection" and the "Conclusion", I situate this study in respect of critical social theory. I assume a position of "simple exteriority", which suspends the task of ethical justification in order to focus on the most rigorous description possible. At the same time, in anticipation of possible critique (or "complex exteriority"), this study already provides the means for describing the stakes, ambiguities and paradoxes associated with the technicity of action. I therefore do not assume a position of a naïve value neutrality, let alone of value indifference, but propose a provisional suspension of critique in the light of the fact that, in this study, I do not dispose of the means by which to provide ethical commitments with justification. This theoretical position is "hermeneutic", without being Ricœur's position.[37]

These three points of divergence warrant my characterisation of this book using the general adjective "interpretative" or "hermeneutic" (rather than the narrower "Ricœurian").

Now the time has come do have a closer look at the steps by which the argument of the book is constructed. The objectives of this study required dividing the book into two parts. Part 1 concentrates on the two major components of the technicity of action, namely acquired capabilities and means of action. Part 2 examines the relation between the technicity of action and the urgency imposed on action by ethical and political concerns (see §5).

4.1 Part 1: The Technicity of Action: Capabilities and Means

The first part consists of a gradual accumulation of insights on the coordination of human capabilities and means of action. The argument fans out between the technicity of the simplest forms of communication and interaction, and the broadest social theoretical overview of collective action and institutions.

The aim of **Chapter 1**, "The Effectiveness of Symbols: Mediology and Hermeneutics", is to outline the specificity of a hermeneutic approach to action and to dismiss the still recurrent notion that hermeneutics is exclusively at home in textual practices. To advance my case, I take up a debate with Régis Debray, who gives a scholarly articulation of the view I reject and offers an attractive alterna-

---

[37] I assume this theoretical stance, drawing on Luc Boltanski, *On Critique: A Sociology of Emancipation*, trans. Gregory Elliot (Cambridge: Polity, 2011) and do not engage here with Ricœur's intervention on the relation between hermeneutics and a critique of ideology in *From Text to Action*.

tive to it. Debray developed a field of study called mediology. Although he argues in favour of a demarcation of this field from other social sciences, such as semiology, sociology, history and communication theory, he often treats hermeneutics with some hostility. This chapter advances a more accurate understanding of the relationship between mediology and hermeneutics by focusing on symbolic efficacy. Three areas of converged interest are identified and discussed: (1) the mutual implication of the technical milieu and the world of technology, (2) the process of autonomisation and re-appropriation of media or texts, and (3) vigilance in politics.

The aim of exploring these convergences is not to sidestep the differences, but rather to make of my erstwhile opponent an ally to help me make the case for a hermeneutic approach to the technical dimension of action. This strategy requires this chapter to demonstrate how Ricœur understands the transition from theorizing text to theorizing action ("from text to action", as a volume of his essays is called). In fact, *From Text to Action* serves as a guide providing a first entry into a hermeneutic approach to action, and more specifically to the place of capabilities and means in interaction. This provisional overview is explicitly elaborated in Chapter 2.

Under the title "Habitus – Means – Worldliness," **Chapter 2** takes over the general anthropological perspective on human action from Chapter 1 and theorizes the fact that action is mediated. The mediation of action is described as essential to human reality. However, this fact takes on different forms in different times and places. In critical engagement with Norbert Elias, I describe hominization as the collection of "civilizing processes" by which people of different cultures in different times and places are formed. This happens through the changing combination of three interdependent anthropogenetic components: society, signs and technics.

The manner in which the third of these components, technics, is constitutive of all cultural events deserves special attention. I argue that action, and more specifically, its technical dimension, consists of three interdependent elements: habitus (capability or technical disposition), instruments (the system of technical objects) and worldliness (the understanding interaction with people's social and material environment). The changing interrelation of these elements through a structural sequence of prefiguration, configuration and refiguration describes a hermeneutics of action, comparable to the hermeneutic structure of narrativity demonstrated by Ricœur. As such, the technical dimension of action is an aspect of all civilizing processes: not only is all culture dependent on the technical means of its existence, but all technical events, by virtue of their instrumentality, carry meaning, transmit, and humanize (in the sense of contributing to the form of human existence). Consequently, any experience by which people must negotiate cultural difference presupposes and depends on the threefold technical dimension of interaction. Each instance of such negotiation amounts to an intervention in the processes of civilization. The self-reflective potential of such interventions can be theorized as part of the problem of symbolic efficacy (cf. Chapter 1).

The complex of habitus, means and worldliness examined in Chapter 2 is further explored in **Chapter 3** under the title "Human Capabilities in the Light of Incapabilities". In this chapter, most is made of the central term of Ricœur's later philosophy, capability, but I fill in the gap left largely unfilled by Ricœur – a theorizing on incapability.

Let us examine this in more detail. Central to Ricœur's later hermeneutics of the self is the "I can". While he explores the range of capabilities, the notion of capability itself nevertheless remains underdetermined from what one may call the "technical" point of view (in the sense I developed in the first two chapters). In this chapter, I defend the claim that the hermeneutics of the capable human being requires a development of its technical dimension, in other words, a reflection on the skills and means related to the "I can". To support this claim and to assert that incapability is the practical horizon of the action of the capable human being, I examine five dimensions of incapability. Subsequently, the tension between ability and inability is described as the originary finitude of the human agent. This conclusion makes it possible to demonstrate that the capable-incapable human being reveals the technicity of the human being over the entire range of his/her social interactions.

In the action theoretic framework deployed in Ricœur's later philosophy (as dealt with in Chapter 3), acting agents reveal their capabilities when these are activated in interaction, face-to-face with others and through institutional mediation. Between these extremes of personal and anonymous interaction, there remains an intermediate form of human interaction that cannot simply be described as either personal or anonymous, namely organized, collective action. This is already a problem for Ricœur's action theory, however, in the light of the later chapters of the book, we will gain a better sense of the significance that this has for a sociological and political understanding of collective action. This shortcoming in Ricœur's action theory is dealt with in **Chapter 4**, "Organized Action: Agency, (In)capabilities and Means".

While I recognize the absence of a thoroughly systematic treatment of this question by Ricœur, I argue that his work nevertheless contains a number of passages in which valuable insights into the phenomenon of organized action are given. This is demonstrated by an analysis of five relevant parts of his work: first, the notion of institution from *Oneself as Another*, and, second, in the same book, the notion of practices as adopted from MacIntyre, third, the idea of an advisory team as used now and then in Ricœur's reflections on medical ethics, fourth, the theorizing of the representation of social collectivities under the term "participative belonging" (*appartenance participative*) in *Time and Narrative 1*, and fifth, the hermeneutics of "social capabilities" in *The Course of Recognition*. What is at stake in exploring these five passages lies not only in doing them justice in their quite divergent contexts, but also in testing the possibility of a synthesis of these insights.

The constructive part of this chapter consists in transposing the categories of capability and incapability already developed in Chapter 3 to the agency of groups or organizations. Some of the same complexities are to be found in the case of the group action.

By the time we arrive at **Chapter 5**, the reader should possess a good view of Ricœur's action theory and the way in which I have elaborated it with a focus on the technicity of action. It is then time to situate Ricœur in the broader field of sociological action theory. I do so by means of a comparison of key notions from Ricœur's work with those of Anthony Giddens's theory of structuration. Hence the title of the chapter: "The Hermeneutics of Human Capabilities and the Theory of Structuration". The aim of this chapter is to consolidate the work of the first four chapters and to suggest a number of points at which Giddens's early theoretic project could be used to strengthen and elaborate the theoretical construction assembled thus far.

This chapter, then, is set up as a dialogue between Ricœur and Giddens, in particular between the hermeneutics of the capable human and the theory of structuration. The chapter starts with an exploration of the key concepts on the basis of which to compare the two authors' views on the relation between actors and systems. On Ricœur's side, I comment on the concepts of institution and practice, and on Giddens's, I examine notions selected to present the "duality of structure". In the course of this exploration, four tasks are identified by which to refine the social theory of Ricœur's *Oneself as Another:* first, surpassing its ultimately teleological schema of action, second, exploring the stabilisation of action despite the uncertainty attributed to the teleological schema, third, reinvesting the notion of constraint, and fourth, clarifying the ambiguity in the notion of institution. In the chapter's conclusion, the contribution of a Ricœur-Giddens dialogue to the accomplishment of these four tasks is demonstrated.

In all this action theorizing, two crucial elements are still lacking. The first is the complex composition of compromises in action by agents in the heat of the action. Then, this theorizing makes quite general anthropological claims (as I pointed out from the beginning) and for this reason we would do well to confront this mode of thinking with the second crucial missing element, which is experienced from outside of the "default" academic orientation to the West. Both of these points can be dealt with simultaneously. To clarify the way I have chosen to deal with these matters, I need to return to the example evoked at the beginning of this introduction: protest action.

5 The Heat of Action

Looking back on the wide range of social movements world-wide since the Arab Spring of 2011, Bertrand Badie tries to capture the historical novelty of these events as "globalization, act 2".[38] One could indeed consider these events from a macro perspective and comment on the increasing integration even of marginalized peoples in course of historical events on a global scale, the interdependence of societies and the mobility of masses of individuals. This is what Badie does when he describes the broad tendency of society to become more powerful than politics. But the same author could equally consider these movements on a micro perspective. Here he is struck by the fact that they are "constituted by an infinite number of micro strategies and distinct social behaviours are aggregated".[39] This alternative understanding opens by taking a different point of view, the one I also adopt in the last two chapters of this book.

Looking more closely, one observes that with all the significant changes of global politics and the living conditions of local societies, a number of persistent aspects of these micro strategies remain. In fact, these aspects are so persistent that one finds them in social movements and political contestations throughout human history. This dimension of the composition of capabilities and means, of the technical dimension of action with ethical concerns – a difficulty which all people have to face in all spheres of life – has been explored in Part 1 of this book. In Part 2, I continue this exploration, with the "heat of action", dramatically presented in contemporary social movements, as a magnifying glass. Indeed, the question of extreme means – the recourse to violence – gives us a singular view on the complex composition of action and brings the dramatic role of ethical considerations in action to the fore better.

---

38 Bertrand Badie, "L'acte II de la mondialisation a commencé," interview with Marc Semo, *Le monde*, 8 November 2019, https://www.lemonde.fr/idees/article/2019/11/08/bertrand-badie-l-acte-ii-de-la-mondialisation-a-commence_6018418_3232.html, last accessed 5 February 2021. The theses advanced in this interview fit into Badie's broader perspective on international politics as developed in a series of recent books, for instance, *L'hégémonie contestée. Les nouvelles formes de domination internationale* (Paris: Odile Jacob, 2019).
39 My translation.

I am certainly not the first philosopher to be drawn into protest movements with an action theoretical interest. To name but two examples, half a century ago Hannah Arendt and Jürgen Habermas both developed some of their most important political philosophical ideas in confrontation with protest movements. Considering the student protests, the anti-racist movements and the anti-war movement in the United States in the late 1960s, Arendt[40] distinguishes the essence of power as generated when many people "act in concert", rather than from the deployment of powerful instruments and arms. In his long view of human history, Habermas[41] describes the social mutations of, and changing relation between, two forms of human rationality and their corresponding forms of action: one instrumental, the other communicative. The instrumental reason focuses so intently on the means by which to realize pre-set aims that it marginalizes the agreement-seeking and value-affirming practices of communicative reason. While Marx set his hope on the proletariat as the force of liberation from the strictures of capitalism, Habermas set his hope on the student movement of the late 1960s to rejuvenate and energize the social, indeed the political, exercise of communicative action.

In my studies, I am quite close to Arendt and Habermas in adopting an action theoretical view on these events. I also embrace the way in which they hold on to philosophical reflection and social science, in such a way that their conceptual developments remain dialectically bound back to the detail of real historical events. However, I do not follow them in their action typologies,[42] which undermine the description of action, as these distinctions can be quite difficult to maintain in analysing cases in detail.

To get a still closer view on what I propose, let us consider a more recent example of philosophical commentary on particular events. I am thinking of the way in which Habermas and Jacques Derrida reflected on the terror attacks in the USA in September 2001.[43] These attacks are, of course, not initiatives of social movements, but in so far as they are attempts to coordinate strategic considerations and normative aspirations, the philosophers' responses to it are, for

---

[40] Hannah Arendt, "On Violence," in *Crises of the Republic: Lying in Politics, Civil Disobedience, on Violence, Thoughts on Politics and Revolution* (San Diego, CA: Harvest/Harcourt Brace Jovanovich, 1972), 134–84.
[41] Jürgen Habermas, "Technology and Science as 'Ideology'" [1968], in *Toward a Rational Society: Student Protest, Science, and Politics* (London: Heinemann, 1972), 81–121.
[42] As I have already argued, inspired by Hans Joas, in Ernst Wolff, "'Technology' as the Critical Social Theory of Human Technicity," *Journal of Philosophical Research* 41 (2016): 333–69.
[43] Giovanna Borradori. *Philosophy in a Time of Terror: Dialogues with Jürgen Habermas and Jacques Derrida* (Chicago, IL: University of Chicago Press, 2003).

my purposes, instructive. In a true philosophical fashion, both strive for maximum understanding of the perpetrators while condemning the acts perpetrated. This is the first interesting point: in order to understand these initiatives, one has to situate them in the broader historical context of international power relations and institutionalized violence. Moreover, such a critical view on the long-term events calls for a self-critical view on the West in its relations to its "others". Thus they perform a hermeneutic gesture, which always forms the backdrop to my own contribution.

However, there is a second significant dimension of these interviews. In their respective philosophical ways, they confirm that these events compelled the West – and in particular, those who work with its intellectual heritage – to scrutinise this heritage in the most energetically self-critical way. In this sense, the arguments of both are in continuity with the spirit of the Enlightenment. Moreover, both attach to this self-critique the need for open discussion with the cultural other; Habermas does so directly,[44] whereas Derrida does so by critiquing a lack of dialogue.[45] Self-critique, they argue, requires encountering the other. And yet, remarkably, they both immediately proceed by evading this task.[46] This performative contradiction is as glaring as it is puzzling. This is, in any case, the negative lesson I derive from them.

When, in the last chapters of this book, I turn to acts of political contestation, my aim is not to offer an encompassing political or political philosophical schema for interpreting such events. Rather, in continuity with the first five chapters of the book, I consider such events bearing in mind the four action theoretical questions mentioned above in §1. In line with the authors I have cited, I attempt to expand and refine my theoretical understanding in a close dialectical loop with concrete historical events. For this purpose, I examine suggestive examples, rather than document general tendencies. I am not asking the historical question of contextualisation, nor a sociological question in the sense of identifying factors contributing to certain forms of movements. Nor am I asking a political scientific or legal question (although, corresponding with the design of my project, significant points from these disciplines are dialectically bound up in this project). Rather, my focus is the action theoretic and hermeneutic question as to the way in which such actions take shape as meaningful for agents in their interaction and in their confrontation with particular contexts.

---

44 Jürgen Habermas and Giovanna Borradori, "Fundamentalism and Terror – A Dialogue with Jürgen Habermas" in Borradori, *Philosophy in a Time of Terror*, 25–43, here 36 ff.
45 Jacques Derrida and Giovanna Borradori, "Autoimmunity: Real and Symbolic Suicides – A Dialogue with Jacques Derrida," in Borradori, *Philosophy*, 85–136, here 121 f.
46 The interviewer did not seem to notice this either.

At the same time, as I have pointed out from the outset, action theoretical claims have a general anthropological reach. And since this is the case, I do my best to avoid Habermas's and Derrida's performative contradiction. On the contrary, I hope to illustrate the value of at least some openness to authors and actors who are not part of the Western philosophical "library".[47] When Habermas and Derrida claimed the need for such intercultural openness, it was not because of naïve exoticism, and I do not succumb to naïve exoticism when I apply the lesson they forgot. Furthermore, if, as I have claimed from the outset, action theoretical claims have a general anthropological reach, then the openness to the cultural other is a first step in precautionary self-relativisation.

5.1 Part 2: Finding Compromises in Practice

The second part of this book consists of three studies. As in the first five chapters, Ricœur is my main interlocutor, serving sometimes as a partner and sometimes as an adversary in advancing my reflection.

In the centre position I place not a philosopher, but an agent, someone who has had to traverse and negotiate the difficulties and complexities of going over to action. I submit to scrutiny a self-interpretation that Nelson Mandela wrote on his own turning to action. What can we learn from Mandela, from the period of peaceful protest, but even more from his decision to adopt violent strategies? Hence the title of **Chapter 7:** "Acts of Violence as Political Competence? From Ricœur to Mandela and Back".

In the third section of his *The Course of Recognition*, Ricœur famously engaged in a debate with Axel Honneth's *Struggle for Recognition*.[48] A careful reading of the debate shows how Ricœur subscribes to Honneth's understanding of struggles for recognition, even to the point of integrating it into Ricœur's own political philosophical. However, he argues for the possibility of exceptional, ephemeral experiences of truce in such struggles. These "states of peace" provide a special vantage point from which to grasp the meaning and aims of polit-

---

[47] I use the term in the sense in which Mudimbe speaks of the colonial "library" in *The Invention of Africa*, 175, 181.
[48] Axel Honneth, *Kampf um Anerkennung: Zur moralischen Grammatik sozialer Konflikte* (Frankfurt am Main: Suhrkamp, [1992] 1994) / Axel Honneth, *The Struggle for Recognition: The Moral Grammar of Social Conflicts* (Cambridge: Polity Press, 1995).

ical struggles. Following Luc Boltanski,[49] Ricœur sees acts of radical love (*agapé*) as a category of social action which reveals the logic of a "state of peace"; for Ricœur, Willy Brandt's genuflection in Warsaw on 7 December 1970 serves as a paradigmatic example.

In scholarship on *The Course of Recognition*, the question regarding which traits of "states of peace" qualify them to provide this exceptional perspective on political struggles has not received sufficient attention. A systematic examination reveals a startling theoretic possibility that is not entertained by Ricœur, namely that their major characteristics (particularly the fact that they are based on a logic of non-equivalence) may be shared by another family of actions. In his book *Love and Justice as Competences* (in the same sections from which Ricœur draws insights on *agapé* as category of social action), Luc Boltanski argues that certain acts of violence also remain true to a logic of non-equivalence.

In Chapter 7, I do not examine the entire range of violent acts. Rather, the focus is be on one particular kind: violent acts of resistance against institutionalized violence. Insights on the way in which such acts are to be understood are drawn from Nelson Mandela's speech at the Rivonia trial. I argue that Mandela's gradient strategy of ways of "answering violence with violence" provides us with suggestions on how to expand Ricœur's phenomenology of ways by which political struggles for recognition may be legitimately interrupted and by which insight into these political struggles may be gained.

In this central chapter of Part 2, I am careful to avoid viewing Mandela as a political icon, one, perhaps, without comparison, and to zoom in on him instead as agent. My objective is to maintain this focus when considering the action possibilities and dilemmas of those citizens of the same country who, half a century later, are faced with similar problems, even though they are no longer in a pariah state, but what has been hailed as a model democracy instead. Unsung, ambiguous agents, like those referred to by Badie, whose faces we may see for (at most) a split moment on the daily news programmes. I learn from some of these people in **Chapter 8**, "Justice Despite Institutions. Struggling for a Good Life from the Destitute Edge of Society."

Continuing the previous chapter's exploration of Ricœur's relevance for political protest and contestation, Chapter 8 aims to clarify the pursuit of justice by people who live at the very edge of society, on the brink of utter destitution. We

---

49 Luc Boltanski, *L'amour et la justice comme compétences. Trois essais de sociologie de l'action* (Paris: Métaillé, 1990) / *Love and Justice as Competences. Three Essays on the Sociology of Action*, trans. Catherine Porter (Cambridge: Polity Press, 2012).

are still pursuing the core objective of this book, namely theorizing the limited capabilities of people and the means by which they interact.

The chapter starts with an exploration of the place of conflict and violence in Ricœur's political philosophy as framed by his later hermeneutic anthropology. I argue that Ricœur assigns a major role to conflict in his political thought. But conflict is not always violence, and it is important to see exactly how he demarcates the place of violence within "the political."

Subsequently, I pursue my line of enquiry with an excursion through labour sociology written in Johannesburg during the last decade or so. The rationale for this inclusion is twofold: these empirical studies help us to retain the practical philosophical thrust that Ricœur's hermeneutics calls for, and they help to question Ricœur's strange limitation of reflection on conflict (in the context of a general hermeneutic anthropology) to a debate in Western democracies. I reject the unspoken assumption – still so prevalent in political philosophy – that one can sufficiently think through something as broad as democracy by focusing on Western examples alone. One positive consequence of my other-than-Western orientation is that this provides a much better vantage on the pursuit of justice from the miserable edge of social co-existence. Accordingly, I can present and reflect on "violent democracy", which provides the background necessary to introduce a distinction between violence relatively close to the centres of privilege, and violence closer to the precipice of destitution. I explore two ways of pursuing the aim of justice from this "edge", the first responding to injustice by means of violent action, and the second responding by contestation, closer to the peaceful possibilities of democracy. In violent democracies, it is impossible to understand one without the other. They are both ambiguous attempts at prudent[50] strategies to improve justice where institutions are failing people. Each is defined in relation to the other, and for each the other remains a viable alternative.

Finally, a number of conclusions are drawn regarding the value of this segue for the attestation by capable and suffering humans of their ability to act and to pursue justice. This will also have implications for those whose profession requires thinking about this quest for justice in the second order of theory or philosophy.

But I have been in academia too long to ignore the scepticism which still often greets attention to "African" events. Anticipation of this scepticism, in **Chapter 6** (the first chapter of Part 2) serves as a justification of my approach. Correspondingly, it is entitled: "Of What is 'Ricœur' the Name? Or, Philosophis-

---

[50] The very specific sense of "prudence" used throughout this book is explained in Chapter 8, §1.

ing at the Edge". In that chapter, I demonstrate how natural it is to look for help and derive a number of insights from Ricœur, in thinking for and about a plural globalised world. Also (while remaining alert to the pitfalls of a simplistic, moralistic view on dialogue between civilizations), I demonstrate how a careful reading of Ricœur's hermeneutics indicates the necessity of listening to others, a project which he himself cannot complete. Once this has been established, the deployment of his hermeneutics of human capabilities in the second and third studies of Part 2 comes quite naturally.

Philosophising, we may recall, is also a practice. In this chapter I wish to contribute to the conflict of interpretations of Ricœur's work. Taking his early anti-colonial tract as a point of departure, I trace two lines of development in his thought: I start with his geopolitics for the post-independence world and then move on to his cultural critical view on modernity as revealed by decolonization. I highlight the significance of these two lines of thought for understanding Ricœur's hermeneutics as a response to disillusioned modernity. A vital implication of this view on Ricœur's work is that it requires completion by the cultural and geopolitical other.[51] I offer an illustration of how such an intercultural philosophical debate could be reconstructed, taking Okolo Okonda as an exemplary partner in debate.

The political nature of philosophising is explored by showing how it can be motivated by the fate of people living "at the edge" of society, demonstrating how Ricœur's own philosophy is invigorated by political concerns, and insisting on the political implications of Eurocentric theorizing. The last three chapters of the book attempt – apart from their stated objective – to experiment with ways by which to oppose such Eurocentric theorizing in ways that brings theoretical rewards.

6 Intermediary Reflexion and Conclusion: Towards an Integrated Theory of the Technicity of Action

The contribution of this book consists of the insights documented in its various chapters, but the Conclusion serves a better purpose than mere compliance with convention. Together with the Introduction and the "Intermediary Reflection" be-

---

[51] Taking Ricœur's philosophy as point of departure, the openness is to African events and scholarship. How valuable such reconstructed dialogues may be is demonstrated in Ernst Wolff, *Lire Ricœur depuis la périphérie. Décolonisation, modernité, herméneutique* (forthcoming). Note that my own point of departure is neither simply Western nor simply African.

tween Part 1 and Part 2, the Conclusion looks more directly at the project as a whole.

One of my points of departure is the fact that action has meaning to the people who engage in action. The limited perspective on the technicity of action changes nothing regarding this fact – quite the contrary. I demonstrate how the capabilities and means of action are simply part of the meaningful fibre of action. Furthermore, at numerous places in the book I show how the central concern of technicity, namely efficacy, remains in relations of mutual implication with the normative or ethical aspects of action.

A first important consequence of the fact that action is thus composed of divergent aspects is that it justifies the circumscribed view I adopt on one aspect, its technicity, in this book. However, this limitation comes at a price: every such focus on one aspect of action has to account for its integration with other dimensions of action. While I am cognizant of this challenge, it has to be borne in mind that the intellectual means appropriate to this examination of the technicity of action cannot give a full view on other aspects, here notably the ethical aspect. This second important consequence of the composition of action is responsible for the fact that, in this book, I do not engage with the meta-ethical philosophising required to clarify the ethical dimension of action in isolation. This means that I have to adopt a descriptive view on action and renounce the ambition of developing it into a full critical theory of the technicity of action. I give an outline of this position in the form of an **"Intermediary Reflection"**, which forms the hinge between Part 1 and Part 2 of the book. The precise nature of the point of view from where I write – the limitation of the promise of what this book could be – informs the **Conclusion** too.

After developing my views on the technicity of action in a constant debate with Ricœur and contributors from the social sciences throughout the book, it seems useful to let those debates recede into the background in order to provide a retrospective view on the gains of these labours. The first aim of the Conclusion is to give a synthetic view of the technicity of action, not to replace the detailed exploration throughout the book.

Then, this brief synthesis again brings to the fore the entanglement of technicity and ethnicity of action, a second point to which I come back in the Conclusion.

This allows me, finally, to advance a hypothesis (which silently forms throughout the book) on responsibility. This hypothesis is that responsibility is best understood as part of the technicity of action, more specifically as the technical dimension of ethical and political action – action which can and should never be reduced to the technical dimension. The preceding chapters allow me to consider reflection on responsibility as grappling with the question: how do we, situated as we are in socio-historical reality, realize our ethical aims (whatever they may be) in full awareness of the difficulties of action? Considered in this way, responsibility is open to the question of the justifiable ethical views, without being the meta-ethical justification of any ethical value or concern. Understood in this way, responsibility would be the opposite of moralism, in two ways: it takes into account the context and difficulties of action and efficiency; and it assumes a hermeneutic (that is, a perspectival, context-determined) view on its own normative concerns. To put it another way: responsibility is the middle way between moralism and cynical realism (something is at stake in action, and the mere pursuit of efficiency of will is a reductive way to view this).

In this way, the Conclusion refers back, albeit obliquely, to Max Weber, who has already been invoked in this Introduction. A century ago, Weber grappled with the dilemma of the irreconcilable opposition of an ethics of responsibility and an ethics of conviction. My book is certainly an attempt to contribute something to our understanding of this dilemma, but on my own terms. Exploring the difficulties of giving a sophisticated descriptive account of the technical dimension of human action, *in view of* the practical dilemmas of finding compromises between normative and strategic considerations in action, aims at achieving this.

Part 1: **The Technicity of Action:
Capabilities and Means**

Chapter 1:
The Effectiveness of Symbols: Mediology and Hermeneutics

1 Introduction

As I explained in the Introduction, my approach in this book combines social theory of action and hermeneutics. The term "hermeneutics" is not new in social theory – it is often used in expositions of comprehensive sociological theories.[1] However, the integration of the philosophical subdiscipline of hermeneutics into social theories is still sometimes met with scepticism. Is philosophical hermeneutics not the study of how to read texts? Is it not fatally bound to tradition? In this chapter, I want to pre-empt this possible objection and in this way also take the first steps in explicating my approach to action.

Hermeneutics did indeed start out as the study of thorough reading. But more than a century's philosophical research has expanded the field of hermeneutics to include all aspects of human reality. Action is certainly included. My primary interlocutor in this book, Paul Ricœur, is one of the philosophers who mastered the scholarly tradition of hermeneutics, but expanded it explicitly to a hermeneutics of agents and action, or as he often said, the acting and suffering human. The title of his book, *From Text to Action*, succinctly captures this point – this book is our major reference to his work in the present chapter. Making action an object of hermeneutic study simply means that it is studied not as a series of impersonal events, but as forms of doings that have meaning for those concerned in and by it. Here, hermeneutics is thus the study of meaning in action and of the interpretation of action. Accordingly, Ricœur's hermeneutics of human capabilities (also called a hermeneutics of the capable human) will remain with us throughout this book.[2] However, instead of simply proclaiming the usefulness of a hermeneutic approach to a social theory of action, I would like to defend it. In order to do so, I chose as my second interlocutor in this chapter someone who has explicitly expressed his doubts about the value of hermeneutics: Régis Debray.[3] Debray is an interesting fencing partner for two very spe-

---

[1] See, for instance, the Gadamer-Habermas debate of half a century ago.
[2] See the sort introduction to the hermeneutics of human capabilities in Chapter 3, §1.
[3] My point is neither to exaggerate his importance as social scientist, nor to use him simply as a weak opponent.

∂ OpenAccess. © 2021 Ernst Wolff, published by De Gruyter. [CC BY-NC-ND] This work is licensed under the Creative Commons Attribution-NonCommercial-NoDerivatives 4.0 License.
https://doi.org/10.1515/9783110725049-003

cific reasons: for one thing, he had an eventful career of political action behind him[4] before he started developing the theory which interests us here; for another, he offered an alternative view on texts from that of hermeneutics, namely mediology. My first aim in engaging with his thought, then, is to demonstrate that hermeneutics, in the broad sense adopted here, is linked to human practice from the beginning. My second aim is to do so by starting from the (historical) core concern of hermeneutics: texts and text-like phenomena.

From the wealth of human capabilities and action, we can narrow down our view to the production and reception of utterances in language. If I can demonstrate that hermeneutics is integrally linked with concerns of action even in this apparently linguistic core, then we have good reason to assume that hermeneutics is integrally linked with human action wherever we may want to explore it. This chapter's focus on speech, texts and transmission is therefore intended as a starting point from which to indicate the full expansion of the approach that I follow in the other chapters.

2 Enter Mediology

But I need clarify my particular interest in Debray's project a bit further. One may consider his theory of mediology as an exciting new actor on the stage on which language and linguistic phenomena are being presented.[5] The unique promise of mediology is that it will clarify the *transmission* of meaning as an aspect of language. This contribution has to take its place in the drama of love and conflict between semiology, linguistics, communication theory, the theory of literature and other disciplines that are evaluated by the community of academic spectators.

At times, however, one gets the impression that Debray is determined to deny hermeneutics (as one of the other actors) its claim to a place on the stage. His dismissive references to hermeneutics create the impression that mediology stands in opposition to hermeneutics, or is at least totally separated from

---

[4] Cf. Keith Reader, *Régis Debray: A Critical Introduction* (London: Pluto, 1995) and Jean Tellez, *L'âme et le corps des idées. Introduction à la pensée de Régis Debray* (Meaux: Germina, 2010), 39–115.

[5] For background see Frédéric Vandenberghe, "Régis Debray and Mediation Studies, or How Does an Idea Become a Material Force?" *Thesis Eleven* 89, no. 1 (2007): 23–42, here 23–25; the same article is also a useful overview of mediology. Maryam Bolouri, *Medial Transformations: Theorising the Intelligent Mediation Sphere* (Tübingen: Eberhard Karls-Universität Tübingen 2019) situates Debray in relation to other media theories.

it.⁶ Admittedly, it is necessary to define the mediological perspective in order to give it its own voice within the "council of disciplines".⁷ But it is equally important to go further than insisting on "why we are not ..."⁸ if we want to prevent the council from becoming a cacophony of monologues. Besides, this opposition does not sit well with the orientation of mediology as *one* of several valid perspectives on reality. Rather, the search for dialogue is a defining characteristic of the methods of mediology. Louise Merzeau summarises this openness, which is reflected in many of the articles in the *Cahiers de Médiologie* and in *Médium*,⁹ when she states that mediology

> is averse to practicing exclusion. Anyone who would like to explore it can do so, without necessarily forfeiting their membership of their original discipline. [...] Double lanes are even strongly recommended, since it is true that mediology cannot be practised in the self-sufficiency of institutionalized knowledge. [...] [M]ediology must cultivate its *impurity* in order to guarantee its effectiveness."¹⁰

The nature of the mediological perspective is such that it offers a perspective on other fields of study, while at the same time it is subjected to the perspectives of those other fields.¹¹ However, this gives us more than only two perspectives, since a successful dialogue produces more than the two original viewpoints, without their being dissolved in a harmonious whole. Such a dialogue between mediology and hermeneutics has not yet taken place and this is precisely what I intend to start, with a view to the broader set of questions about action in this book.

But where should one start? Consider the following two questions:
– How do ideas become effective, or practice?
– How are cultural products understood?

---

6 See, for example, Régis Debray, "Un dialogue manqué," *Médium* 5 (2005): 116–31, here 116, 129.
7 See Régis Debray, *Introduction à la médiologie* (Paris: PUF, 2000), Chapter V, "Le conceil des disciplines," in which the author discusses the demarcation of mediology in respect of other disciplines. On these demarcations, cf. Tellez, *L'âme et le corps des idées*, 174–77.
8 This is the refrain repeated in the subdivisions of the abovementioned chapter by Debray: Why are we not (semiologists, psychologists, sociologists, pragmatists, historians)?
9 The *Cahiers de Médiologie* (published between 1996 and 2004), was the first mediology journal. Since October 2004 its function has been taken over by *Médium*.
10 Louise Merzeau, "Ceci ne tuera pas cela," *Cahiers de Médiologie* 6 (1998): 27–39, citation 28. Unless otherwise indicated, all translations are my own.
11 See Pierre Lévy's attempt at situating mediology in respect of a variety of communication disciplines, and thereby also in the field of all the disciplines, in "La place de la médiologie dans le trivium," *Cahiers de Médiologie* 6 (1998): 43–58.

The first question is typically mediological, the second is hermeneutic. Two different points of view, two procedures, two goals. But the two disciplines have a shared interest in that a message that did not belong to anyone becomes someone's, in other words, it is appropriated and thereby becomes meaningful. Both want to know how a message is formed and received. Based on this significant overlap, I would like to single out three areas of shared interest to explore: the subject or agent who is surrounded by technology, which shapes his/her milieu or world (§3), the autonomy of the message or writing and reading (§4) and the opening towards politics (§5).

3 The Technical *Milieu* and the *World* of Technology

At the centre of mediology, Debray places the study of the human being as someone who transmits (*l'homme qui transmet*).[12] Where can this human being be found? What are the minimum requirements for transmission characterising the *homo transmettans?* Transmission takes place where that which is "spoken" (*dit*) survives or endures because of the way it is spoken, its "speaking" (*dire*). This coordination of "spoken" and "speaking" stands metonymically for all utterances of meaning, including, for instance, writing or the production of video material.[13] One may thus reformulate: transmission takes place where the emitted message endures because of the way it continues to be conveyed. Such survival requires that (a) the uttered words or produced images have to be deposited in a support mechanism or prop (*support*), and (b) that this prop has to be simultaneously transformed by institutions into a carrier or conveyor (*vecteur*). In short, the "speaking" must be reinforced to become a medium.[14]

---

[12] Debray, *Introduction à la médiologie*, 2.

[13] The two concepts *le dire* (to say, the saying) and *le dit* (the said, that which is / was said) are used in widely divergent theories and philosophies in Francophone academic writing. They refer to a meaningful *event* and the related *meaning* of the event. I translate them with "speaking" and "the spoken", in quotation marks. For my current purposes, this conceptual pair is useful because it is used by both Debray and Ricœur, and in quite similar ways. However, since they cause quite awkward phrases, I restrict my use of them to the minimum.

[14] A detailed survey of Debray's concept of "medium" is offered by Luo Shicha, "Media as Mediation: Régis Debray's Medium Theory and Its Implications as a Perspective," *Empedocles: European Journal for the Philosophy of Communication* 9, no. 2 (2018): 121–38. Andrea Miconi and Marcello Serra's article "On the Concept of Medium: An Empirical Study," *International Journal of Communication* 13 (2019): 3444–61 is not dedicated to Debray, but the references to his work in the article are helpful to situate him in the broader landscape of theories of media.

Correspondingly, a medium, consists, then, of a conveyor with two sides: (a) the prop, as a technical conveyor or expression, i.e. as organized matter (*matière organisée*); and (b) the institution, as a social conveyor, i.e. materialised organization (*organisation matérialisée*). Likewise, a medium is both a form of technical artefact and a kind of practice. Thinking through these two aspects of media opens the way to a study respectively of the logistics and the strategy of transmission.[15] Hence Vandenberghe correctly concludes that "The medium is not [only – EW] a thing, but a dynamic, dialectical *praxis* and process that interrelates and integrates objects, peoples and texts."[16]

An additional specification of transmission consists in distinguishing it from communication.

3.1 Transmission and Communication

If Debray is concerned with the survival of emitted messages, what is his view on the production and reception of the message? In his mind, this question requires a distinction that is fundamental to his understanding of the mediological enterprise. This distinction consists of contrasting communication (the attempt to transmit a message as effectively as possible over a distance) and transmission (the attempt to ensure that a message will be heard for the longest possible time). Communication is regarded as nothing more than an aspect of transmission. All transmission involves communication, but not all communication transmits, according to Debray.[17]

Not only do I find problematic the way in which Debray makes this basic distinction, I also think that a more careful reconstruction thereof would help us to gain a view on the mutual implication of mediology and hermeneutics. In arguing this point, I stay as close as possible to Debray's conceptual frame. Let us launch this reconstruction by examining what one may consider the most minimal instance of transmission.

Given the way in which Debray made the communication/transmission distinction, there is nothing obvious about my counterclaim that the most basic,

---

15 Cf. Debray, *Introduction à la médiologie*, 127; Régis Debray, *Transmitting culture*, trans. Eric Rauth (New York, NY: Columbia University Press, 2000), 10–15.
16 Vandenberghe, "Régis Debray and Mediation Studies," 29.
17 So important is the communication/transmission distinction thus made that Krämer presents her whole introduction to Debray from this perspective, cf. Sybille Krämer, *Medium, Messenger, Transmission: An Approach to Media Philosophy* (Amsterdam: Amsterdam University Press, 2015), 63, likewise 77. However, she does not subject this premise to critical examination.

minimal transmission phenomenon can be found where two people are speaking to each other, or that dialogue or communication in the physical presence of another always involves transmission, and that if we wish to understand what transmission is, we first have to learn to recognize transmission in communication. In order to justify my claim, it is necessary to explore this minimal scenario carefully. At the core of this phenomenon of minimal transmission is a message: that which is "spoken". By speaking, a person deposits this message in a prop which conveys it to another person. In this case, the prop, on the speaker's side, is the language, which was not invented by the interlocutors, the ability to inflect verbs correctly, practices of courtesy, skilful accentuation and so forth, while on the recipient's side it is the ability to listen, concentrate, understand the type of language or register used, remember, etc. Finally, the two people involved in the conversation form a micro social conveyor that transmits the content of the message and the code used for transmission. The existence of the aforementioned code has already been ensured by the surrounding society and those involved in the conversation are participating in the survival of this code by using it for their mutual communication. Therefore, by communicating a message, the two participants in the conversation are explicitly taking part in the transmission of that message and are implicitly transferring the ability to communicate and receive a message.

3.2 Transmission in the Mnemosphere

This simple examination of a situation of dialogue already suffices to raise questions about the mediological resistance to thinking of communication as a transmission event.[18] It would even become impossible to deny the transmission dimension of communication, by situation communication, as Debray does, within the broader context of mediaspheres.[19] In Debray's work, a mediasphere is defined as an enormous socio-technical milieu of transmission. Mediaspheres correspond with stages in the technical development of humanity; the logosphere, the graphosphere and the videosphere (the three mediaspheres discussed in detail by Debray), which are historically telescoped into each other. In *Introduction à la médiologie*, further reference is made to Louise Merzeau's hypothesis of a hypersphere that would be the full development of the video-

---

18 Even though Debray would have to agree with my analysis – cf. Régis Debray, *Cours de médiologie générale* (Paris: Gallimard, [1991] 2001), 24.
19 See, for instance, Debray, *Transmitting Culture*, 103–104, 115–16.

sphere,[20] but this was later more completely expounded by Debray in collaboration with Merzeau.[21] My point about communication as transmission could be substantiated further by due consideration of the mnemosphere – identified but, strangely, neglected by Debray.[22]

The mnemosphere, which only makes its appearance fairly late in Debray's mediological discourse, is mentioned only in passing and disappears quickly from his agenda.[23] This sphere does not receive the attention it deserves – for instance, one searches in vain for the type of table used to describe other mediaspheres – and there is no justification for this oversight. We are simply informed that, following a vague period of hominising, the logosphere appears as "the period that is introduced by the discovery of the technique of writing".[24] Each time, a mediasphere is opened up by a technical invention, and Debray urges us to agree that "the phenomenon of technique [...] does not start [...] with electronics, not even with typography, but with the first forms of writing and the first readings".[25] One might have been able to agree with this contention, if "writing" and "reading" were to be understood in the very broad sense that I use in §2, according to which all technical artefacts are inscriptions that lend themselves to reading and being read (in which case, Debray's claim would simply amount to an analytical truth), but as a historical indication, the claim is simply not true. Debray neglects, amongst other things, the technical dimension of communication in physical presence (although he is not unaware of it) and does not engage with the techniques of the body. These techniques are essential to an understanding of the performative and transmitting nature of communication, which is the most important socio-technical conveyor of the mnemosphere. Hence the significance of reflecting on this mediasphere in the context of the question of the relation between communication and transmission.

In the mnemosphere (in the socio-technical milieu prior to the development of writing on which the logosphere is based), transmission occurs mainly in dia-

---

20 Debray, *Introduction à la médiologie*, 45.
21 See Louise Merzeau and Régis Debray, "Médiasphère," *Médium* 4 (2005): 146–52.
22 Very revealing of this inexplicable neglect of the mnemosphere is the absence even of this term in authors who nevertheless discuss Debray's mediaspheres: cf. Bolouri, *Medial Transformations*, 162; Shicha, "Media as Mediation," 128; Vandenberghe, "Régis Debray and Mediation Studies," 35; and Melinda Turnley, "Towards a Mediological Method: A Framework for Critically Engaging Dimensions of a Medium," *Computers and Composition* 28, no. 2 (2011): 126–44, here 130.
23 See Debray, *Introduction à la médiologie*, 44.
24 Merzeau and Debray, "Médiasphère," 147.
25 Debray, *Cours de médiologie générale*, 26.

logue and other forms of direct communication, for example, oral traditions, dances, ceremonies, decorating practices, etc. In the mid-1990s, I attended the inauguration of a Venda chieftain named Stalin Boy. On that occasion, we listened to a recital of Venda history going as far back as six or seven hundred years: centuries of oral transmission of history – the most valuable source for contemporary historiography covering the distant history of a part of the world where methods of transmission were disastrously affected by progress in other mediaspheres.[26] In the long term, the success of the other mediaspheres in contrast to the mnemosphere was catastrophic for the transmission of forms of socialization, ideas regarding authority, crafts, moral values, etc. which were transmitted via the mnemosphere. The mnemosphere should not be neglected; it still exists alongside the logo-, grapho- and videosphere, and, arguably, the hypersphere. The messages transmitted through the mnemosphere are considerable. We can think about the wearing of clothes, make-up and adornments, smoking, knowledge of edible plants, the practice of music, sexism and the idea of the supernatural, to name but a few of the most important messages whose continued existence will increasingly be ensured by other forms of transmission. This first mediasphere that preceded the development of writing is therefore of paramount importance for the entire mediological project. For the purposes of the current argument, it confirms the transmitting dimension of communication. At a later stage, we will see that the transmission in communication can be explained by the fact that spoken language has a "text-like" dimension, which accords it a form of autonomy, on the basis of which it can function as a medium.

My insistence on the transmitting character of all types of communication should not be seen as a contradiction of the communication/transmission distinction maintained by Debray (on the contrary, I maintain it explicitly in §2, below). However, it is important not to look for transmission only in the more technologically impressive forms in which it appears. Just as we have found *homo transmettans* in dialogue, he/she is also present in numerous interactions which involve implicit or explicit learning. Here the basic phenomenon is the techniques of the body (Mauss) or the habitus (Bourdieu).[27] All artefacts are mnemotechniques, and, in general, artefacts tend to impart a mnemotechnical

---

[26] Further on oral tradition, cf. Okolo Okonda and Jacques Ngangala Balade Tongamba, *Introduction à l'histoire des idées dans le contexte de l'oralité: théorie et méthode avec application sur l'Afrique traditionnelle* (Louvain-la-Neuve: Academia-L'Harmattan, 2018).

[27] Also see Debray, *Introduction à la médiologie*, 122: "The human body remains the first and last mediator of meaning." On the technical aspect of the body in Mauss and Bourdieu, cf. Ernst Wolff, "Technicity of the Body as Part of the Socio-technical System: The Contributions of Mauss and Bourdieu," *Theoria* 76, no. 2 (2010): 167–87.

effectiveness to the body. In the extension of techniques of the body, which include the most basic forms of communication, the transmission of all the other techniques can be revealed. In this regard, clothes can serve as a useful paradigm.

3.3 Clothes: Transmission and Understanding

Almost every single technical artefact transmits something, even if it only the possibility of using natural objects in a technical way. My point is not to simply rephrase McLuhan's "the medium is the message"[28], but to give a basic phenomenological description of the transmitting quality of technical artefacts, a description which should allow us to see the overlap between and validity of the hermeneutic and mediological view on it. Let us hone in on this issue.

Through their transmitting character, technical artefacts create sociocultural ties. The following observation by Jean-Pierre Séris about clothes highlights this point:

> Clothing is a perfect example of the dialectic of necessity and exigency that takes place in technical production. To the object responds a world that is not reduced to the material world, but is a humanized world, the social and historical world, spoken and written. Clothing and gesture introduce the individuals into this world.[29]

This observation is of considerable importance to understand why clothes are a paradigmatic example of objects invested with socio-historical meaning. Clothes may satisfy physical needs, but at the same time they offer an entrance to that which is not only physical but human, in other words historical, social and meaningful. Furthermore, I argue that clothes are not only objects, but an extension of the wearer's body. This allows them to be both medium and message, which means that wearing clothes therefore amounts to transmitting and simultaneously signifying and understanding. On which grounds can these claims be made?

Clothes are vehicles for messages (for instance, of cultural belonging, social status, a protocol to express resistance to established values); they are the technical props (e.g. this specific shirt; that specific hat) that are mobilised to become a medium by a social wearer involved in the transmission (e.g. the social

---

28 On the convergences and divergencies of Debray with regard to McLuhan, see Shicha, "Media as Mediation," 124–26.
29 Jean-Pièrre Séris, *La technique* (Paris: PUF, 1994), 68.

consensus regarding the proper way to clothe yourself in different situations, penalising practices for ignoring taboos with regard to what is considered appropriate). But to wear and see clothes is also to understand (e.g. I see myself as belonging to this cultural group and other people identify me as such; I understand that the event is formal and that the concert is an elegant occasion which I help to create through my dress; I present myself as sporty to the woman I am trying to impress and she sees me as either genuine or artificial). Clothing inserts wearers into a milieu of media that transmit cultural values and ideas; at the same time they insert them into the totality of references to which we as people who understand are open and which, in phenomenology is referred to as the *world* (in the rest of this book I use the term "world" in this specific sense). The fact that there is not an explicitly formed message in each case does not detract from the fact that something is being transmitted, and that whatever is being *transmitted* (and its context) is *understood*.

3.4 No Mediology without Hermeneutics. No Milieu without a World

I have now (a) questioned Debray's articulation of the communication/transmission distinction, (b) explored the mediological significance of identifying transmission in all communication, with reference to the mnemosphere and (c) demonstrated the mutual implication of transmission and understanding with the example of clothing. There is a very good reason why I allowed myself this space: I needed to show how *the core concern of hermeneutics emerges logically from the very conceptual framework of mediology*.[30] It may now be safely claimed that it is impossible to see *the person as transmitter* in the person wearing clothes unless he/she is also recognized as the *person who understands*. The person who understands is the one who continuously sees and understands everything around him/her, either consciously or unconsciously. A part of what is understood, often the largest part, is what is being transmitted. In other words,

---

30 I would therefore recommend caution when reading Krämer's claim that "[w]hat Debray achieves with this approach is that he does not need to pit matter against ideas [...], but rather he is able to trace the interconnection of both. Wherever culture is found there is obviously *both* and – if you will – the traditional, hermeneutic-semiological dematerialisation, which proceeds from the tangible to the intangible, is thereby put in its relatively proper place" (Krämer, *Medium, Messenger, Transmission*, 65). Nor is Debray able to explore fully the passage "from the tangible to the intangible" (i.e. reading), nor does the categorical tag of "dematerialisation" apply to the hermeneutics of Ricœur.

3 The Technical *Milieu* and the *World* of Technology — 43

each *milieu* or sphere that is created by people who transmit also contains a *world* thanks to people who understand that milieu and who understand themselves through that particular milieu. Because people understand more than the isolated transmitted message (they also understand that which surrounds the transmission, subject as it is to changing circumstances), the meaning of the transmitted message changes along with the changes in context of its reception. And that is why the institutions and other social conveyors that watch over the transmission are compelled to react by adapting their methods and means of transfer in as far as they strive to stabilise the message. If people, unlike animals, do not only communicate but also transmit,[31] and if "I *am* my milieu",[32] it is possible simply because people do not merely have a situation, but also a world,[33] or rather, *belong* to a world. Our milieu is like an enormous garment that leads us into the world and clothes us with meaning, even if (as with clothes) we are often not aware of it.

Belonging (*appartenance*) is the condition of the human being as the one who understands, according to Ricœur's hermeneutics. Before we examine what this means for Ricœur (see §2), allow me to explore this point first with a view to clarifying its mediological significance. At any given moment, a human being understands and understands him-/herself in a milieu that calls forth his/her world. People bathe in meaning to which they are open, together with others. Different milieus support different worlds: the world of the home, the world of work, the world of recreation, etc. Technical artefacts represent an enormous part of the milieu. In reality, any object can be a prop for signs, and I cannot agree with Debray's assertion that there is no transmission in the interaction with all technical objects.[34] The bath and the fork (Debray's examples of non-transmitting artefacts) are mnemonics (*mnémotechniques* as the French aptly say) which, in coordination with social conveyors, are the media of messages about shame, cleanliness, hygiene, or an understanding of food and good manners (see the discussion of this below).

---

[31] Régis Debray, "Technique," *Médium* 3 (2005): 162–69, here 164. The author of the particular column is not named, but it is probably Debray.
[32] Debray, *Introduction à la médiologie*, 93.
[33] Paul Ricœur, *Du texte à l'action. Essais d'herméneutique II* (Paris: Editions du Seuil, 1986), 211 / Paul Ricœur, *From Text to Action: Essays in Hermeneutics II*, trans. Kathleen Blamey and John Thompson (London: Athlone, 1991), 149.
[34] See Régis Debray, "Histoire des quatre M," *Cahiers de Médiologie* 6 (1998): 7–24, here 20.

The understanding human is an embodied being and understands, above all, with his/her body.³⁵ This body gives specificity to one's understanding, which, however, is never solely one's own. It is not one's own in as far as it is through interaction with other people and the surrounding media that one has learned and continues to learn to understand. It is because people understand, and because in their own way they belong to their milieu and their world, and because their understanding constitutes them as social beings, and because as social beings they simultaneously participate in the construction of the existence of society, that people can transmit, knowingly or unknowingly. At the same time, the understanding belonging to the world through complex techniques of the body can only be understood if it is constituted through transmission. One therefore cannot transmit if one does not also have an understanding³⁶ of that which is being transmitted: first, one understands in one's capacity as a social conveyor accompanying the transmission, and second, one understands through one's belonging to, or appropriation of, that which is being transmitted.

The sphere of *media*, as a gigantic milieu consisting of numerous means of transmission, is therefore the *socio-technical dimension of the world*. However, the world is always larger than the mediasphere. This is of great importance to mediology, since people's understanding of their worlds always has an impact on their reception of mediated messages. This is why transmission always involves transformation. The struggle for the survival of the emitted message requires modifications of the media by which it is transmitted, in the form of mediological innovations that inevitably lead to the metamorphosis of that message. (In Chapter 3, §5, I explore this as an instance of the technological paradox.)

By establishing the relationship between mediology and hermeneutics, the mediologist should obtain a better understanding of our belonging to a mediasphere, and the socio-technical transmission of understanding is clarified in turn for the hermeneuticist.

---

35 As has been so carefully described by Merleau-Ponty. Through the techniques of the body, understanding depends on transmission in the same person – a baby's nervous system remains underdeveloped until it is developed by the involvement of those in whose care it is, in other words through songs, dances, jokes, etc., which are cultural products that are supported by techniques of the body and other communal techniques. I owe this insight to Jörn Rüsen.
36 "*An* understanding" obviously does not remotely imply "*full* comprehension".

4 Autonomy and Appropriation

The preceding exposition has brought to light how human beings simultaneously belong to mediaspheres and to worlds of meaning – spheres and worlds that are mutually dependent. In order to emphasise the way in which people are surrounded by milieus and worlds all the time, I have highlighted the overlap between communication and transmission in practice. However, the difference between the two cannot be ignored without damaging our understanding of both transmission and interpretation. What is at stake here is the autonomy of the medium (seen from the mediological perspective) or of the text or writing (from the hermeneutic perspective) in respect of the situation in which the message was originally formed.[37]

Mediology and hermeneutics both distinguish equally between "speaking" and the "spoken". The mediologist asks how the "speaking" makes it possible for the "spoken" to survive – how the "spoken" succeeds in being received later by way of its socio-technical "speaking". The hermeneuticist asks how the "spoken" that has been detached from its milieu of living meaning and acquires its own mode of existence in the socio-technical "speaking" can be absorbed in the meaning for someone, which is how it can be appropriated as having sense. Let us now look at the connection from the perspective of hermeneutics. Paul Ricœur serves as our reference.

The hermeneuticist does not strive only to learn more about the phenomenon of understanding, but also about interpretation. Here, *understanding* refers to the spontaneous, often unintended grasp which is constitutive of belonging to a world of meaning, while *interpretation* refers to the second order capacity of reflecting on understandings. This means that interpretation requires a distancing or distantiation[38] [*distanciation*] with regard to one's belonging to the world of meanings. Distantiation[39] thematizes what is understood and is only possible if that which in this way becomes the object of interpretation is supported by

---

[37] In Chapter 2, §3.2 (Point 1) autonomy is discussed further and argued to be a characteristic of technical artefacts in general.

[38] The English translation of *From Text to Action* writes "distanciation". I follow *Oxford English Dictionary* which writes "distantiation".

[39] Distantiation is the hermeneutic variant of the phenomenological reduction. One would be able to identify a mediological version in Debray's work (only in the spirit of the text, since the letter of the text will object to the somewhat scholastic nature of the phenomenological method), namely in Debray, *Introduction à la médiologie*, 48, where the author uses it to describe how the understanding of spontaneous participation in a mediasphere could, as it were, be placed in brackets by a disturbance of the normal functioning of that sphere.

some or other medium. According to Ricœur, the "original trait" (*trait primitif*) of distantiation is discourse: verbal expression, or simply putting things into words. In discourse *someone says something to someone*. Thus discourse forms a dialectic of an *event* that occurs and which is understood as *meaning*.[40] This is equally valid for spoken and written discourse (which, in Ricœur's opinion, both represent archetypes of discourse). Thus a situation develops that is paradigmatic for hermeneutics: written text that must be read, or more generally formulated, inscription that has to become an event of meaning again.

If we consider spoken discourse as a medium for the transmission of a message, as we did in § 3 (above), it would be possible to note that the message has a certain autonomy even in dialogue.[41] In this way, the dialogical exchange could be seen, at least partially, as an event of writing and reading, where "writing" is metonymic for an event during which meaning obtains autonomy in respect of its origin, and "reading" is metonymic for any event involving the appropriation of meaning. In dialogue, writing and reading, communication and transmission, are more condensed than in cases with a more elaborate socio-technical structure. But when one has learned to view each of these elements in dialogue, it becomes easier to recognize them in other instances.

4.1 Discourse as Action

All discourse emits meaning. However, the event or act of discourse itself exceeds the spoken meaning with its own meaning. To get a good grasp on this fact, Ricœur borrows from the *speech act* theories of Austin[42] and Searle, in particular Austin's distinction between three discourse actions: the locutionary act (the fact that something is being said), the illocutionary act (the way in which

---

[40] Cf. Ricœur, *Du texte à l'action*, 115–17, 123–24 / *From Text to Action*, 77–78, 81–82.

[41] However, Ricœur might not agree – in his expositions on discourse, he emphasises the difference between the spoken word and text. But this seems to me a matter of stressing the autonomy of discourse as a dimension of distantiation. Once this point is granted, one has to accept that there is distantiation in spoken discourse too.

[42] Also used by Debray in *Introduction à la médiologie*, 112, 114. I would like to point out that Ricœur had been working on his own version of a "speech act theory" even before J. L. Austin's famous book, *How to Do Things with Words*. The William James Lectures Delivered at Harvard University 1955 (Oxford: Clarendon, 1962). See Paul Ricœur, "Travail et parole" [1953], in *Histoire et vérité* (Paris: Seuil, 1964), 238–64 / "Work and the Word," in *History and Truth*, trans. Charles A. Kelbley (Evanston, IL: Northwestern University Press, 1965), 197–222. I have commented in detail on this interesting essay in a monograph, *Lire Ricœur depuis la périphérie. Décolonisation, modernité, herméneutique* (forthcoming).

something is said) and the perlocutionary act (that which is done or brought about by saying something).[43] In each of these three modalities by which meaning is produced, speaking is also doing – Austin's book is fittingly entitled *How to Do Things with Words*, and is aptly translated into French as *Quand dire, c'est faire* (When saying is doing). This embedding of speech act theory in Ricœur's reflection on interpretation is of the utmost importance for the objective of this chapter, since it creates the hinge between a hermeneutics of text and a hermeneutics of action – the latter opens in turn to the broader theme of my whole book.

According to Ricœur, these three aspects of the action of meaning form a descending hierarchy of the possibility of being captured in writing:[44] the more speech is doing, the less this act can be inscribed in words. Why is this so? Ricœur does not give us a reason, but Debray may help us to work it out for ourselves. The reason is that from locution to illocution to perlocution, speaking gradually becomes more dependent on other forms of technical support: illocution is concerned with the techniques of prosody; in perlocution everything that is needed to ensure the desired effect on the persons who are addressed is used. From locution through illocution to perlocution, discourse increases in sociotechnical density, which is nothing other than the combination of organized matter and materialised organization (as Debray calls it). Therefore Debray is quite right in claiming that "the object of transmission does not pre-exist the operation of its transmission"[45] – in other words, there is no message without a socio-technical embodiment. However, one should not conclude from this that all dimensions of a message are equally prone to be transmitted equally successfully. If the discourse should not merely be written down, but should remain an effective way of doing things with words, then the discourse has to retain this socio-technical logistics and strategy.

4.2 Autonomy and the Effectiveness of Symbols

Ricœur does not investigate further how and in which forms speaking can be doing,[46] and can continue doing over the course of time, which is exactly where the interest of mediology lies. However, the most general condition for

---

43 Ricœur, *Du texte à l'action*, 208 / *From Text to Action*, 147.
44 Ricœur, *Du texte à l'action*, 119, 209 / *From Text to Action*, 79, 147.
45 Debray, *Introduction à la médiologie*, 18.
46 My comment applies to the texts in *From Text to Action*. What one can do with words has already been thematized in Ricœur, "Work and the Word" referred to above.

"continuing to do over the course of time" holds his attention. Informally, this condition is called writing, but it would be incorrect to limit the writing to which Ricœur refers to textual inscriptions. When considering writing, Ricœur thinks about the core features of all forms of inscription. He sees writing as the archetype of all inscriptions, as it informs us about the *autonomy* of the message mediated by the medium or media.

Autonomy emerges when inscription dislocates the dialectic of the "speaking" event and "spoken" meaning. Inscription has this dislocating effect on discourse regardless of whether the inscription is done orally,[47] in writing, or visually, or by means of any other socio-technical support mechanism. By being written down, the discourse loses its character as an event, or rather as an event of meaning, and continues its existence merely as potential meaning that can only be realized when a recipient appropriates it again as a message. In more mediological terms, autonomy is the mode of existence of the transmitted message. Through the autonomous medium, the message survives, despite, but also as a result of, its autonomy (a) in respect of its original formulator-sender, (b) in respect of its first milieu of reference, i.e. the socio-cultural circumstances of its production, and (c) in respect of the original addressees.[48] In other words, the autonomous inscription decontextualises what it has inscribed. It is a transformed version of discourse. In this decontextualised state, the discourse is maintained in practice by that with which Ricœur's understanding of the discourse must be completed: discourse is the event during which someone tells something to someone *by means of something*. No discourse is possible without organized matter and materialised organization, and without an element of autonomy. That is why I argue that dialogic discourse can also be examined according to the model of inscription and transmission (I once again refer to the above explanation of transmission in communication, §3.1).

Debray is, of course, quite familiar with using the text as paradigm, as the following statement proves: "For the dependence of the spiritual on the material, the history of writing serves as a parable".[49] If the text can serve as a paradigm or archetype, this can be attributed to the fact that it is the example of the autonomy of the message that can be most easily analysed. I have not forgotten that here the "text" is metonymic for the entire milieu associated with it: the school, the books and newspapers, the libraries, the academies, the publishers, etc. And

---

[47] The idea of "oral inscription" is not a contradiction in terms: all verbally transmitted formulas, narratives, languages, etc., which are at least partially repeatable and recognizable, correspond with this term. Oral history (mentioned above) illustrates this point.
[48] Ricœur, *Du texte à l'action*, 207 ff / *From Text to Action*, 146 ff.
[49] Debray, *Introduction à la médiologie*, 43.

no one considers neglecting the particularities of the other media, even though they are also regarded as "texts".[50] In Debray's view, "texts" are that which (a) emanates from a general symbolising procedure (*procédé général de symbolisation*), (b) uses a social code of communication (*code social de communication*), (c) is supported by a physical aid, (d) benefits from a distribution system (*dispositif de diffusion*),[51] (e) is transmitted together with other "texts" thanks to institutions' efforts to manage transmission; and (f) forms milieus that in turn form groups in the mediasphere. But Debray demands more detail and asks: How and by which means can the transmission of "texts" enable us to do things with them? Or, "How does an idea become a material force?" (in the formulation taken up in the title of Vandenberghe's 2007 article). Debray is explicitly concerned with *the effectiveness of symbols*.[52]

Ricœur, for his part, is not at all ignorant about the significance of the effectiveness of symbols. In the Introduction we saw the importance he attached to the combination of a "spirituality" and a "technology" – that art which Gandhi mastered so well (see Introduction, §3.1). For this reason, I would not hesitate to venture that the question about the effectiveness of symbols is one of the sources from which his interest in hermeneutics emerged. Be that as it may, in his hermeneutic essays in *From Text to Action* he is satisfied with not spending too much time contemplating the nature of the means of discourse; he accepts text/writing as a paradigm and moves on to other important questions: how does it happen that that which had been "spoken" is *recontextualised*, in other words, how does the autonomous discourse become reintegrated into a dialectics of event and meaning, and how does this fact become interpretation? Therefore Ricœur's hermeneutics remains occupied with the effectiveness of symbols, but in a different way.

---

50 There is therefore no reason to protest, for example, with reference to Debray, *Introduction à la médiologie*, 161–62, that visual images cannot be interpreted as a written discourse – here we are not ignoring the differences between the media, but we are concerned with pointing out their common characteristic, which is autonomy.
51 Cf. Debray, *Introduction à la médiologie*, 35.
52 See, for example, Debray, *Introduction à la médiologie*, the title of Chapter IV – *L'éfficacité symbolique*. The French "efficacité" embraces both effectiveness and efficiency. If there were an exact English equivalent, I would have used it. Since there is not, I try to distinguish as well as possible in each case which term to use, if not both, taking as my guide the idea that effective transmission requires effective conveyors, and that may be so because they are also efficient, but not necessarily.
    Translating "éfficacité symbolique" directly poses another problem: "symbolic effectiveness" could create the misunderstanding if the phrase is contrasted with, say, "real effectiveness". Hence the decision rather to use "effectiveness/efficacy of symbols".

Whereas Debray places more emphasis on the *effectiveness* of symbols, Ricœur tends to stress the *symbolic* aspect of their effectiveness. Mediology examines the ways in which meanings are transformed into media; hermeneutics attempts to decipher the media environment that offers itself as having meaning. Mediology places more emphasis on everything that relates to the text (but not exclusively), whereas hermeneutics emphasises everything that relates to the reading of the text (but not exclusively).

I therefore conclude that there is a symmetrical relation of mutual implication between the hermeneutic and mediological views. There can be no Beethoven without scores, without concert halls, without conservatories, but the scores, concert halls and conservatories remain deadly silent without the performance and the interpretation. Writing and reading go together – for hermeneutics as much as for mediology – since both are interested in the effectiveness of symbols. Reading is impossible without writing, but until writing has been read, it has not transmitted anything. Therefore, when Sybille Krämer paraphrases Debray as saying that "[t]o transmit something means *to embody the immaterial*"[53] she renders accurately his fundamentally truncated view on transmission,[54] an error which can easily be pointed out with the hermeneutic means deployed here. No reception, no transmission.[55]

4.3 On Reception: Reading Texts and Artefacts

If the inscription suspends the life of the meaningful event, the text remains dead as long as there is no reader to give it life again. Who is the life-giving reader? It is not only the person to whom the message was originally addressed, but any person who gains access to the message, whether consciously or not, intentionally or not. Moreover, a person never reads alone. Ricœur quite correctly

---

53 Krämer, *Medium, Messenger, Transmission*, 65.
54 Debray concludes his chapter on symbolic effectiveness with the words: "Mediology as discourse can be summarised as a trajectory of [...] message, medium, milieu and mediation"[" *La médiologie comme discours peut se ramener à un parcours [...] message, médium, milieu et médiation*"] (Debray, *Introduction à la médiologie*, 137 and also Debray, "Histoire des quatre M"). One might ask whether he does not perhaps stop too soon on his trajectory. The transmission trajectory does not lead anywhere unless appropriation takes place.
55 In fact, one could see how Debray fails on this point, by considering his own description of Glen Gould's reception of Bach – cf. discussion by Constantina Papoulias, "Of Tools and Angels: Régis Debray's Mediology," *Theory, Culture & Society* 21, 3 (2004): 165–70, here 168–69.

points out that "every reading of a text always takes place within a community, a tradition, or a living current of thought, all of which display presuppositions and exigencies – regardless of how closely a reading may be tied to the *quid*, to 'that in view of which' the text was written."[56] The message is read by a reader who participates in a social formation of readers, who keep an eye on what he/she reads and influences his/her way of reading it. Stated in more mediological terms, the institution that changes the deposited meaning into a conveyor does it by reading and by transmitting and/or examining the way in which meanings should be attached. Reading means making the text one's own or interpreting it. If the "effectiveness" of "the effectiveness of symbols" means anything, it is to be sought in the appropriation of meaning. The purpose of transmission is appropriation, and without appropriation transmission remains unaccomplished.

Through appropriation the autonomy of the message is dissolved and the dialectic of the event of meaning and the meaning itself is restored. The message again says something to someone, but this reception is subject to the receiver's specific socio-cultural context and world. It is therefore inevitable that what the transmission delivers to be understood is simultaneously transformed as a result of the circumstances in which the transmission takes place. Appropriation is always taking place, albeit to different degrees, through an active intervention called *reading*. Here we again have a paradigmatic word that joins together a large number of appropriations, whether intended or not, where the rejection of the message is merely a derived form of reading. To substantiate this claim, let us look at the appropriation of the meaning of technical artefacts in general.

In my opinion, it is possible to identify three types of meaning when reading or appropriating any *technical object* or transmission medium.[57] I derive all three from Ricœur's textual hermeneutics:

1. *Comprehension* through use. Let us look at the example of the fork: I appropriate the fork by using it to eat with, regardless of whether this happens consciously or unconsciously. At the same time, I appropriate a series of re-

---

[56] Paul Ricœur, *Le conflit des interprétations. Essais d'herméneutique I* (Paris: Seuil, [1969] 2013), 7 / *The Conflict of Interpretations. Essays in Hermeneutics*, trans. Don Ihde et al. (Evanston, IL: Northwestern University Press, 1974), 3.
[57] The last two of these together form the dialectic of reading, as analysed by Ricœur (*Du texte à l'action*, 163 / *From Text to Action*, 113). If I slightly adapt his scheme, it is to place his ideas in a context in which technical objects constitute the "text". In other words, the three types of appropriation as I describe them (which are in essence reconcilable with Ricœur's textual hermeneutics) are developed in the direction of a hermeneutics of technique. This theme is developed further in Chapter 2, §3.

lated objects that belong to the milieu (see 2.) and the world (see 3.) of the fork.

2. The *explanation* of the way in which apparatus and devices work, i.e. the literal or direct technical references involved in such artefacts. Thus one can explain how the fork works by referring to the materials from which it was manufactured, its intended relation to other cutlery, the differences between different kinds of forks, the ergonomic or aesthetic logic of its design, its hygienic maintenance, etc.

3. The *interpretation* of the world of the artefact,[58] i.e. of the myriad of meanings the artefact and its milieu call to mind. In a certain sense, I dress myself with my forks, as with my clothes. The forks convey a meaning of which their designer is not the (only) author and which cannot be reduced to their direct reference; that is the meaning of the reader who interprets him-/herself in relation to the object.[59] Here I am concerned with interpretation not only in relation to a fork, but also in relation to the entire milieu into which the fork is integrated. Simultaneously, this involves an interpretation by the reader as being shaped for it through my belonging to a tradition of interpreters.[60] Thus a communal bond of ideas and values is created between the forks and their users and is also transferred and transformed. The work of the hermeneuticist is to explain "the type of being-in-the-world unfolded *in front of* the text"[61] and also before everything that has the textual structure that I described here. This world is always a mixture of intentionally transmitted meanings and of particular or contingent interpretations within a specific historical context. We will study the hermeneutic circle of the interpretation of technical means in more detail in the next chapter (see §3).

If this is valid for that which apparently does not carry any message (such as the fork), it is even more valid for newspapers, radio, television, the internet and social media. All the media elicit an understanding appropriation that removes the autonomy of the message and gives new meaning to the message. But the initial understanding can also be enhanced through explanation. A typical element of Ricœur's hermeneutics is the conclusion regarding the dialectical coordination

---

[58] I use this phrase as an equivalent to Ricœur's "the world of the text" (cf. e.g. Ricœur, *Du texte à l'action*, 125–27 / *From Text to Action*, 84–86).
[59] Compare with the way in which the reader interprets him-/herself in front of a text, according to Ricœur (*Du texte à l'action*, 128 / *From Text to Action*, 86).
[60] Think how people could say, for instance, "We don't eat with our hands like barbarians" or "The Thompsons could really have taken out their best silver for the occasion…".
[61] Ricœur, *Du texte à l'action*, 128 / *From Text to Action*, 86.

between explanation and understanding in the act of reading: the more we explain, the more we understand (*expliquer plus, c'est comprendre mieux*).[62] Explanation strengthens and mediates understanding through the study of the internal functioning of a particular message in its autonomy.[63] Explanation helps us to re-understand our appropriation of a message, which in turn advances our interpretation of what we ourselves are, of what we were made to be by our socio-technical milieu and of the extent to which such a reading of ourselves is possible.

5 Vigilance and Politics

If it is true, for Ricœur as for Debray, that symbols can acquire effectiveness, then we have to ask by whom that effectiveness is used. With a view to achieving which goals is the effectiveness mobilised? At the expense of whom have these symbols become effective, rather than those? It is hard to deny the immediate social critical and political implications of the idea of the effectiveness of symbols. So significant is this socio-political dimension of the hermeneutics of action that I devote the whole Part 2 of this book to it. Still, a number of comments are called for here.

Debray and Ricœur agree that we do not have direct access to ourselves as beings who understand the world and that self-understanding and understanding others are always mediated.[64] The conveyors of messages that surround us exert considerable influence on our understanding – "machinery transports its own perspective on the world".[65] That does not mean that we are programmed by our milieu, but rather that the milieu influences the possibilities of our understanding.[66] One could say that the person who appropriates messages stored in the media has already been appropriated by the milieu to which he/she belongs, and which has taught him/her to accept or reject, distinguish, evaluate, interpret. This is not only because of the predispositions that are needed for the use of technical artefacts and in this way are encouraged in readers and users of each artefact, but also because the institutional conveyor is concerned about the re-appropriation of the autonomous technical conveyors – an appro-

---

62 Ricœur, *Du texte à l'action*, 25 / The translation omits this passage in *From Text to Action*, 9.
63 See Ricœur, *Du texte à l'action*, 195, 201 / *From Text to Action*, 138, 142.
64 See, for example, Ricœur, *Du texte à l'action*, 170 – 71 / *From Text to Action*, 118 – 19; Debray, *Transmitting Culture*, 7.
65 Debray, *Cours de médiologie générale*, 401.
66 Cf. Debray, *Introduction à la médiologie*, 88.

priation that is desired for the long term. Therefore, through reading, understood as a complex socio-technical event (rather than as a private activity), efficient symbols have the ability to influence the way someone understands him-/herself in a particular milieu. The will to influence this reading that people do of themselves is a political reality. This point obviously holds for explicit, linguistic messages; it equally holds for the implicit influence on people through a whole technical milieu, as has been convincingly demonstrated by Foucault.[67] Politics in the broadest sense is concerned with mediology and hermeneutics, since the core of both disciplines – the effectiveness of symbols in social interaction – constitute the matter of which politics and its means and power are composed.

Admittedly, mediology "does not practise politics" and "morality is forbidden to the mediologist".[68] Its task is to describe and explain. Nevertheless, "political and moral reflection on the limits, ends and abuses of power will increasingly have to pass through the *technical study of the power of means*, which would not be a bad definition of our project [that is, of mediology – EW]".[69] Hermeneutics can be situated in the same way: it is not simply political philosophy, but a spontaneous extension of the hermeneutic project is the investigation into that which occurs politically during the interpretation events, and with a view to interpretation of the connections between narrative, action and the ethical-political complex.[70] This is amply demonstrated in Ricœur's published *Lectures on Ideology and Utopia*,[71] but he also traces the way to such engagement with political matters in *From Text to Action* and comes explicitly back to it in examining the socio-political dimension of his hermeneutics of the capable human, for instance, in *Oneself as Another* (Studies 7–9). But for those who have taken his early philosophy seriously (see Introduction), this comes as no surprise.

Mediology and hermeneutics, each in its own way, examine people's position in the socio-technical whole that can never be completely unravelled since it is shaped by people while it simultaneously shapes them. As heirs of Marx on this point, hermeneuticists and mediologists do not believe in the autopositioning (*autoposition*) of the subject, since subjects are shaped through

---

[67] Notably in Michel Foucault, *Discipline and Punish: The Birth of the Prison* (New York, NY: Pantheon, 1977).
[68] Debray, *Cours de médiologie générale*, 417 and Régis Debray, *Vie et mort de l'image. Une histoire du regard en Occident* (Paris: Gallimard, 1992), 506, respectively.
[69] Debray, *Cours de médiologie générale*, 46.
[70] See Ricœur, *Du texte à l'action*, 9 / *From Text to Action*, xv.
[71] Paul Ricœur, *Lectures on Ideology and Utopia*, ed. George Taylor (New York, NY: Columbia University Press, 1986).

the mediation of the products of their hands, which also made their hands.⁷² The production of people (and both meanings of this ambiguous expression should be understood) lends itself to two types of interpretation – the practice of recollection of meaning and the practice of suspicion which Ricœur discusses at the beginning of *De l'interprétation*.⁷³ The practising of these two interpretation strategies in the hermeneutics of technical artefacts, and more specifically the hermeneutics of the media, can help us to examine every mediasphere as "a transcendental technique that sets *a priori* the conditions for the production of meaning and events for whoever wants to use it", but only while bearing in mind "the mastery of the medium over its masters".⁷⁴ The aim is clearly not to draw up a political programme, but rather to assume a stance of vigilance: "Hermeneutics is not the name of a philosophical project that aspires to absolute intelligibility, but the name of a vigilant thinking based on its absence."⁷⁵

The time has now come for a number of provisional conclusions.

6 Conclusion

In this chapter I attempted a first alignment of philosophical hermeneutics with social scientific theory. This was undertaken with the book's aim of clarifying the relation between human capabilities and the means of action in mind, namely by concentrating on the interactions involved in the emission, transmission and reception of messages. On Ricœur's side, I offered a reconstructive reading of his hermeneutics in *From Text to Action* and an elaboration on the hermeneutics of technical artefacts. Throughout, this was done in tandem with a critical interpretation of Debray's mediology, from which I also drew out some unexplored implications. It would certainly have been possible to work with another author in media studies, but the succession of arguments above suffices to demonstrate the merits of my choice. What are the most important gains from this chapter for the overall argument of the book?

---

72 See the way in which Cornelius Castoriadis situates Marx's contribution to the philosophy of technique, in Cornelius Castoriadis, "Technique," *Les carrefours du labyrinthe* (Paris: Seuil, 1978), 221–48.
73 Paul Ricœur, *De l'interprétation. Essai sur Freud* (Paris: Seuil, 1965), 38–46 / *Freud and Philosophy. An Essay on Interpretation*, trans. Denis Savage (New Haven, CT, and London: Yale University Press, 1970), 28–36.
74 Debray, *Cours de médiologie générale*, 440, 437.
75 Jean Grondin, *Le tournant herméneutique de la phénoménologie* (Paris: PUF, 2003), 115.

First, critical debate with a sceptic served to dispel doubt as to the rightful place and utility of philosophical hermeneutics in studying human interaction.[76] From the point of view of hermeneutics, I developed the argument from its very historical core: the understanding of texts. "Texts", we saw, may well be technical artefacts, but we can only grasp what they are as social phenomena if we consider them as an integral part of complex events of human interaction. From the point of view of mediology (the social scientific relevance of which I never questioned), I showed how consistent reflection on its own core concepts compels it to accept and openness to hermeneutic questioning; indeed, that it requires hermeneutics to complete its own work (see the discussion of communication, the mnemosphere and reception). This was not a boxing match in which hermeneutics scored a knockout. Using mediological insights into the formation and transmission of media, and the mediological dimension of technical artefacts and milieus in general, I was able to develop Ricœur's understanding of textual autonomy and reception into an outline of a hermeneutics of technical action and means. This outline is, moreover, in agreement with his own understanding of strategy and technology in his earlier socio-political thought (cf. Introduction, §3).

Second, I need to emphasise that recognizing the symmetrical relation between mediology and hermeneutics is not merely a matter of academic courtesy. For all the importance accorded to hermeneutics in this book, I do not consider it a master paradigm. In order for it to shed its clarifying light on social phenomena, it needs to be used in combination with insights from other social sciences. That Ricœur steadily did so, and that I consider it essential to the research documented in this book, has already been stated in the Introduction (§§1 and 2). Hermeneutics is, amongst other things, an approach to interdisciplinary integration.

Third, I need to circumscribe carefully the place of everything "technological" in this chapter. In speaking about media of transmission in their full breadth (materialised organization and organized matter) and in considering the transmitting quality of technical means and action in general, we quite clearly

---

[76] In this respect it is not irrelevant to point out that Debray accepted an earlier version of this chapter of my book for publication in his journal, *Médium*. He placed an editor's introduction on the first page of the article conceding that "[b]etween hermeneutics and mediology, there is evidently proximity and complementarity. The 'dialogue' published in our last issue (*Médium* n° 5) was too obviously caricatural to give an account of these complex relationships, between sisters who are not enemies but accomplices. Let us thank Ernst Wolff for having reacted appropriately, by identifying important avenues of research to shed light on our common goal: symbolic effectiveness." Untitled editor's introduction to Ernst Wolff, "Transmettre et interpréter," *Médium* 6 (January-March 2006): 30–47, citation 30 (the author is not named, but it is probably Debray).

enter the domain of a philosophy of technology and of science and technology studies. However, the general sense and objective of the chapter is oriented beyond the interdisciplinary contributions that may come from these disciplines. What is at stake is rather an exploration of social interaction, of which the coordination of human capabilities with means is a central dimension. I call this the technical dimension of action or the technicity of action. With this chapter in mind, it becomes much easier to substantiate the claim that all action has a technical dimension; it even begins to outline the profile of that technical dimension and give an impression of why one would take a specific interest in it.

Fourth, let us reflect again on the core notion of "the effectiveness of symbols". Everything in this chapter speaks for the embeddedness of communication, transmission and interpretation in human interactions. This accords the efforts to bring a message home a pervasive place throughout society. Yet, one limit of this notion should not escape our attention. The question regarding the *validity* of the message for which efficient symbols are sought has not been addressed, and for a very good reason: neither the elements of hermeneutics mobilised here nor mediology has the competence to deal with this question. The closest we came to this point is to indicate the vocation that both mediology and hermeneutics have for caution or vigilance. Both are animated by the conviction that something is at stake in their research. However, they cannot go further, and in this book I will also keep myself to this delimitation (which is not to say that the question is insignificant!). I will look closer at this point in the "Intermediary reflection".

Fifth, all along it has been assumed that, unless explicitly specified otherwise, the claims made are sufficiently general to apply to all people in all contexts. This holds as much for everything related to the historical genesis of socio-technical systems as it does for the more narrowly defined human interaction with such systems. It holds as much for mediology as it does for hermeneutics. As stated in the Introduction, I do not object to the quest to identify such anthropological similarities. However, it should be evident that openness to the cultural other would make an invaluable contribution in such a quest, both to test the generality of such claims and to suggest other claims.

But this chapter is clearly still very limited in its scope and the task is now to turn much more explicitly to Ricœur's broader philosophy to gain solid insights.

Chapter 2:
Habitus – Means – Worldliness

1 Introduction: "Civilizing Processes" as Processes of Hominization

The human being that we are today has not always existed. It came into existence through a double process of hominization. Initially, this happened through the very long process of biological evolution, which resulted in the single human species we know today. Subsequently, this biological process was overtaken by a much shorter diversifying process of ethological or cultural change[1] that has filled the earth with a great multiplicity of modes of human existence and their cultural expressions. The roots of the latter process lie in the times before *homo sapiens*, and the process continues to change modes of existence and their cultural expressions towards open, unknown futures. One might call these processes by which human beings become what they are "processes of hominization". To contextualise the current chapter, I also refer to the second phase of hominization as "processes of civilization", a notion I adopt (and slightly adapt) from Norbert Elias.[2]

---

[1] I reject any evolutionary perspective on the subsequent changes of *homo sapiens* that would imply a natural, hierarchical ordering of worth between cultures. The sequence of the ethological change of *homo sapiens*, unlike biological evolution, is not irreversible; and it is unjustifiable to hold one culture and its development up as the future of others – cf. Hans Jonas, *Das Prinzip Verantwortung. Versuch einer Ethik für die technologische Zivilisation* (Frankfurt am Main: Suhrkamp, 1979), 200–203; see also Anthony Giddens's deconstruction of evolutionist theories of social change in *The Constitution of Society. Outline of the Theory of Structuration* (Berkeley and Los Angeles, CA: University of California Press, 1984), 227–43. This does not, however, mean that the question of evaluating cultural changes and differences should be rejected. But it does call for the utmost vigilance with regard to the cultural specificity of the means of evaluation or comparison of cultures. A valuable overview of historical trends in the appropriation of evolution theory in social theory is Richard Machalek and Michael W. Martin, "Social Evolution," in *Handbook of Contemporary Sociological Theory*, ed. Seth Abrutyn (Cham: Springer, 2016), 503–26.

[2] While Elias has received relatively modest recognition in the Anglo-American academic world, he is considered a seminal author in such countries as Germany and the Netherlands. Teresa Koloma Beck, "Mehr als der Mythos vom Zivilisationsprozess. Warum es sich lohnt, Norbert Elias' bekanntestes Werk neu zu lesen," *Zeithistorische Forschungen* 15, no. 2 (2018): 383–90, provides an overview on the history of reception of Elias and an interesting view on the contemporary interest of this work. Hermann Korte, *On Norbert Elias – Becoming a Human Scientist*, ed. Stefanie Ernst (Wiesbaden: Springer VS, 2017) is a detailed examination of the historical and intellec-

Evidently the term "civilization" requires clarification. I am of course cognizant of the European history from which Elias developed his theory, but what I am after is the "fact-oriented, ideologically cleansed concept of civilisation",[3] as he formulates it later. We all know that people have often succumbed to the temptation of considering civilization something that is acquired only by some, while others allegedly still lack it.

It would be much more accurate to consider "civilizing" a process that includes, or processes that include, *all of humanity*, albeit in different forms, in different times and in different places – as Elias explicitly argues in his later writings.[4] Since "civilization" refers here to the processes by which human beings take on a specific form of existence as human beings, the expression "an uncivilized human being" is a contradiction in terms. Still, the processes of civilization always entail greater or smaller episodes and phases of falling back, that is, of *decivilization*. My interest in using the term "civilization" thus resides in (a) opening a view on humanity in its entirety, (b) without disqualifying *a priori* all normative assessment of changes.

According to Elias, civilization is the complex of processes by which the biological "given" of the individual human being is shaped by learning the societal

---

tual background of Elias's *The Civilizing Process*. For a valuable literature review of recent scholarly publications on Elias, see Marta Bucholc and Daniel Witte, "Transformationen eines Klassikers: Norbert Elias Zwischen Kanonpflege und Kanonverschiebung," *Soziologische Revue* 41, no. 3 (2018): 384–99.

The adaptations I make are motivated not only by my own research problem, but also by an attempt to respond to the criticisms formulated against Elias's work. For an overview of this criticism, see Stephen Mennell, *Norbert Elias. Civilization and the Human Self-image* (Oxford, and New York, NY: Blackwell, 1989), 227–50, and Robert van Krieken, *Norbert Elias* (London, and New York, NY: Routledge, 1998), 118–34.

3 In "What I Mean by Civilisation: Reply to Hans Peter Duerr" [1988] in Norbert Elias, *Essays II. On Civilising Processes, State Formation and National Identity*. The collected works of Norbert Elias, volume 15, eds. Richard Kilminster and Stephen Mennell (Dublin: University College Dublin Press, 2008), 8–13, here 9. This is also the sole key of interpretation that would take us through his view on colonialism without disgrace – cf. Norbert Elias, *On the Process of Civilisation. Sociogenetic and Psychogenetic Investigations*. [1939] The collected works of Norbert Elias, volume 3, eds. Stephen Mennell, Eric Dunning, Johan Goudsblom and Richard Kilminster (Dublin: University College Dublin Press, 2012), 425–26.

4 Cf. "If one surveys the development of humanity, one encounters a comprehensive, humanity-wide process of civilisation. Up to now – that is, from the Stone Age to our time – this process has remained dominant in a continuous conflict with countervailing, decivilising processes," in Norbert Elias, "Civilisation" [1986], in Norbert Elias, *Essays II*, 3–7, citation 4. The same view is reflected in "What I Mean by Civilisation: Reply to Hans Peter Duerr" [1988] in Elias, *Essays III*, 8–13.

standards of co-existence, which in turn results in a kind of individual behaviour that could be called civilized or cultivated, in other words, behaviour more or less adapted for living with other people.[5] But the coming into existence of a particular kind of behaviour in an individual is not the result of a programme, neither his/her own nor that of his/her parents (but not without these either), but first of all the result of the position in which that person grows up in a particular society. Wherever individuals enter the world, they do so by entering into social *figurations* that describe a particular mode of co-existence, a network of interdependency, and thus also the power relations of a society. A figuration is like a dance:[6] it does not exist independently from the individuals that constitute it, but nor does it depend for its existence strictly on any particular individual. It is therefore only within such figurations that a new human being is *socialized*, but also obtains the means for his/her *individualization*. And as socialized individuals take the initiative, they in turn influence the process of sociogenesis, that is, the figurations in which they interact, so that the same people could form different figurations, or different people could participate in the same or similar figurations at different times and in different places. Mostly, the changing of figurations takes place over long periods by means of social processes spanning generations.[7] This happens, as Elias succinctly states, "[f]rom plans arising, yet unplanned; by purpose moved, yet purposeless".[8]

Civilization as event (*Zivilisierung*, civilizing[9]) is then, on the side of the individual, a process of psychogenesis, namely as "an individual self-regulation of behavioural impulses that are momentarily conditioned by drives and affects or a redirection of those impulses thereof from the primary to the secondary goals

---

[5] In what follows, I, unlike Elias (*On the Process of Civilization*, 13–57), use the terms "civilization" and "culture" interchangeably, as has become the convention in anthropology, cf. Georg Bollenbeck, "Zivilisation," in *Historisches Wörterbuch der Philosophie*, Band 12 (W-Z), eds. Joachim Ritter, Karlfried Grunder and Gottfried Gabriel (Basel: Schwabe, 2005), 1365–79. It should also be stated categorically that I could use the words "civilization" and "culture" only devoid of prejudice regarding claims to progress, as was still present in the earlier work of Elias, but from which he too departed later on – on this subject, see the commentary of Danilo Martucelli, *Sociologies de la modernité* (Paris: Gallimard, 1999), 258–59, or claims to cultural superiority.
[6] As Van Krieken explains in *Norbert Elias*, 58.
[7] Cf. In "Figuration," in Norbert Elias. *Essays III. On Sociology and the Humanities*. The Collected Works of Norbert Elias, volume 16, eds. Richard Kilminster and Stephen Mennell (Dublin: University College Dublin Press, 2009), 1–3, here 2.
[8] Norbert Elias, *The Society of Individuals*. [1987] The Collected Works of Norbert Elias, volume 10, ed. Robert van Krieken (Dublin: University College Dublin Press, 2010), 62.
[9] And not the end-point, as Korte, *On Norbert Elias*, 181, correctly emphasises.

and if need be also the sublimating reshaping thereof".[10] In other words, psychogenesis is that aspect of the civilizing process by which the constraints inherent in a social figuration are interiorized to form personal or self-constraints. This does not mean that all external constraints (*Fremdzwänge*) are directly converted into the acquisition of personal constraints (*Selbstzwänge*), but to the great extent that they are, this acquisition results in the enablement of a form of coexistence. Individuals acquire the habit, the stable and durable disposition (as Bourdieu would say) or second nature – a *habitus*[11] – of acting in certain ways. The habitus gives a personal style to socially acquired forms of acting. As can be seen from the short definition of the process of civilization above, Elias is particularly interested in self-constraint[12] as a process of mastering and sublimating drives (that is, the psychogenetic aspect of sociogenetic processes). Such a *habitus* is not only formed when young individuals enter a social figuration, but it is also formed under the influence of the powers inherent in the gradual change of figurations. To summarise, Elias presents us with a vision of the nature of change of social existence in which human beings are "conceptualized as *interdependent* rather than autonomous, comprising what he called *figurations* rather than social systems or structures, and as characterised by socially and historically specific forms of *habitus*, or personality structure".[13] On the one hand, this describes a process in which all people are involved, on the other hand, it accounts for the great variety of forms of existence that makes of humanity plural, constantly generating more variations even within single societies.

It is this perspective on the processes of the socio-individual formation of human beings that is of interest to me, rather than Elias's thesis that civilizing is an attenuation of habits and an augmentation of sympathy due to the double

---

10 My translation of "...eine individuelle Selbstregulierung momentaner triebe- und affektbedingter Verhaltensimpulse oder deren Umleitung von den primären auf sekundäre Ziele hin und gegebenenfalls auch deren sublimatorische Umgestaltung" (Norbert Elias, "Zivilisation," in *Grundbegriffe der Soziologie*, ed. Bernard Schäfers (Leverkusen: Leske & Budrich, 1986), 382–87, here 382). The standard translation is in Elias "Civilisation" [1986] in Elias, *Essays II*, 3–7, 3.
11 This term will be one of my central notions in the section on technics in this chapter. For Pierre Bourdieu's definition of the term, see *Le sens pratique* (Paris: Editions de Minuit, 1980), 88–89. Ricœur explicitly appropriates it in *La mémoire, l'histoire, l'oubli* (Paris: Seuil, 2000), 316 / *Memory, History, Forgetting*, trans. Kathleen Blamey and David Pellauer (Chicago, IL: University of Chicago Press, 2004), 245.
12 In his reading of Elias, Ricœur accords the central position to the notion of self-constraint (see Ricœur, *La mémoire, l'histoire, l'oubli*, 261–66 / *Memory, History, Forgetting*, 206–209).
13 Van Krieken, *Norbert Elias*, 55.

mechanism of a concentration of state power and the concomitant interiorization thereof as a mastering of biological urges.[14] Elias provides us with a theory of civilization as a non-monolinear process of hominization that is without any specific beginning, and that remains open-ended. However, whereas Elias concentrates especially on *society* as an anthropogenetic factor, one could engage in a quest for similar theories of the two other anthropogenetic factors,[15] namely *meaning* and *technics*.[16] To put it another way: civilization or hominization is not only a process by which societal processes take shape, but also a process by which the creation of meaning and technicization take place. Society, meaning and technics are interdependent factors of hominization – none of them exists without the others – and all three share the same double structure of generality and particularity: society/individual (in the case of human socialization), language system/language usage (in the case of human signification) or technical system/technical action (in the case of human technical praxis).

These historical processes by which the nature and interrelation of the biological, the social, the meaningful and the technical in human beings change are the conditions for anthropogenesis or hominization, that is, the formation of human beings. Since times immemorial, human beings have reflected on their own human condition – the condition in which these processes leave people – be it through philosophy or science, ritual or narration. They have done so in attempts to intervene in the processes of hominization. Any such intervention requires a view on what a human being *is*, what people may *become* and how human existence *should ideally be*. And in order to answer these questions, each person draws on his/her particular position in a historically contingent, social, meaningful and technical figuration.

At least three factors give rise to such reflection about human existence and its meaning. First, people almost incessantly pursue the good life, rather than mere continuation of existence. One of the main factors that frustrate this pursuit is the difficult coordination of normative concerns and the question for efficacy

---

[14] I am especially uncomfortable with the remnants of a link between civilization and progress that marks Elias's earlier work. For a study of how this idea was gradually attenuated by Elias, see again Martuccelli's chapter on Elias in *Sociologies de la modernité*. On the ambiguity of the state with regard to the reduction of violence, see Florence Delmotte and Christophe Majastre, "Violence and *Civilité:* The Ambivalences of the State," in *Norbert Elias and Violence*, eds. Tatiana Savoia Landini and François Dépelteau (New York, NY: Palgrave Macmillan, 2017), 55 – 80.
[15] See also Ernst Wolff, "'Technology' as the Critical Social Theory of Human Technicity," *Journal of Philosophical Research* 41 (2016): 333 – 69, here 352.
[16] As a first approximation, consider that the word "technics" designates the whole complex of technical action, procedures, artefacts, sources of energy, systems and institutions. Then follow the discussion below.

in the same action (a problem that will occupy our attention explicitly in Chapters 7 and 8), a fact that can be appreciated better once we get a grasp on the paradoxical nature of the technical and institutional means of action (see Chapters 3, §5 and 4, §4.1). Second, acquired civilization as the ability to live with others always remains fragile. Here we think of the "breakdown of civilization" which Elias theorized with the history of Nazism in mind[17] (but other cases – colonization, apartheid and labour exploitation – will form the backdrop of the last three chapters of this book). The threat or reality of civilization's degenerating has an impact on how people understand themselves and arrange the course of their life. Third, when confronted with others who live in other, incompatible ways, people may sometimes question their views on what they are or should become, but more often seek ways by which to confirm their current views.[18]

2 Human Technicity and the Civilizing Processes

How does one know what a human being is or could become? Certainly one learns of the human being by personal experience, but these experiences are mediated, from very early childhood onward, and they are mediated especially by *stories*.[19] I learn what I am, could and should be and what others are through the imaginative variations of actions and manners of being that are transmitted in the stories of my culture. This statement summarises the essence of Paul Ricœur's theory of narrative hermeneutics. The importance of stories (fictional or

---

[17] Already present in Elias, *On the Process of Civilization*, 422 (the "counter spurt" to the process of civilization), and captured in the (late) definition of civilization in Elias "Civilisation" [1986] in Elias, *Essays II*, 3–7 and worked out in "The Breakdown of Civilization" in Norbert Elias, *Studies on the Germans. Power struggles and the development of habitus in the nineteenth and twentieth centuries.* [1989] The Collected Works of Norbert Elias, volume, 11, eds. Stephen Mennell and Eric Dunning (Dublin: University College Dublin Press, 2013), 223–330. For discussions of this theme see Jonathan Fletcher, *Violence and Civilization: An Introduction to the Work of Norbert Elias* (Cambridge: Polity Press, 1997) and Delmotte and Majastre, "Violence and *Civilité*," 66–71.
[18] A substantial body of recent Eliasian research turns to these questions, with reference to his work, co-authored with John Scotson, *The Established and the Outsiders*. [1965] The Collected Works of Norbert Elias, volume 4, ed. Cas Wouters (Dublin: University College Dublin Press, 2008). On this literature, see Bucholc and Witte, "Transformationen eines Klassikers," 391–94. An exemplary study is Michael Dunning, "'Established and Outsiders': Brutalisation Processes and the Development of 'Jihadist Terrorists'," *Historical Social Research / Historische Sozialforschung* 41, no. 3 (157), Special Issue: Established-Outsider Relations and Figurational Analysis (2016): 31–53.
[19] What is presented here with reference to stories should, in a more complete exposition, be complemented by parallel claims about games.

scientific) for reflection on civilization and humanity hardly needs to be argued. However, we know that stories are not transmitted in isolation: the stories of early childhood are often accompanied by games (playing out a narrative); many stories are enacted or danced; others stories are recited, accompanied by ritual actions and objects; many stories are learned off by heart in poetic form; others are written down in books and sold or stored in libraries, to be studied by students, researchers and teachers. In short, stories have a *Sitz-im-Leben* that is not made of the same narrative material as the stories themselves; stories are supported, amongst other things, by technical support, as has been discussed in the previous chapter. In fact, by changing the perspective slightly, one could consider stories as being technically supported by things that form part of a larger technical system (a book, for instance, is part of the education process, the library, the editing and printing industries, etc.).

If this is the case, one can ask oneself whether stories are the only things that are carried by these technical objects and procedures; or to put the question differently: are the technical objects themselves not perhaps telling a "story" of what a human being is or could become? And indeed, it is well known that technical artefacts are not only mnemonics or mnemo-technics (support for not forgetting things, like stories); but any artefact, to be efficient for any use of it, presupposes a *history* of its use, and all technical artefacts summarise, while simultaneously hiding, a history of their invention, development, production, wear-and-tear and maintenance. If one concedes that technical objects and procedures "tell stories" (in this metaphorical way), one could well ask whether people do not perhaps know what human beings are, not only through the mediation of socially transmitted constructs of meaning (such as stories), but also from the *means* by which these ideas about humanity are transmitted. And if this is the case, could it not be possible that all technical experiences mediate, albeit implicitly, ideas about what a human being is or could be? This is indeed the *hypothesis* I would like to support: *the process of the acquisition and use of technical objects and technical know-how brings about an intervention or mediation analogous to that of stories in our ideas and lived experience of what it is to be human.* This hypothesis states, in other words, that the technical aspects of the processes of civilization are *de facto* processes by which people learn how to be human.

Perhaps the most important objection that one might raise against this hypothesis is that stories are symbolic and even fictional entities, whereas technical objects and procedures are practical entities. I shall use Ricœur's hermeneutics to problematise this objection and to argue that human interaction with technical means shares with the interaction with stories the element that, in both, the user and the reader are confronted with a world of references that transcend the internal references of either the story text or the technical means.

Taken together as a whole, the references of the story and of technics beyond themselves will be called the *world* and the fact of its enactment, *worldliness*.

In order to embark on my project, I need to specify what I mean by "*technics*". The following demarcation serves a three-fold purpose: first, to accommodate as far as possible the plurality of legitimate, but partial, perspectives provided on technics in the history of philosophy;[20] second, to avoid reducing human technicity from the outset to its instrumental rational aspect;[21] and, third, to give a descriptively neutral or general rendering of technicity, in the sense that this rendering would be able to account for both beneficial and malignant aspects of human technicity.[22] Technics is a complex that consists of three interdependent aspects: *habitus* (the technical capabilities and disposition of the technical agent), instruments or *means* (the system of technical objects and accompanying human procedures) and *worldliness* (the understanding interaction of the technical agent with the technical system).

Human technicity as a whole, the nature of each of these three elements, as well as the nature of their interaction, are always *changing*. They change, first, whenever an individual child acquires skills that he/she did not have as a newly born baby and throughout his/her life in the acquisition of new skills or in the gradual loss of them.[23] They change, second, "naturally" across an entire cultural group during the process of civilization (albeit sometimes at a slow transgenerational pace). But, third, technicity also changes in smaller or larger interventions in the "normal" flow of events – nowadays this is what often happens when we speak of "development" or of a "transfer of technology", for instance. Technical change, but also the everyday technical use of technics, is therefore considered here as analogous to the transmission of stories.

---

20 As already pleaded for by Hans Lenk in *Zur Sozialphilosophie der Technik* (Frankfurt am Main: Suhrkamp, 1982), 21–22.
21 Against such reduction see Wolff, "'Technology' as the Critical Social Theory," 357.
22 For this too, see Wolff, "'Technology' as the Critical Social Theory".
23 The "imperfectness" of learning is due to (a) the "imperfectness" of rule-following in technical judgement – see Wolff, "'Technology' as the Critical Social Theory," 346 and (b) the incapabilities associated with capabilities – see Chapter 3, §2.1.

3 Technics and Narrativity

Using the transmission of narration as an analogy, I would like to adapt Ricœur's transcultural theory of narrativity[24] to develop an outline of a hermeneutics of technics and technical change, in other words, the general anthropological pattern of changing human technicity that is an element of the formation of all civilizations.[25] Ricœur presents his hermeneutics of narrativity in three phases: (1) a pre-understanding of narrativity embedded in everyday life, (2) text/writing and (3) reading. These phases are also called (1) the prefiguration, (2) the configuration and (3) the refiguration of understanding respectively. In passing through these three phases, human beings change the manner of their understanding, not only of the stories and histories transmitted to them, but also of their understanding of themselves. My basic hypothesis, as formulated above, is that a similar hermeneutic circle of prefiguration, configuration and refiguration structures human engagement with the technical milieu.[26] Consequently, changes in this

---

[24] Cf. Paul Ricœur, *Temps et récit 1. L'intrigue et le récit historique* (Paris: Seuil, 1983), 105 / *Time and Narrative*. Volume 1, trans. Kathleen Blamey and David Pellauer (Chicago, IL: University of Chicago Press, 1984), 52. In doing so, for the explorative purposes of this chapter, I limit myself to Ricœur, *Temps et récit 1*, 105–162 / *Time and Narrative 1*, 52–87; what I say here and later on about narrativity depends on this text (and some others) by Ricœur. The adaptation of Ricœur's thought on time and narrative has been facilitated by his own adaptation of this theory to space in architecture, in his article "Architecture et narrativité," *Urbanisme* 303 (Nov/Dec 1998): 44–53 / "Architecture and Narrativity," *Études Ricœuriennes / Ricœur Studies* 7, no. 2 (2016): 31–42. The hermeneutics of technics in the present chapter develops what has been proposed in a nutshell in my contribution to Montagu Murray and Ernst Wolff, "A Hermeneutic Framework for Responsible Technical Interventions in Low-income Households. Mobile Phones for Improved Managed Health Care as Test Case," *The Journal for Transdisciplinary Research in Southern Africa* 11, no. 3 (2015): 171–85, here 178–81.

[25] By doing so, I respond (amongst other things) to Lenk's challenge, which has not lost any of its relevance: "If social science is able to bring to light and 'enlighten' such hidden self-evident facts, attitudes and preconceptions that are effective in everyday life, it gains all the more significance for a carefully balanced theory of the technical and of technology and also for the philosophy of technology, given that technical and systems-technological interrelationships increasingly influence our environment, which has become largely artificial, and also our social coexistence" (Lenk, *Zur Sozialphilosophie der Technik*, 23, my translation). My blueprint of a hermeneutics of human technicity should serve, *inter alia*, as a general theory for the manner in which the forces of everyday existence affect technical events.

[26] Such a threefold perspective on technics is not entirely new. It is already suggested by Benjamin in "Das Kunstwerk im Zeitalter seiner technischen Reproduzierbarkeit" [Zweite Fassung] in *Walter Benjamin, Gesammelte Schriften*, Band I, 2, eds. Rolf Tiedemann and Hermann Schweppenhäuser (Frankfurt am Main: Suhrkamp, 1974), 471–508, here 500–501 (n.26), where Benjamin explains that every form of art is situated at the point of interference of three developmental

milieu also change people's understanding of themselves and their world. Finally, over long periods, the cumulative effect of all such changes has an impact on the processes of civilization that are responsible for shaping diverse forms of human life.

3.1 Prefiguration

Understanding narrations about actions, and coming to a new understanding of oneself as an agent through the experience of understanding a narration, can occur only on the basis of a non-explicit pre-understanding of action. According to Ricœur, this pre-understanding of action is situated in a threefold familiarity:
- familiarity with the semantics of action – that is a person's capability to use a network of notions by which human actions are distinguished from general physical movements; they are notions denoting the "who", "how", "why", "with whom", etc. of actions;
- familiarity with the symbolics of action – people act in a regular way, and this regularity forms an implicit symbolics that makes it possible for other people to understand what they are doing and why they are doing it;[27] this readability of action testifies to its social setting and production, and to its conformity with social norms that give action its rule-like character;
- familiarity of the agent with his/her own temporality – the fact that the agent is himself/herself temporal means that the agent knows temporality as something different from a succession of "nows"; one could say that the agent is him-/herself like a "plot" that unfolds without being narrated.

---

lines – that of the transmitted effort or quest of which it is the provisional end-point, that of its technical support, and that of its changing reception. Similarly, Hegel, in his Jena lectures analysed three dialectical relations between the subject and the object, namely patterns of speech, utensils and the family (cf. Jürgen Habermas, "Arbeit und Interaktion. Bemerkungen zu Hegels Jenenser 'Philosophie des Geistes'," in *Technik und Wissenschaft als "Ideologie"* (Frankfurt am Main: Suhrkamp, 1969), 9–47, in particular 9–10. However, these suggestions are completely reworked here within the framework of a phenomenological hermeneutics.

27 Ricœur situates this notion of symbolicity, widely used in anthropology, between two other notions of symbolicity, namely that of simple notation and the symbolics of double meaning inherent in metaphors (Ricœur, *Temps et récit 1*, 113 / *Time and Narrative 1*, 57). In this regard, it is useful to consult Clifford Geertz, "Thick description. Toward an interpretive theory of culture," in *The Interpretation of Cultures: Selected Essays* (New York, NY: Basic Books, [1973] 2000), 3–30, and also the very lucid essay by Charles Taylor, "To follow a rule..." in *Bourdieu. A Critical Reader*, ed. Richard Shusterman (Oxford, and Malden, MA: Blackwell, 1999), 29–44.

Human beings, then, live every day in a narrative way, and their experience of living is structured in a pre-narrative manner[28] (in the sense of a lived-through pre-comprehension of action). Now I will argue that they also live in a technical way, that living is structured in a pre-technical manner (in the sense of a lived-through pre-comprehension of technicity). My point is not at all to advance an action typology.[29] Rather, I argue that action has a technical *dimension* that may be more or less pronounced, depending on what agents do. Narrativity and technicity are two *aspects* of action, with similar hermeneutic structures:
- although human pre-technicity is informed by a semantics of action, the hermeneutics of the technicity of action moves the means of action and of that semantics to the centre of its concern; there is a "vocabulary" of possible actions with means (i.e. not words) over which every agent disposes;
- although technical action is just as symbolic as other actions, *as* technical action the concern is the normativity (i.e. the compatibility with other actions and events) and the practicability of that action; even though action is symbolic, it cannot be reduced to its symbolicity; and
- temporality is as much part of narrativity as of technicity, but the emphasis in the latter case is more on functionality than on plot;[30] this implies that at the level of prefiguration, the human being's temporality is, as I argue discussed below, the condition of "I can".

Between narrativity and technicity the emphasis is different, but, in considering the pre-technical experience of living in this manner, one notices that all three of Ricœur's elements of narrativity rely on, or presuppose, a technicity. Likewise, all technical actions, even if they are only the practice of a bodily technics, have a narrative quality that gives meaning to them, even if only episodically. Thus, neither technicity or narrativity is more original than the other. Furthermore, what draws together this three-fold technical pre-comprehension is the phenomenon of habitus. *Habitus* is the essence of the human pre-comprehend-

---

28 "structure pré-narrative de l'expérience" (Ricœur, *Temps et récit 1*, 141 / *Time and Narrative 1*, 74).
29 On my anti-typological stance, see Ernst Wolff, "'Technology' as the Critical Social Theory".
30 In his presentation of the temporality of pre-understanding, Ricœur borrows from the "in-structure" of "Within-time-ness" at the end of Heidegger's *Sein und Zeit*. Without in the least taking away from this temporality, the exploration of the in-character of understanding in technicity would take as its first point of reference the in-character of being-in-the-world as introduced by Heidegger in his small phenomenology of instrumentality: using something as something that unfolds the basic pre-predicative understanding or hermeneutic mode of existence.

ing of technicity (and equally of the pre-comprehending of sociality and signification); it is our technical second nature.

But what does this mean, in more concrete terms, for changing human technicity? We know that a human infant that is not stimulated by games, dances and stories will not develop repeatable, and (at least partially) reliable means of doing things. These culturally specific forms of social interaction not only socialize young human beings and initiate them into the world of meaning of the particular cultural group they are born into (as I explained in respect of the processes of civilization in §1, above), but infants also learn how to use something *as* something – whether this is those initially alien masses of human flesh that are used as a means of perambulation, teeth that are used as a means to bite, crayons that are used to express innate artistic genius on lounge walls. Young human beings acquire the capability to use their bodies with and against the forces of nature (gravitation, the impulses of their own bodies, the brute biological given of speech equipment, etc.), with and against objects, with and against other people. This continual process of stimulation and learning from earliest childhood on results in the formation and transformation of a habitus.[31] As will become clear, the habitus is always already taken up in a hermeneutic spiral of interaction with the technical events that transform it.[32]

The habitus is then a name for the growing and changing range of capabilities incorporated in the body of the developing child, and later in the developing adult, by means of cultural forms of implicit or explicit learning. It is a set of durable dispositions that do not predetermine action, but that predispose an agent to embark on a certain kind of action – the habitus is the name of its possibility (it is the "I can this or that"). It is like a feeling for the game(s) that one plays (Bourdieu's *le sens du jeu*), whatever "game" or situation of life that might be. The *habitus* is the bodily, pre-reflective, pre-predicative mode of existence of "I can" (Merleau-Ponty). *I can* is the way in which the body is familiar with the *world* – familiarity in a non-intellectual, non-consciousness-centred way, but

---

[31] The technicity of the habitus has been thoroughly described under the name "bodily technics" since Marcel Mauss's essay, "Les techniques du corps" (1934), in *Sociologie et anthropologie* (Paris: PUF, 1950), 365–86. See also especially the work of André Leroi-Gourhan, *Evolution et techniques*, Tome 1: *L'homme et la matière* (Paris: Albin Michel, 1943) and that of André-George Haudricourt, *La technologie science humaine. Recherches d'histoire et d'ethnologie des techniques* (Paris: Editions de la maison des sciences de l'homme, 1987). Contemporary studies abound, see, for instance, the journal *Technologies & Culture* (https://journals.openedition.org/tc/, last accessed 22 February 2020).

[32] The point here is not at all to reduce the experience of bodily efficiency to a form of instrumentality; I simply want to highlight that even if one were to claim that "I don't have a body, I am a body", this bodiliness has a specific technicity associated with it, namely as habitus.

without excluding consciousness; *I can* means having to do with matters in such a way that a horizon of familiarity takes form, not only in my consciousness, but in my action. The metaphor used in phenomenology to describe this acquaintedness with one's very being in the world is dwelling. The *dwelling* metaphor helps me to illustrate what this technical prefiguration or pre-understanding is like: it is familiarity or socially and symbolically (culturally) formed know-how. For example, my acquaintedness with my shower (with opening the tap, locating the soap, standing without slipping, etc.) is just one element out of a whole bodily "vocabulary" or "semantics" of the kind of action that would be possible for me as agent.

In all of this, the symbolic and social (and biological) aspects of the habitus, of the technical prefiguration, is explicitly affirmed; the anthropogenetic triad of society, meaning and technicity is maintained.

3.2 Configuration

People's lives and events might have a pre-narrative structure, but narratives exist only when they are told or written down or portrayed in film. And it is by this process of formation of a narrative that one enters the domain of the "as if".[33] "As if" does not mean that all narration is fictional; the domain of "as if" covers fiction as well as historiography. In fact, Ricœur prefers the notion of "as if" to that of "fiction" to refer to the most general category of the process by which one takes a step away from the events "themselves" in order to re-present them narratively. According to Ricœur, the process by which a narrative is formed (that is, a set of events is represented) consists of
- an intrigue or plot – drawing a configuration from a succession of events that simply follow each other, i.e. putting into a plot or relating events;
- a syntax of action – putting together heterogeneous elements such as agents, interactions, circumstances, means, goals, unexpected turns, etc. This is where the transition is made from a semantics of action to a syntax of action, there is a telling of the fact that someone did something when…; and
- followability – at the same time, the creation of a plot that configures heterogeneous elements brings about a temporal line that could be followed or understood.

---

33 Ricœur, *Temps et récit 1*, 125 / *Time and Narrative 1*, 64.

In this three-fold process, there is an imaginative schematization of events at work along traditional lines, implying that at the same time there are movements toward a *sedimentation of forms* and *innovation* at work in the creation of a narrative.

In this form, the configured narration mediates between the prefiguration of the lived pre-narrativity and what follows, namely the audition or reading of the narrative, that is, the application or appropriation of the narrative to the receiver's lived narrativity. Thus, if we want to follow this analogy, we would have to ask whether there is also such mediation in technicity. I would wager that this mediation is realized by the technical system (by the set of artefacts and procedures that could exist independently from any specific individual technician, if not from human technicians as such).

I do not wish to embark on a detailed analysis of technical artefacts and systems here. It would be impossible in any case, since here we find ourselves in the domain in which competence regarding the internal coherence of the technical system is the speciality, not of philosophers, but of carpenters and chemists, engineers and artisans. I would rather pursue the analogy between technicity and narrativity by indicating one similarity between the narrative and the instrument and then two dissimilarities.

1. Autonomy – The most general term that can be used to name the commonality between narrative and the technical system is *autonomy*, in the sense developed in the previous chapter.[34] "Writing" (or "text") is the typical form of autonomy of any narration or discourse: it is autonomous in respect of, or decontextualised from, the intention of the author, from the socio-cul-

---

[34] The notion of autonomy is not drawn from my guiding text (Ricœur, *Temps et récit 1*), but from *Du texte à l'action / From text to action* (as discussed in Chapter 1, §4). Whereas this volume was published after Ricœur's *Temps et récit 1*, all but two of the essays in it predate *Temps et récit*. This is true also for my references to the notion of autonomy that had been written when Ricœur wrote *Temps et récit*. I suspect that the reason Ricœur does not use the notion of autonomy here (in Ricœur, *Temps et récit 1*) in his theory of narrative, as he did in his more general theory of textual hermeneutics, is that he associates autonomy very closely with the textual form of discourse (with writing), and not with oral discourse (with speech). However, recall that in Chapter 1, §§3.1 and 3.2, I demonstrated that what he describes as the autonomous state of discourse characterises speech (or does so at least in principle), just as it does with writing.

Bruno Latour also deploys the metaphor of text or script (see "Where Are the Missing Masses? The Sociology of a Few Mundane Artefacts," in Wiebe Bijker and John Law, *Shaping Technology/Building Society* (Cambridge, MA: MIT Press, 1992), but he does so to describe the agency of technical objects, whereas I connect this issue to the facilitation structure of the autonomous socio-technical system.

tural conditions of its production and from the original addressee.[35] Practically all technical artefacts and procedures are stamped by this writing-like character, or are at least partially constructed of elements that are like writing in this sense. Everything in the technical life of humanity that has durability or existence that in one way or another transcends the life of the individual technician should draw our attention here. It is easy to name tools and machines, toys and means of transport, processes and the channelling of sources of energy; less evident perhaps are alphabets and grammars, the bodily technics as social heritage and divisions, practices, procedures and programmes of work. What all of them share is that they could be decontextualised and recontextualised, very often due to the training and information that accompany the selling, learning and/or transmission of technical procedures and instruments; the decontextualisation maintains or safeguards a practical essence of the instrument. Just like a written story keeps in stock the "what it is about", so the instrument keeps in stock the "what it is for". But as will be seen later, this does not mean that the reading of what is written entails merely taking over the stock – reading always implies an element of transformation.

It is about this aspect of technics especially that technical specialists learn in their textbooks. Explaining how things work, how to maintain their working, how to use them, and even how to get rid of them, is made possible by the *technical* knowledge of technics (whereas I incorporate that kind of knowledge here into a *hermeneutic* interpretation of technics). Just as there is a science that studies the constitution of narratives – narratology – so there are sciences explaining the constitution of technical things. An umbrella science of the socio-technical system may be called a technology.[36] So much for the similarity.

2. Usability – At the beginning of the discussion of configuration, I said that the narrative configuration is the domain of the "as if". Now, it would be no use denying that technical artefacts are capable of supporting "as ifs": my mobile phone, for instance, is not only a means of mobile communication, it is also a status symbol; it is a means by which I introduce myself into a symbolic or even fictional space of social esteem, that is, a space of "as if". This secondary or external reference of technical objects transcends the internal or technical reference of the parts of the technical system and is an

---

[35] Cf. Ricœur, *Du texte à l'action*, 207 ff / *From Text to Action*, 146 ff.
[36] Günther Ropohl gives an excellent analysis of the socio-technical system in its autonomy in Chapter 3 of his *Allgemeine Technologie. Eine Systemtheorie der Technik*, 3rd ed. (Karlsruhe: Universitätsverlag Karlsruhe, 2009).

integral part of technics (as such, this phenomenon will reappear in the discussion of refiguration below). But as an autonomous technical configuration, it has its own mode of existence, which I would like to call its "usability". One discovers usability as the mode of existence of technical means when its "as if" is lost from sight and the conditions for its functionality are highlighted. The autonomous technical system does not, like a narrative, represent something, it does not stand for something; it organizes things, namely objects, sources of energy, institutions, agents. It channels power; it divides and coordinates actions; it synchronises or sequentialises procedures. The usability which characterises instruments is especially made up of a normativity, the tendency to form networks and a traditionality and historicity that have the same dialectics of improvisation and sedimentation of form as narration has.[37] In short, whereas the story is created when a syntax of action forms a plot, the creation of a technical artefact coordinates or configures heterogeneous elements together in specific manners in order to form a usable means.

3. Facilitation – On the basis of its usability, the technical instrument, procedure, institution or source of energy is an implicit proposition of what could be done or how something could be done. The technical means makes one kind of action possible, stronger, finer, smaller, quicker, etc. and makes others impossible or difficult (both with greater or smaller side effects).[38] However (as will become clear in §3.3 below), this does not determine or exhaust its practical application. The "could be" suggested by the technical means is very often accompanied by a social means of instruction

---

[37] As Jean-Pierre Séris describes the threefold essence of the technical phenomenon *La technique* (Paris: PUF, 1994), 45–105. This text gives an excellent description of what others term "functional" normativity, as opposed to moral or aesthetic normativity (see Ibo van de Poel and Peter Kroes, "Introduction: Technology and Normativity," *Techné: Research in Philosophy and Technology* 10, no. 1 (2006): 1–9, and their whole thematic volume of *Techné* 10, no. 1 on "Technology and Normativity"). A suggestion for the coordination of the different forms of normativity is Maarten Franssen, "The Good, the Bad, the Ugly... and the Poor: Instrumental and Non-instrumental Value of Artefacts," in *The Moral Status of Technical Artefacts*, eds. Peter Kroes and Peter-Paul Verbeek (Dordrecht: Springer, 2014), 213–34.

[38] This theme is discussed further in Chapter 3, §2.1 (Point 5) and Chapter 4, §3 (Point 5). The classic analysis on the amplification/reduction effect of technical events is that of Don Ihde, *Technics and Praxis* (Dordrecht, Boston, MA, and London: Reidel, 1979), 38, 48 and *Technology and the Lifeworld. From Garden to Earth* (Bloomington, and Indianapolis, IN: Indiana University Press, 1990), 78. More recently this has been taken up by Peter-Paul Verbeek, *What Things Do: Philosophical Reflections on Technology, Agency, and Design* (University Park, PA: Pennsylvania State University Press, 2005), 186–97.

that opens up the "could be" by teaching how to use something and what to use it for. Just as the storyline of a narrative creates a followability to the heterogeneous elements that are configured together, so the technical instrument facilitates certain usages (while making others more difficult or impossible).

The formation of typical technical actions and instruments is amongst the most visible traits of cultures and civilizations – a fact which was already appreciated by Hannah Arendt when she wrote that "[t]ools and instruments are so intensely worldly objects that we can classify whole civilizations using them as criteria".[39] Wherever there are processes of civilization, processes of the transformation and transmission of culture, technics is involved. I say more about this in the next section. However, it is important already to note here that the metaphor of writing invites us to a whole series of critical questions pertaining to the transfer of technics. These involve particularly the interests that are carried over during the transfer of technics, the prejudices sedimented in technics and the effects of particular technical conditions on the users. When one puts it this way, it soon becomes clear that as long as one limits one's reflection to the level of *technical* knowledge of technics and ignores its social and symbolic implications and the appropriation of technics in the use of it, a vast domain of critical questions concerning technics is simply lost. A full critique of technics can only be undertaken if the recontextualisation of autonomous technics is considered. That is why technics is not only a matter of concern for whoever contemplates the processes of the formation of human beings and how they should live together, but also why such a reflection should have a cross-cultural dimension.

3.3 Refiguration

Thus far, I have isolated, in turn, the first two elements of the technical whole: first the habitus or technical pre-understanding (that is, the *I can* that dwells in the world), and then the configuration of technical means. In order to present the third aspect of technicity (namely worldliness), the interaction of all three aspects of human technicity should now be considered. The guiding metaphor for this process of refiguration is *reading*.

In this context, reading is a metaphor drawn from textual practices, like the reading of stories. In reading, the pre-narrative disposition (or habitus) is con-

---

[39] Hannah Arendt, *The Human Condition* (Chicago, IL: University of Chicago Press, 1958), 144.

fronted with a configured narrative. This confrontation of the reader's expectation or pre-judice by the followability of the text elicits a response in the form of a reactualisation of the plot which the configured narrative invites its reader to follow. This reactualisation of the narrative in the reading event entails an application or understanding of the narrative, leading the reader either to accept or to reject it. Of course, the reader never reads as a simple individual, but rather reads as a member of a community of readers[40] that invests its members with a specific type of reading culture; it accompanies the reading with the know-how of reading over which the reader disposes (which is not to say that there is no singularisation of interpretation in reading, but only that all reading is socially mediated to some extent). Furthermore, one reads within a particular context, a horizon, that gives further meaning to the reading event. Thus the socially and contextually influenced reader enters into a fusion between his/her own horizon of understanding. That horizon of understanding is offered by the "as if" of the story. Thus, in reading, something is offered that goes beyond the text, namely a world. The *world*, says Ricœur, "is the whole set of references opened by every sort of descriptive or poetic texts that I have read, interpreted and loved"[41] and it should be added that "what is interpreted in a text is the proposing of a world that I might inhabit and into which I might project my ownmost possibilities [*pouvoirs*]."[42] Thus, one's preconfigured, pre-narrative existence is reconfigured through reading.

It is much the same in human interaction with technical means. In the same sense as there is no story if the book is not read, no music if the score is not played, there is no technical event without the *use* of technics, be it by the handling of tools, monitoring and maintenance of processes, administration of institutions, etc. Reading, as a metaphor applied to human technicity, refers to the confrontation of the agent's technical pre-understanding or habitus with the technical configuration of an object embedded as it is in the technical system. In this event, the agent responds to the "could be" that is facilitated by the technical object, by reactualising it or by reactivating it as a means to do something. What was a mere instant ago still a lifeless object is now used *as* a saw, *as* a table, *as* an oven. This holds equally for more complex examples such as air-conditioning, nuclear power plants, and banks. By using the technical configuration, the agent suspends the configuration's autonomy and inserts it into a con-

---

40 Cf. Paul Ricœur, *Le conflit des interprétations. Essais d'herméneutique I* (Paris: Editions du Seuil, [1969] 2013), 7 / *The Conflict of Interpretations. Essays in Hermeneutics*, trans. Don Ihde et al. (Evanston, IL: Northwestern University Press, 1974), 3 (also discussed in Chapter 1, §4.3).
41 Ricœur, *Temps et récit 1*, 151 / *Time and Narrative 1*, 80.
42 Ricœur, *Temps et récit 1*, 152 / *Time and Narrative 1*, 81 (translation modified).

text in which it is used with or in coordination with other things in order to attain a certain goal. It is this "using something as" (what Heidegger called the "hermeneutic as"[43]) that opens up the *world* of technics. In the use of a technical object, the technical agent makes use of a technical object and thus recontextualises the facilitation offered by the technical object; the range of technical possibilities open to the technical agent when using an object depends on the complexity of the technical pre-understanding of the agent. At the same time, in using technical means, the agent is *disciplined* into how to use it and thus his/her technical habitus is refigured. In this sense, this two-way "dialogue" between a human being and the technical means could be considered a fusion of horizons.[44] One could also say that in engaging in technical activity, the agent is confronted by a proposal of ways to do things and at the same moment his/her *I can* is refigured. In learning how to use and master the use of certain objects in certain ways, the way in which one dwells in the world is transformed.

Of course, just as is the case with texts where one does not read alone, one does not use tools alone either.[45] The know-how of technical activity is to a large degree mediated by socially acquired skills (for example, a master craftsmen teaches apprentices how to use the tools of the trade). This, again, does not exclude singularising innovation, which could be seen in the style of an individual, his/her failure to meet the requirements of his/her training or in the excellence of brilliant technicians. Also, the use of technical means, and thus the meaning of the means, depends on the context or project in which it is used. The input from society and the context of the technical procedure co-determine the nature and meaning of that technical event. This situatedness of technics is responsible for the fact that when technics is understood purely *technically*, it is not fully understood. To be precise, technics have a *threefold reference*. First, there is the internal reference of the different elements of the technical object or procedure to one another, due to their technical qualities and design. One might call this the *tech-*

---

[43] Martin Heidegger, *Sein und Zeit* (Tübingen: Max Niemeyer Verlag, [1927] 1993), especially §32.
[44] This "dialogue" should certainly be taken metaphorically, since a lot of the interaction between human beings and the technical configuration takes place without the technical agent's being conscious or fully conscious of the entire scope of that interaction – hence I introduce the Foucauldian notion of "discipline".
[45] François Caron's book, *Les deux révolutions industrielles du XXe siècle* (Paris: Albin Michel, 1997), does not use only the intimate relation between the social and the technical as a grid for his historiography of the more recent developments in the socio-technical system (see 14 ff): one could equally read this book as a justification for the thesis that a technical community accompanies and guides the technico-hermeneutic process. The same could be said for his follow-up volume: François Caron, *La dynamique de l'innovation. Changement de technique et changement social (xvi-xxe siècle)* (Paris: Gallimard, 2010).

nical reference. Second, there is the reference of *usage* that identifies a technical means *as* this or that by using it in the context of a certain project, by using it for this or that. Third, there is the *symbolic* reference by which technics refers to social values of precision, aesthetics, fashion, sophistication, consumability, and so forth. The first of these corresponds to the observer perspective on technical configurations; the second and third depend for their description on a hermeneutics of action and constitute the worldliness of technics.[46]

4 Conclusions

I shall allow myself two concluding remarks by which to emphasise the sociopolitical significance of the proposed hermeneutics of technics. First, I want to clarify how this aspect of the hermeneutics of action sheds light on the formative effect of technical change on people's view of what human beings are and can (or cannot) become. Second, processes of technical change result in people's living under divergent, incompatible or unequal conditions. This may lead to strife and conflict, which has an obvious technical dimension. But I would like to clarify how more peaceful approaches to dealing with these difficulties are equally constituted in a technical way.

In the third phase of my presentation of the hermeneutic circle of technics, I indicated that the interaction between the technical habitus and the configured technical means is characterised by the emergence of worldliness, that is the threefold reference of technical action. It should already have become clear that the meaning of technics is certainly not only determined by the *technical* qualities of the technical objects, but also by the qualities and usage of the technical agent, which are socially formed, and by the context, which includes interaction with the social and symbolic aspects of human life. But this interaction of the diverse factors that shape technical events does not simply happen in a haphazard way – the changing life of technics is *stabilised* by the slowly changing habitus of the technical agent, by the practical given that one's life condition

---

[46] The description of the second or usage reference develops what Merleau-Ponty called concrete actions, whereas the description of the third or symbolic reference develops what he called abstract actions. See Maurice Merleau-Ponty, *Phénoménologie de la perception* (Paris: Gallimard, 1945), 127–30. For an elaboration of the threefold reference and detailed examples, cf. Ernst Wolff, "Hermeneutics and the capabilities approach. A thick heuristic tool for a thin normative standard of well-being. Practices of spatial arrangement as example," *South African Journal of Philosophy* 33, no. 4 (2014): 487–500, here 491, Murray and Wolff, "A Hermeneutic Framework," 181–82 and Wolff, "'Technology' as the Critical Social Theory," 351–52, respectively.

or occupation remains *fairly constant*, by the *stability* of the community that transmits the know-how, by the society that *maintains* certain symbolic values. We see this daily in the fact that children and students spend time acquiring skills and use those skills later on to practise a profession which has a place and status in society. But we also see it in other practices in which an interaction with technics and the acquisition of a habitus is involved, such as the acquisition of social roles, including, for instance, gender roles (for example, knowing how to walk in high-heeled shoes), religious roles (for example, who does what in a particular religious community), age roles (for example, how one walks with a frail body and a cane). One's engagement in the hermeneutic circle of technics is a constitutive element of one's identity, of what one is to oneself and for others. Just as we can be introduced to someone by means of a narrative ("this is Susan; she is the person I met at the conference in Essen"), we could also be introduced to someone by means of a name relating to the position that he/she takes in the technical system ("this is John, he is a computer programmer"). My point is, of course, not to reduce professions and other social roles to their technical aspect, but to caution that we need to guard against forgetfulness regarding that technical aspect. *Human beings typically occupy relatively stable, socially and symbolically shaped technical roles.*[47] At the core of such a role is the habitus, the second nature, the manner in which one is predisposed to act.

In the introduction to this chapter (§1), I have used Elias's theory to show that civilization is the process by which the habitus as mediation between the social and the individual is accomplished on a cross-generational scale. The habitus is not only formed by culturally specific objects, or by a culturally specific training on how to use the objects, but also, and at the same time, of the *virtues* involved in using them. When one learns carpentry, one learns not only how to saw and chisel wood, but also to be patient in doing so – an impatient carpenter is a second-rate carpenter. All technical training involves such virtues, since the excellence of technical execution depends on them (but negligence in this regard is also a form of training about virtues). Think of consistency, fidelity, precision, perseverance, collaboration, patience with oneself, with the instruments and materials and with one's co-workers, parsimony, prudence, etc. It should be clear that with these requirements for technical excellence and the requirement that they all be incorporated into the habitus, we have come very close to the domain

---

47 One should thus radicalise Jonas's conviction (as developed in *Das Prinzip Verantwortung*) that contemporary technics has changed the range of action and the context of application of action that are susceptible to ethical judgement – the agent him-/herself and the constitution of his/her role in society could be changed by developments in the domain of technics. I have taken a step in this direction in Wolff, "'Technology' as the Critical Social Theory".

of ethics. In fact, in many cases, it would be impossible to distinguish whether a virtue is more technical or more ethical.[48] What is certain is that training in the technical virtues of patience, consistency, etc. makes it possible to act with those same virtues outside of our daily professional domain. In fact, I posit that we know what those virtues mean, first of all, not through a theoretical understanding of them, but by our acquisition of them on the level of our dwelling *I can*. It is practically impossible to teach someone how to become a good artisan without at the same time offering that person an entry to the teacher's culture or civilization and thus teaching the apprentice something of what that culture or civilization constructs as being a good human being. Conversely, it is practically impossible to ignore the fact that imposing exploitative, meaningless and degrading modes of labour on people has detrimental effects on their self-esteem and expectations regarding personal and social improvement.[49] Thus I come back to my conviction, expressed in the introduction, that the cycle of technical change constitutes a hominization, in the sense of forming someone as a human being and transmitting to that person what a good human being is supposed to be like, or reducing the hope that one may be able to nurture for a better life. We only need to think here of the global discourse and practice of *development* in all its different forms in order to be convinced of the magnitude of this cross-cultural process of civilization and hominization by means of technical transfer.

My first point is thus to claim that the processes of technical change are processes of civilization that transmit culturally specific elements of ideal human existence (or pathological distortions thereof) and my hermeneutics of technical change proposes a schema for understanding how this happens. I would like to make a second point, focused on inter-cultural dialogue as an intervention in the processes of civilization and on the technical requirements for its effectiveness in order to indicate aspects of its dependency on its technical means of existence. But human cultures are numerous and so are the conditions under which people live, even in the same region. If we want to make general anthropological claims about the hermeneutics of technics, as part of divergent processes of civilization, then we have to reflect on the relation between people. That such difference often leads to aggressive interaction (military interventions, brutal imperatives of development, etc.) is beyond dispute. However, I would like

---

48 See further Wolff, "'Technology' as the Critical Social Theory," 356–60.
49 This has been demonstrated, for instance, in the classic work of Anson Rabinbach, *The Human Motor. Energy, Fatigue, and the Origins of Modernity* (Berkeley, CA: University of California Press, 1992), recently extended in Anson Rabinbach, *The Eclipse of the Utopias of Labor. Forms of Living* (New York, NY: Fordham University Press, 2018).

to show that technical differences also condition the most well-intentioned attempts to construct peaceful interaction. This is the dilemma I wish to clarify as my second point of conclusion, using intercultural dialogue as an example.

From the point of view of technics, the problem of intercultural dialogue or strategic negotiations to establish partnerships could be summarised as a problem of the *effectiveness of symbols* – the principal point of overlap between mediology and hermeneutics, discussed in Chapter 1 (especially §4.2). Such a dialogue seeks to be a discourse on culture, humanity and values (that is the symbolic aspect) and it wants this discourse to be an intervention in human sociality, symbolics and technicity (the aspect of efficiency). Whatever that intervention might entail, of necessity it depends on a transmission of its symbolic content. Transmission, as we saw in Chapter 1, §3, is the event by which symbols are enabled to cover not only space, but more particularly, time. Transmission consists of a number of stereotypical elements. In my opinion, they follow a trajectory that is very close to the hermeneutic circle of technics that I have developed above. *Firstly*, the message or the "what it is about" is deposited (inscribed in some or other form of support). By means of this process, the message gains autonomy, which is made possible by the autonomy of the technical configuration that supports it. From the point of view of the transmission, this autonomy is simultaneously the best and the worst of all possible things: on the one hand, its autonomy makes it susceptible to being uprooted from the situation in which the message was created and to being recontextualised elsewhere at another time; but on the other hand, it is the trajectory that links the decontextualisation with a recontextualisation that exposes the message to transformation. Hence transmission is not only an attempt to safeguard a message against disappearing, but also an attempt to supervise and control its transformation. *Secondly*, transmission consists of mechanisms by which the support of the message is changed into a conveyor that will take charge of the movement of the message through time. This conveyor has a dual character: it is both technical and institutional, in other words, it relies on both equipment and organization.[50] Both dimensions change and take shape as part of a broader technical and institutional (and therefore symbolic) milieu. *Thirdly*, the means of transmission mediates its messages, in other words, energizes it with its transmissive energy, which amplifies the impetus of the message to a level at which the message never was. Inevitably, this mediation constitutes a transformation of the message and aims to accompany the last phase of transmission, the reception or reading. *Fourthly*, then, (an area unfortunately neglected by Debray) there is the appropriative or

---

50 Cf. Régis Debray, *Introduction à la médiologie* (Paris: PUF, 2000), 126. See also Chapter 1, §3.

rejecting reading of the message, under the influence of its very means of transmission. The reception of the message already constitutes a further extension of the life of the message, that is, of its transmission.

In respect of any ideas that may emerge from negotiations or dialogue between people of divergent settings, what can we conclude from this trajectory of the means by which such ideas would become effective? Any intercultural dialogue worthy of the name would also have to include a technics, in the sense that it would have to be structured by a means of transmission that could convert its theory into practice.[51] This is true not only because what is formulated in the dialogue has to be transmitted, but also because efficient transmission has to mediate between old culture-specific ideas concerning human existence from all corners of the world (transmit whilst transforming the ideas inherited from the past).

I would not be surprised to find that what I say about transmission sounds quite obvious here, in Germany.[52] The reason for this is that the very milieu in which we find ourselves (the German university and research environment) is to a large degree the fruit of a cultural project that understands itself since the beginning as an endeavour of transmission and that has been very successful in what it does. But the obviousness of this system of transmission is undercut once it has to relativise itself as only one among other partners on an intercultural forum. In simple terms: whatever agreement could be reached on humanity and values has to be transmitted to cultural specific locations; but since this is an intercultural dialogue, the means of transmission has to be culturally specific and thus transforms the message in diverse, culturally specific ways; and the original agreement is in danger of falling apart in practice. Thus the diversity of praxes and technologies of transmission threatens the possibility of a coherent and honest intercultural dialogue.[53]

Let me rephrase this point. People who are searching for new ways of co-existence for our culturally diverse humanity, and who understand that this en-

---

51 Cf. Debray, *Introduction à la médiologie*, 114.
52 This chapter was written during a period spent as research fellow of the Kulturwissenschaftliches Institut in Essen.
53 Cf. Wim van Binsbergen, who observes from a southern hemisphere perspective: "It is the irony of many identity constructions and identity claims outside the North Atlantic today, that in order to succeed, in order to be taken seriously by their actual and potential adherents and by others including national and international governmental bodies, they need to be formulated in the academic and commodified format stipulated (even imposed) under North Atlantic hegemony." (Wim van Binsbergen, "Ubuntu and the Globalization of Southern African Thought and Society," *Quest. An African Journal of Philosophy* 15, no. 1–2 (2001): 53–90 (https://www.quest-journal.net/Quest_2001_PDF/binsbergen.pdf, last accessed 23 February 2020), citation 66.

deavour has an intercultural dimension, implicitly want their ideas to become practice – if they did not, everybody could just have remained human and humane in their own way, in their own corner of the world. If one then supposes that the means to reach this goal, for the transmission of the acquisition of an intercultural dialogue, already exists in Europe in the form of schools and universities, libraries and bookshops, etc., one has to consider the question of whether the technologies for the transmission of such acquisition also exist elsewhere.[54] Or will they have to be provided, from the outside, as it were? That would imply, at the same time, the provision of a technics with a concomitant implicit culturally specific civilizing force that would change people's culture in the name of making them ready to participate in an intercultural dialogue. Or if the means for an intercultural dialogue are already present or possible in other regions, is it not perhaps already only on the basis of a universal mono-cultural technics of transfer that spreads itself over the globe in a very non-dialogical, non-intercultural manner?

What I am trying to convey is the idea that any intercultural dialogue which is not at the same time a technology (in the sense of an essential reflection on its means of transmission) runs the risk of using and propagating culturally specific means of transmission that will transform an intercultural symbolic invention according to its own homogenising logics in a naïve way. Or to put it positively, a global intercultural dialogue would be worthy of this name (on a descriptive level) only if it is effective as a result of a truly intercultural dialogic practice in all three of the elements of hominization: society, signs *and technics*.[55] And if this holds for the most peaceful attempts at negotiating human differences, then it surely holds equally for more strategic negotiations and bargaining in trade, humanitarian aid or alliance formation.[56]

---

[54] Or could such an inter-cultural dialogue be invented that it would suit the existing means of transmission of other parts of the world? Debray has expressed his own reservations (and hopes) concerning inter-cultural dialogue in *Un mythe contemporain: le dialogue des civilisations* (Paris: CNRS Editions, 2007).
[55] The question of dialogue and cultural diversity is picked up again in Chapter 6, §§5 and 6.
[56] The chapters of Part 2 are devoted to a closer look at examples of these difficulties.

Chapter 3:
Human Capabilities in the Light of Incapabilities

1 Introduction: A Hypothesis on the Technicity of Capabilities

In the first chapter, I demonstrated the affinity of philosophical hermeneutics to questions related to the human ability to act, and the means by which humans act. Anyone who wants to understand the transmission of ideas will, sooner or later, have to study the efficacy of symbols, which depends on the technicity of those who articulate meaning, those who inscribe it and those who receive it. The second chapter considered how, throughout the history of the species, human beings have attempted to intervene in what human beings are, or could become, by means of a narrative reconfiguration of their lived existence. We saw that, intentionally or not, the sphere of technical actions and systems of artefacts has a similar reconfiguring effect on human beings as agents. In this chapter, we zoom in on the agent, in other words, on human beings, from the perspective of what they are able to do, or do not succeed in doing.

In *Oneself as Another* and much of Ricœur's later work, he elaborates a hermeneutics of the self, or, as he puts it, the acting and suffering human. The notion of capability or "I can" receives a central place in this project, which is also called a hermeneutics of the capable human [*l'homme capable*]. In essence, this hermeneutics explores four central capabilities that are telescoped into each other: saying, doing, narrating and imputing action to oneself as good/bad, just/unjust, prudent/irresponsible. These capabilities belong to the agent in the first person (*I* or *we*), but they require activation in interaction with others – both in interaction with people in the sense of a physical presence (*you*) and institutional others (that is, the institutional mediation of *it*). In this chapter and the remaining chapters of this book, I repeatedly come back to this grid which plots the range of capabilities on the threefold activation (I – you – it). Nevertheless, although Ricœur explores a range of human capabilities, the notion of capability itself remains underdetermined from what one may call a "technical" angle. In this chapter I transform this lacuna in his hermeneutics into a task. My aim is to deploy something that is already present in his philosophy, but in the negative, or in the form of fragmentary thoughts, and to examine this aspect more fully. The *hypothesis* guiding this chapter is that the *hermeneutics of human capabilities requires more detailed development of the technical dimension of capabilities, that is, a reflection on, first, the skills and, second, the means of the "I can"*. This is thus a development of the hermeneutics of capabil-

	I (capabilities)	*you* (close-by others)	*it* (institutional mediation)
saying			
doing			
narrating			
imputing			
(etc.)			

relations of embedding ↓

Figure 1: Grid plotting capabilities on activation in relation with others

ities that we do not find in *Oneself as Another*.[1] Ultimately, the interest of this hypothesis exceeds the hermeneutics of human capabilities, taking it into the political and ethical dimensions of interaction. This link is made by Ricœur himself when he claims that it is their "capabilities that make human beings worthy of respect," and when he argues that the development of capabilities by the institutions of the state is its first political obligation.[2] We will come back to this point in the conclusion of the chapter (§5, below).

In formulating my hypothesis, I identified two dimensions of "I can": the *skills* deployed or activated, and the *means* used in the action. From the series of capabilities studied by Ricœur – speaking, doing, narrating, imputing, plus

---

[1] In this chapter, I limit myself to the philosophy of Ricœur's last two decades. All insights from the earlier work and notably Paul Ricœur, *L'homme faillible*, in *Philosophie de la volonté 2. Finitude et culpabilité* (Paris: Edition Points, [1960] 2009), 37–199 / *Fallible Man*, trans. Charles A. Kelbley (New York, NY: Fordham University Press, [1965] 1986)) would require reintegration into the *hermeneutic* investigation to the self, which I adopt here.

[2] Paul Ricœur, *Lectures 1: Autour du politique* (Paris: Seuil, 1991), 164. I take note of the critique of the emergence of capability policies (which is directed at Ricœur's philosophy, sometimes directly, sometimes implicitly); however, since this chapter is a reflection on the nature of the capabilities in question, this critique may be placed into parentheses. See, for example, Jean-Louis Genard and Fabrizio Cantelli, "Êtres capables et compétents: lecture anthropologique et pistes pragmatiques," *SociologieS* [Online], Théories et recherches, online on 27 April 2008. http://sociologies.revues.org/1943, last accessed 29 February 2020. I will come back to this point at the end of the Conclusion to this book (§3.3b).

remembering and promising³ – let us take the ability to speak as an example of what this is about. Ricœur studies numerous dimensions thereof in depth, for instance
1. the person capable of speaking, which involves
2. the addressees,
3. the medium or institution of spoken language,
4. the forms and types of verbal and written speech,
5. the fact that by speaking, things are done (the pragmatics of language), and
6. the autonomy of the text abstracted from the conditions of its writing and reading.

But there is no development of a similar scale in his argument on the *means* by which we speak (such as telephones, text support, conference rooms, counters or satellites). Nor does he discuss the institutional forms of speech, which are highly dependent on socio-technical networks (such as publishing industries, libraries, global networks of communication technologies and everything on which they depend). Only rarely⁴ does he ponder the nature of the *capability* to speak and write – or the degrees to which capable people would be capable of speaking or writing – which may vary as people work to improve their spelling, learn to send emails, try to integrate educational institutions that would allow them to address students, use institutions that guarantee the durability of a document, etc.

My hypothesis can be reformulated as follows: A phenomenological analysis of the capability to speak – an analysis that examines the *what?* and then the *how?* and finally the *who?*⁵ of speech *as an aspect of the hermeneutics of the capable human* – remains insufficient as long as it is limited to an analysis that passes from statements (*what?*) to speech-acts (*how?*) to the speaker (*who?*), while ignoring two crucial elements. These two elements are the *technical supports* that make speech and writing possible (to say nothing of other forms of language expression), and the ways in which a capable human figures out

---

3 Remembering and promising are added in Paul Ricœur, *Parcours de la reconnaissance* (Paris: Stock, 2004), 179–214 / *The Course of Recognition*, trans. David Pellauer (Cambridge, MA: Harvard University Press, 2005), 109–34.
4 Cf. Paul Ricœur, "Autonomie et vulnérabilité," in *Le juste 2* (Paris: Esprit, 2001), 85–105 / "Autonomy and Vulnerability," in *Reflections on the Just*, trans. David Pellauer (Chicago, IL: University of Chicago Press, 2007), 72–90.
5 According to the reformulation that structures the second part of Ricœur, *Course of Recognition*.

how to cope with his/her *limited abilities* to express him/herself and use those means of expression.

In other words, we would lose sight of an important aspect of the capable human – of what "capabalises" humans – if the two elements added above are omitted. This holds, *mutatis mutandis*, also for the other capabilities that Ricœur has identified, namely those of doing, narrating, imputing, remembering and promising.

In order to formulate my hypothesis, I have to assume that "technicity" is not a type of action, but an attribute of action in general.[6] How then can we understand the technical aspect of action within the framework of Ricœur's hermeneutics of human capabilities, of which it should have been an essential component? I would argue that giving *incapability* its rightful place is one way to achieve this.

2 The Capable Human is the Incapable Human

There is almost an admission of the lacuna that I will try to fill in a passage in *The Course of Recognition* when he introduces the two additional capacities to the four listed in *Oneself as Another* – namely remembering and promising:

> We thought we were justified in treating the different modes of doing things, the ability to speak and act, the ability to recount, up to and including imputability, *without giving an equal weight to the inabilities* that correspond to them – something that would be open to criticism if we had to take into account the psychological, the sociological, and especially the pedagogical dimension in the effective exercise of these capacities. [...]

The rest of my chapter shows why this lacuna must also be considered philosophically questionable – as Ricœur admits when he continues the previous citation:

> [...] But we cannot allow such a deadlock in the cases of memory and promises. Their opposite is part of their meaning: to remember is to not forget; to keep one's promise is not to break it.[7]

---

6 This has been argued partially in Chapter 2, §2, but in more detail in Ernst Wolff, "'Technology' as the Critical Social Theory of Human Technicity," *Journal of Philosophical Research* 41 (2016): 333–69, here 342–44, where I adopt this anti-typological critique from Hans Joas, *Die Kreativität des Handelns* (Frankfurt am Main: Suhrkamp, 1992), 213.
7 Ricœur, *Parcours de la reconnaissance*, 180 / *Course of Recognition*, 110 (my emphasis).

What we are implicitly invited to do is to show that what Ricœur insists on in respect of remembering and promising also applies to other capabilities. I thus propose to enrich the phenomenological movement from the *what* to *how* to the *who* of the capable human, by elaborating the "I cannot."

On the outset of this undertaking, this discourse on the incapability of agents must be qualified in order to help readers to guard against three possible misunderstandings. Firstly, the aim here is not to develop yet another dimension of the suspicion directed at the claim of being able to act, the kind of suspicion that threatens the already fragile *attestation* of varieties of "I can", which Ricœur himself has already dealt with in his preface to *Oneself as Another*.[8] The point is completing our understanding of the very attestation of "recognizing oneself as being capable." Secondly, the exploration of the figures of incapability is not an elaboration on ignorance [*méconnaissance*], although we will see that incapability is not always recognized as such during the action. Finally, this elaboration on the "I cannot" is about something other than a reflection on the "absence" of capability, as Ricœur often presents it when he speaks of suffering, fragility or vulnerability. In this sense, what is discussed here is the in*ability* of the human being even in his/her optimal condition(s), rather than a pathological absence or deprivation of abilities.

2.1 Five Figures of Incapability

The time has come to flesh out the preliminary considerations by exploring in more detail that which limits capacity. I would like to call this set of limitations by the abstract name "incapability" and speak about it in a personifying way, to make the presentation easier. Strictly speaking, incapability is nothing in itself, and it is certainly not a counter-power. I can identify five elements of incapability[9]:
1. Any capability to act is a capability of the body (as we have seen in the discussion of the *habitus* in the previous chapter, §3.1). Here, I borrow from Marcel Mauss the notion of "bodily techniques" to which I nevertheless give a significantly different meaning. I concur that these are the great series

---

[8] Paul Ricœur, *Soi-même comme un autre* (Paris: Seuil, 1990), 33–34 / *Oneself as Another*, trans. Kathleen Blamey (Chicago, IL: University of Chicago Press, 1992), 21–22.
[9] These five elements correspond broadly to the five dialectics of technicality and aspects of human existence other than the technicality of the body in Ernst Wolff, "'Technology' as the Critical Social Theory of Human Technicity," 352–55.

of dispositions and skills to perform this or that activity, often learned through socio-cultural learning. However, the discussion that follows will show that the Maussian definition of "traditional and effective acts" [*actes traditionnels et efficaces*][10] errs, both by ignoring the individualization of these techniques and by exaggerating the effectiveness that they lend to action. These abilities are recognized by the relative consistency of their execution: one recognizes someone who walks when one sees the person walking; one recognizes Australians by the unique way in which they form the words of the English language, etc. This tendency to do things as if we were following rules is due to the fact that by learning to do something, we learn to do it in a particular way, in *this* way and not in another. And even if we can decide to do this or that action differently, we cannot perform all our actions otherwise at the same time or otherwise all the time. Technicity is what makes it possible to act, but as the seat of capability, it is a seat that is predisposed to do something in a particular way, without, however, determining the action. By making us more skilled at acting in some ways than others, capabilities make it comparatively more difficult for us to act in any other ways. Thus, the body's techniques also forge incapabilities, not in an absolute way, but by disposing us not to act in any other way.

2. Upstream of the acquired skills is the *biological body*, which is relatively homogeneous between people, but still differs in many aspects. At the beginning of human life, the infant human body is a wriggling body; little by little the agent manages to impose a discipline on these wriggling movements;[11] part of this discipline is inherited from traditional practices or instilled by interpersonal learning processes, but not only from these: there is also learning that takes place "all by itself" (e. g. learning how to sit). Yet this range of skills never becomes complete mastery, nor an omnipresent social control over action.[12] Action, made possible and improved by the acquired skills, re-

---

10 Marcel Mauss, "Les techniques du corps" (1934), in *Sociologie et anthropologie* (Paris: PUF, 1950), 365–386, here 371.
11 This "discipline" is what Aristotle calls *hexis meta logou*, which is common to *praxis* and *poiesis*. I have demonstrated elsewhere that Aristotle greatly exaggerates the difference between the two species of *hexis meta logou* (cf. *Nicomachean Ethics* 1140a, 3–5), see Ernst Wolff, "Aspects of technicity in Heidegger's early philosophy: rereading Aristotle's *techné* and *hexis*," *Research in Phenomenology* 38, no. 3 (2008): 317–57.
12 In this respect, I agree with Laurent Thévenot, who considers "too strong the current hypotheses that rule out these difficulties [of coordination between agent and environment – EW] by assuming coordinated action through routines, rules or social norms that would only require to be implemented in the situation". *L'action au pluriel. Sociologie des régimes d'engagement*

mains forever exposed to the vagaries of the physiological body from which the disciplined body derives its strength or momentum to act:[13] one learns to a certain extent to do something like others in a way adapted to one's own physical condition, or in accordance with one's ability to persevere, and not necessarily as well as others. Add to this all the factors that make one's physical condition unstable, unsteady – hormones, fatigue, exercise, health, pregnancy, stress, age, etc. – and it becomes clear that the physical condition contributes to differentiating between capacity and non-capacity. In addition, physical fitness is a factor in the individualization of bodily techniques. Perhaps no phenomenon shows this as clearly as the style of an action: mannerisms, gait, accent, etc. retroactively designate their author,[14] distinguishing the agent from his/her counterparts.

3. So far, I have considered identifiable actions in isolation. However, the capacities that are at play in actions which can be isolated for analysis are entangled in the flow of actions. Sometimes it is necessary to train to combine different actions; sometimes the combination of a number of isolatable actions is done "all by itself". However, it is not possible to coordinate every action or way of doing things with every other. Here we are dealing with both the limits imposed on the combination of two or more quite different and sometimes incompatible actions (e. g. concentrating on driving a car while talking on your mobile phone, imputing an action without indicting your partners, telling your life-story without demeaning your adversaries), and the difficulties or impossibilities of reconciling certain competing specifications of actions (e. g. working with a machine quickly and safely, saving

---

(Paris: La Découverte, 2006), 95. The subsequent discussion above gives my own argument in support of this position.

13 In this statement, I implicitly take up the Aristotelian notion of *orexis* – a key notion in connection with the *hexis meta logou*, which, whether in the form of virtue or in the form of ability, transforms bodily energy into capacity. Marc Breviglieri's interesting study, "L'espace habité que réclame l'assurance intime de pouvoir. Un essai d'approfondissement sociologique de l'anthropologie capacitaire de Paul Ricœur," *Études Ricœuriennes / Ricœur Studies* 3, no. 1 (2012): 34–52, reflects on this phenomenon, which I point out by taking up the notion of *orexis*, and which I present as already related to its transformation into capabilities. Inspired by the philosophy of life in *Freedom and nature. The voluntary and the involuntary*, Breviglieri shows the importance of recognizing "the intimate assurance of being able" [*l'assurance intime de pouvoir*] and "feeling oneself alive to which one can only consent" (39). This assurance *precedes* any capacity to act and is situated in the agent's biological life.

14 As Ricœur would say in another context, namely Paul Ricœur, *Du texte à l'action. Essais d'herméneutique II* (Paris: Seuil, 1986), 123 / *From Text to Action: Essays in Hermeneutics II*, trans. Kathleen Blamey and John Thompson (London: Athlone, 1991), 82.

energy without losing performance, developing an argument in a conference without exceeding the time limit, etc.).[15] Thus the coordination of different actions makes them limit each other: a new dimension of the "I cannot" in action is identified. This creates conflict and the challenge of finding compromises. And given the contingencies of acting in response to the requirements of each particular context, the successful combination of isolable actions represents a skill of a higher degree of complexity than the techniques learned in themselves, which is an additional factor in the individualization of a skilled act.

4. Ricœur explains clearly that the capacities of the self (the "*I*") are realized in interaction with other people (the "*you*", as he calls it) and in institutions (the "*it*", as he calls it). But interaction, to remain at least roughly intelligible – to be *inter*action and not simply a juxtaposition of non-coherent actions – must limit or form the action of agents. For instance, we try to avoid interrupting each other; we do not respond to a gift too quickly with a return gift; we have to keep up with the set pace of work in team collaboration, or we manage to get official documents in due time from state bureaus, etc. In short, the coordination of interaction introduces a dimension of inability to act, and we all know the interpersonal conflict that can arise from this situation and the resulting attempts to find compromises.[16]

5. Finally, when we act, we often act by means of something. The characteristics of these means and our ability to use them reveal and extend the dialectic of the capacity and incapability of human action in general. This interplay of increasing and reducing our capabilities through the means of action has been analysed by the American phenomenologist Don Ihde, and has already been touched on in the previous chapter (§3.2[3]).[17] Let us take the microscope as an illustration of this point: by using it, we increase our ability to inspect the details of an object, but at the same time we are

---

[15] This is the central problem examined in Chapter 8, by means of a case studies on labour action.

[16] The capability of agents to coordinate their actions and find compromises between the adverbial specifications of their actions is complex and limited, as shown by the example of sociopolitical justifications, see Luc Boltanski and Laurent Thévenot, *De la justification* (Paris: Gallimard, 1991).

[17] Ihde first proposed this idea in an analysis of observational tools – see Don Ihde. *Technics and Praxis* (Dordrecht, Boston, MA, and London: Reidel, 1979), 38, 48. It is easy to demonstrate that the phenomenon of augmentation-reduction is applicable far beyond this field of technical objects – see Don Ihde, *Technology and the Lifeworld. From Garden to Earth* (Bloomington and Indianapolis, IN: Indiana University Press, 1990), 78. Nevertheless, it remains to be seen how the scope of the validity of this phenomenon should be delineated.

subjected to a reduction in our ability to observe a wide field of view. Let us rephrase this: the increase in capability is coupled with the imposition of incapability. This coupling of capacitation with incapacitation is achieved not only in the use of tools, but also in our interaction with technical complexes, which are an integral part of the organizations and institutions in which we live (schools, bureaucracies, hospitals, etc., each with their own networks of electricity, transport, sanitary equipment, cleaning, administration, etc. – see the elaboration below). To assess the significance of human interactions with "tools" for a philosophical anthropology of the capable human, it seems useful to consider that the hominization of humans as a historical process has involved interaction with tools, of slowly increasing sophistication, which have allowed for increased differentiation of capacities to act (as I have discussed in Chapter 2).[18] The sophisticated techniques which are typical of organizational and institutional systems are an extension of this process, but one has to reject categorically reducing them to their technical aspects.[19]

Let us conclude. To say that incapability and capability are not two mutually exclusive dimensions of action, but that they are constitutive of each other, implies that incapability, despite its *"negative"* character, contributes to an agent's capability to do things. In the weak sense in which the term "incapability" is used here, it is not *a priori* pathological and cannot be separated from action. Similarly, capability, despite its *"positive"* character, contributes to an agent's incapability to do other things or do them in other ways. This is one of the sources of the unintended consequences of actions.

2.2 Incapability as a Practical Horizon of Action. (In)capability as a Mark of Uncertainty

Thus, the incapacity, even if it is overlooked, forms at least the horizon of the *practical* intelligibility (not the conscious or theoretical intelligibility) of the action – in a way comparable to the interaction between the focus and the horizon in Merleau-Ponty's perception:[20] just as there is a need for part of the field of per-

---

[18] As already theorized more than half a century ago by André Leroi-Gourhan in *Le geste et la parole* (Paris: Albin Michel, 1964–1965), or more recently by François Sigaut in *Comment Homo devient faber. Comment l'outil fit l'homme* (Paris: CNRS Éditions, 2013).
[19] Organized action and the technicity of organizations is examined in Chapter 4.
[20] Maurice Merleau-Ponty, *Phénoménologie de la perception* (Paris: Gallimard, 1945), 81–86.

ception practically to disappear, in order to function as a horizon against which the object aimed at can be perceived, so the unrealized or unrealizable dimension of actions in the vanishing point of feasible actions serves as a *practical horizon for the intelligibility of the actions performed*. As such, this horizon of incapacity (even if it is consciously unknown) would already inform the almost unconscious acts of adaptation, judgment and invention required by the fact that by acting, one deploys one's habitual abilities in non-identical circumstances.

That is why, in the course of action, the relation between capability and incapability remains to some degree uncertain. The degree of capability may be anticipated in routine action; or people may strive to shift the limits of capability by concentrated effort. This uncertainty is only dispelled at the moment when an action is performed; action splits capability from incapability. After the act has been completed, one may retrospectively trace the degree of capability, that is, the shifting point of differentiation between capability and incapability attested to in that act.

For this reason, I claim that paying attention to the interplay of capabilities and incapabilities is an important aid in the difficult task of understanding action *as* action.[21] Furthermore, it necessitates due attention to the numerous "*adverbial increments*" which singularize each specific action in relation to its specific context of application.[22] Finally, the incapability as the horizon of the practical intelligibility of action and the uncertainty of the practical distinction of (in)capability contributes to the inherently interpretative nature of action, as performed by situated and finite agents.

If we lose sight of this implication of the dialectic of capability-incapability, we also fail to appreciate what I refer to later as the "paradox of the technicity of

---

[21] This notion was dear to Pierre Bourdieu, see *The Logic of Practice* (Stanford: Stanford University Press, 1990), 52, and his critics, cf. Theodore Schatzki, "Practices and Actions. A Wittgensteinian Critique of Bourdieu and Giddens," *Philosophy of the Social Sciences* 27, no. 3 (1997): 283–308.

[22] This idea is derived from Michael Pakaluk's reading of Aristotle's understanding of the choice for an appropriate mean (*mesotés*) in action (see Michael Pakaluk, *Aristotle's Nicomachean Ethics. An Introduction* (Cambridge: Cambridge University Press, 2005), 110 ff.) When Aristotle describes the capacity of the virtuous agent to decide on an appropriate mid-way between two vices, he describes this mid-way as "relative to us", in other words, dependent on who we are and the context in which we find ourselves. Correspondingly this "mean" can be qualified as situated somewhere on the discernible increments on the continuums of all the categories that determine the particular quality of an action (the agent, object, instrument, manner, time, place, duration, reason, purpose).

action." But before we embark on this topic, let us consider some of the implications of the preceding presentation.

2.3 The Capable Human is the Finite Human

In the light of the five dimensions of incapability that I proposed above, we can gauge the extent to which a hermeneutic of "I can" is dependent on such a hermeneutic of "I cannot" (and *vice versa!*). In addition, it is then possible to consolidate this acquisition with a small thought experiment. Let us try to elevate capability to an absolute status: if we eliminate the "I cannot," we lose sight of the fact that the "I can" is most often realized as "I can this, but not that," "I can do something up to that point, but not further," etc. Once these restrictions are eliminated, both the isolated actions and the entanglement of actions would be unlimited; an agent who is capable without limits[23] would be an omnipotent agent.[24] Conversely, saying that "I cannot" is constitutive of "I can" only translates the notion of finitude into terms of capability and action. The tension between power and powerlessness is the *originary finitude* of the human agent.[25]

If incapability originates as much in the finiteness of the human agent as capability does, it follows that, by granting importance to incapability, one becomes aware of the complexity of the dialectic of recognition and misrecognition of capabilities,[26] since, henceforth, in recognizing one's capabilities, it should be considered possible also to recognize one's incapabilities. Similarly, when Ricœur speaks of misunderstanding [*méprise*][27] as the "ability to fail" ["*pouvoir-*

---

[23] Just the "conjugation" of acting with more specific verbs – singing, justifying, knitting, stammering, etc. – testifies to this limitation of the infinitive; adverbs and other adverbial phrases add additional details.
[24] Raising the "I cannot" to the absolute rank would result in complete impotence. Moreover, unlike omnipotence, absolute impotence cannot be recognized.
[25] The question of the finiteness of the capable human was addressed in another way by Johann Michel, "Crise de soi et substitution narrative," *Archivio di filosofia* 1 (2013): 281–90. He remobilised the philosophy of the will of the young Ricœur to interpret the "structural crisis" of an actor forever unequal to himself as the fact that humankind is "the intermediary between finitude and infinitude." Despite this difference in approach and wording, Michel's statement on this point seems to me to be generally compatible with mine.
[26] This subject is discussed by Ricœur in *Parcours de la reconnaissance*, 391; *Course of Recognition*, 256.
[27] "Admitting that every capacity has as its counterpart a specific incapacity is easy to accept in its generality. The details of these incapacities, on the basis of the distinct registers of the power to act, reveals ever more concealed forms of incapacity whereby misunderstanding [*méconnaissance*] leads to 'self-deception.' The mistake [*méprise*] then is to mistake oneself, to take oneself

faillir"] that is ignored,[28] he comes close to formulating my concern, but his formulation does not reflect sufficiently the relationship between capabilities and incapabilities. A hermeneutic of the abilities of the capable human must, as a hermeneutic of the finite human, relate the notions of recognition-misrecognition and capability-incapability, in order to be able to account for the recognition of both capability and incapability, as well as the misrecognition of capability and incapability.

If this conclusion is accepted, it becomes clear that the Ricœurian notions of "suffering,"[29] of "fragility",[30] of "vulnerability"[31] (and perhaps also of "fallibility"[32]), sometimes referred to by him as figures of powerlessness or incapacity, despite their relevance, are insufficient to clarify this field, since their mutual implication in the agent's finitude is not properly understood. Whenever the capable human recognizes himself/herself as capable, he/she recognizes himself/herself as (only) capable of something in particular and capable to a certain extent. *Thus, the recognition of incapability is constitutive of the act of recognizing oneself as capable (in other words attesting to one's capabilities), because these are two interdependent dimensions of the same act: the act of recognizing oneself as a finite agent.* It would be too ambitious to attempt an explanation of this entire network that conjoins competence-incompetence with recognition-misrecognition here. In what follows, I only raise a few relevant points to come back to my hypothesis on the technicity of the capable human.

3 The Capable-Incapable Human Discloses the Technical Human

I embarked on an exploration of the dialectic of capability and incapability, positing that this would make a significant contribution to our understanding of the

---

for what one is not" (Ricœur, *Parcours de la reconnaissance*, 392–393 / *Course of Recognition*, 257 and see the development of this idea in the following pages).

28 Ricœur, *Parcours de la reconnaissance*, 392 / *Course of Recognition*, 257.
29 Cf. Paul Ricœur, "La souffrance n'est pas la douleur," *Autrement*, "Souffrances" 142 (February, 1994): 58–69.
30 Cf. Paul Ricœur, "Fragilité et responsabilité," in *Eros and Eris. Contributions to a hermeneutical phenomenology*, eds. Paul van Tongeren et al. (Dordrecht: Kluwer, 1992), 295–304 / Paul Ricœur, "Fragility and Responsibility," *Philosophy & Social Criticism* 21, nos. 5–6 (1995): 15–22.
31 Cf. Ricœur, "Autonomie et vulnérabilité" / "Autonomy and Vulnerability".
32 In terms of the limited scope of this chapter, I suspend my judgment on Ricœur's *Fallible Man*. See, however, the reference to fallibility in *Parcours de la reconnaissance*, 392 / *Course of Recognition*, 256.

technicity of action. My contention was that a clearer view on this dialectic would provide us with new notions that would firstly be appropriate within the framework of the hermeneutics of the capable human, but that would, secondly, at the same time allow us to grasp the technical aspect of both capabilities and action. Relying on the previous analyses, I will now show how what I call primary and secondary technicity are part of this dialectic of capacity-incapacity, at the heart of self-recognition – self-misrecognition.

3.1 Misrecognition of Incapability, Practical Horizon and Primary Technicity

While affirming that in action, a person's capabilities are intertwined with his/her incapabilities, I have no reason to believe that the *attestation* of incapability accompanies each action – often we simply act in misrecognition or ignorance of the incapability, as long as we act spontaneously. In fact, as I suggested above, incapability forms part of the practical horizon of the intelligibility of action. If this is the case for our spontaneous action, it furnishes us with a vantage point from which to understand what I call the *primary technicity of action*[33]:

1. The effects of more or less stable acquired bodily capabilities on the daily flow of action (driven by bodily vitality) are in their exercise always a (more or less appropriate) response to the requirements or opportunities of a specific practical context (as tacitly interpreted by the agent).
2. This context refers both to the physical and social field of action and to the limits of capabilities that the agent can attest to after the event.
3. Since primary technicity is, therefore, the effect of the dialectic of spontaneously exercised capability-incapability (which implies tacit acts of judgment and invention), conscious planning of action is not part of its definition; primary technicality must therefore be described as non-teleological.

3.2 Reflection, Level of Competence and Secondary Technicity

But, as suggested above, it happens just as often that *we do recognize that we are unable* to do something or do it as we wish. This occurs when our course of action is disturbed, whether this is due to the state of our capacities, the condition

---

[33] The notions of primary and secondary technicity are discussed in detail in Ernst Wolff, "'Technology' as the Critical Social Theory of Human Technicity," here 345–47.

of our body, the difficult coordination of various actions, the complexity of the interaction or the challenges of the technical mediation of action. When this happens, agents are confronted with their incapability. At such a point, the observer in oneself as agent is awakened and one's attention is reflected towards oneself. In phenomenology (at least since Heidegger's "pragmatism"[34]) as much as in American or French pragmatism, it is the range of failures that invites or prompts the self to recognize itself, and even to recognize itself as being capable.

And yet, it is not only the confrontation with incapability in all its dimensions that triggers the "reduction" or reflection, because even if one is used to one's limitations, one can still be confronted in an unexpected way with one's capabilities. Think of the surprise of an unexpected accomplishment, the pleasure of a very difficult performance, the joy of learning to use new skills, but also the fatigue of repeated actions that are too well-known. In these cases, the usual or anticipated *relationship* of capabilities and incapabilities in a specific context is disrupted. Capability is therefore no more a determinant for action than incapability is; a determinant (speaking "technically"[35]) is the fluctuation between capabilities attested against a background of incapabilities, and incapabilities attested within the horizon of capabilities (both are regimes of primary technicity) – relationships that then undergo disruption.

These small and large disturbances, small and great pleasures, so frequent in the flow of action, are responsible for the fact that a "reflexive monitoring of action" (Giddens) is produced or awakened in agents, albeit in a discontinuous, sometimes inconsistent and of variable intensity. This in turn makes possible what I call the *secondary technicity of action*. This notion is defined as
1. the transformation of primary technicity, in response to disturbances (French pragmatists would rightly call them tests, "*mises à l'épreuve*") of the non-teleological flow of action,
2. disturbances to which the actor is sensitised or awakened and which the actor attests as disturbances of the anticipated ratio of capacity to incapacity in a specific practical context,
3. the actor's becoming aware of this frustration with his/her action (or the instances when he/she recognizes him-/herself as finite), and the fact that this

---

[34] See, for example, the sections on Heidegger in Rudolf Bernet, "La réduction phénoménologique et la double vie du sujet," in *La vie du sujet. Recherches sur l'interprétation de Husserl dans la phénoménologie* (Paris: PUF, 1994), 5–36.

[35] Non-technical aspects of action, such as the primacy of life, are left out of consideration here. Their intimate attestation remains a condition for the development and exercise of capacities – see again Breviglieri, "L'espace habité".

awareness subsequently makes it possible to reflect on action and to plan an appropriate response to this event, and
4. the deliberation implied by this planning regarding a goal of the action and calculation of the capacities and means to achieve that goal in this context (in other words, teleological technical competence is generated in this way).

In this argument, I do not claim in any way that the capable human can be reduced to the technical human. I hope I have made plausible my initial hypothesis, which can be succinctly reformulated by a double negation: the capable human *cannot* be a capable human *without* being a technical human.

4 Social Theoretical Horizon

I would like to recall how all these reflections are linked to the social dimension of the hermeneutics of the capable human being. Let us take up two aspects of the capacity-incapability dialectic presented earlier (§2.1): that of the *mediation* of action through technical inventions and that of the unfolding of action in *interaction*. The other three aspects of this dialectic – the biological body, the disciplined body and the entanglement of isolable actions in the flow of action – also have a social dimension or are socially constituted in part, but it is technical mediation and interaction that give human action its full social dimension. As recalled already in the introduction to this chapter, Ricœur argues that the capacities of the individual agent are deployed when the *I* interacts with the *you* and the *it*.[36] This fact applies to all capabilities, but in particular also to imputation – to the responsibility for "the good life with and for others in just institutions". Thus, Ricœur gives a key place to interaction in his hermeneutics of the capable human, as I have already mentioned above. Let us, however, emphasise a dimension of interaction that Ricœur does not elaborate on: its technical constitution. It is not that he would have denied that action was technical right up to institutional interaction. What he calls the *it* in interaction with which one deploys one's capabilities on the largest social scale does indeed refer to "the large-scale organizations that structure interaction: technical systems, monetary and fiscal systems, juridical systems, bureaucratic systems, pedagogical systems,

---

[36] See Ricœur, *Soi-même comme un autre*, 212 / *Oneself as Another*, 181; *Le juste 1* (Paris: Esprit, 1995), 34 / *The Just* (Chicago, IL: University of Chicago Press, 2000), 5; *Parcours de la reconnaissance*, 387 / *The Course of Recognition*, 252.

scientific systems, media systems, and so on."[37] It is obvious is that these forms of interaction are all to some extent technical systems. This does not mean that these systems are limited to their technical aspect, but it does mean that they do *not* exist *without* this technical aspect (the double negation is again key here). Therefore, what remains for us to do is to propose a way of exploring the dialectic of capability-incapability extending to the largest social scale (a task for which I will offer a response in outline in Chapter 4) and with it, the range of the technicity of action.

A "theory of the agent and structure," suitable for analysing the incapability-capability dialectic and the mediation of action on all scales of social interaction must therefore be proposed in order to describe, in a way compatible with Ricœur's hermeneutics of the capable human, the technical mediation of the interaction of the individual agent with others (close, but also and especially distant), as well as the constitution of the skills required by this interaction. While acknowledging the various attempts to put Ricœur's thinking to work in social theory – in "French pragmatism"[38] and, more recently, in Johann Michel[39] – I limit myself here only to suggesting an alternative possibility, namely the extension of the hermeneutics of the capable human by Anthony Giddens's theory of the constitution of society. I highlight some elements of Giddens's theory that are directly relevant to the current purpose.

Giddens shares with Ricœur the approach of the social reality through action. As with Ricœur, Giddens is attentive to the face-to-face interaction or interaction between the *I* and the *you*, which gives rise to "social integration," which Giddens defines as the "[r]eciprocity of practices between actors in circumstances of co-presence, [co-presence] understood as continuities in and disjunctions of encounters."[40] This reciprocity in interaction produces, reproduces and transforms rules and resources of interaction that give interaction form on a scale larger than that of the individual agent, and that are called structures. In turn,

---

37 Ricœur, *Le juste 1*, 36 / *The Just*, 6–7; Ricœur, summarising Jean-Marc Ferry with approval. The place of the other institutional partner in Ricœur's work is obviously much more complex. On this subject, we consult Johann Michel's article: "Le sens des institutions," *Il Protagora* 39 (2012): 105–17.
38 Cf. Dosse, *L'empire du sens. L'humanisation des sciences humaines* (Paris: La Découverte, 1995), especially Chapter 14, "Une philosophie de l'agir: Paul Ricœur," 170–79, and Breviglieri's short overview in "L'espace habité," 34–36.
39 Johann Michel, *Sociologie du soi. Essai d'herméneutique appliquée* (Rennes: Presses Universitaires de Rennes, 2012).
40 Anthony Giddens, *The Constitution of Society. Outline of the Theory of Structuration* (Berkeley, and Los Angeles, CA: Polity, 1984), 376.

these structures serve as media in which people act and exercise an organizing function on the interaction between people. This interaction is repeated, back and forth, between agents and structures, and may be called a "duality of structure". It is responsible for the fact that structures are always of variable stability or variable structurality. Thanks to the fact that rules and resources – the structures – can be reinforced and extended in their spatial and temporal dimension, which is done mainly through the *technologies of transport and communication*,[41] social integration can generate a broader "systemic integration," which Giddens describes as "[r]eciprocity between actors or collectivities accross extended space-time, outside of conditions of co-presence."[42] Now, this definition seems to me acceptable to describe what Ricœur refers to in his practical philosophy as the domain of the interaction of the *I* with the *it*, understood as the condition of anonymous plurality, "the extension of interhuman relations to all those who are left outside of the face-to-face encounter of an 'I' and a 'you' and remain third parties."[43]

Once the correspondence between Giddens's theory and Ricœur's philosophy has been suggested, it should be stressed that, for Giddens, structures, in their entire spatial and temporal extension, have a double effect on action: they make action possible while limiting it.[44] This fact recalls the double effect of augmenting and reducing which technical means have on human capacities, as Don Ihde argues (Giddens's theory can be understood as a socio-theoretical extension of Ihde's analyses on this point), and it also points to the *social dimension of the dialectic of capability and incapability*. Thus, all the contributions of this dialectic to a better hermeneutics of human capabilities can be translated to the level of social interaction.

This brief reference to Giddens's theory suffices to suggest that reading his theory of the agent and systems as a development of the Ricœurian view of social action may be a fruitful exercise. Thus, what Ricœur refers to as the interaction between the *I*, the *you* and the *it* could be investigated further and enriched with Giddens's explorations of social and systemic integration, while providing an appropriate conceptual framework in which to reflect on the capabilities and means – the technicity – of social interaction. Chapter 5 will be devoted to an exploration of the relation between Ricœur and Giddens.

---

41 See, for instance, the discussion in Anthony Giddens, *The Nation-state and Violence*. Volume 2 of *A Contemporary Critique of Historical Materialism* (Cambridge: Polity, 1985), Chapter 7.
42 Giddens, *The Constitution of Society*, 377.
43 Ricœur, *Soi-même comme un autre*, 228 / *Oneself as Another*, 195.
44 Giddens, *The Constitution of Society*, 171.

5 Conclusion: The Technical Paradox and its Political Relevance

Agents are characterised by capabilities of which the shadow of incapability reveals the technical aspect of their action. This is discernible throughout all the degrees of complexity of action in society, as schematized by the personal pronouns, *I*, *you* and *it*. In other words, the technicity of action, located in acquired *skills* and the *mediations* by technical inventions, finds expression in the variable levels of ability to do something in a specific way within different contexts of action. Just as the acquired capabilities and technical means are essential to give efficacious power to interpersonal and institutional action, so too they increase the consequences of the variability of capabilities and incapabilities. Thus, the action and interaction of the capable human reveals a structure that I would call a *technical paradox*. This paradox is in force on all scales of human action: to be effective, it is necessary to integrate dynamic abilities and powerful means into action, but these do not always serve the best interests of the agents nor do they always accurately reflect the intention of the action, the spirit in which the skills were taught or the purpose of the invention of the means. In this way, the augmentation and reduction that technicity brings about in the relationship between capability and incapability accords a dramatic, even tragic, potential to human action.

An example of this phenomenon is the paradox that rapid growth in the power and complexity of technology leaves the capacity for imputation and therefore responsibility far behind.[45] Moreover, I would argue that a variation of the technical paradox is Ricœur's political paradox (first presented in the Introduction, §3.2):[46] pursuing life together as a political good, people invest the

---

[45] A recurrent theme in Ricœur. See Ricœur, "Postface au *Temps de la responsabilité*," in *Lectures 1*, 271–94, here 286, "The Concept of Responsibility. An Essay in Semantic Analysis," in Paul Ricœur, *The Just*, 11–35 / *Le juste*, 29–40 and *Parcours de la reconnaissance*, 170–77 / *The Course of Recognition*, 104–109. This is the reason for his rejection of the Enlightenment notion of the makeability (*Machbarkeit*) of history (see Paul Ricœur, *Temps et récit 3. Le temps raconté* (Paris: Seuil, 1985), 384–85 / Paul Ricœur, *Time and Narrative*. Volume 3, trans. Kathleen Blamey and David Pellauer (Chicago, IL, and London: University of Chicago Press, 1988), 213.
[46] At least the first formulation of this paradox – Paul Ricœur, "Le paradoxe politique," in *Histoire et vérité* (Paris: Seuil, 1967), 294–332 / "The Political Paradox," in *History and Truth* (Evanston, IL: Northwestern University Press, 1965), 247–70. In later chapters we will discover the derivatives of the technical paradox, the organizational paradox (cf. Chapter 4) and the institutional paradox (cf. Chapter 5). On Ricœur's own development of the political paradox see Pierre-Olivier Monteil, *Ricœur politique* (Rennes: Presses Universitaires de Rennes, 2013), 27–68.

state with power and legitimacy, but all too often the political decisions that are supposed to give effect to the will of the people often simply turn against the people, to their detriment. The most efficient means by which to pursue the flourishing of a political community can in fact mutate into the means of the most brutal oppression. The point is not to reduce the political to the technical, but to grasp the technical dimension of the political to its full paradoxical extent.

This implies that the consequences of the technical paradox extend beyond the political evils resulting from the paradox of political power alone, to everywhere where the optimal relationship between capability and incapability is disrupted. In the sphere of law, for instance, Ricœur clearly recognizes what is at stake: a real subject of the law, he says, needs "the conditions for the actualization of its capacities. These have need of the continual mediation of interpersonal forms of otherness and of institutional forms of association in order to become real powers to which correspond real rights."[47] These conditions, one has to add, are partly technical conditions.

Finally, if it is "capabilities that make a human being worthy of respect" and if the development of such capabilities by state institutions is the first political obligation, as Ricœur claims,[48] then my proposed broadening of the hermeneutics of the capable human can bring to light the hidden critical potential of Ricœur's thought. Drawing inspiration from Sen and Nussbaum and their theorization of *capability deprivation*,[49] it should now be possible to deploy the hermeneutics of the capable human as a heuristics by which to identify defects in the internal and external conditions of the formation of capabilities and the activation of capabilities in action. Questions such as "who has (or is deprived of) a competence to speak or act in a particular context?" or "who has access to what means to tell or judge a series of actions?" should be more fully thematized (see also other possible developments of this negative side of capabilities in the Conclusion, §2). These questions inform the indignation that is the driving force behind the struggle for recognition. In this way, Ricœur's transition from self-recognition to mutual recognition requires and benefits from such a critical

---

47 Ricœur, *Le juste 1*, 33 / *The Just*, 5.
48 Ricœur, *Lectures 1*, 164.
49 A useful overview of the debates on "capability deprivation" in the scientific study of (the alleviation of) poverty, is provided by Rod Hick and Tania Burchardt, "Capability Deprivation," in *The Oxford Handbook of the Social Science of Poverty*, eds. David Brady and Linda M. Burto (Oxford: Oxford University Press, 2016), https://doi.org/10.1093/oxfordhb/9780199914050.013.5, last accessed 5 February 2021.

force of the enriched notion of capability. These issues are central to our concern in the three chapters of Part 2.

Chapter 4:
Organized Action: Agency, (In)capabilities and Means

1 Organized Action as Part of the Technicity of Action

One of the main features of human life is the organization of interaction. Our social existence simply cannot be imagined without clubs, companies, religious communities, protest movements, schools, factories, administrations, hospitals, etc. It is thus quite evident that organized action has to form part of a study on human capabilities and the means by which people act.

Before we go further, I need to explain why I speak about "organized action" from the outset.[1] Using this term allows me to keep *action* central to my approach, so as to gain a view on the full variety of a specific aspect of action. On the one hand, organized action is a much more general phenomenon than actions within organizations such as bureaucracies or companies, which are formalised under the name "organization". On the other hand, the varieties of organized action display a range of levels of formality, which is important to account for if one wants to understand what is "organizational" about them. Both of these points may be illustrated with the example of the "informal economy"[2]: its informality is also a version of organized action, albeit less structured than "organizations" in the narrower sense.

While my approach remains a theorizing of *action*, I will not refrain from using the word "organizations". This is not merely due to convention. Part of the discussion consists of advancing an action theoretical ontology of organizations – variations in the size and complexity of organizations can only be properly accounted for by studying them as extensions of organized action. This first approximation of organized action is required in order to demarcate the theme of the current survey. I defend two theses. The *first* is that organizations, as the outcome of and basis for organized action, have a *specific agency*, of which the ac-

---

[1] I originally derived the notion of "organized action" from Crozier and Friedberg, cf. Michel Crozier and Erhard Friedberg, "Organizations and collective action," in *Studies of Organization in the European tradition*, eds. Samuel B. Bacharach, Pasquale Gagliardi and Bryan Mundell, (Greenwich: Jai Press, 1995), 77. However, since I could not make peace with their "methodological utilitarianism," I restrict my reference to their concept to the two formal traits of organized action that follow.

[2] Cf. the short retrospective on this notion in Chris Hann and Keith Hart, *Economic Anthropology. History, Ethnography, Critique* (Cambridge, and Malden, MA: Polity, 2011), 112–16.

tion theoretical concepts used here can give an account. The *second* thesis is that organized interaction is characterised by structures of *capacity and incapacity comparable to those of individual action and studying these (in)capabilities reveals the technicality of collective action, of which the utilization of technical means is an important part.*

At first sight, Ricœur's later practical philosophy could be immediately helpful in thinking through this dimension of human interaction. In the previous chapter, we saw how he sought an appropriate way to articulate the individual capability to act and the institutional embeddedness of action (see Chapter 3, §1). Agents' capabilities remain mere potential until they are "activated" in interaction with others. The notion of "others" is differentiated into an interpersonal form (in *I-you* relations) and an institutional form (in *I-it* relations).

Yet, one soon realizes that, on its own, this schema remains inadequate to allow us to grasp the specificity of organized action. There are two reasons for this: the understanding of the "other" and the view on "capability":

1. Organized action involves face-to-face interaction and the mediation of anonymous institutions, but the other encountered in organizations cannot be reduced to either of these forms, or to a combination of them.
2. Organized action represents a form of human capability that would be distorted by reducing it to individual capability (and this applies even when we take into consideration the institutional embeddedness of this capability). The kind of capabilities concentrated by organized action are just as distorted when the means of individual and collective action are not accorded due attention.

Nonetheless, I would argue that this is not a dead-end for the question of the hermeneutics of human capabilities and organized action. Quite the contrary. In continuity with the previous chapters, I can now outline the place of organized action in my broader examination of the technicity of action. To do so, I work on the two shortcomings just mentioned.

1. I start by clarifying my view on the specificity of organizational interaction, this "intermediary" between *I-you* and *I-it:* it can be wider and more formal than interpersonal relations, taken in isolation, and can be more restricted and more personal than anonymous society-wide institutions. Understanding this intermediary relation will improve our understanding both of who the subject of organization is and of the sense in which agency may be ascribed to organizations. To be clear, I need to establish two things. First, what and how are the relations between people that account for the establishment and maintenance of an organization? Second, in which way may we attribute agency to the organization? The attribution of agency to the or-

ganization is a condition for the next shortcoming that I address. It turns out that fragments from Ricœur's own work provide stimulating material to advance this point.
2. Next, having established established what the agency of organizations consists of, I can ask how the relation of capability/incapability applies to organizations. The exposition on capabilities/incapabilities in the previous chapter serve as guide, but I am not insinuating that organizations are just individual agents writ large. I will highlight the question of relating *(in)capabilities* and *means* of action as part of this discussion.

It is perhaps in order to circumscribe the limits of this discussion – I do not claim to have digested the mountains of sociological and managerial studies on organizations.[3] My focus remains the place that organizations deserve in my broader exploration of the capabilities and means of action.

2 Organized Action and the Agency of Organizations

Before embarking on our examination of collective (in)capabilities, we first have to clarify the tricky term "collective". Admittedly, a thoroughly systematic treatment of this question is absent from Ricœur's work, but it nevertheless contains a number of passages in which valuable insights into the phenomenon of organized action are given. This can be amply demonstrated by drawing on five relevant examples: (1) the theorizing of the representation of social collectivities under the term of "participatory belonging" (*appartenance participative*) in *Time and Narrative 1*, (2) the notion of the institution in *Oneself as Another*, and, (3) in the same book, the notion of practices as adopted from MacIntyre,

---

3 Some helpful guides are the twin volumes by Paul S. Adler, *The Oxford Handbook of Sociology and Organization Studies: Classical Foundations* (Oxford: Oxford University Press, 2010), and Paul S. Adler, Paul Du Gay, Glenn Morgan, and Michael I. Reed, *The Oxford Handbook of Sociology, Social Theory, and Organization Studies: Contemporary Currents* (Oxford: Oxford University Press, 2014), as well as Richard W. Scott and Gerald F. Davis, *Organizations and Organizing: Rational, Natural, and Open System Perspectives* (Upper Saddle River, NJ: Pearson, 2007). Other useful sources are Walter W. Powell and Christof Brandtner, "Organizations as Sites and Drivers of Social Action," in *Handbook of Contemporary Sociological Theory*, ed. Seth Abrutyn (Cham: Springer, 2016), 269–92; Peter Preisendörfer, *Organisationssoziologie. Grundlagen, Theorien und Problemstellungen*, 4th ed. (Wiesbaden: Springer VS, 2016); Alfred Kieser and Mark Ebers, eds., *Organisationstheorien*, 8th ed. (Stuttgart: Kohlhammer, 2019). From a behavioural perspective see Stephen P. Robbins and Timothy A. Judge, *Essentials of Organizational Behavior*, Global 17th ed. (Upper Saddle River, NJ: Pearson Prentice Hall, 2017).

(4) the idea of an advisory team as used occasionally in Ricœur's reflections on medical ethics, and (5) the hermeneutics of "social capabilities" in *The Course of Recognition*.[4] The challenge in exploring these five instances lies in not only doing justice to them in their quite divergent contexts, but also testing the possibility of a synthesis of the insights gleaned from them.

2.1 Entities of Participatory Belonging and Institutions

What is the epistemological status of the entities of collective action, the "social entities"[5] that we encounter in historiography and the social sciences? In *Time and Narrative*, Ricœur argues that these entities share the trait that a multitude of people participate in their formation and maintenance – they are entities of "participatory belonging".[6] In social scientific research, such entities are embedded in causal explanations. One may call this kind of causal chain the "quasi-plots" of causal explanation. The social entities may thus also be called "*quasi-characters*".[7] Such "quasi-characters" cannot be broken up into a "dust cloud of individual actions"[8] – in other words, one cannot trace exhaustively the contribution of each individual person's action to the formation of the social entity. While doing similar work as Coleman's bathtub,[9] the specificity of Ricœur's position resides in the narrative character that he ascribes to social entities and the hermeneutic circle by which agents appropriate these entities understandingly as they belong participatively to them.

Now, although these quasi-characters cannot be de-composed to their constituent participators, they do contain "indirect references" (*références obliques*)

---

[4] This selection does not mean that I have exhausted the possibilities in Ricœur's work for my question. See for instance also archives as social spaces in *La mémoire, l'histoire, l'oubli* (Paris: Seuil, 2000), 209–230 / *Memory, History, Forgetting*, trans. Kathleen Blamey and David Pellauer (Chicago: University of Chicago Press, 2004), 166–181.

[5] Paul Ricœur, *Temps et récit 1. L'intrigue et le récit historique* (Paris: Editions du Seuil, 1983), 340 / *Time and Narrative*. Volume 1, trans. Kathleen Blamey and David Pellauer (Chicago: University of Chicago Press, 1984),193.

[6] Ricœur, *Temps et récit 1*, 321, 340–41 / *Time and Narrative 1*, 181, 193.

[7] Ricœur, *Temps et récit 1*, 321 / *Time and Narrative 1*, 182.

[8] Ricœur, *Temps et récit 1*, 340 "*indécomposables* en une poussière d'actions individuelles" / *Time and Narrative 1*, 190.

[9] On this and other versions of the same schema, see Werner Raub and Thomas Voss, "Micro-macro models in sociology. Antecedents of Coleman's diagram," in *Social Dilemmas, Institutions, and the Evolution of Cooperation*, eds. Ben Jann and Wojtek Przepiorka (Berlin, and Boston, MA: Walter de Gruyter, 2017), 11–36.

to individuals. On this basis it is possible to examine how they are constituted as communities through a method of "questioning back",[10] also called genetic phenomenology.[11] While historians and other social scientists are justified in speaking of large-scale quasi-characters, phenomenologists must concern themselves with the real ties between the "members [of]…" or participants composing these quasi-characters. In other words, the phenomenologist has to examine the ontology of the entities of participatory belonging. In this passage of Ricœur's, social ontology consists in

- prioritizing one specific "historical community", namely society,[12] as well as entities that are most often also of national extension such as the "nation, class, people, community, or civilization".[13] The three main traits of societies – territorial organization, institutional structure and temporal continuity (taken from Mandelbaum) – refer indirectly to the constituting existence of individuals: dwelling, role-taking and the succession of generations respectively.[14]
- establishing the mode of existence of participatory members to be of the order of *action* (this corresponds to pre-figuration or *mimesis I*, discussed in Chapter 2, §3.1), and the mode of existence of quasi-characters to be of the order of *narrative* (which corresponds to the configuration or *mimesis*

---

[10] Ricœur, *Temps et récit 1*, 318 / *Time and Narrative 1*, 179.
[11] Summarised as follows: "It is always starting from the pole of an assumed identity that the work of constitution unfolds behind this pole. Consequently, the work of constitution never begins from a tabula rasa, it is in no way a creation. It is only starting from an already constituted object that one can retroactively, retrospectively, unfold the layers of sense, the levels of synthesis, making the passive syntheses behind the active syntheses appear, and so on." Paul Ricœur, *From Text to Action: Essays in Hermeneutics II*, trans. Kathleen Blamey and John Thompson (London: Athlone, 1991), 234 / *Du texte à l'action. Essais d'herméneutique II* (Paris: Editions du Seuil, 1986), 320.
[12] Ricœur, *Temps et récit 1*, 343 / *Time and Narrative 1*, 195: "The irreducible object of history is of a *societal* order".
[13] Ricœur, *Temps et récit 1*, 357 / *Time and Narrative 1*, 203. Likewise a "governing board, a state, a nation, a people, a class" in Paul Ricœur, *Temps et récit 3. Le temps raconté* (Paris: Seuil, 1985), 302n21 / Paul Ricœur, *Time and narrative*. Volume 3, trans. Kathleen Blarney and David Pellauer (Chicago and London: University of Chicago Press, 1988), 207n1 – the first element breaks the rule. This is not yet in itself a sufficient basis for typifying Ricœur's position as a "methodological nationalism". Besides, this notion is itself a complex of difficulties, cf. Daniel Chernilo, "Social Theory's Methodological Nationalism: Myth and Reality," *European Journal of Social Theory* 9, no. 1 (2006): 5–22.
[14] Cf. Ricœur, *Temps et récit 1*, 349 / *Time and Narrative 1*, 199.

II, also discussed in Chapter 2, §3.2).[15] By implication, the agents often understand each other through these narrative entities.[16]
- laying bare the underlying "ontology of being in common" (*ontologie de l'être en commun*).[17] This is done in *Time and Narrative 3*,[18] where Ricœur writes:

> "I am following the broad distinction in Schütz's analysis between a we-orientation and a they-orientation, between a direct kind of orientation and an anonymous form based on typifications [= between interaction of agents and quasi-characters – EW]. Schütz takes great care to nuance this opposition with a careful study (at which he excels) of the *degrees of anonymity* in the world of contemporaries."[19]

However, despite his praise for Schütz, Ricœur evades a discussion of the "progressive enlargement of the sphere of direct interpersonal relationships to include anonymous relationships".[20] Still, this ontology of being in common sketched in *Time and Narrative 3* reflects the pattern of *Time and Narrative 1*, in which the instituting interaction is contrasted with the anonymity of quasi-characters, which nevertheless refers indirectly to the instituting interaction.

Subsequently, in *Oneself as Another*, Ricœur takes over this basic framework for his social thought. He focuses on the *I-you* (interpersonal) and the *I-it* (institutionally mediated) dimensions of human interaction, again *at the expense of* a

---

15 Ricœur, *Temps et récit 1*, 351 / *Time and Narrative 1*, 200.
16 A similar position is taken by Luc Boltanski, who writes that "a sociology whose object is modelling the way in which social actors fashion society can indeed regard communities (or, in general, collectives) as *fictions*, but on condition of recognizing that these fictions seemingly have a *necessary* character and must therefore, at least by this token, find a place in sociological theory." Luc Boltanski, *On Critique: A Sociology of Emancipation*, trans. Gregory Elliot (Cambridge: Polity, 2011), 36 / *De la critique. Précis de sociologie de l'émancipation* (Paris: Gallimard, 2009), 65 (my emphasis).
17 Ricœur, *Temps et récit 1*, 350n1 / The English translation renders it as "ontology of the we-relation," *Time and Narrative 1*, 261n17.
18 Cf. Paul Ricœur, *Temps et récit 3. Le temps raconté* (Paris: Seuil, 1985), 203–209 / *Time and narrative*. Volume 3, trans. Kathleen Blamey and David Pellauer (Chicago and London: University of Chicago Press, 1988), 112–114.
19 Ricœur, *Temps et récit 3*, 207n1 / *Time and Narrative 3*, 392n21 (my emphasis). See also *Temps et récit 3*, 204 / *Time and Narrative 3*, 302.
20 *Temps et récit 3*, 204 / *Time and Narrative 3*, 112. Cf. also Paul Ricœur, *Soi-même comme un autre* (Paris: Seuil, 1990), 228 and 234 / *Oneself as Another*, trans. Kathleen Blamey (Chicago, IL: University of Chicago Press, 1992), 195, 200–201.

phenomenology of degrees of anonymity in the world of contemporaries for which he praises Schütz.

Instead, Ricœur coordinates these two dimensions of interaction by considering institutions as constituted by *power in common*, a notion he gets from Arendt.[21] We will discuss this in greater detail in the next chapter (see Chapter 5, §2.1a), but a few comments on this point are in order here. Power in common enables Ricœur to account for the *event* by which a plurality of individuals generate *institutions* and it introduces the social factor of *power* in institutions. However, Arendt's understanding of action remains artificially detached from "work" and "labour" and thus predisposes Ricœur to give a one-sidedly political view of institutions.[22] Moreover, the question of the relative stability of action is settled by moving directly from "action in concert" to institutions which buttress actions. In this way, the impression is created that Ricœur's view on the constitution of institutions leans to the individualistic, or even voluntaristic, side.

Yet Ricœur does not believe he has succumbed to individualism, and thanks to the Rawlsian notion of *participation/distribution*[23] that he introduces at this point.[24] Through "participation", action can bridge the gap from the interpersonal level of *I-you* (where all power in common originates) to the societal level of institutions, the *I-it* relations. In short, the notion of participation, firstly, (implicitly) marks the place of a full theory of the degrees of anonymity from the interpersonal to the societal, and secondly, (explicitly) seals the fate of the presumed opposition between the individual and society.

Nevertheless, this solution smuggles in three biases:
- In harmony with the trend in *Time and Narrative*, Ricœur prioritizes a notion of "society", which he understands to be as extensive as the inhabitants of a country or region, *at the expense of* a plurality of societies or associations of varying sizes.
- Ricœur's presentation of institutions follows the same trend.
- When Ricœur defines institutions as structures of living together held together by common mores,[25] this contention remains in harmony with the

---

[21] Hannah Arendt, "On Violence," *Crises of the Republic: Lying in Politics, Civil Disobedience, on Violence, Thoughts on Politics and Revolution* (San Diego, CA: Harvest/Harcourt Brace Jovanovich, 1972), 103–198, here 143.
[22] Nevertheless, he refers to all three terms from Arendt's *The Human Condition* in Ricœur, *Soi-même comme un autre*, 229n1 / *Oneself as Another*, 196n38.
[23] See especially Part 2, "Institutions" in John Rawls, *A Theory of Justice*. Rev. ed. (Cambridge, MA: Harvard University Press, [1971] 1999).
[24] Cf. Ricœur, *Soi-même comme un autre*, 234 / *Oneself as Another*, 200.
[25] Ricœur, *Soi-même comme un autre*, 227 / *Oneself as Another*, 194.

narratological status of the quasi-characters in *Time and Narrative 1* in the sense that it is *to the detriment of* the organizational meaning of the institution.

From these biases arise Ricœur's excessive attention to the two poles of initiating or instituting events of collective action on the one hand, and the already existing, instituted structures on the largest scale on the other – this, *at the expense of* what binds the two together. What do I have in mind? What is missing here[26] are
- processes of formalisation and codification (and deformalisation and decodification) of the structure,
- the generation and disintegration of teleological structures,
- attention to the introduction of agents into their roles,
- attention to the degree to which agents are mobilised for the accomplishment of collective aims, and
- the mechanisms by which the systems of participation/distribution are maintained.

What is at stake in these five shortcomings is the core of organized action itself, namely the *degree of integration, formalisation and stability of varying scales of acting in common.*

Interim Conclusion: Individual and Collective Agency of Organized Action

Despite the limitations indicated, the two texts discussed just now are instructive regarding the agents of organized action.

In reflecting on organized action, it is always possible to zoom in on the *individual agent*, who interacts with others. Even on this scale, organized action is structured by *I-it* relations.[27] But the individual agent's relations to others in organized action has another dimension, corresponding to the degrees of anonymity between direct interpersonal and completely anonymous institutional relations. These intermediate kinds of relation vary and fluctuate according to the five factors listed at the end of the previous paragraph. How these varying mediations of interaction impact on the (in)capabilities exercised by individuals acting in an environment of organizational counterparts, and of organizational

---

[26] Here I borrow from Erhard Friedberg, "Les quatre dimensions de l'action organisée," *Revue française de sociologie* 33, no. 4 (1992): 531–57.

[27] Although these are not saturated by institutional relations, as Laurent Thévenot points out in meticulous studies in *L'action au pluriel. Sociologie des régimes d'engagement* (Paris: La Découverte, 2006).

infrastructure, can be described using the exposition of (in)capabilities in the previous chapter (see Chapter 3, §2). Such variations of individual action in organization can be illustrated, for instance, in considering networking, which is a major contribution that individuals make to their organization. Networking as interaction can be facilitated or obstructed by an organization; it can happen more or less formally; it could be more inside-inside oriented or more inside-outside oriented. Each time the organization has an impact on the precise character or "adverbial increments" of this type of networking interaction.[28]

More important still is the perspective opened on *collective action*. If we accept Ricœur's view on the constitution of entities of "participatory belonging", then one has to consider the quasi-character formed by organized action to be "organization" in the broadest sense. This view facilitates a complex view on organizations. Consider, in particular, the recurrent claim that "[o]rganizations are made up of individuals pursuing a common goal, such as producing a good or service or advocating for some cause".[29] It would be much more circumspect to say that, (a) in as far as people consent to have their efforts taken up in a broader movement of organized action, they do indeed participate in the pursuit of that organization's goals, and yet, (b) many people are in organizations in pursuit of many other goals (and those of the organization may in extreme cases be irrelevant to them). Moreover, one can say that (c) all their activities and the unintended consequences of their actions contribute to shaping the organization, but that finally, (d) the organization is not simply the overlap of individual projects. Ricœur's idea of participatory belonging can account for all of these facts.[30] On the strength of this conclusion, I claim that organizations, as quasi-charac-

---

[28] Cf. Powell and Brandtner, "Organizations as Sites and Drivers of Social Action," 281, 286. On "adverbial increments", see again Chapter 3, §2.2.
[29] Powell and Brandtner, "Organizations as Sites and Drivers of Social Action," 270.
[30] This is not without political relevance: consider what organizations do to people, how sometimes people are forced to participate. Or conversely, consider the fact that organizations need a minimum of buy-in (power in common, if you will) to function.

In his work before *Oneself as another* Ricœur made abundant use of Max Weber's action theory (coupled with Husserl's phenomenology of intersubjectivity), cf. Paul Ricœur, "Hegel et Husserl sur l'intersubjectivité" in *Du texte à l'action*, 311–34) / "Hegel and Husserl on intersubjectivity" in *From Text to Action*, 227–45. This provides material for a direct comparison with Thomas Schwinn's Weberian piece, "Interaktion, Organisation, Gesellschaft. Eine Alternative zu Mikro-Makro?," in *Interaktion – Organisation – Gesellschaft* revisited. *Anwendungen, Erweiterungen, Alternativen*. Sonderheft der Zeitschrift für Soziologie, eds. Bettina Heintz and Hartmann Tyrell (Stuttgart: Lucius & Lucius, 2015), 43–64. However, despite the similarity in structure with what I reconstruct here from Ricœurian material, because the 1990 book relativises the significance of Weber for Ricœur, I do not engage with Schwinn's position.

ters formed by organized action, acquire a functioning that is not reducible to a myriad of individual courses of action and practices. I will call this the *(quasi-) agency of organizations*.

Having thus established the specificity of organizations as collective agents, one may venture that this agency has its own, corresponding (quasi-)capabilities through which organizations can speak, act, narrate, be responsible, remember and promise. The specific qualities of these capabilities vary according to the specific characteristics of each form of organized collective action. And one may already assume that for each of these quasi-capabilities there is as corresponding quasi-incapability (a point I will demonstrate later in this chapter).

Having provisionally clarified the two modes of agency involved in organized action, let us see what Ricœur can teach us in respect of what agents do and how they act in organizations.

2.2 Practices and the Example of Advisory Bodies

As part of a "revision of the concept of action",[31] Ricœur examines composite units of action such as professions, games, arts.[32] Practices are "units of configuration"[33] and are structured by "embedding relations".[34] Complex actions are governed by "laws of meaning"[35] and are made up of constituent actions that follow "constitutive rules".[36] These rules imply that actions can be seen as actions *of* a specific practice, and that they can clearly be recognized and acknowledged as such. Furthermore, practices are interactions, or even "internalized interaction",[37] in which agents take each other into account in the form of competition, cooperation, conflict, etc.[38] Agents also learn practices in relation to and with others, in traditions of education.[39] Practices are then embedded in *life plans* (*plans de vie*), such as family life, professional life, or recreation and these in turn are embedded in the narrative *unity of one's life*.

---

[31] Ricœur, *Soi-même comme un autre*, 181 / *Oneself as Another*, 152.
[32] Ricœur, *Soi-même comme un autre*, 186 / *Oneself as Another*, 157.
[33] Cf. Ricœur, *Soi-même comme un autre*, 182 / *Oneself as Another*, 153.
[34] Ricœur, *Soi-même comme un autre*, 182 / *Oneself as Another*, 153. The published translation renders "relations d'enchâssement", as "nesting relations".
[35] Ricœur, *Soi-même comme un autre*, 182 / *Oneself as Another*, 154.
[36] Ricœur, *Soi-même comme un autre*, 183 / *Oneself as Another*, 155.
[37] Ricœur, *Soi-même comme un autre*, 185 / *Oneself as Another*, 156.
[38] Ricœur, *Soi-même comme un autre*, 185 / *Oneself as Another*, 156.
[39] Ricœur, *Soi-même comme un autre*, 185/ *Oneself as Another*, 156.

Clearly, Ricœur's borrowing from the Aristotelian tradition is of interest to the current question. Yet the exact nature of this inchoate theory of organized action has to be qualified.

On the positive side, *practices* allow individual agents to attest to their capabilities when these are activated in the agents' interaction with close-by others (*I–you*, e.g. in interactions that involve collaboration, conflict, etc.), and others far away (*I–it*, e.g. in through traditions).[40] Through practices, instituted interaction on scales *other than* that of national societies are introduced in the discussion. Therefore, practices could be considered to fill the place of the "degrees of anonymity" as Schütz calls them, in as far as practical roles account for the particular mediations that constitute the organizational self and other. In short, the exploration of practices shows the way to a fuller understanding of *institutionalization* and of the *alterity* involved in organized action.

On the negative side, the concerns of Study 6 of *Oneself as Another* steer Ricœur to focus on the structure of embedding: actions – practices – life plans – narrative unity of a life. In this way, a series of other components of organized action are lost from view: agents' belonging(s) to different organized complexes, the relationships between different organized action complexes, the mode of existence of rules and configurations of practices, as well as the reasons for their inertia and resistance to change in organizations, the cumulative adverse effects of actual practice, and so on. Other components of organized action remain underdeveloped: the degrees of formalisation (present in the relationship between tradition and innovation), the specification of organizational otherness (even if the notion of "internalised interaction", and the forms of interaction – competition, cooperation, conflict – point to it), conflicts over the constitutive rules,[41] etc. Yet, if narrative identity is essential in connecting the descriptive to a normative approach to action (as Ricœur argues in *Oneself as another*, Study 6), it is surprising that Ricœur presents the practising of practices as coordinated only in the narrative unity of a life and its quest for being good, and not in the narrative unity of organizations in and with which people live and which has a direct influence on institutions. One misses out on important gains that can be had from the previously examined passages too, in particular the notion of collectivities as quasi-characters. In Ricœur's discussion one finds, for instance, the practice of the farmer without reference to the quasi-character, the farm (the example of the practice of judging without looking at a court of law illustrates the problem even more clearly).

---

40 See again Chapter 3, §1, Figure 1.
41 Ricœur, *Soi-même comme un autre*, 207 / *Oneself as Another*, 176.

Together, these two points confirm that Ricœur's discussion of practices is about the practices of individuals acting in organized contexts, but not about the actions of organizations. This point may be missed if one considers an apparent counter-example, where the hermeneutics of the capable human suitably accommodates reflection on the action of a small organization. Concluding his discussion on "prudential judgement" in bio- and medical ethical cases, Ricœur points to the fact that decisions of practical wisdom can be prepared with the full benefit of advice and debate with specialists in the field, in other words, as groups, not as individuals.[42] Ricœur argues that doctors, like judges, make their judgements supported by an advisory body (*cellule de conseil*).[43] What is this advisory body then, if it is not diverse social role players, each contributing a specific competence? To paraphrase in terms close to those in *Time and Narrative 1:* the advisory body is a quasi-character, however, one so small that its actions can to a great extent be decomposed into the actions of the individuals who constitute it and to which this quasi-character always refers indirectly.

However, the point remains that this case is an outlier that cannot be generalised to all organized action. But elsewhere one does find Ricœur reflecting on collective agency. Let me turn to such a case.

2.3 Social Capabilities

In the second study in *The Course of Recognition*, Ricœur revisits his hermeneutics of the "I can" and extends it with an excursion on what may be called a hermeneutics of the *"we* can", which he identifies in social capabilities and practices. Whereas individuals are capable of affirming reflexively their ability to act through attestation, collectivities do so through public evaluation and approval,[44] through ethico-legal justification, or disputes and claims about social justice.

The identity of collective actors is reflected by symbolic mediation in representations of the practices as competences for social action.[45] The identity of social entities is the (disputable) agreement that coordinates social actions and

---

42 Ricœur, *Soi-même comme un autre*, 318 / *Oneself as Another*, 273 and Paul Ricœur, *Le juste 2* (Paris: Esprit, 2001), 252–253 / *Reflections on the just*, David Pellauer, trans. (Chicago: University of Chicago Press, 2007), 219–220.
43 Ricœur, *Le juste 2*, 253 / *Reflections on the Just*, 220.
44 Paul Ricœur, *Parcours de la reconnaissance* (Paris: Stock, 2004), 215 / *The Course of Recognition*, trans. David Pellauer (Cambridge, MA: Harvard University Press, 2005), 134.
45 Ricœur, *Parcours de la reconnaissance*, 219–20 / *Course of Recognition*, 137–38.

practices, even when the relevant identity is still under construction. Ricœur implicitly revisits the question of the ontology of collectivities in a way close to that of *Time and Narrative:* agents and their coordination in collective action do not have the same ontological status – collective identity is narratological (*Time and Narrative*) or representational (*The Course of Recognition*), and in both cases, they are in the process of being established by agents' actions. This difference between the two ontologies is reflected in the "interplay of scales"[46]: by concentrating on the *micro* level, one gets a glimpse of the strategies by which agents attempt to reduce the unpredictability of events; by focusing on the *macro* level, one observes the long-term anonymous structures and constraints which nevertheless stand under the influence of social action.[47] The difference of ontological status, reflected in the interplay of scales, is responsible for the fact that social capabilities cannot be recognized by direct attestation, but are recognized rather by "second-order reflection reconstructing them".[48]

An illuminating example of this complex of ideas is identified by Ricœur in Amartya Sen's thought on "rights to certain abilities".[49] In this valuable expression are linked "capabilities" – which refer to the positive freedom of each individual for his/her life choices (as opposed to both negative freedom and exclusively self-interested action) – and "rights", that is, claims in the name of *social justice*. If one follows Sen and Drèze's scientific finding that an improvement in the conditions for the exercise of positive freedom (capabilities) actually prevents famines from occurring, then one could say that preventing famines is a manifestation of a capacity to act, that it is a collective capability, that it is good to be capable in this way, and that it is good that this capability be guaranteed (for example, in the form of rights), since it makes the realization of social justice possible. Thus, it is not a question of directly attesting an individual capability, the "I can", but of a "second-order reflection reconstructing" a social capability, of the "we can" in the form of a public appreciation and approval, ar-

---

46 Ricœur, *Parcours de la reconnaissance*, 220 / *Course of Recognition*, 139, the phrase is borrowed from Jacques Revel.
47 Ricœur, *Parcours de la reconnaissance*, 221 / *Course of Recognition*, 139.
48 Ricœur, *Parcours de la reconnaissance*, 223 / *Course of Recognition*, 140.
49 Ricœur, *Parcours de la reconnaissance*, 228 / *Course of Recognition*, 144. See also Paul Ricœur, *La critique et la conviction. Entretien avec François Azouvi et Marc De Launay* (Paris: Calmann-Lévy, 1995), 187 / *Critique and Conviction. Conversations with François Azouvi and Marc De Launay*, trans. Kathleen Blamey (New York, NY: Columbia University Press, 1998), 123 for the connection with these ideas and "collective guilt" and "collective memory". Another elaboration of social imaginary that could be linked to the current discussion is that of ideology and utopia in Ricœur's *Lectures on Ideology and Utopia*, ed. George Taylor (New York, NY: Columbia University Press, 1986).

ticulated in the claim of a right. This right, when it is claimed, would be, according to Ricœur's argument, the second degree "attestation" or reconstructed representation of a social capability to act. Using some other terms considered here, it could be said that if a famine does occur, it would be because, from the *micro* point of view, individual actors are not able to exercise their life choices in order to obtain food; or because, from the *macro* point of view, the absence of rights creates a social injustice, preventing the population from feeding itself.

2.4 Scales of Organized Action, its Capabilities and Means

We have now been able to develop further the findings of the "interim conclusion". We have seen that the subject of organized action is, on the one hand, the self, who can attest to his/her own capabilities to act in interaction with others under organized conditions, on the other hand, quasi-characters ("organizations") of varying sizes and complexities whose capabilities are identified in a work of reconstruction (in fact, the collective agent itself is derived from the demonstration that collective capabilities have been used). It is therefore no contradiction when Powell and Brandtner[50] attribute agency to organizations (as they do when they refer to organizations as equalisers, stratifiers, stabilisers, movers, shakers, etc.), *while* passing in review, amongst others, micro behavioural or ethnomethodological studies on individuals in organizations. Ricœur gives us a means by which to coordinate these two forms of discourse.

Yet, up to *The Course of Recognition*, Ricœur maintains his preferential treatment of the two extremities on the spectrum of the interplay of scales.[51] Accordingly, we may sometimes focus on the individual agents, their interaction, their practices, and the constraints to their action, and sometimes on the largest collective agents, which do not exist without the individual actors, but still cannot be broken up into a "dust cloud of individual actions". It is then up to us to insist on the whole range between these two ends of the spectrum of scales and on the variety of collective actors and organizations it covers.

But how can one get access to this *variety*? Ricœur's understanding of the embedding of actions into practices may give us some direction, but we have al-

---

[50] Powell and Brandtner, "Organizations as Sites and Drivers of Social Action".
[51] This is also Ricœur's way of coordinating what David Lockwood called "systems integration" (in Ricœur's terms, the formation and relation between quasi-characters) and "social integration" (in Ricœur's terms, the interaction of individuals with other individuals and with organizations).

ready noted the limitations of such an approach. I would now like to suggest an alternative.⁵²

(A) This alternative starts out from the basic components describing *what* organizations of various scales are. Following the classic textbook presentation of Scott and Davis,⁵³ organizations consist of transactions between people, their work with technology, the organization's formal organization and its informal organization – together driven by an almost external factor, namely goals. With my previous chapters in mind, one cannot fail to notice that each of the four components has a technical dimension: the habitus of the participants, the work they do with available technologies, the technical "software" of the organizational structure (both formal and informal). Without these, strategic aiming at goals and ends would not mean much. While Scott and Davis have more formally institutionalized organizations in mind, it would be possible to demonstrate that their model applies to all organized action, even if in some cases, this would be less evident than in others.

(B) But this point would remain almost trivial, if we do not consider *how* organizations act in pursuit of their goals (the fact that the action(s) of organizations cannot be reduced to the mere pursuit of goals and that they do not always achieve the goals they pursue, need not detain us now). Pursuing its goals, an organization takes on an organizational structure that is supposed to facilitate the efficient attainment of those goals. Robbins and Judge list six typical traits of organizational structure,⁵⁴ as ways of organizing the four components of the organization (and thus, following our previous point, the technical capabilities and means deployed in the organization). The six traits are work specialisation, departmentalization, chain of command, centralization and decentralization, formalisation and boundary spanning. Note that each of these traits of organizational structure allows for a spectrum of variable increments (for instance, the chain of command and reporting may restrict sensitive information to a larger or smaller group of collaborators and the authority to make decisions may be shifted higher or lower on the hierarchy; or a greater or smaller number of roles may be created to cross the boundaries of formalised working groups with greater or lesser freedom to exercise their own initiative). The ways in which they vary determine the features of an organization and consequently

---

52 This remains true to the spirit of Ricœur's phenomenological studies, which proceed from an examination of the *what*, through the *how*, to the *who*. However, this procedure is based on the phenomenology of individual agents, not collectives. In another way, I remain true to his hermeneutics, namely by advancing via a detour through scientific work outside of philosophy.
53 Scott and Davis, *Organizations and Organizing*, 20, discussion 20–25.
54 Robbins and Judge, *Essentials of Organizational Behavior*, 276–82.

has a vital influence on what the organization is able to do and how it will act. Although subject to change, these traits may be relatively stable (it is the point of intersection between these changing traits that identifies the organization for what it is and reflects the ways it acts.) This means that by comparing the cluster of traits of organizations, we may also identify the key differences between them and (partially) account for the different ways in which they act. But organizational structures are also modified, which means that the identity of an organization changes over time, and allows us to account for gradual change in the appearance and action of each organizational quasi-character.

These two considerations (the four components of organizations and the six traits of their structure) combined, give us a first clue as to how one could account for the variety of organizational agents as subjects of "social capabilities" (in the terms of *The Course of Recognition*). The particular traits of each organization's structure become the pieces of a mosaic which reflect the actional capability of the collective. However, this does not mean that the organization's structure equals its capabilities, since, up to this point, we have left out the real-life *action* (power in common) which invigorates the organization. Once this factor is added, the organizational structure may serve as a means by which to converge individual agency with collective agency and to represent that claim to collective agency (as the claim to rights does for social capabilities, according to Ricœur's reading of Sen). Each time an organization delivers a service or a product, this retroactively confirms the claim to that organization's having collective agency, corresponding to the variations of its traits.

From their side, the agents bring more to an organization than just the power to act in harmony with the relatively bulky and slowly changing features of the organization (solidity due to the consolidation of certain practices or the use of heavy and expensive equipment). The individual agents' action(s) may vary over the course of a day, or over a cycle of financial reporting, differ between individuals, fluctuate according to team spirit, change according to the institutional culture, etc.[55] All these variables have an impact on the way in which interacting individuals continually institute their organization.

Finally, having made these distinctions clear for the purpose of greater precision, we have succeeded in getting a better grasp of the rich variety of interactions and collective action that lie between face-to-face interaction and the anonymity of institutions.

---

[55] Nor should the fact that we can give a name to an organization as a quasi-character give the impression that the frontiers are sharply drawn or stable.

(C) Individual agents' continual buy-in or cooperation thus remains a necessary condition for organizational agency. Whereas the variations in agents' behaviour in organizations can be described, often people have an interest in controlling it, in as far as the organization serves to pursue a set of aspirations. Hence, we also need to consider interventions in view of steering organizational behaviour. Drawing on insights from agency theory in organizations, Preisendörfer distinguishes four "instruments for disciplining agents":[56] (1) direct behavioural control, (2) rewards that depend on results, (3) bonding or guarantee arrangements, and (4) improvements to the information system. Two things should strike us in these strategies. Firstly, they are a means by which to change *action*. Secondly, the variables that they can introduce into action can have an impact on the agents' biological body, their trained body, their coordination of actional qualities, the coordination of their interaction with others or their use of means or technologies – in short, any of the five *aspects of human (in)capabilities* discussed in the previous chapter (and summarised below).

Two further consequences of this chain of thought (Points A to C above) have to be spelt out. *Firstly*, speaking about interventions in organizational behaviour (Point C), we consider interventions in the (in)capabilities of agents as *individuals* participating in organization. One would expect that, as the scale of organization increases, our ability to break up the cumulative effects of such changes in behaviour or interventions on the individual agents' change of behaviour would decrease. This then again raises the question about the nature of collective agency, which I discuss next. Secondly, attempts to control individual agents' action (Point C), through the structuring characteristics of organizations (Point B), may be expected to change the whole organization (Point A) in its likely behaviour, in what it is able to achieve, and the limits of that achievement. Or one may simply claim that organizations as collective agents have their own capabilities and incapabilities (which are not reducible to those of the individuals who act in them). This is what I would like to develop in the next section.

3 Capabilities and Incapabilities of Organizations

Having thus clarified the question of the subject of organized action, the time has come to return to the original question: how, then, are we to understand the relationship between capability and incapability in organized action? A short recapitulation at this point may help to contextualise the discussion.

---

[56] Preisendörfer, *Organisationssoziologie*, 119–24.

Under the term "technicity", I have studied one of the aspects of human interaction, namely that which involves the conscious or unconscious exercise of dispositions and capabilities, often through the use of specific means. Reflecting on the technicity of *capabilities*, I discovered the importance of a very specific notion of *incapability*. This was discussed in the previous chapter. I use the term "incapability" such that the negative prefix "in-" refers neither to doubting the capacities attested to, nor to ignoring capabilities, nor to a lack of capabilities in fragility or suffering – it simply points to a weak notion of incapability as a constant companion of capability: the incapability in question shows itself only as *correlated to capabilities,* and *in action.* This approach provides a way to get closer to the ever unattainable goal of a theoretical grasp of the *action as action.* More specifically, it is by considering how the event of action correlates capability and incapability that one can, firstly, see exactly *what* is done (and what is not done) or the *degree* to which one is able to do something, secondly, discern the kind and level of *competence* of an agent to do something in particular, and thirdly, open a useful window on the *means* that intervene in the execution of actions.

To visualise this role of incapability in action better, let us briefly recall its five dimensions, as discussed in Chapter 3, §2.1.

1. Capabilities are exercised by the biological *body*, which is never completely *mastered*. Therefore, when exercising his/her physical capabilities, the agent will simultaneously be confronted with the incapability completely to control his/her acting body. This incapability characterises the particular manifestation of action no less than the capability does.
2. Insofar as we have abilities to do things, these *acquired abilities* dispose us to do something in particular and in a particular way. It does not always become impossible to do it otherwise, but in practice it becomes more difficult: it is less likely that we will act against our dispositions, and in this sense, represent a weak incapability.
3. By acting, we *combine* actions. However, even if the capable agent can combine his/her actions in many different ways, not all combinations are practically feasible; one is incapable of performing certain combinations. In consequence, the way in which actions are finally combined speaks as much about capabilities as about incapabilities.
4. Similarly, the coordination of one's actions with those of others imposes limits on our actions: although we may be able to do something with others, this action receives part of its meaning from the qualities of *interaction* that we are, by definition, incapable of producing ourselves.

5. The mediation of our actions by *means* has an effect of simultaneously increasing and reducing our capability. In action, the means amplify the distinction between what I can and cannot do.

The individual capable human in an organized context essentially displays the (in)capabilities just recalled. The five dimensions of individual (in)capability will now be used as a heuristic framework to reflect on the collective (in)capabilities of organizations. When we speak about (in)capabilities, the whole series of capabilities to which they correspond (such as saying, doing, narrating, imputing, remembering and promising) is implied, even if this is not illustrated in the examples that follow.

1. The organization as a quasi-character constantly refers, obliquely, to the agents whose power-in-common institutes the organization. However, its existence and therefore its capacity to act is, at its inception, ephemeral. Without a certain formalisation (and technical support, see Point 5. below), it is incapable of ensuring its action in the long term (see Points B and C above). Even then, the management of organizations remains incapable of completely mastering the common power that institutes the organization. Moreover, even if it is true that organizations need common action to maintain themselves (and this is whence their agency comes), it is impossible to keep this fact permanently in mind – the formalisation of organizations leads to the forgetting[57] of the power-in-common, that is, to the incapability to remain in the act of instituting, and to taking collective action for granted. A number of phenomena testify to this limitation of capability: the formation of informal structures, nepotism and to some degree the organizational culture, etc. However, efforts to steer this force of organized action lead to varying degrees of "structural inertia",[58] which may in turn limit the organization's capabilities, and notably its ability to change.

2. The internal structuring of each organization makes it easier for this quasi-character to do certain things, and in certain ways (see Point B above). It is possible to maintain this claim without committing a teleological reduction of the organization: the organization is what facilitates X, as a result making Y more difficult to execute; it is what predisposes the quasi-character to do A in an A^1 way, so much so that it becomes improbable, even impossible, to do A in an A^2 way. Moreover, like individual agents, organizations can exercise their capacity to act, or even achieve intended outcomes, only by surrender-

---

57 On "forgetting" as a technical term in Ricœur's social thought, see Chapter 5, §2.1c.
58 Robbins and Judge, *Essentials of Organizational Behavior*, 318.

ing to the incapability of avoiding all unintended adverse effects. Finally, organized action may well intensify people's efforts to set goals, to plan and to maximise the outcome for their efforts, but this still does not mean that organizational agency (individual or that of the organization) has to be construed according to the lines of rational action theory or utilitarian action theory.[59]

3. Organizations not only combine the effort of different members and groups, but also combine different actions or adverbial determinations. Not all combinations are possible. This seems to me, for instance, to be the dilemma faced by the Catholic Church at the time of Benedict XVI: finding an answer to how to convince the world once again of the greatness and weight of the Church as a millennial institution, while at the same time presenting her as a humble servant of humanity. Another instance is the challenges faced in management regarding how to balance the organizational strategies of innovation *and* cost-minimisation, when they ideally require organistic and mechanistic structuring of the organization respectively, and how to find a compromise between this balance and a third strategy, that of imitation, which requires a combination of the two forms of structuring.[60] In the course of action, the exercise of capabilities results in the manifestation of incapabilities – the specific relationship between capability and incapability revealing the degree of competence of an organization in carrying out a set of actions.

4. Similarly, the ability of an organization to act in one way but not another, which depends on how it coordinates its action with that of other organizations. A crowd that is not at least minimally organized is not able to assert itself in the face of other social forces (think, for instance, of a group of labourers engaged in a dispute with the managerial powers of the sector of industry they work in[61]). Once their power in common is consolidated by the symbolic mediation of a claim considered just or good, a unification of individuals may occur (however, at the price of excluding opposition, with the concomitant risk of weakening support for the group). In turn, this assessment of action (or, as Ricœur calls it, "imputing" action as praiseworthy

---

[59] One could get this impression, for instance, from Preisendörfer's exposition on agency theory in the sociology of organizations, Preisendörfer, *Organisationssoziologie*, 114–29. On this point, see again the distinction between primary and secondary technicity in Chapter 3, §§3.1 and 3.2.
[60] This example is derived from Robbins and Judge, *Essentials of Organizational Behavior*, 289.
[61] In Chapter 8, §3.1 an example is explored in detail.

or blameworthy to agents[62]) makes the formation of coalitions easy or difficult (the group becomes capable of some coalitions, while others become difficult). Also, the group becomes unable to reconcile its claim to fight for a cause with certain behaviours (such as whether the ends justify the means). Finding a trade-off between pre-election promises and post-election coalition formation illustrates the point – Belgian politics offering a wealth of instances. Finally, the organization's adopted strategy has to be coordinated with the broader social environment (its means, its expectations, etc.). The relation between organized action and its social environment shifts the degree of (in)capability of the organization, in relation to the capacity, volatility and complexity of the environment.[63]

5. I have already touched on the *means* of action of the organizations – much more than the proverbial desk and fax machine (see Point 1. and Points A and B, above). The means play a major role in the coordination of actors in organizations; they serve, in the form of a relatively stable framework, as an identifiable representation by which the agents implicitly reconstitute the social bonds that have been established; and thus form ensembles or devices of habit that also facilitate the forgetting of the continuous institution of organizations by the power in common. If quasi-characters refer obliquely to the interactions of individual agents, it is because the relaying of their actions by technical devices makes this possible (in the same way symbols do).[64] At the same time, this instrumental aspect of organizations prolongs the effect of augmentation and reduction of action: a city library, capable of offering a large collection to its readers, will be incapable of bringing these books to the readers; the mobile library, in order to maintain its mobility, will have to forego a large collection. Finally, whereas the material and organizational infrastructure of organized action can never sufficiently account for the agency of organizations, it certainly is a key point where the organization remains irreducible to the behaviour of the agents which function in it.

---

62 See again Chapter 3, §1
63 This example is drawn from Robbins and Judge, *Essentials of Organizational Behavior*, 290.
64 Cf. Régis Debray on transmission in Chapter 1 and Anthony Giddens on "time-space distantiation" in Chapter 5.

4 Conclusion. Paradoxes, Risks, and Political Implications of Organized Action

In this chapter I have tried to clarify the notion of organized individual and collective action. The relationships of capability and incapability involved in the action of the quasi-characters that are organizations were also examined. Nowhere have I simply equated organizations to agents writ large. Yet, the structural similarities between the (in)capable agency of individuals and organizations justifies a transfer of other conclusions from individual agency to this discussion of collective agency. In both cases, (in)capability is a feature of the *finitude* of agency. Moreover, the flip side of this is the *situatedness* of agents, both individual and collective. Then, incapability functions as the *practical horizon of intelligibility* of action in both cases. Finally, in the course of action, the shifting difference between capability and incapability remains *uncertain*, until executed actions have marked that difference.[65] These four characteristics together help us to understand *action as action* and to appreciate the *interpretative* make-up of action. These are all aspects of the technicity of collective action, the study of which can clearly benefit from a hermeneutic approach.

Agents know practically that their capabilities to do things are shadowed by incapability. Every attestation of capability is an affirmation of an inability to do otherwise. Hence the impression – often obscured in more routine actions – that something can go wrong, that there is something at stake in action. This is certainly also true for organized action. In conclusion, I would like to highlight this point by looking at the paradox of organized action and the concept of risk.

---

[65] Interestingly, despite my affirmation of two types of organizational agency (individual and collective) the cumulate effect of the five incapabilities, as they bear on capabilities, is to relativise the agent as the core of initiative and power. Accordingly, this draws a picture of power as more diffuse than my terminology of agency may have suggested. My exposition shows that power arises primordially "from below"; it has a relational structure, and the myriad of interactions generate shifting fields of power. At the same time, it accounts for the "crystallization" of power as effects of many interactions, which in turn account for concentrations of power (as in revolutions or states) and, more generally, the formation of power hegemonies. All these terms are directly derived from Michel Foucault's theory of power, or at least in its reformulation in Michel Foucault, *Histoire de la sexualité 1. La volonté de savoir* (Paris: Gallimard, 1976), 121–29. The most important difference seems to reside in the fact that I do not shy away from directly examining and theorizing the agency of powerfully organized action.

4 Conclusion. Paradoxes, Risks, and Political Implications of Organized Action

4.1 The Paradox of Organized Action

This analysis of the (in)capabilities of organizations can help us to understand better the complex relationship between the intentions of agents, the plans of organizations and the whole range of adverse effects that accompany individual and collective action.[66] For this reason, I argue that this general interplay of capabilities and incapabilities in collective action is the basis from which a more pronounced paradox emerges: where organization consolidates the power of people to act in common always lurks the likelihood that the organization may generate unintended, adverse or detrimental effects. This is not a declaration of an *a priori* pessimism about organizations. I simply underscore the unavoidable (but still varying and partially malleable) ambiguity of action in common.

In a previous chapter (Chapter 3, §5), I have already argued for a general paradox of the technicity of action. If there is a paradox of organized action, it is due to the technical constitution of organized action ("technical" in the sense developed in this chapter). If the basic structure of the paradox of organized action then also corresponds with what Ricœur calls the political paradox (discussed in the Introduction, §3.2), it is because the political paradox is a particular manifestation of the broader paradox of organized action and the latter of an even broader paradox of the technicity of action. There is a paradox in each of these cases, because the power, abilities, initiative and means that make it possible for individual or collective agents to achieve certain things (bring forth a product, results, outcomes), can turn against the initial spirit and intention of the action. In the case of organized action, the instituting work by which a plurality of actors become capable of stabilising, consolidating and giving effect to their power in common can in turn veer away from the project or plan for which the collective action was organized, or can even stifle the sources of its power to which organizations obliquely refer. Thus organization can lead to forms of disempowerment or decapabilisation (as I illustrate in the Conclusion, §2).

There is no theoretical solution for this paradox; provisional compromises can only be found in practice. The ability to avoid the worst to emerge from this paradox is itself a sliding point on the spectrum of (in)capability. In the context of his discussion of the political paradox, Ricœur advocates compromises that reflect an "ethics of limited violence". The challenge of democracy, he says, is to find "the techniques" or "technologies" to make the exercise of power possible and abuse impossible. For organized action, broadly speaking,

---

[66] Unintended consequences are explored further in Chapter 5, §3.2 (Point 2).

I would say, the stakes are the continuous trade-off between norms and efficiency. This means that the only way by which to steer organized action to safety from the more harmful possibilities entailed in the paradox of organized action is by other organized action, which is equally subject to paradox. This is explored further in the chapters of Part II of this book.

4.2 Organized Action in the Social Sciences

As I have pointed out, the uncertainty involved in the relation between incapability and capability and amplified by the paradox of organized action leads us directly to the phenomenon of risk. The problem of risk magnifies the fact that, in action, something is at stake. I do not intend to open a larger discussion of this topic here. Rather, I want to show how the terms developed in this chapter can help to clarify the notion of risk even beyond the theoretical frame I have adopted, in other words also within discussions that respond to *other* theoretical commitments.

It is well known that Ulrich Beck gave an important impetus to the social scientific research and theorization of risk in his book *Risk Society*.[67] Let us translate one of the main theses of this book into the terms proposed here and extend it to some conceptual implications not found in Beck's argument. Whatever the definition of "risk", this term implies the relationship between the capability to act and an inability to prevent, or even cope with, the consequences that result precisely from putting this capability into practice. A "risk society" would be a quasi-character that is constituted (a) by recognizing its social (in)capabilities by "second-degree reflection of the order of reconstruction",[68] (b) a reconstruction centred on the category of risk, attributed to society as its salient contemporary characteristic, and (c) where risk brought to light by the social scientist. But risk(s) also say(s) something about the context of society, in particular, the urgency of a collective response. The transition from a class society to a risk society corresponds to a change in the internal arrangement of participation of the members of society.

In order to respond to the risks generated by modern industrialization, society takes recourse to science – yet another quasi-character. On the one hand, science is characterised by an increased capacity for interpretation and relevant advice to society – so much so that it would benefit from a "monopoly of

---

[67] Ulrich Beck, *Risk Society: Towards a New Modernity* (London: Sage, 1992).
[68] My translation, Ricœur, *Parcours de la reconnaissance*, 223 / *Course of Recognition*, 140.

definitions" (this extraordinary capacity of science is matched by a widespread incapacity of other members of society). On the other hand, the complexity of the causal relationships revealed by science makes it impossible for it to rationally control the complexity of the consequences of planned actions on which it must express its expert opinion.

The point that risk is not *a priori* an evil is defended later by Niklas Luhmann.[69] Whereas a danger is a possible disaster of which agents are unaware, a risk would be a danger that has been acknowledged, it is integrated into the calculated sphere of response (the inability to master the consequences of actions impromptu leads to an increased capacity for awareness). Thus an increased capacity to identify risks would increase the ability to respond to world events in a decisive manner.

More recently, Elísio Macamo[70] has identified a whole series of questions relating to the "monopoly of definition" of risks, the importance of which can be gauged, for instance, in the context of humanitarian interventions in so-called developing countries: who defines the risk? for whom? in the name of which concerns? in relation to which emergency measure? etc. One could describe the spirit of Macamo's project as a study of the politics of allocating risk to quasi-characters. Furthermore, if risk identification is a factor that makes actors capable of (re)acting (Luhmann) and if the whole society is marked by the role of risks (Beck), then quasi-characters specializing in risks – the sciences, consulting firms, sometimes non-governmental organizations, etc. – could become disproportionately important in the exploration of the phenomenon of risk, to the detriment of the general public/agents. Hence the forgetfulness, or even ignorance, that Macamo notes among many researchers about the issue of risk among individual agents, or in regions of the world that have limited mastery of Western science (hence the importance of intercultural dialogue and negotiations as opposed to unilateral impositions that I touched on at the end of Chapter 2, and that is thematized in Chapter 6, §§5 and 6). Thus, Macamo indicates the passage from incapability to fragility and suffering, and suggests the social-critical potential of studying risk.

---

[69] Niklas Luhmann, "Die Moral des Risikos und das Risiko der Moral," in *Risiko und Gesellschaft. Grundlagen und Ergebnisse interdisziplinärer Risikoforschung*, ed. Gotthard Bechmann (Opladen: Westdeutscher Verlag, 1993), 327–38.
[70] Elísio Macamo, "Conclusion," in *Risk and Africa*, eds. Lena Bloemertz, Martin Doevenspeck, Elísio Macamo and Detlef Müller-Mahn (Vienna, Berlin: LIT Verlag, 2012), 265–72.

Chapter 5:
The Hermeneutics of Human Capabilities and the Theory of Structuration

1 Introduction

The previous four chapters have gradually developed our view on the coordination of human capabilities and the means by which people act. I have made abundant use of insights from Ricœur's hermeneutics, but I have also critiqued and completed his views, often taking recourse to insights drawn from other social theorists to do so. In this chapter, I proceed in a similar way, turning my attention to the broader social-theoretical frame of the insights gathered in the previous chapters. Here, I explore two major structuring features of Ricœur's view on social action: the teleological structure of interaction and his understanding of institutions. My critical views on these two themes open the way for a detour through Anthony Giddens' structuration theory and lead us back to a revision of the initially considered theoretical framework. Since the choice of Giddens as an interlocutor may not be immediately obvious, and to avoid misunderstanding, let me start by laying out my rationale for choosing him.

As I pointed out in the Introduction, it is not the coordination between Ricœur's hermeneutics and a social theory that poses the problem. After all, Ricœur was both a great specialist in the dialogue of traditions and an important philosopher of social action. Still, with some exceptions,[1] he seems to have developed his thinking without taking into account the enormous body of thought on these topics on social theory written in English. Given the breadth and depth of Ricœur's work, it would be ridiculous to present an absence of dialogue with this or that author or intellectual movement as sufficient reason to point out any inadequacy. Nevertheless, his work contains a multitude of possibilities that remain unexplored, to which a reconstruction of such omitted dialogues could

---

[1] See, for instance, his work on Clifford Geertz: Paul Ricœur, *Lectures on Ideology and Utopia*, ed. George Taylor (New York, NY: Columbia University Press, 1986), 254–68. To a lesser degree, consider also Alfred Schütz, who wrote most of his work after settling in the United States and whose texts were first known in English. Ricœur seems to prefer to use the English versions (see particularly Paul Ricœur, *Temps et récit 3. Le temps raconté* (Paris: Seuil, 1985), 203–209 / *Time and narrative*. Volume 3, trans. Kathleen Blamey and David Pellauer (Chicago and London: University of Chicago Press, 1988), 112–16 and *La mémoire, l'histoire, l'oubli* (Paris: Seuil, 2000), 159 f., 688 / *Memory, History, Forgetting*, trans. Kathleen Blamey and David Pellauer (Chicago: University of Chicago Press, 2004), 130 f, 395.

draw our attention. And this is exactly what I expect from Giddens in this chapter: relating his social theory to Ricœur will help us to find, and also to develop, such unexplored possibilities, specifically in respect of the broader social-theoretical frame in which our explorations on human capabilities and means are to be set. A number of other social theorists have already been used in a similar fashion – for instance, Bourdieu, Schütz, Geertz or Foucault.[2] My chapter complements these studies, but they do oblige me to justify my comparison with Giddens more clearly.

Although he is sometimes criticised by his peers in sociology for his lack of empirical work, Giddens can nevertheless be considered the most important British sociologist of his generation in the field of social theory.[3] My point is not to elevate him to the status of ultimate authority in social theory, but to use his work for the heuristic objectives outlined here. In Chapter 3, §4, I have already explained the promise that such a confrontation may hold. I argued that Gid-

---

[2] Johann Michel, "L'*habitus*, le récit et la promesse," in *Ricœur et ses contemporains: Bourdieu, Derrida, Deleuze, Foucault, Castoriadis* (Paris: PUF, 2013), 15–43. Francesca Sacchetti, *Alfred Schütz e Paul Ricœur. Percorsi della soggettività tra fenomenologia ed ermeneutica* (Acireale-Roma: Bonanno Editore, 2012). Thiemo Breyer, "Handlung, Text, Kultur. Überlegungen zur Hermeneutischen Anthropologie Zwischen Clifford Geertz und Paul Ricœur," *Meta: Research in Hermeneutics, Phenomenology and Practical Philosophy* 5, no. 1 (2013): 107–29. Simon Castonguay, "Michel Foucault et Paul Ricœur, vers un dialogue possible," *Études Ricœuriennes/Ricœur Studies* 1, no. 1 (2010): 68–86; or Sébastien Roman, "Hétérotopie et utopie pratique: comparaison entre Foucault et Ricœur," *Le Philosophoire* 44, no. 2 (2015): 69–86.
[3] This is the assessment reflected in the position accorded to Giddens in the landscape of sociological theory by George Ritzer and Jeffrey Stepnisky, *Modern Sociological Theory*, 8th ed. (Los Angeles, CA: Sage, 2018). This view is corroborated by the four volumes of commentaries on his work in the series "Critical Assessments": Christopher Bryant and David Jary, eds. *Anthony Giddens: Critical Assessments* (New York, NY: Routledge, 1997), and his inclusion in a reader: Craig Calhoun et al., eds., *Contemporary Sociological Theory*, 3th ed. (Malden, MA: Blackwell, 2012), Chapters 18 and 35. For similar views from outside the anglophone world, see Hans Joas and Wolfgang Knöbl, *Sozialtheorie. Zwanzig einführende Vorlesungen* (Suhrkamp: Frankfurt am Main, 2004), 393–439 and Philippe Corcuff, *Théories sociologiques contemporaines: France, 1980–2020* (Malakoff: Armand Colin, 2019), 56–62. Nevertheless, this can be contrasted to Plamena Panayotova, ed. *The History of Sociology in Britain: New Research and Revaluation* (Cham: Palgrave Macmillan, 2019), which contains almost no reference to Giddens.

Giddens has also been criticised for his political commitment to Tony Blair and his entry into the House of Lords. These facts are not relevant here, since the phase of formulation of his theory of structuration, the phase to which I confine myself here, predates these facts. An interpretation of the relation between Giddens's academic work and politics is offered by Peter Kolarz, "Introduction: Anthony Giddens – Social Theory and Politics" in *Giddens and Politics Beyond the Third Way* (London: Palgrave Macmillan, 2016), 1–17. It also offers a contemporary "Giddensian" view on politics.

dens's structuration theory lends itself for this kind of exploration, first, because of the centrality of *action* which it shares with Ricœur's hermeneutics of human capabilities. Structuration theory may offer a sociologically informed view on the action-theoretical structure of human *capabilities*. Second, Giddens describes how face-to-face socially integrated interaction is extended to systems integrated interaction by time and space transcending *means*. In this way, he offers a useful view on the relative stabilisation of human relations of interaction in institutions, and we have already seen how significant the place is which Ricœur accords to institutions.[4] Third, by furnishing ways by which to understand the full social breadth of the technical constitution of human actional capabilities, Giddens's structuration theory promises to help us understand the dialectic of capabilities and incapabilities which is central to Chapters 3 and 4, above.

With these points in mind, the best way to set up a debate between these two authors is by comparing their main formative concepts: *institutions* and *practices* in Ricœur and the *duality of structure* in Giddens.[5] In both cases, these terms anchor a broader view of social interaction, that is, their views on the relationship between agents and society. Once I have completed this comparison, I suggest some contributions that such a dialogue could make for those of us who are working on the unfinished construction site of Ricœur's work.[6]

To keep this undertaking manageable, I mainly limit myself, as for Ricœur, to his hermeneutics of human capabilities. For Ricœur, I focus on *Oneself as Another* (1990) and later texts; for Giddens, I refer mainly to *The Constitution of Society* (1984), the culmination of a decade of theoretical work in the 1970s and

---

[4] For instance, in Chapter 3, §1.
[5] When the first version of this chapter was published, no systematic comparison of Giddens's work with Ricœur's existed. John Thompson's remarks in *Critical Hermeneutics. A Study in the Thought of Paul Ricœur and Jürgen Habermas* (Cambridge: Cambridge University Press, 1981), 143–49, precedes the publication of the major texts considered in my chapter. However, subsequently, two doctoral dissertations took up this challenge: Darryl Scott Dale-Ferguson, *Capable Agents and Just Institutions. A Reconstruction of Paul Ricœur's "Ethical Aim" Using Anthony Giddens' Theory of Structuration* (PhD diss., University of Chicago, June 2019) and Jana Alvara Carstens, *Complacency: An Action Theoretical Approach via Paul Ricœur and Anthony Giddens* (PhD diss., University of Pretoria, November 2019).
[6] The present discussion is not intended to be exhaustive. A broader discussion would have to take into account not only the semantics and ontology of action, but also the debates in which Ricœur develops the position of *Oneself as Another* – debates with Weber, Walzer, Boltanski and Thévenot, Honneth, Sen, and others. See the useful orientation by Laurent Thévenot, "Des institutions en personne. Une sociologie pragmatique en dialogue avec Paul Ricœur," *Études Ricœuriennes/Ricœur Studies* 3, no. 1 (2012): 11–33, here 11–18.

1980s, during which the theory of structuration was developed.[7] Following an internal critique by the Giddensian Rob Stones, I limit myself to the "true" theory of structuration by omitting Giddens's work from the same period in which conceptual articulation links with structuration theory were not convincingly established.[8]

2 Ricœur: Individuals and Society in the Hermeneutics of the Capable Human

The relationship between the individual and society is a key theme that structures a large part of Ricœur's thought. But this view evolved gradually. Upstream from *Oneself as Another*, the Ricœurian approach to social ontology is clearly Husserlian: he subscribes to Husserl's (and later Schütz's) "working hypothesis", according to which it is always possible

> to generate all the higher-level communities, such as the State, solely on the basis of the constitution of others in an intersubjective relation. All the constitutions have to be derivative: first, those of a common physical world, then those of the common cultural world,

---

7 See Joas and Knöbl, *Sozialtheorie*, 403–405; Christopher Bryant and David Jary, "Anthony Giddens," in *The Wiley-Blackwell Companion to Major Social Theorists* (Volume 2), ed. George Ritzer and Jeffrey Stepnisky (Malden, MA, Oxford: Wiley-Blackwell, 2011), 432–63, here 433. I do not review all the critiques of structuration theory –instead, my selection of themes and overall interpretation responds to some of these points. Useful overviews of these critiques are those by Lars Bo Kaspersen, *Anthony Giddens: An Introduction to a Social Theorist* (Oxford: Blackwell, 2000), 157–87; and Jean Nizet, *La sociologie de Anthony Giddens* (Paris: La Découverte, 2007), 87–100.

8 Rob Stones, *Structuration Theory* (New York, NY: Palgrave MacMillan, 2005). According to him, many of the concepts developed by Giddens "remain either cut off from, or only very weakly informed by, the central concepts of structuration" (41). I also agree with Stones's assessment that Giddens got carried away "with the thought that it [structuration theory] is grander and more global than it really is. Consequently, he has extended its nominal remit into areas in which it cannot perform [...] the majority of Giddens's broad-ranging substantive explorations of historical sociology, the institutional processes and contours of modernity, and of the trajectories and possibilities within the political spheres of late modernity, are not in fact, despite what Giddens himself suggests, studies that draw on structuration theory in any significant sense. Rather, they are best characterised as pluralistic and non-reductionist studies that do indeed draw from various ontological insights but ones that have little, if anything to do with the structural-hermeneutic nexus at the heart of structuration" (13). Stones's proposition of a new "strong" version of structuration, as well as its debate with Mouzelis, Archer, Parker, etc., falls beyond the scope of this chapter.

conducting themselves in their turn in relation to one another as higher-order selves confronting others of the same order.[9]

In the previous chapter, we have examined Ricœur's understanding of the relation between individual agents and social entities or "quasi-characters" (see Chapter 4, §2.1). However, Ricœur reconsidered this "methodological individualism" of phenomenological and partially Weberian inspiration to adopt a modified position on the "acting and suffering human" (*l'homme agissant et souffrant*) as social being in *Oneself as Another*. Two important features give us access to this revised social theoretical orientation: the way it deals with institutions (§2.1) and its understanding of practices (§2.2).

2.1 First Approach: Ricœur on Institutions

Let us first read Ricœur's proposed definition of "institution":

> By institution, we are to understand here the structure of *living together* as this belongs to a historical community – people, nation, region, and so forth – a structure irreducible to interpersonal relations and yet bound up with these in a remarkable sense which the notion of distribution will permit us [...] to clarify. What fundamentally characterizes the idea of institution is the bond of common mores [*moeurs*] and not that of constraining rules.[10]

This definition contains a number of essential features of Ricœur's exploration of institutions in *Oneself as Another:*
- they are "structures";
- they are structures of "living together", as opposed to "imposed" structures;[11]

---

9 Paul Ricœur, "La raison pratique," (1979), *Du texte à l'action. Essais d'herméneutique II* (Paris: Seuil, 1986), 263–88, here 284 / Paul Ricœur, "Practical Reason" in *From Text to Action: Essays in Hermeneutics II*, trans. Kathleen Blamey and John Thompson (London: Athlone, 1991), 188–207, here 204.
10 Paul Ricœur, *Soi-même comme un autre* (Paris: Seuil, 1990), 227 / *Oneself as Another*, trans. Kathleen Blamey (Chicago, IL: University of Chicago Press, 1992), 194 (translation slightly modified).
11 Taken in isolation, this claim of Ricœur's is highly questionable. However, note that elsewhere in the same book, Ricœur explicitly comes back to the constraining character of institutions. On this point one may consult the classic work of Michel Dobry, *Sociologie des crisis politiques*, 3rd ed. (Paris: Presses de Sciences Po., 2009), 100–103, which convincingly argues that the limitations of actions in particular social sectors cannot be attributed to the sole consensus (implicit or explicit), or to a common agreement about the rules of the "game" of each sector.

- the "collective entities" or "historical communities" are "linked" to interpersonal relations, but are explicitly "irreducible to interpersonal relationships";
- what in the institution goes beyond interactions are common mores, or an *ethos*, which gives content to the notion of "structure"; and finally,
- "participation" would be the appropriate term to refer to coordination between actors who share common mores and historical communities within which they practice them.

I insist on the detail of this dense passage because it involves a number of theoretical *tensions*, which Ricœur hopes to keep in balance, or even overcome, in the "theory social" of the 1990 book:
- The tension between the *reduction* or *non-reduction* of institutions to the interaction between individuals is explicitly mentioned (we will see that Ricœur rejects methodological individualism and sociologism with equal vigour).[12]
- There is a tension between the institution, considered as a set of *rules of participation* on the one hand, and on the other hand as that *in which one participates* by following the rules, i.e. historical communities.
- *Common mores* are opposed to "*constraining rules*," thus opposing capabilisation to coercion. Curiously, the claim that a common *ethos*, and therefore structures of living together, is non-binding, is settled by definition.
- Here, Ricœur leaves intact the question of the relationship between the *expected consequences* and the unforeseen or *unintended consequences* of the interaction.

Subsequently, in developing this understanding of institutions, Ricœur examines three themes: first, power-in-common, then society as a system of participation or distribution, and finally, the pair "forgetting" [*oublie*] and "authority." Let us explore these three themes.

2.1a Power-in-Common

First, if participation is a key concept in the social-theoretical vision adopted and promoted by Ricœur in *Oneself as Another*, it is nevertheless necessary to appreciate the care that Ricœur takes to support this notion by using the Arendtian

---

[12] This is discussed explicitly in Ricœur, *Soi-même comme un autre*, 234 / *Oneself as Another*, 200.

notion of power or, more precisely, of "*power-in-common*".[13] This approach is important for two decisive reasons. First, since *Oneself as another* as a whole is a hermeneutic of human capabilities – of the power to act –, redeploying this notion of power-in-common allows Ricœur to theorize the social and political extension of the individual's capabilities. Second, the notion of "power-*in-common*" gives Ricœur other argumentative means to remain in line with Husserl's precept – namely to reduce collective entities to events[14] – even if it no longer fits in with the methodological individualism he has previously recommended. As constituted by a common power, the institutions are established primarily from the bottom up, instead of being imposed from the top down.

Nevertheless, I consider this borrowing from Arendt an uneven success. On the negative side, by recalling the conceptual context of *The Human Condition*, one can easily demonstrate how Ricœur is smuggling in a reductive view of human interaction: he implies that institutions as the structure of living together are established by "action" and not by "labour" or by "work" (in the Arendtian sense of these terms). Even if we accepted Arendt's anthropological typology of action, labour and work,[15] it seems to me quite debatable to reduce the generative function of living together (the institution of all collective entities) to "action" alone, characterised as it is by plurality and consultation, while excluding labour and work.[16] To name but one reason: labour and work are subject to rule-following, however, according to the five principles of imperfect mastery of such practices (reflected in the (in)capability structure of action, see Chapter 3, §2.1), they never merely repeat learned actions. Quite the contrary: the small and large deviations have cumulative, often unintended, consequences with generative, or at least transformative, effects on institutions.

On the positive side, borrowing *plurality* as anthropological trait of action opens up the sphere of the relevance of interaction, in principle, to all humanity. Doing so firmly roots the relation of agents to "third parties who will never be

---

13 Cf. Ricœur, *Soi-même comme un autre*, 227–30 / *Oneself as Another*, 194–97.
14 Paul Ricœur, "Hegel et Husserl sur l'intersubjectivité" (1977), dans *Du texte à l'action*, 311–34, here 334 / "Hegel and Husserl on Intersubjectivity" in *From Text to Action*, 227–45, here 244–45.
15 I could list numerous reasons to be suspicious about it, but this is not the place to develop this point.
16 However, in the notes in *Soi-même comme un autre*, 228n3 and 229n4 / *Oneself as Another*, 195n37 and 196n38, Ricœur seems to contradict this implication of his borrowing from Arendt; we will see further on that framing the actions (including labour and work) in a reflection on practices implicitly contradicts this vision of the instituting of institutions.

faces"[17] in interaction. Or, in more Ricœurian terminology, in all face-to-face interaction between an "I" and a "you", an essential place is accorded to the institutional other, the "it". We have already seen how this schema of *I, you* and *it* structures Ricœur's entire hermeneutics of human capabilities (see Chapter 3, §1, Figure 1). But the point goes still further. In as far as capable agents react to the fragile and ephemeral nature of the power they generate by common action, this desire for durable or stable power is realized by institutions. Ricœur points out that "[i]t is from the institution, precisely, that power receives this temporal dimension [i.e. duration – EW]."[18] Those who interact in such a way that without their interaction there would be no institutions are already passively constituted by their participation in the institutions. Furthermore, the partnership with Arendt helps Ricœur to confirm, as in some of his previous writings,[19] that institutions are not only constraining, but that they are precisely mediations of freedom. In *Oneself as Another*, this Hegelian moment of Ricœur's "social theory" is strongly affirmed when he states that it is "only in a specific institutional milieu that the capacities and predispositions that distinguish human action can blossom; the individual [...] becomes human only under the condition of certain institutions; and [...] if this is so, the obligation to serve these institutions is itself a condition for the human agent to continue to develop."[20]

2.1b Participation and Distribution

However, Ricœur also accepts the Rawlsian notion of society as a system of regulated *participation*, maintained by social institutions. If Arendt's theory of power helps him to express the fact of "communality" in life-together structured by institutions,[21] the Rawlsian notion of participation fills a gap in the idea of wanting to live together, namely the idea of "distribution" it implies. Admittedly, Ricœur adopts the notions of participation and distribution initially in reflecting on pol-

---

17 Ricœur, *Soi-même comme un autre*, 228 / *Oneself as Another*, 195. However, I do not see clearly how third parties are really introduced – if not simply by a choice of definition.
18 Ricœur, *Soi-même comme un autre*, 228 / *Oneself as Another*, 195.
19 E.g. Ricœur, "La raison pratique," 283 / "Practical Reason," 204.
20 Ricœur, *Soi-même comme un autre*, 296–97 / *Oneself as Another*, 254–55. This is already the decisive point of the political good, argued in "Le paradoxe politique," in *Histoire et vérité* (Paris: Seuil, 1967), 294–32 / "The political paradox," *History and Truth* (Evanston, IL: Northwestern University Press, 1965), 247–70. Today this position is strongly supported by Axel Honneth – see *Freedom's Right: The Social Foundations of Democratic Life*, trans. Joseph Ganahl (Cambridge: Polity, 2014).
21 According to the definition cited above from Ricœur, *Soi-même comme un autre*, 227 / *Oneself as Another*, 195.

itics and law, but we must fully recognize the broader socio-theoretical significance which the notion has for him. Accordingly, Ricœur explains that distribution "denotes a feature fundamental to all institutions, to the extent that they govern the apportionment of roles, tasks, and advantages or disadvantages between the members of society."[22] Thus, the members of a society "participate" (*prennent part*) or "have a share" (*ont part*) in the institutions and the society from which they receive their shares through the "distribution" (*répartition*) by the institutions. Reinforcing this double-sided image of distribution, Ricœur describes society, in line with John Rawls, as a "cooperative enterprise" (*entreprise de coopération*). Thus, the notion of "participation", already introduced in the first definition of institution (above), serves as the key to overcome the alternative between sociologism and methodological individualism: "The institution as the regulation of the distribution of roles, hence as a system, is indeed something more and something other than the individuals who play these roles. In other words, the relation is not reduced to the terms of the relation. But at the same time, a relation does not constitute a supplementary entity."[23] From this view of society, Ricœur derives two features of institutions: they are regulators of role distribution (probably referring to the organizational side of institutions) and the very rules of these distributions. Clearly, the point of understanding society as a "cooperative enterprise" resides in capturing this bi-directional complex of agents' participation and institutions' distribution of shares – however oppressive and exploitative these relations may be – and not in some Pollyanna-ish idealization of social relations. Ricœur does not use the phrase, but one may consider it his version of social integration.

2.1c Forgetting and Authority

Ricœur characterises institutions by the terms "forgetting" and "authority". These are two key terms in his political thought,[24] the redeployment of which in this context requires some clarification.

---

22 Ricœur, *Soi-même comme un autre*, 233 / *Oneself as Another*, 200.
23 Ricœur, *Soi-même comme un autre*, 234 / *Oneself as Another*, 200.
24 For the development of these notions in dialogue with Arendt, see especially Paul Ricœur, "Pouvoir et violence," (1989), in *Lectures I. Autour du politique* (Paris: Seuil, 1991), 20–42 / Paul Ricœur "Power and Violence," trans. Lisa Jones, in *Theory, Culture & Society* 27, 5 (2010): 18–36 (published shortly before *Soi-même comme un autre*) and *La critique et la conviction* (Paris: Calmann-Lévy, 1995), 147–56 / Paul Ricœur, *Critique and Conviction: Conversations with François Azouvi and Marc De Launay*. Trans. Kathleen Blamey (New York, NY: Columbia University Press, 1998), 95–101 where Ricœur comments on these same ideas a few years later.

Knowing that society does not function as a gigantic board meeting (even if the emphasis on the Arendtian notion of consultation[25], outside its political context, in a broader, social-theoretical context, could lead to such a misunderstanding), Ricœur acknowledges that participants (without whom there would be no institution) often *forget* the constituted nature of institutions. Thus the status of being forgotten in the course of interactions belongs to the mode of existence of institutions and equally to the will to live together.[26] This insight could be rephrased by saying that social agents, most often forget how, by participating in a life together with others, they constitute institutions. They do so by hypostasizing[27] the events of participation to a model of agents in relation to collective entities. At the same time, it must be stressed that "this forgetting, inherent to the constitution of that consent which creates power, does not refer back to any past which could have been lived as present in the transparency of a society conscious of itself and of its engendering(s)".[28] In short, "forgetting" is not a loss of memory of something that was once present in mind to society as a plan. Therefore, institutions would, like power, be constituted in a way that could be characterised as pre-contractual and pre-juridical (in the sense that Heidegger has accustomed us to understand the prefix "pre-" in the "methodological" paragraph of *Being and Time*, since taken up by Lévinas, Lyotard, etc.). One only notices what is generally forgotten when it is threatened, or even undone.[29]

Let us also explain what Ricœur means by associating the term *authority* with institutions.[30] Above, we already saw how institutions ensure the durability of people's capability of power to act. Still, durability is not enough to legitimate either action or institutions. Power, created by action and transmitted by institutions, must therefore be supplemented or augmented by a legitimate reference to the instituting action, i.e. the legitimate foundation. This "augmentation" is called "authority". Thus politics – and by implication institutions – reveals an ambiguity: it exercises here and now power in common, while drawing on the

---

25 As in "acting in concert", Hannah Arendt, *The Human Condition* (Chicago: University of Chicago Press, 1958), 162.
26 Ricœur, *Soi-même comme un autre*, 230 / *Oneself as Another*, 197. In the other places in this book where this term is used (*Soi-même comme un autre*, 278, 299, 303 / *Oneself as Another*, 239, 256, 260), it is deployed each time to qualify a mode of the existence of political power.
27 In the terminology Ricœur uses in the 1970s, cf. *Du texte à l'action*, 334 / *From Text to Action*, 244–45.
28 Ricœur, "Pouvoir et violence," 29 / "Power and Violence," 25.
29 Cf. Ricœur, *La critique et la conviction*, 153 / *Critique and Conviction*, 99 and *Soi-même comme un autre*, 230 / *Oneself as Another*, 197.
30 This exposition is primarily based on "Pouvoir et violence."

legitimacy provided by past, founding actions. This reference to the foundation of authority is not necessarily conscious or articulated, but rather, is most often forgotten.[31] At the same time, each key foundation event refers to the foundations (previous institutionalizations) by a logic of endless regression of what is nonetheless still present.[32] Ricœur concludes that authority is not the result of tradition, but that authority itself is transmitted. To be clear, Ricœur's point is the transmission of authority, not the authority of tradition, transmission or institutions.[33] Finally, the importance of talking about the authority of institutions would reside, it seems, for Ricœur, in an understanding of the legitimacy they can command, rather than in the description of their origin. Acting-in-common surely requires stabilisation by institutions, but to be legitimate, institutions must be more than mere constructions: they must first and foremost be institutionalized as repetitions of previous legitimate foundations (or at least be assumed to be such).[34] At stake in the schematization of manufacturing-repetition is our understanding of the capacity of institutions to assert rules and regulations, as well as the practices to which they give durability (capacity being understood as either the capacity or the right to command).[35]

2.1d Provisional Conclusion: The Institutional Paradox

It is not easy to assess the alignment between institutions and politics that informs Ricœur's discussion. Does he imply that political institutions provide the paradigm to understand other institutions (including, for example, the family)? Would all institutions therefore be essentially political? Or should we rather conclude that the key concepts – action, power-in-common, forgetting, authority, etc. – apply to politics only because they are first typical of institutions in general and, therefore, typical of politics as an institution?

Let us leave this question open to examine the formal proximity between the political and institutions. How should we orient ourselves in Ricœur's thought on the delicate relationship "between" agents and institutions if the agents are

---

31 Cf. Ricœur, *Le Juste 2* (Paris: Esprit, 2001), 113 / *Reflections on the Just* (Chicago: University of Chicago Press, 2007), 96.
32 Ricœur, *La critique et la conviction*, 154–155 / *Critique and Conviction*, 100–101.
33 Ricœur, "Pouvoir et violence," 41 / "Power and Violence," 31–32.
34 He states that "the foundation is paradoxically, not something that is to be made, but repeated", Ricœur, "Pouvoir et violence," 41–42 / "Power and violence," 34.
35 Cf. Ricœur, *Le Juste 2*, 107–108 / *Reflections on the Just*, 91–92. For further discussion, see "Le paradoxe de l'autorité" in *Le Juste 2*, 107–23 / "The Paradox of Authority" in *Reflections on the Just*, 91–105.

sometimes given an active position ("acting," "power-in-common," "consultation," "participation"), and sometimes a passive position ("forgetting," "distribution," or even "authority")? I suggest the following: if first, power-in-common, which first explains the power-dominance relationship within the state, can be used to clarify the power with which social agents in general invest authority-bearing institutions,[36] and if, second, the two sides of power-in-common (active and passive) can be forgotten while remaining operational, then we could consider Ricœur's famous *political paradox*[37] as a model for understanding the agent-institution relationship proposed in *Oneself as Another*. I call it the *institutional paradox*.

This claim is based on the following observations, *from the point of view of agents* involved in the interaction –
- agents live to a large extent by conforming to the mores that structure their interaction;
- by doing so, collectivities (institutions) are generated;
- within these collectivities, individuals participate and institutions participate in a controlled [*réglée*] manner;
- despite their interaction, which establishes institutions, the inter-acting agents forget the instituting force of their action; and
- the life of institutions often precedes and continues after that of participants.

Since this is the case, then, *from the point of view of the institutions* –
- the institutions established come to be something else and more than just the cumulative effect of agents who interact;
- institutions achieve a longevity and durability and agents experience them not only as regulations for distribution, but also as hypostasised;
- this durability does not exclude the transformation of institutions, since, if every institution is preceded by other institutions, this means that institutions are changing gradually; and
- while denying institutions any subjectivity, they acquire in this way a stability and capacity that I may call "personified", as is evidenced, for example, in the phenomenon of authority.

From these characteristics of institutions arise two contradictory effects – hence the paradox: *on the one hand, institutions can exist at the expense of individuals*[38]

---

[36] Ricœur, *Soi-même comme un autre*, 299 / *Oneself as Another*, 196.
[37] The political paradox was discussed in the Introduction, §3.2 and subsequently invoked in Chapters 3, §5 and 4, §4.1.
[38] As is illustrated in the Conclusion, §2.

and, on the other hand, the effectiveness of institutions nevertheless remains essential to enable individuals to live fully with others. If we now page back to Chapter 3, §5 it appears that institutions display exactly the same paradoxical structure as the technical dimension of action in general. And again, we noted a similar paradoxical structure in organized action in Chapter 4, §4.1. The fact that institutions are partially technical entities gives them the traits of a specific kind of technical paradox.

Clarifying though this view on the relation between agents and institutions may be, it does not explain the *mode of existence* of institutions. During the discussion, we encountered institutions as rules and as regulators of distribution, as ephemerally regulated action and as support of durable action, as repetitions of instituting action, but also as constructions. Furthermore, even if we place the emphasis on the "tradition of authority" which provides institutions with legitimacy, this dimension of institutions is not yet sufficient to explain their durability and stability, which can hardly be imagined without an effort of construction and of organization. Finally, there is a certain ambiguity in the way Ricœur uses the term institution: first and foremost as a "rule", but sometimes also as a "historical community".[39] To clarify this ambiguity is the *first task to be accomplished in our conclusion* (see §4 below).

2.2 Second Approach: Practices Between "Basic Actions" (Danto) and "Narrative Unity of Human Life" (MacIntyre)

Having explored Ricœur's understanding of institutions, we can now turn to his view of practices. As we saw in the Chapter 4, §2.2, Ricœur undertakes "a revision in the very concept of action" in *Oneself as Another*.[40] In order to do so, he claims, "[a] hierarchy of units of praxis must be made to appear, each unit on its own level containing a specific principle of organization, integrating a variety of logical connections".[41] This discussion presents us with an alternative approach to the socio-theoretical question in Ricœur, namely the action-theoretical coordi-

---

[39] Thus my exposition complements Johann Michel's discussion of the "conceptual floating" of the "institution" in Ricœur. See Johann Michel, "Le sens des institutions," *Il Protagora* 39 (2012): 105–17.

[40] Ricœur, *Soi-même comme un autre*, 181 / *Oneself as Another*, 152. I tear this sentence out of its context (which is an exploration of narrative identity), but restore its function in *Oneself as Another*, as discussed here. For Ricœur's double debt to Aristotle, see *Soi-même comme un autre*, 203 / *Oneself as Another*, 172.

[41] Ricœur, *Soi-même comme un autre*, 181 / *Oneself as Another*, 153.

nation of agents and their action on the one hand, and of social actors mutually on the other hand.

Ricœur argues that human actions are coordinated by a principle of embeddedness (*enchâssement*). Thus, basic actions (in the sense of Danto) are embedded in larger actions with a view to something. Or to spread out the whole array of embeddings: from "partial actions" to "total actions" (i.e. practices), and then from practices to larger life-plans, to the overarching narrative unity of a life – action forms an intricately embedded complex which aims at realizing the good life. Hence Ricœur (in line with Aristotle and MacIntyre) subscribes to a fundamentally *teleological* vision of action.[42] It is essential to indicate the limits and shortcomings of such an orientation in order to account for social action:

- Even in cases where one would expect to see the teleological scheme confirmed by the reality of action, for example, work in organisations, it has been shown that the scheme remains incomplete as a representation of the course of interactions.[43]
- The distinction between practices as total actions and the "partial actions" by which they are constituted cannot do justice to the way of life of a large part of humanity in which partial actions, the "non-practices" if you will, are the main daily activity, for example, in the semi-slavery of sweatshops.
- Undergoing and suffering cannot enter into a teleological vision of action and remain (despite Ricœur's attempt to do the opposite[44]) outside of actions, since they retain the status of consequences of actions.
- The excellence of virtuoso practices can certainly serve as a benchmark for measuring the tragedy of lives that seem to have lost all direction, but the teleological scheme does not succeed in sufficiently accounting for the actions of people such as the unemployed who have fallen into despair or disoriented refugees.
- In a teleological scheme of action, there is no place for children and their way of doing things.[45]

---

[42] The fact that we follow Ricœur here in a rather Aristotelian train of thought should not make us forget other references (particularly phenomenological sociology) that have played a role in the formulation of his thought on social action.

[43] Cf. the interpretation of Niklas Luhmann's writings on the sociology of organizations and on the notion of goal(s) developed by Hans Joas, *Die Kreativität des Handelns* (Frankfurt am Main: Suhrkamp, 1992), 149 ff.

[44] Ricœur, *Soi-même comme un autre*, 186 / *Oneself as Another*, 157.

[45] Psychoanalyst Donald Winnicott, for example, emphasises the non-teleological nature of children's playing – *Playing and Reality* (London, and New York, NY: Routledge, [1971] 1996), 55.

Here, then, is a *second task* in response to Ricœur: to go beyond the fundamentally teleological scheme of action (see §4 below). More precisely: it is not a question of rejecting *en bloc* the Ricœurian appropriation of MacIntyre's thought (which underlies the discussion of practices) in the service of a reflection on the ethical aim of life,[46] but of questioning the teleological scheme itself in so far as this scheme is proposed as a "revision in the very concept of action".

Although nothing in Ricœur's argument calls into question this teleological scheme, it is nevertheless worth mentioning three points that give this scheme a certain flexibility. First, for Ricœur,

> the practical field is not constituted from the ground up, starting from the simplest and moving to more elaborate constructions; rather it is formed in accordance with a twofold movement of ascending complexification starting from basic actions and from practices, and of descending specification starting from the vague and mobile horizon of ideals and projects in light of which a human life apprehends itself in its oneness.[47]

In addition, the vocabulary of Ricœur pertaining to the course of life remains suspended between "project" and "uncertain", between "plan" and "mobile", between "oneness" (*unicité*) and "fragmentary", between "governed" (*régi*) and "indeterminacy" (all Ricœur's terms). For Ricœur, acting is therefore not to add one isolated act to another and yet another, as one stacks Lego blocks on top of each other; acting means to be caught in the heart of the hermeneutical tension between the whole and the parts.[48]

Secondly, let us insist on a decisive factor which, that, in Ricœur's case, complicates the vision of a simple teleological sequence of actions. This factor emphasises the actors' interpretative and judging capacities, namely the social constitution of action and practices and consists of five elements. In the first instance, through *interaction* with others, we do not act without context. Then, the aiming or directed action of some may result in others undergoing the consequences of that action or even suffering because of that such action – these *passivities* are not easy to arrange in a teleological perspective. Moreover, if it is true that interaction can be *internalized*, as Ricœur asserts, then the presence of ab-

---

[46] We also notice here a similarity with Honneth, who recognizes in MacIntyre one of the rare authors who have theorized non-legal conditions of social justice – Axel Honneth, *Das Recht der Freiheit. Grundriß einer demokratischen Sittlichkeit* (Berlin: Suhrkamp, 2011), 126 and Axel Honneth, *Leiden an Unbestimmtheit* (Stuttgart: Reclam, 2001), 8–9.
[47] Ricœur, *Soi-même comme un autre*, 187 / *Oneself as Another*, 158.
[48] Cf. Ricœur, *Soi-même comme un autre*, 187, 210 / *Oneself as Another*, 158, 179.

sent others may limit what the isolated agent can project as meaningful action.[49] In addition, the *traditional* nature of the practices and their standards of excellence inform the practices and the arrangement of life plans. Finally, the *indeterminacy* and uncertainty that disrupts or complicates the exercise of practices makes absolute initiative impossible for a hypothetical agent-master-of-self-and-circumstances. These five elements converge in limiting the autonomous action of the individual agent.

It is therefore necessary to theorize constraint in the context of Ricœur's theory of social action – a theme which is still present in his thinking on social action in the early 1970s,[50] but then slides away. To comment further on this point is the *third task* of the conclusion (see §4 below).

Thirdly, Ricœur complicates the teleological aim of action by insisting on the uncertainty of its hermeneutical construction and the contextuality of action. *If* the endpoint to which action aims – namely the good life – is "for each of us, the *nebulus of ideals* and dreams of achievements with regard to which a life is held to be more or less fulfilled or unfulfilled"[51], and *if* the desire to live (well) together has the status of "forgotten," as Ricœur says explicitly, and *if* "this constitutive element can be discerned only in its discontinuous irruptions onto the public stage",[52] *then* it must be conceded that the ethical aim, the ultimate teleological point, is "firstly and mostly"[53] mobile, eclipsed or fuzzy. As a result, the "top-down specification" of the teleological structure by the ethical aim (mentioned above) remains very much in the background in a large part of daily life.

If this is the case, one may wonder what maintains the relative stability of social and institutionalized action despite the uncertainty associated with its ul-

---

49 Here, a dialogue can be established with Bourdieu on the notion of *habitus*. See Ricœur, *La mémoire, l'histoire, l'oubli*, 266 / *Memory, History, Forgetting*, 542–43, Gérôme Truc, "Une désillusion narrative? De Bourdieu à Ricœur," *Tracés* 8 (2005): 47–67, and Michel, "L'*habitus*, le récit et la promesse," 17–27.
50 Paul Ricœur, "Le modèle du texte: l'action sensée considérée comme un texte" [1971], in *Du texte à l'action*, 205–36 / Paul Ricœur, "The Model of the Text: Meaningful Action Considered as a Text" in *From Text to Action*, 144–67.
51 Ricœur, *Soi-même comme un autre*, 210 / *Oneself as Another*, 179, my emphasis.
52 Ricœur, *Soi-même comme un autre*, 230 / *Oneself as Another*, 197, my emphasis.
53 I intentionally use this expression, a translation of Heidegger's "zunächst und zumeist" in *Being and Time*. By his Aristotelianism (including his criticism of Aristotle's instrumental aspect), his reflections on the teleological structure and concern, and through the importance given to oblivion – Ricœur invites comparison with Heidegger (which is, however, beyond the scope of this chapter).

timate anchoring. Attempting to answer this question is the *fourth task* of the conclusion (see §4 below).

3 Giddens: Individual and Society in Structuration Theory

Before addressing the four tasks identified in this discussion of Ricœur, let us turn our attention to Giddens's theory of structuration. I begin by presenting a general perspective of his theory of action on the basis of which to demonstrate the broad compatibility of the two authors on this point. Thereafter, I discuss in more detail some aspects of Giddens's social theory relevant to our conclusion.

3.1 Giddens: Action, the Original Sociological Problem

At the centre of the theory of structuration is action.[54] However, the view advanced by Ricœur and MacIntyre, that single actions would be embedded in broader practices and these in turn in encompassing life plans, is completely avoided by Giddens: "Human action occurs as a *durée*, a continuous flow of conduct [...] 'Action' is not a combination of 'acts': 'acts' are constituted only by a discursive moment of attention to the *durée* of lived-through experience".[55]

Such action belongs to an agent who is driven by bodily motives, but for the rest acts "knowingly". This *knowledgeability* in action is obviously mostly tacit, but Giddens acknowledges in it an ability to "rationalize": when they are challenged, the agents can give more or less precise reasons for what they are doing.[56] The ability to rationalize their actions implies a practical form of attention to the flow of action. Between the practical know-how of actions and its discursive rationalization, agents also have an intermediary awareness of action

---

[54] For this entire section, see also Anthony Giddens, "Agency, structure," in *Central Problems in Social Theory: Action, Structure and Contradiction in Social Analysis* (London: Macmillan, 1979), 49–95, and Anthony Giddens, *New Rules of Sociological Method: A Positive Critique of Interpretative Sociologies,* 2nd ed. (Stanford, CT: Stanford University Press, [1976] 1993), Chapter 2. See also Theodore Schatzki's review, "Practices and Actions. A Wittgensteinian Critique of Bourdieu and Giddens," *Philosophy of the Social Sciences*, 27, 3 (1997), 283–308, which we cannot explore here.

[55] Anthony Giddens, *The Constitution of Society. Outline of the Theory of Structuration* (Cambridge, and Malden, MA: Polity, 1984), 3 (all translations mine). See also Giddens, *New Rules of Sociological Method*, 86–87 on the identification of individual actions.

[56] Giddens, *The Constitution of Society*, 5–6.

which Giddens calls "reflexive monitoring of action".[57] Through reflexive monitoring, agents can observe more or less consciously their own actions, the actions of others, and the context in which all these actions take place.[58]

The details that Giddens provides of this capacity for reflexive monitoring are rare and insufficient.[59] Even so, it is clear that he sees this capacity as a specialization of the practical conscience of knowledgeable action,[60] as "chronically" linked to the flow of action[61] and as an integral part of the "reflexive capacities"[62] of agents. By drawing from phenomenology and pragmatism, one could quite easily propose a clearer description of reflexive monitoring, while remaining close to Giddens's programme. Competent action can be disrupted[63] and is indeed very often disrupted during its execution. These disruptions cover the entire range of intensity, from very low to overwhelming, and can be very different in nature (physical, practical, perceptual, temporal, modal, cultural, etc.). They direct or reflect the actor's attention to the action itself. These events are sufficiently recurrent to accompany actions (certainly, with interruptions, although Giddens does not state it explicitly) – hence the term "monitoring". At the same time, in their most intense manifestations, these disruptions represent challenges which require that attention, once reflected back to action, be transformed into a "strategic" judgment serving to redirect action, if necessary.

With this clarification in mind, we can now join Giddens again. Reflexive monitoring of action makes possible and sometimes encourages "reflexive self-regulation".[64] Through such reflexive self-regulation, agents modify a part of the flow of action so as to aim at a purpose. The teleological orientation or *purposiveness*[65] of many actions enters only gradually into the course of action.[66] In

---

57 Giddens, *Central Problems in Social Theory*, 51.
58 Cf. Giddens, *The Constitution of Society*, 3, 5
59 Cf. for instance Giddens, *The Constitution of Society*, 44. It is not even certain that the definition provided in *The Constitution of Society*, 376, captures this idea correctly.
60 Giddens, *The Constitution of Society*, xxiii.
61 Giddens, *The Constitution of Society*, 5.
62 Giddens, *The Constitution of Society*, xxii.
63 Cf. Giddens, *The Constitution of Society*, 281.
64 This notion is, in my opinion, very important for Giddens's theory, although it is barely mentioned in the text of *The Constitution of Society*. However, its definition can be found in the glossary: "Causal loops which have a feedback effect in system reproduction, where that feedback is substantially influenced by knowledge which agents have of the mechanisms of system reproduction and employ to control it," *The Constitution of Society*, 376.
65 On the hierarchy of ends, see Giddens, *New Rules of Sociological Method*, 84, 89–91.
66 And explicitly not from the outset, as in the voluntarist theories – *The Constitution of Society*, 3.

other words, the whole action of agents is not teleologically organized from the outset, but is rather capable of (partial) modification in view of realizing purposes or carrying out tasks. Although Giddens can therefore claim repeatedly that agents are able to intervene in a state of affairs and bring about changes, in other words, to exercise transformative power,[67] he is obliged to specify that "[t]he knowledgeability of human actors is always bounded on the one hand by the unconscious and on the other by unacknowledged conditions/unintended consequences of action".[68]

Giddens explores this bounded rationality and contextuality of action further by using Merleau-Ponty's analyses in the *Phenomenology of Perception*. He states that the bodily agent is formed internally by each specific activity, directed towards a world (or being "in the world") and oriented towards others.[69] One "faces" someone or something,[70] is situated in relations to the past (and, one may suppose, to the future),[71] takes into account one's social position,[72] recognizes a relational, actional and routine framework that "gives meaning" to the action, etc.[73] Thus, the situated interaction is oriented interaction that seeks to reflexively adapt its course of action. This course of action presupposes a practical rationality.

Two important consequences follow from these descriptions. On the one hand, agents cannot interpret themselves directly, but must go through the reflexivity that accompanies action and gives an image, not of an "I", but of a "self" or a "me".[74] On the other hand, consequently, the philosopher or scientist

---

[67] Giddens, *The Constitution of Society*, 15. Power precedes subjectivity and reflective monitoring of action (see *The Constitution of Society*, 15), i.e. that power is above all a capability (and in this case Giddens seems to me to be relatively close to Ricœur).
[68] Giddens, *The Constitution of Society*, 282.
[69] Cf. detail Giddens, *The Constitution of Society*, 64–68.
[70] Giddens, *The Constitution of Society*, 67, 112.
[71] Giddens, *The Constitution of Society*, 49.
[72] Giddens, *The Constitution of Society*, 84.
[73] Giddens, *The Constitution of Society*, 87.
[74] Giddens, *The Constitution of Society*, 7, 51. Giddens's thought on this point is far from being sufficiently elaborated. Nevertheless, the passages devoted to this question show at least a "family resemblance" with the hermeneutics of the self, thematized with such sophistication by Ricœur. See Giddens, *The Constitution of Society*, 52: "The 'I' is an essential feature of the reflexive monitoring of action but should be identified neither with the agent nor with the self. [...] The 'I' has no image, as the self does. The self, however, is not some kind of mini-agency within the agent. It is the sum of those forms of recall whereby the agent reflexively characterises 'what' is at the origin of his or her action."

who wants to explore human action afterwards, encounters the object of exploration as already meaningful – a fact which Giddens refers to as the "double hermeneutics" typical of the social sciences.[75]

3.1a Giddens and Ricœur: Profile of a Significant Overlap

Let us interrupt the discussion of Giddens's social theory at this point in order to take stock of the *correspondences (and of one difference)* with Ricœur's social theory. (a) The key role given to action of more or less competent agents, (b) the double hermeneutics, (c) and the reflexive hermeneutic structure of action, which aims to avoid a metaphysics of the subject without evacuating the acting subject, show a major overlap between these two attempts to find an alternative to objectivist or subjectivist theories. Let us anticipate also that the two authors (d) agree on the centrality of the notion of power[76] to understanding the ability to act socially (see Point 10 below in §3.2) and (e) present a comparable view of institutions as structures of action and systems of distribution (see Point 8 below in §3.2). Both points confirm the proximity of the two authors. This very substantial overlap, I argue, allows us to borrow additions, or even corrections, from the one to the other, without violence to their respective projects. This is a decisive point, since it could already be indicated that this important overlap goes hand in hand with at least one considerable point of *disagreement:* Ricœur and Giddens discuss the internal structure of the action in two significantly different ways, the keywords "embeddedness" and "flow" representing their respective points of view.

3.2 Giddens: Action and Duality of Structure – Some Specifications

Giddens gives us a whole series of specifications that elaborate on and complexify the central part of structuration theory. An advanced discussion of the elements most relevant to our current concern is essential to prepare the conclusions that will follow.
1. *Body, certainty, routine.* A particularity of human action (compared to the inconsistent use tolerated by tools) is that the acting bodily agent needs a con-

---

75 See Giddens, *The Constitution of Society*, 284, 374; Giddens, *New Rules of Sociological Method*, 86. It should be noted here that Giddens refers to many of Ricœur's texts. However, these references are too rare and too brief to conclude that Ricœur had an important influence on Giddens.
76 Compare Point 10 below, with the central notion of "I can" in Ricœur.

text of relative certainty – provided by a framework of relatively predictable routines – in order to mobilise the relatively autonomous capacity of the body.[77] According to Giddens's thesis, "[a] sense of trust in the continuity of the object-world and in the fabric of social activity [...] depends upon certain specifiable connections between the individual agent and the social contexts through which that agent moves in the course of day-to-day life".[78] It is the regular exercise of the body in the execution of routines that provides this basic trust or confidence,[79] also known as "ontological security". The relative vagueness of this description will need to be clarified in the conclusion.[80]

2. *Unexpected consequences and recursiveness.*[81] We have seen that agency is defined by the possibility of making a change in a sequence of events. However, this does not mean that the results of this intervention all correspond with the intention of the agent.[82] From a social theory perspective, these unintended consequences are essential to explore "the mechanisms of reproduction of institutionalized practices".[83] These unintended consequences of actions (coupled, one should add, with the intended consequences) can consolidate subsequent action plans or gradually change them. This fact, called "*recursiveness*", is easily illustrated by an example from language:[84] people conversing in English (most often) do not speak *in order to* consolidate the grammar and vocabulary of this language; however, the consolidation of this grammar and vocabulary is an unintended consequence of the use of English. The English language is not only the *consequence* of the conversation, but also the *medium* that makes this conversation possible. And

---

[77] Cf. Giddens, *The Constitution of Society*, 50, 51–64.
[78] Giddens, *The Constitution of Society*, 60, see also 86–87, 282, and Giddens, *Central Problems in Social Theory*, 123–28.
[79] Cf. Giddens, *The Constitution of Society*, 36: "All social systems, no matter how grand or far-flung, both express and are expressed in the routines of daily social life, mediating the physical and sensory properties of the human body."
[80] Giddens, *The Constitution of Society*, 60.
[81] The theme of unintended consequences has been touched on in both discussions of incapability (see Chapter 3, §2.1 and Chapter 4, §3).
[82] Here, Giddens is not far from Norbert Elias, when Elias says that the figurations are "[f]rom plans arising, yet unplanned; by purpose moved, yet purposeless," *The Society of Individuals*. [1987] The Collected Works of Norbert Elias, volume 10. Robert van Krieken (ed.) (Dublin: University College Dublin Press, 2010), 62 (see my discussion of this point in Chapter 2, §1). More explicitly, he uses texts by Raymond Boudon.
[83] Giddens, *The Constitution of Society*, 14.
[84] Giddens, *Central Problems in Social Theory*, 67, 77–78; Giddens, *The Constitution of Society*, 170 – or the example of chess (cf. *Central Problems in Social Theory*, 65).

this applies even if it must be added right away that (having reached the point where they are able to speak English thanks to the English language) the interlocutors gradually modify this medium.

3. *Structure and duality of structure.* Recursiveness describes how social interaction "follows rules" while being carried out in "full knowledge of the facts." Giddens prefers the notion of structure for this phenomenon and specifies that structures include both rules and resources. Thus, he can define structures as "recursively organized sets of rules and resources [...] out of time and space [i.e. they exist virtually[85]], save in its instantiations and co-ordination as memory traces and is marked by an absence of the subject".[86] In addition, structures are characterised by a duality that is generally recognized as the core of the theory of structuration.[87] Giddens describes this duality as follows: "Structure as a *medium* and *result* of conduct that it recursively organizes; the structural features of social systems do not exist outside action but are chronically involved in the production and reproduction of action."[88] It is important to note that the processes of change and reproduction extend as far as the structure itself: from individual actors to the largest communities or institutions.[89] The three main types of structures – meaning, domination (allocative or authoritative) and legitimization – govern the differentiation of institutional orders (see Point 8).

4. *Enabling, constraining.* Giddens insists that the unintended consequences, as well as lasting social structures, may well exercise a constraining effect on the action of the actors through their power extended in space-time (see Point 6). But this constraint is in principle always accompanied by facilitation or enablement, albeit always to varying degrees.[90] Thus the enablement is associated with constraint from the level of the individual agent's body, up

---

85 Cf. Giddens, *Central Problems in Social Theory*, 55: "structure" as equivalent of "virtual space-time" (also Giddens, *Central Problems in Social Theory*, 64; *The Constitution of Society*, 17).
86 Giddens, *Central Problems in Social Theory*, 25.
87 See the references provided by Stones, *Structuration Theory*, 4–5.
88 Giddens, *The Constitution of Society*, 374 (my emphasis). Giddens defines his notion of "structure" in opposition to the definitions used in functionalism, Marxism or structuralism – cf. Giddens, *The Constitution of Society*, 16–17 and Steven Loyal, *The Sociology of Anthony Giddens* (London, Sterling: Pluto Press, 2003), 71–74.
89 Stones, *Structuration Theory*, 5, 16, proposes, following McLennan, the use of the term "duality of structure-and-agency." This is an acceptable proposition: if the structure is "dual" or double by being both medium and result, agents are also "dual," being both constrained and capable – these two facts mutually imply each other.
90 As Giddens claims, *The Constitution of Society*, 31–32, approving's Foucault's understanding of discipline.

to that of interaction with systems[91] and must be considered in consequence of the fact that, at all these levels, actions are structured by rules and resources. In fact, enablement-constraint is only another way of talking about the duality of structure.

5. *Systems or social systems.* The duality of structure implies that through structured action, something is reproduced or transformed, called "system"[92] or "social system". Giddens understands social systems to refer to relatively stable patterns of *activities* or *situated practices*, which are generated and reproduced by rules and resources (= structures) of action, and which in this way reproduce relatively stable *relations* and *patterns of relations* between agents or collectivities, with the latter being formed to varying degrees of coherence (systemness). It is difficult to deny that the notion of system is very close to the definition of structuring or structuration. Does this justify the recurring complaint that there are too many concepts in Giddens? I don't think so. On the contrary, I propose to read "structuration" as including both structure and system: as a substantivized verb, "structuration" refers to the performance of (virtual) structures, which become concrete or instantiated as the transformation of (real) systems. Structuration and "systematization" imply each other, structures (in the process of becoming) being properties of systems (in the process of becoming).[93] The proximity of the notions of structure and system is not a flaw – it is the essential point. The structure-system pair thus captures the ambiguity of the term "institution" (see Point 8).

6. *Time-space distantiation.*[94] The relative stability of these systems and the practices that constitute them may, depending on the case, be increased in spatial and temporal extension. This extension is made possible and carried out by the characteristics of the resources that structure systems. Technologies that enhance the efficacy of actions in the dimensions of space and time (notably transport and communication technologies) thus play a central role in distantiation. Therefore, the extension of the systems is at the

---

91 Cf. Giddens, *The Constitution of Society*, 117, 172–73.
92 Cf. Giddens, *The Constitution of Society*, 19.
93 Giddens, *Central Problems in Social theory*, 66. See also *The Constitution of Society*, 25, where structuration is defined as "[c]onditions governing the continuity or transmutation of structures, and therefore the reproduction of social systems."
94 Giddens writes "distanciation". I follow the *Oxford English Dictionary*'s spelling: "distantiation".

same time the extension of their power,[95] of the enablement and constraint exercised by their structures.

7. *Social and system integration.* Structured action, we have said, reproduces systems, understood as practices and patterns of relationships between actors. For this reason, interaction often has an integrating effect between actors. Integration must be understood as regularised links or reciprocal practices – it does not necessarily imply cohesion or consensus.[96] Giddens distinguishes two types of integration: that which is achieved when actors interact in "co-presence" and that which is achieved when actors interact through resources of the spatio-temporal extension of the action, i.e. without "co-presence".[97] For this distinction, he uses David Lockwood's terminology: social integration and system integration.[98] The impression Giddens leaves is that these are two distinct processes; this is unfortunate.[99] On the one hand, the presentation of his theory thus far allows us to appreciate that even the most intimate face-to-face interaction can gradually contribute to the reproduction of social systems (strictly speaking, there is a system from the moment there are at least two agents, very similar to what we have seen in debate with Debray, there is transmission as soon as there is communication, see Chapter 1, §3).[100] On the other hand, the most anonymous, the most mediated interaction can inform the action in co-presence. Therefore, the two forms of interaction deserve to be designated *both* social *and* systemic, albeit to varying degrees.[101] It is important to distinguish between the two dimensions of integration, because it gives us the means to describe the range of relationships between what Ricœur calls the *I* and respectively the *you* and the *it*, while avoiding assigning the *I-you* exclusively to a micro-sociology and the *I-it* exclusively to a macro-sociology.[102]

---

[95] Cf. Giddens, *The Constitution of Society*, 258–60.
[96] Giddens, *Central Problems in Social Theory*, 76.
[97] See the definitions in Giddens, *The Constitution of Society*, 376–77.
[98] "Social integration" refers to the relationships between actors, "systemic integration" refers to the relationship between the parts of the social system. For a critical discussion of this adoption of these constructs by Giddens, see Nicos Mouzelis, "Social and System Integration: Lockwood, Habermas, Giddens," *Sociology* 31, no. 1 (1997): 111–19.
[99] To some extent this is conceded by Giddens, *The Constitution of Society*, 28, and implicitly *The Constitution of Society*, 36.
[100] Cf. Giddens, *Central Problems in Social Theory*, 73.
[101] This has been well described by Alfred Schütz – see the discussion of degrees of anonymity in Chapter 4, 2.1.
[102] Cf. Giddens on this subject, *The Constitution of Society*, 139 ff.

8. *Institution*. If one considers the importance of the distinction between systems (regular and reproduced practices) and structures (rules and resources), it is disappointing that Giddens did not clarify his understanding of institution better. If "institution" corresponds to practices, as he claims at some places,[103] then it is a notion of system; if "institution" corresponds to "chronically reproduced rules and resources", as he claims elsewhere,[104] it is a notion of structure.[105] In my view, it is only by accepting and coordinating both of these *two* visions of the institution (as both structure-like and system-like) that consistency can be restored to the presentation of institutions. *As practices*, the notion of "institution" refers to practices with the greatest spatial and temporal extent,[106] their extension being made possible by space-time distantiation. That institutions pre-exist individuals and remain after them[107] is an additional consequence of their extension and stabilisation.[108] However, this "long duration" of institutions[109] must be attributed to the same degree to the fact that they are structures: *as structures*, institutions are both consequences (partially unintentional) and media or mediations of individual actions[110] that structure their long-term practices, also called "institutions". Let us recall on this point that while Ricœur defines institutions as structures and therefore as "irreducible to interpersonal relationships", he insists on the fact that institutions are nevertheless linked to interpersonal relationships (quoted at the beginning of this chapter). Thus, whatever the differences between them may be, the two authors agree that institutions are constituted in a way that cannot simply be decomposed into intangible rules and interpersonal relationships (even without co-presence).

9. *Society(-ies)*. The term *society* is very close to the idea of a set of institutions. Actually, Giddens accepts a dual use of the term "society": equally as a

---

103 Giddens, *The Constitution of Society*, 17; Giddens, *Central Problems in Social Theory*, 65.
104 Giddens, *The Constitution of Society*, 375.
105 Supported by Giddens, *The Constitution of Society*, 24; Giddens, *Central Problems in Social Theory*, 65.
106 Giddens, *The Constitution of Society*, 17.
107 Giddens, *The Constitution of Society*, 170.
108 Social systems are "articulated sets" of institutions and are difficult to change because of their relative stability (Giddens, *The Constitution of Society*, 170–71). Social life is, however, not limited to institutions. These are only "the more enduring features of social life" (Giddens, *The Constitution of Society*, 24).
109 Cf. Giddens, *The Constitution of Society*, 35–36.
110 Cf. Giddens, *The Constitution of Society*, 27, 36; Giddens, *Central Problems in Social Theory*, 95.

"bounded system" and as a social association in general.[111] A society is therefore not simply the aggregate of all the inhabitants of a state, since within the state itself there is overlap of a variety of societies (or processes of associating).[112] Rather, societies are open, but limited by relationships with other systems[113] and by the internal articulation of institutions. Giddens identifies and explores four kinds of typical institutions – symbolic, political, economic and legal institutions.[114]

10. *Power.* The phenomenon of power cuts across all the notions discussed so far. Let us therefore finally underline some of its features, according to Giddens's very complex thinking about it. First, power is defined not as the pursuit of the interests of a section of actors, but as a feature of any (inter)action, namely the possibility of producing results.[115] This understanding of power, already involved in the Giddensian idea of action as the ability to introduce a difference into a sequence of events, is very close to that of Ricœurian capability, that is, the power of "I can". In that sense, power cannot be transcended.[116] In fact, the power *practised* is involved in the full extent of structural duality as a consequence and a means of action. So, power is involved in both enabling and constraining action.[117] As a result, power is (with meaning and normativity) a modality of structuring that is exercised through resources.[118] This includes both "allocative" and "authoritative" resources – both essential for increasing power and its spatial and temporal extension,[119] which infiltrates social and system integration.[120]

---

111 Giddens, *The Constitution of Society*, xxvi.
112 Cf. Giddens, *The Constitution of Society*, 283.
113 Cf. Giddens, *The Constitution of Society*, 164, 165. The discussion of the types of "societies" and related concepts such as "time-space edges" and "structural principles" fall outside of my use of Giddens, in which I follow Stones, as explained above.
114 Giddens further develops his theory of institutions in Chapter 3 of *Central Problems in Social Theory*.
115 Giddens, *New Rules of Sociological Method*, 116–20; Giddens, *The Constitution of Society*, 16, 257; Giddens, *Central Problems in Social Theory*, 83, 88.
116 Giddens, *The Constitution of Society*, 32.
117 Giddens, *The Constitution of Society*, 169.
118 Giddens, *The Constitution of Society*, 16.
119 Giddens, *The Constitution of Society*, 260.
120 Cf. Giddens, *New Rules of Sociological Method*, 118 ff.

4 Conclusion: Contributions of Structuration Theory to the Hermeneutics of the Capable Human

Through the exposition of two important moments of the social theoretical framework of *Oneself as Another*, I have identified four tasks to be accomplished:
1. to transcend the fundamentally teleological scheme of the action;
2. to explore the stabilisation of action despite the uncertainty inscribed in the teleological scheme;
3. to reinvest the notion of constraint; and
4. to clarify the ambiguity of the notion of institution.

In order to show how Giddens helps us to accomplish these tasks, I propose to experiment with a graft, formulated in the following thesis: the description of action as a continuous flow subject to the duality of structure could be transplanted into the hermeneutics of human capabilities, without essential loss. On this basis, I wish to coordinate Ricœur's hermeneutics of action and Giddens's structuration theory.

Task 1. The argument by which to overcome the fundamentally teleological scheme of action (in as far as this scheme serves the "revision in the very concept of action"[121]) in favour of an alternative is made in two steps.

First, it must be demonstrated that the patient and donor have *compatible* bodies. By emphasising, above, the overlap of Giddens's and Ricœur's views in respect of (a) the centrality of action for theory, (b) the double hermeneutics, (c) the reflexivity of the post-metaphysical subject, (d) the conjunction of power and action starting from the capabilities of agents and (e) the dual approach to the constitution of institutions (as a rule and as practice), I believe that I have argued their compatibility sufficiently (to be qualified below).

Then, it is necessary to demonstrate that the transplant would not cause violence to the patient and that the result would be able to do the same job as what it replaces. Giddens's account of the flux of action, which allows for teleological modification without being fundamentally teleological, can do just this. Commenting on the flux of action, Giddens says that its "unintended consequences are *regularly 'distributed'* as a side effect of regularized conduct and reflectively supported as such by the *participants*".[122] This citation demonstrates

---

121 Ricœur, *Soi-même comme un autre*, 181 / *Oneself as Another*, 152.
122 Giddens, *The Constitution of Society*, 14 (my emphasis) – however, unlike Ricœur, without reference to Rawls.

that the flux of action can account for the duality of structure. The duality of structure in turn accounts for the "mechanism" of participation/distribution in the relationship between agents and their institutions. In other words, Ricœur's view of social integration through participation/distribution does not have to depend on the overstated teleology of action, but can be accounted for from a view of the flow of action and the duality of structure. And this modification remains completely compatible with the hermeneutics of human capabilities.

If these two points are accepted, then we may anticipate good convalescence for the patient. I do not ignore the fact that structuration theory does not provide a view on the ethical aim of life, which plays such an important role in Ricœur's understanding of action. Nevertheless, since structuration can account for teleological modifications of the action flow,[123] the grafting of a Giddensian view of action onto Ricœur's understanding of action does not require the abolition of the ethical aim. After all, it is one thing to claim that ethics is fundamentally actional and exercises an effect of teleological modification on action; it is another to claim that action as such is fundamentally teleological – one may reject the second claim, while holding onto the first. Rather, our understanding of this ethical aim needs to be completed in order also to include the non-teleological and non-praxis-shaped ways of acting (i.e. forms of action that do not constitute sets of embedded actions as in Ricœur's notion of practice).

The other contributions of structuration theory to Ricœur's social-theoretical framework stem from this successful "transplant".

Task 2. We have seen in Ricœur the uncertainty of the "top-down specification" with which the ethical aim of life weighs on the teleological structure of practices. The question on what stabilises life despite the absence of a sure and unchanging life plan can, in my view, be addressed by a Giddensian rehabilitation of routine. I speak here only about relative stability, the opposite of which would be random actions. Routine-based action, I would argue, is the fluctuating intermediary between a life that is wholly structured by embedded practices aiming at one clear aim and a life of a chaotic sequence of gestures. Therefore, routine could provide the "ontological safety" without which neither consistently successful practices nor striving for the good life are possible.

---

[123] This modification has been captured by my terms "primary technicity" and "secondary technicity" of action – see Chapter 3, §§ 3.1 and 3.2 and Ernst Wolff, "'Technology' as the Critical Social Theory of Human Technicity," *Journal of Philosophical Research* 41 (2016): 333–69.

However, we cannot agree with this proposal if the notion of routine (left rather vague by Giddens) is not clarified. Let us consider the two nuclei of meaning of this term, identified by Marc Breviglieri: "one refers to a gesture that is mechanically accomplished by habit, the other to a sequence of action aimed at an outcome in a technical procedure".[124] In the first sense, the teleological dimension is negligible, in the second it is essential. My proposal that routine can buttress life, despite the uncertainty imposed by the vagueness of the ethical aim on the teleological structure of the action, cannot be valid if routine is itself defined teleologically (second sense). Routine can support "trust in the continuity of the world of objects and in the fabric of social activities"[125] only as long as the non-teleological (but not shapeless, accidental or hazardous) takes precedence over teleology, planning or programming. For the large part, it is therefore a matter of the routine of "intimate and bodily habituation with an environment".[126] In addition, it seems plausible that daily interactions are at least partially marked by such routine habituation (yet without participating in planning). François Dubet captures this idea of routine very precisely: "None of us can live in a state of permanent tragedy and hardship [*épreuve*] in which one should constantly make fundamental choices, prioritize one's interests, stage oneself [*se mettre en scène*], solve a host of cognitive and normative problems [in other words: consciously arrange one's entire life teleologically – EW][...][s]o we have a set of routines that are not internalized programs, but conduct carried out in a state of very attenuated vigilance".[127]

Task 3. A third contribution by Giddens to the hermeneutics of the capable human would be a reflection on constraint. This is not developed by Ricœur in *Oneself as Another*,[128] but we are invited to explore this question by his

---

124 My translation. Marc Breviglieri, "Le fond ténébreux de la routine. À propos des morales du geste technique au travail," in *L'ordinaire et le politique,* eds. Sandra Laugier and Claude Gautier (Paris: PUF/Curapp, 2006), 189–217, here 189.
125 Giddens, *The Constitution of Society*, 60.
126 Thévenot, "Des institutions en personne," 20.
127 François Dubet, *Le travail des sociétés* (Paris: Seuil, 2009), 291–92. One should certainly confront this idea of routine with Ricœur's own reflection on habit, ever since *The Voluntary and the Involuntary* (Paul Ricœur, *Philosophie de la volonté 1. Le volontaire et l'involontaire* (Paris: Point, [1950] 2009) / *Freedom and Nature: The Voluntary and the Involuntary,* trans. Erazim Kohák (Evanston, IL: Northwestern University Press, 1979)).
128 Of course, the theme of the human being as suffering from or undergoing the effects of events and others' actions marks the place which constraint can be reflected upon throughout this book. And here too one could gain insights from Ricœur's earlier work, notably by examining the figures of the "involuntary" in *The Voluntary and the Involuntary.* The question of being

view of society as a distribution system: is the ability of each actor to take part in this system not restricted by the part he/she receives? Giddens provides us with a morphology of constraint in three parts: (a) constraints imposed on action by the physical conditions of the body and the space of action, (b) constraints due to the exercise of authoritarian power, and (c) constraints that result from the structuration of agents' interaction.[129] In all three cases, Giddens tries to demonstrate that these hamper or obstruct agents' ability to act knowledgeably, rather than impose ways of acting.[130]

Task 4. The last contribution of a Giddensian readjustment of the field of action in the hermeneutics of the capable human relates to the two aspects of structure. On the one hand, they are the *rules* of interaction (which correspond to the place Ricœur gives to "constitutive rules of practices" and mores [*moeurs*][131] – and which he also describes as the "structure" of living-together[132]); on the other hand, they are *resources*, which in turn cluster resources of authority and resources of allocation. It should be remembered that "resources" refer to what generates and propagates power, either by the domination of nature, objects or material phenomena (in the case of allocative resources), or by the domination of agents by others (in the case of resources of authority).[133] Having already discussed authority in Ricœur (above), let us focus on the resources called allocative.[134]

In Chapter 3, §§1 and 3, I have demonstrated that there is a significant omission in the hermeneutics of the capable human, namely the skills and means of

---

conditioned by history, is also discussed in Ricœur, *Temps et récit 3*, 391–414 / *Time and narrative 3*, 216–29 under the title of "Being-affected by the Past".
129 Giddens, *The Constitution of Society*, 174–179 and see *The Constitution of Society*, 113 for Point (a).
130 I do not expand on this point further because Giddens has already been criticised for not giving a sufficiently convincing place to constraints in his theory of action (see Stones, *Structuration Theory*, 58–61, 109–115.) This theme is yet to be explored.
131 Ricœur refers to "the bond of common mores and not [...] constraining rules" (*Soi-même comme un autre*, 227 / *Oneself as another*, 194) – a rigid opposition that finds its meaning only in connection with the specification: "[B]efore constraining, norms order action, in the sense that they configure it, give it form and meaning" (*Du texte à l'action*, 272 / *From Text to Action* 195). In other words, they facilitate and constrain.
132 Ricœur, *Soi-même comme un autre*, 227 / *Oneself as Another*, 194.
133 Cf. Giddens, *The Constitution of Society*, 33, 258, 373 and our discussion above.
134 I acknowledge that Ricœur gives a specific place to authority in his thinking (see, for instance, the standards of excellence and the authority of institutions) and I enter into debates on the virtuality of resources in Giddens here (see Stones, *Structuration Theory*, 68–73).

action.[135] All the previous chapters have been offered to build out this shortcoming. Structuration theory adds to this effort. By linking resources to rules of action in a single definition of the structure, Giddens integrates precisely the means of action and the context of action (for as long as it is made up of constraints and enablements due to allocative resources). This is already a significant point for the individual agent who embarks on a course of knowledgeable action by means of resources. But then spatial and temporal distantiation spreads the effect of the allocation of resources over all reciprocal interactions without co-presence. Thus, communication and transport technologies,[136] above all, are responsible for the spatial and temporal extension of structures. All along, the allocative resources of structures have an effect of relative autonomisation of practice complexes, in internally articulated institutions or in relatively stable societies. Hence, distantiation[137] gives collectivities a character that is not only linguistic: through distantiation, collectivities acquire an "autonomy" relative to the agents whose action institutes them. This is in a way quite similar to the autonomy of texts, according to the analogy proposed by Ricœur (cf. Chapter 1, §4.2 on this autonomy, and Chapter 4, §2.1 for a development on organizations). Thus, the relative autonomisation achieved by resources clarifies central elements of the Ricœurian vision of institutions: it is only because allocative resources are an integral part of the structure of action and of the spatial and temporal distantiation of action that we can accept that institutions are objectivized, that they support the duration of power-in-common and thus contribute to the development of individuals' action.

However, this autonomy is equally a source of the obstructive functioning of allocative resources. Hence we arrive, by another way, at identifying the technical paradox, of which the institutional paradox is a derivative (see discussion in §2.1d, above).

---

135 Certainly, we have seen Ricœur's adoption of MacIntyre's "standards of excellence". However, if I am not mistaken, there is no analysis of competence as a component of action in the hermeneutics of the capable human.
136 For example, Giddens, *The Constitution of Society*, 201.
137 This theme has yet to be further explored in relation to the hermeneutics essays of the 1970s in Ricœur, *From Text to Action*.

Intermediate Reflection: Tools for Critique

1 Something Is at Stake

A first round of explorations into the technicity of action has now been completed. In Chapter 1, the appropriateness of a hermeneutic approach to this aspect of action has been defended. At the same time, I demonstrated the presence of technicity in the heart of the human interaction of the emission, transmission and interpretation of meaning, in other words, in the efficacy of symbols. In Chapter 2, I examined the technicity of action as a feature of human existence, over the whole span of human civilizations and with all the variation and cultural specificity that capabilities and means may have at any specific place and time. The interplay between capabilities and means has been studied as a dimension of the understanding interaction that people have with their world. Through an exploration of the interrelation of capabilities and incapabilities in Chapter 3, it was possible to get a grip on the contingency and uncertainty of action as action. Chapter 4 expanded this view on the technicity of agency by considering the technicity of organized action: the agency of individuals in organizations and of collectives as organizations. Again, the interrelation of capabilities and incapabilities provided a view on the way adverbial increments of action vary as action plays out. Finally, aspects of the broader social theoretic framework of the previous chapters were studied in Chapter 5. The question of the teleological structure of action and the relation between agents and institutions has been clarified and its technical dimensions have been highlighted.

Looking back over the five chapters in this way, one observes the major thrust as descriptive, clarifying and detailing. Still, each time this descriptive work opened up a view on the *stakes* involved in the respective views on the technicity of action. If symbols have efficacy, as I argued in Chapter 1, this calls for vigilance regarding the use people make of them, the power relations symbolic efficacy draws from, maintains or creates. Hence the question of social asymmetries, and in particular those depending on symbolic violence. Chapter 2 showed how people's self-understanding is influenced by the technical dimension of interaction and how people come to play social roles that are technical acquisitions, as much as normative constructions. But such roles, and the ideals they embody, may also be imposed on people (for example, under degrading and exploitative working conditions from which some people cannot escape). Furthermore, the politics of debate about the improvement of people's fate or about the values to be enforced by technical means is itself co-constituted by a technico-normative milieu that is constantly presupposed in exchanges. In Chapter 3, I identified the paradox of the technicity of action: while it is indispensable in the reinforcement of action to increase its efficacy, the technicity may always turn against those who activate it. There is no escaping this paradox by simply reducing capabilities and means, since this amounts too easily to conditions of relative capability deprivation. The same applies to the agency of organizations, which is subject to a similar paradox, and generates similar issues of deprivation, as can be seen from Chapter 4. Moreover, the sheer power of organized action magnifies the relevance of this paradox, as has been evoked by the complexities of identifying and dealing with risk. Finally, in Chapter 5, we encountered a third version of the same paradox, namely the institutional paradox. It too is a derivative of the structure of technicity of action. Through their long and wide spatio-temporal extensions, institutions allocate resources, means and power and may thus amplify the effects of maldistribution, exclusion, political vulnerability, etc.

These stakes stretch over a very wide range of personal, social and political fields. They do not form a systematic ensemble, but together illustrate the pervasiveness and ubiquity of the sense that something is at stake because of the technicity of action – stakes which could be explored in a more systematic way. It seems as if the discussion leans towards socio-political critique, but stops just short of theorizing such a critique. This impression is not only entirely accurate, it is also a position I have consciously assumed. This position requires some clarification and justification.

2 On Critique

Let us first consider from which perspective and to what extent the previous five chapters may be called critical. Roughly following Luc Boltanski, I distinguish between two kinds of social scientific critique on the basis of their "simple" or "complex" exteriority.[1] One assumes a position of *simple exteriority* by taking a spectator's position, outside of the normal unfolding of social events, in order to subject the phenomena to careful study and reporting. Here, critiquing means bringing to light what may be overlooked, or what may be too vast to be observed by participants in the usual course of events. Critique is then exercised as if the aspect of reality studied appears arbitrary, but has to be clarified as nec-

---

[1] Luc Boltanski, *De la critique. Précis de sociologie de l'émancipation* (Paris: Gallimard, 2009), 23–25.

essary. Furthermore, such scientific work is critical in pursuing accurate and coherent descriptions, learning from experts and falsifiable reporting. By contrast, one assumes a position of *complex exteriority* by first taking the position described as simple exteriority (since critiquing in the second sense depends on the descriptive accuracy provided by the first). But this is coupled with a normative assessment. Critiquing in this sense fulfils the functions of unmasking or denouncing. It typically exposes what things are and the values they have obtained in society as exploitative, dominating or unjust, rather than as just powerful.

Clearly, in the five chapters of Part I, I attempt to be critical in the sense of simple exteriority. But do these chapters assume a position of complex exteriority? Should they?

A first step in the direction of critique in the more incisive sense was taken by examining the articulation and transmission of ideas, including critical ideas, insisting on the quest for the "effectiveness of symbols" (Chapter 1). A second step in this direction consisted in emphasising the uncertainty of action and the fluctuations of (in)capabilities in achieving what agents set out to perform (gradually set out in Chapters 2, 3 and 4). Perhaps the clearest advance towards a critical position was the repeated insistence on the paradox of technicity (in general, but also in organized action and in institutions, as in Chapters 3, 4 and 5). These paradoxes speak to the ambiguity of outcomes which the technical dimension of action enables people to realize. This ambiguity calls for assessment and judgement; the identification of ambiguity itself arguably serves as a springboard for critique. Still, even then, the position of complex exteriority is never fully assumed.

But is this a failure? In developing a theory of the technicity of action into a full critical theory, one would have to hesitate at one very specific threshold, namely the fact that *that in terms of which* one may advance such a critique is not an aspect of the technicity of action. I have touched on this fact in passing. In Chapter 1, I explained that establishing the validity of ethical ideas which are transmitted is a competence neither of a hermeneutics of action, nor of mediology. Likewise, in Chapter 4, we saw that, as much as planning is part of the functioning of organisations, the aims pursued – that which is valued – is not itself part of the technicity of organized action. In general, one would have to concede that a development of a critical theory of the technicity of action would require the deployment of intellectual means appropriate to establishing the normative orientation of such a critique. Clarification and justification of such an orientation fall beyond the scope of a hermeneutics of the technicity of action.

3 Towards the Intricate Relations between Technicity and Ethics

However, this does not at all mean that everything normative or ethical is thereby banished from my exploration. Quite the contrary: the normative and ethical concerns of action are given their due place, and this is the focus of Part II. However, all norms and ethics are approached from a merely descriptive point of view, that is, from the perspective of their functional legitimacy alone, as is required by the assumption of simple exteriority.[2]

What such a position shows up is how significantly, all the time, the technicity of action is infused with normative or ethical concerns. Conversely, that by which ethical "transcendence" has to gain reality is precisely the technicity of action. The three chapters of Part II thus demonstrate how two aspects of action – the technical and the ethical – are both aspects of the meaning of action, albeit more or less evident in particular cases, *and* in this overlap, the one depends on the other. In order to get a good grasp on this fact, one has to suspend one's judgement on the *de jure* or actual validity of norms, while giving due attention to their *de facto* or functional validity. Only in this way can the assumed position of simple exteriority do its work of informing a complex exteriority. I confess that it is ultimately my desire to intervene critically in the fullest sense that informs, in advance, my exploration of the technicity of action (a point to which I will come back in Chapter 6).[3] In other words, refraining from a full critical development of my study is justified as a provisional demarcation of its objective and scope.

Therefore, I do *not* say that the hermeneutics of the technicity of action explores the field of *application* of an ethics that has to be established elsewhere by putting practice out of play. What the normative foundation or orientation of critique could be or should be cannot be determined in abstraction, separate from the social reality in which it can finally come to mean something concrete. Rather, the assumption of the restriction of simple exteriority has to include an examination of the technicity of action *as* an attempt to give efficient effect to "value". Thence comes my insistence, above, on the pointers to complex exteriority already present in Chapters 1 to 5 and the attention I accord hereafter to the ethical dimension of the technicity of action in Chapters 6 to 8. Still, as long

---

[2] Contenders for "transcendence" may be religious, traditional, anthropological, metaphysical or historical. The emergence and legitimation of such values fall outside this demarcation. On this theme, see, for instance, Hans Joas, *The Genesis of Values* (Cambridge: Polity Press, 2000).
[3] This effect of anticipated complex exteriority on the work undertaken in an approach of simple exteriority has been discussed by Boltanski, *De la critique*, 36–37.

as the provisional demarcation is assumed, the means by which to elucidate the normative basis of a critique remains insufficient. This restriction can be lifted only by adopting other theoretical and philosophical means suitable to clarifying the generation of values from the very practices described here,[4] while they are not simply reducible to the perspectivism of each particular context of action. On the one hand, establishing the normative orientation therefore requires a broader theory of society (far beyond the outline offered in Chapter 5, and much more specific than the general anthropological perspective of Chapter 2). On the other hand, critique would gain validity if it can be demonstrated to express more than the frustration of individuals' moral expectations. Some form of exploration on how to evaluate divergent and contradictory ethical claims is thus also required.

With all of the above in mind, a new characterisation of the enterprise of this book is now possible. A hermeneutics of action, and its technical dimension in particular, aims at giving an account of a specific dimension of the common matrix of social interaction from which emerge both the flourishing and the oppression of people, from which both confirmation and critique can become understandable responses. Furthermore, it accounts for the entanglement of these divergent tendencies in human interaction and provides analytical and descriptive means without which the distinction between constructive and destructive tendencies in real life cannot be made, even if these analytical and descriptive means on their own still remain insufficient for this task of critical discernment.

4 Working in Anticipation

But how feasible is it to exclude all normative considerations from the present task? How long could (or should) one persevere in abstaining from judgement in descriptive and explanatory work? Since theoretical work is itself already a form of interaction, and as such is already integrated in circuits of meaning (technical as well as ethical), the feasibility of suspending one's judgement should not be overestimated. In two ways it seems justifiable to have one's descriptive work already informed by a critique (even if it cannot itself theorize this critique yet), lest it undermines the very meaning of the demarcated project itself. First, one has to assume that ethics itself is not devoid of meaning; one has to anticipate that moral nihilism will not have the last word, even if one

---

[4] Cf. Titus Stahl, "The Metaethics of Critical Theories," in *The Palgrave Handbook of Critical Theory*, ed. Michael J. Thompson (New York, NY: Palgrave Macmillan US, 2017), 505–23.

does not yet know how nihilism is to be overcome. Second, if ethics itself is not void or meaningless, one further has to assume that some forms of meaningful compromise between contradictory ethical claims will not remain impossible indefinitely. Let us call these the anticipated *ethicity* and *sufficient decidability* respectively. In other words, by allowing these two points of anticipation to filter through into a descriptively demarcated project, I also anticipate that, once the critical extension of my work is in place (even though I do not yet know how this is to be achieved), it will prove me right in now refusing to theorize as if nothing ethical is at stake.

Chapter 6 deals to a great extent with the kind of social interaction which constitutes philosophising. Like Chapter 1, it is concerned with symbolic efficacy, but now the two points of anticipation will guide the examination. Here the proto-critical nature of our book is situated in a broader proto-critical vocation of hermeneutics in general. From this perspective, hermeneutics aims at furnishing the tools by which to describe the common matrix of action, whether the consequences of action turn out to be beneficial to people's lives or detrimental to them. Hermeneutics is the study of things as meaningful – in the fullness and fragility of meaning. That is why the threat of meaning due to moral uncertainty or due to the plurality of contradicting claims without an instance of arbitration informs hermeneutics.

Hence, Chapter 6 gives an indication of how my entire book is directed by the anticipation of legitimate critique, or in the terms of Okolo Okonda, which are discussed in that chapter, "praxis triggers the hermeneutical process and gives it an orientation".[5] True to the complexity the book strives to account for, human diversity is presented as both a threat and a potential in this process. Besides, the general anthropological set-up of the book requires that human diversity be taken into account as far as possible (as already pointed out at the end of Chapter 2). This fact goes some way toward justifying the very specific social scientific material which I deploy to advance the exploration of the entanglement of technicity and ethics in Chapters 7 and 8.

---

5 Okolo Okonda, *Pour une philosophie de la culture et du développement. Recherches d'herméneutique et de praxis africaines* (Kinshasa: Presses Universitaire du Zaïre, 1986), 46.

Part 2: **Finding Compromises in Practice**

Chapter 6:
Of What Is "Ricœur" the Name?
Or, Philosophising at the Edge

1 What's in a Name?

In 2007, Alain Badiou published a little book with the title *De quoi Sarkozy est-il le nom?* – Of what is "Sarkozy" the name?[1] The delightful rhetorical trick of this wording confronts the reader with a choice: either you respond with a lame analytical truth: "Sarkozy is the name of... Sarkozy", or you take up the challenge of looking for something else, something further and more significant, of which the person, Nicolas, is only a figure-head, the bearer of the name.

In this chapter I ask in a similar way: of what is "Ricœur" the name? Someone who has in mind Ricœur's later hermeneutics of the self may object that this is not a very Ricœurian question. After all, *Oneself as Another* teaches us how *not* to ask the question "*what* kind of *thing* a human being is," but "*who* a *person* is". However, my concern here is not the self-attestation or identification of one specific individual, Paul, but rather the significance of his work. My question is thus in agreement with the spirit of his earlier textual hermeneutics. I want to explore what he called "*la chose du texte*", the thing of the text, that which the text is about, and for which the name "Ricœur" is the simplest metonymic reference. What then are we speaking about, when we speak about Ricœur? To which concerns does the body of work called "Ricœur" direct our attention?

In responding to these questions, I do not attempt to provide a synoptic view of Ricœur's entire work. I rather attempt to increase the *conflict of interpretations* about his work by examining a set of things of which Ricœur is the name, one set of concerns that can be traced in most of his work.

But this question itself is posed by someone, who writes from somewhere, with a part of his life history behind him and his heart full of questions and worries. I confess, then, that this chapter is also a small part of my own attempt to think through life at the social "edge"[2]: living in a country brought to the brink,

---

[1] Alain Badiou, *De quoi Sarkozy est-il le nom ?* (Paris: Éditions Lignes, 2007). Parts of the present chapter have been developed in my *Lire Ricœur depuis la périphérie. Décolonisation, modernité, herméneutique* (forthcoming). This accounts for a few overlaps of content, which will not be indicated each time.

[2] I borrow the polysemic term "edge" from Johan Snyman, "Filosofie op die rand," *Koers* 62, no. 3 (1997): 277–306. The "edge" (*rand*) at which he philosophised is also the "ridge of the

to the edge, of civil war by totalitarian violence, the contemporary omnipresent threat of outbursts of violence, people living on the edge of unbearable trauma through exploitation and poverty, etc.[3] (aspects of which are dealt with more directly in Chapters 7 and 8). But I also reflect on the position of the philosopher as somebody who stands far enough from the edge of action and events to be able to witness them – which also involves being, like other witnesses, somehow traumatised by what one is a witness to – all the while realizing the unspeakable good fortune of escaping the worst trauma oneself.

I think Ricœur found himself in a similar situation shortly after the Second World War. Confronted with recently published articles on the fate of colonized peoples, Ricœur wrote a short reflection entitled "The Colonial Question" (1947).[4] It is an indignant outcry against the "edge" of inhumane life at which the colonized are left to languish; it is written in the awareness of his philosophising in response to this "edge". The influence of this concern reaches deep into the course of Ricœur's intellectual life, as I intend to show.

3 "The Colonial Question"

Ricœur's declared intention in this essay is to clarify, and henceforth to awaken every day, the responsibility of a non-expert in respect of the colonies. Although Ricœur writes here explicitly as a Christian and also for a Christian readership,[5] he declares that the responsibility he has in mind is based on one's citizenship (in this case his French citizenship) and a lack of expertise does not relieve one of this responsibility. In fact, the feeling of responsibility emerges from the plight of the colonized:

---

white waters" (Witwatersrand) – the rich and tragic mining region in South Africa where we both grew up.

[3] Recently, I have given an account of this history in Ernst Wolff, *Mongameli Mabona. His life and work* (Leuven: Leuven University Press, 2020).

[4] Paul Ricœur, "La question coloniale," *Réforme* 3, no. 131 (20 September, 1947). I have prepared a re-edition of this article for the Fonds Ricœur, which is available at https://bibnum.explore.psl.eu/s/psl/ark:/18469/1z0z0#?c=&m=&s=&cv=, last accessed 5 February 2021. The following references are to this edition and the translations are my own.

[5] But later he is more specific: "At least, these principles have the virtue of being half way between belief [*foi*] and politics; which is morality itself, incapable of inspiring as a belief [*foi*] and lacking all the technical competence required by politics." Ricœur, "La question coloniale," 4. However, one may ponder whether "foi" should here be translated as "belief" in a religious or non-religious sense, or as "faith".

...their claim shatters me, when it turns against us the moving themes of national liberation that our struggle brought against Nazism. I'm afraid I may be a Nazi without knowing it. I hear those Germans protesting lamentably when we tell them about Auschwitz: 'We didn't know'. And we condemn them victoriously: 'Your fault is that you didn't know'. I do not know much about the French oppression in the colonies and I fear that my fault is, mainly, the fault of omission to get myself informed.[6]

What perspective does Ricœur offer his readers, then, on the colonial question? He advances five principles:
1. As seen from his perspective in 1947, the only remaining legitimate objective of the entire colonial project is to bring an end to colonization and to guarantee the liberty of the indigenous populations.
2. France, and similarly the other colonial powers, have to recognize the unilateral violence of the colonizing act: "The use of violence by peoples who aspire to freedom does not increase our good right: the colonial enterprise is contaminated/invalidated [*viciée*] from the beginning by cunning and violence. [...] as the occupying force we have from the beginning an indelible priority in violence."[7]
3. Ricœur declares that "[t]he trap of the colonial spirit is racism; the basis of the right of indigenous peoples is universalism."[8] This means that the anticolonial protesters are more "French" than the inheritors of the "Universal declaration of the rights of man and of the citizen".
4. With his typical taste for paradox, Ricœur observes that "[t]he frantic and often premature thirst for freedom that drives separatist movements is the same passion that is at the origin of our history of 1789 and Valmy, of 1848 and June 1940, it is of no use to say that this thirst is frantic and premature".[9] Even a supposedly immature drive for liberty always normatively outweighs the imagined virtue of paternalism. That such a quest for national liberty may lead to disastrous consequences may be read in the pages of European history (cf. World War I). Europeans knew before the other peoples how to fire their desire for liberty to the point where nationalism boils

---

6 Ricœur, "La question coloniale," 2. In 1990, he still writes: "The idea of culpable negligence is of great importance in this type of debate, as has been resoundingly echoed by the tragic events of World War II." Paul Ricœur, *Soi-même comme un autre* (Paris: Seuil, 1990), 339n4 / *Oneself as Another*, transl. Kathleen Blamey (Chicago, IL and London: University of Chicago Press, 1992), 293n89.
7 Ricœur, "La question coloniale," 3.
8 Ricœur, "La question coloniale," 3.
9 Ricœur, "La question coloniale," 3. Ricœur's article was published on the day of commemoration of the Battle of Valmy (20 September 1792).

over, with catastrophic consequences. However, the problem here is that people did not sufficiently relativise the importance of their nation with reference to the whole of humanity; the problem is not the desire for liberty itself. Hence Ricœur's generalization – "[t]hey are right to do as we did, to want to be free ahead of schedule; they are wrong, as we were, to want to take this unnecessary detour through the nation state"[10]. As Ricœur states in his concluding paragraph, first, all people have to be liberated, then, together, all can fight as free people against the danger of nationalism.

5. But one might object that movements calling for independence (Ricœur calls them "mouvements séparatists"[11]) represent only a minority of the population. Still, Ricœur is willing to give these movements the benefit of the doubt, because they articulate the first "awareness" (*prise de conscience*[12]) of the normative dimension of the problem. Here one should take note of the decisive significance of the category "*prise de conscience*" for good political action in Ricœur's early philosophy.

Ricœur's essay is short, but its critique of the colonial enterprise is carefully argued, nuanced and unequivocal. In subsequent years, he never returned to the justification of this principled anticolonial stance. Rather, henceforth, it seems that he thought the injustice of the colonies and the need for decolonization had been sufficiently dealt with to require mere referencing.[13] At the same time, it would be incorrect to think that his essay is like a fireworks display – spectacular, but quickly gone. On the contrary, one may trace two lines of continued reflection on colonization/decolonization in Ricœur's work from this point on: the first is his *political* view on the post-colonial world order (§4); the second is a more philosophical and cultural critical reflection on decolonization and modernity (§5). *If we want to understand what the name "Ricœur" stands for, we need to have a look at the coordination between these two lines of thought.*

---

10 Ricœur, "La question coloniale," 4.
11 Ricœur, "La question coloniale," 4.
12 Ricœur, "La question coloniale," 4.
13 This does not imply that there is nothing to elaborate on, but Ricœur seems to be sufficiently convinced, and could subsequently also count on sufficient consensus, to move on to dealing with other problems, cf. "examples on which there is precisely a consensus: we do not tolerate racism, anti-Semitism, apartheid or, in another area, the sexual exploitation of children for commercial pornography." Paul Ricœur, *Lectures 1. Autour du politique* (Paris: Seuil, 1991), 306.

4 Ricœur's Anticipation of Global Politics after Independence

A snapshot on Ricœur's changing political views is "True and False Peace" (1955).[14] It was published a few months after the beginning of the Algerian war of independence and seven years before its end. It was presented as a paper a few days after the Bandung Afro-Asian conference, which he welcomed as being of great historico-political significance. He devotes several pages of this paper to decolonization.

Interestingly, there is no justification of an anti-colonial stance in this article. Ricœur already writes from a post-independence perspective. His reflection on the burning geopolitical issues of his day is focused on the following paradox: two opposing visions of the economic organisation of human societies – capitalist and communist – hold the same destructive potential – in fact, so massively destructive that outright victory of any one side over the other is likely to entail the destruction of the conditions of life for all the winners too. Since self-destruction is no option, the only remaining option is peace. But will it be a true or a false peace? That is Ricœur's question. False peace is the construction of a balance between a liberal and a communist bloc – presented through Manichean ideological simplification as absolute opposites. A true peace would reveal the underlying similarities and complexities of the geopolitical order.

Decolonization is a central component of Ricœur's understanding of a global political order and the possibility of peace. What the ideology of the "two big blocs" hides was revealed at Bandung, namely the reality of a complex network of international stakeholders. But Ricœur remains perplexed about the means by which these new role-players could assume their rightful position in international politics (cf. Principle 4 of "The colonial question"). Finally, he concedes these nationalisms *may* play a progressive political role, *may* be a legitimate means by which to attain political autonomy, on three conditions:
- *if*, as liberation movements, they articulate the "awareness" (*prise de conscience*) of foreign oppression,
- *if*, as attempts to re-anchor people in history and land, they signal a return to "popular and local culture", and
- *if* they can realize people's aspiration towards modernisation.[15]

---

14 Paul Ricœur, "Vraie et fausse paix" (1955), as republished in *Autres Temps* 76–77 (2003): 51–65.
15 See Ricœur, "Vraie et fausse paix," 58.

Schematically, then, decolonization unleashes the plurality of cultures; nationalisms give geopolitical force to this plurality and in this way undermine the simplistic geopolitical ideology of there being only two opposing camps. Yet, political reality is more complex: small countries tend to align themselves with big powers, even at the risk of losing some of their independence and cultural specificity. In this regard, Ricœur underscores the corrupting potential of American capitalism, but is slightly more positive about the influence of Russian and/or Chinese communism on the African continent. Such a communism is to be approved, provided that the concomitant philosophy of materialism does not smother local "cultures" or "spiritualities", but rather merges with them.[16] By the way, before concluding that this is mere conservative culturalism, remember that we are standing here on the eve of *African* socialisms – as far as African politics is concerned, Ricœur finds himself in very good company.[17]

Therefore, the countries that are struggling for their independence should be assisted in attaining real independence – not a new form of dependence on one of the two blocs. Interestingly, France has a role to play in progressive decolonization (for which Ricœur, surely idealistically, thought that the Union Française provided the framework): by first assuming its own independence completely and not aligning itself with the capitalist or communist bloc, France could strengthen the hand of the newly independent states, and thus prevent them from (over-)aligning with either the communists or the capitalists, for the same reasons. Or, one may conclude that France was to help the nations literally or symbolically gathered at Bandung to remain non-aligned, so that France could align itself with them and by so doing, retain its own independence! This was, as far as Ricœur can see, the surest path to "real peace".[18]

---

[16] Ricœur, "Vraie et fausse paix," 59.

[17] Cf. Introduction to Saïd Bouamama, *Figures de la révolution africaine. De Kenyatta à Sankara* (Paris: Découverte, 2017), 5–18, and William Friedland and Carl Rosberg, *African Socialism* (Stanford, CA: Stanford University, 1967).

[18] A similar position has been confirmed from a contemporary view on the geopolitical order by Bertrand Badie, *Quand le Sud réinvente le monde. Essai sur la puissance de la faiblesse* (Paris: Découverte, 2018). His point is also that the entire geopolitical order should be reviewed in light of the up-to-now insufficiently recognized significance of decolonization.

The importance of France's non-alignment is already anticipated in Paul Ricœur, "Le chrétien et la civilisation occidentale" (1946), as republished in *Autres Temps* 76–77, (2003): 23–36, where Ricœur advocates a positioning of France independent from Russia and America, and drawing its energy first of all from its own inventive core. For background, see François Dosse, *Paul Ricœur. Les sens d'une vie (1913–2005)*. Edition revue et augmentée (Paris: La Découverte, 2018), especially 192–93.

Having thus demonstrated that *"Ricœur" is the name for an anti-colonialism developed into a view of strategic geopolitical alignment with the variety of decolonized states*, I move on to the second line of development.

5 Ricœur's View on the Philosophical and Cultural Critical Consequences of Decolonization

On the one hand, Ricœur was deep under the impression of the epochal change brought about by decolonization; on the other, this new reality was in the first place not to be regarded as a source of conflict or struggle (a "clash of civilizations") but as the emergence of the richness of human existence. A last citation from "True and False Peace" brings together all of these themes:

> the Bandung conference [the rallying point and symbol for decolonization – EW] reminds us that the facts are stubborn and that the world will not let itself be ordered into two battle lines. There is latent, potential diversity that seeks to express itself. Modern reality, in its human depth, is not dualistic, but really pluralistic. So, when we speak of French independence, we are alone only in appearance and at first glance, that glance which is sensitive only to the strategic device of the camps [capitalist and communist – EW] and not to the human richness of our globe.[19]

We gain a better view on this globalized plurality by turning to the 1961 essay: "Universal Civilization and National Cultures".[20] It captures Ricœur's diagnosis of the post-independence world. The same diagnosis applies, albeit in two distinct ways, to what he calls the "industrialized" and the "underdeveloped" nations of the earth.

---

19 Ricœur, "Vraie et fausse paix," 66. The significance of decolonization for a proper, modern European self-understanding is echoed three decades later in Ricœur's reflection in *Time and Narrative:* "Eurocentrism died with the political suicide of Europe in the First World War, with the ideological rending produced by the October Revolution, and with the withdrawal of Europe from the world scene, along with the fact of decolonization and the unequal – and probably antagonistic – development that opposes the industrialized nations to the rest of the world", Paul Ricœur, *Temps et récit 3. Le temps raconté* (Paris: Seuil, 1985), 369–70 / *Time and narrative 3.* Transl. Kathleen Blamey and David Pellauer, (Chicago, IL: University of Chicago Press, 1988), 204.
20 Paul Ricœur, "Civilisation universelle et cultures nationales," in *Histoire et vérité* (Paris: Seuil, 1967), 322–38 (cf. "mondialisation", 324) / "Universal Civilization and National Cultures," in *History and Truth* (Evanston, IL: Northwestern University Press, 1965), 271–84.

Everybody witnessed the rise of a "single world civilization",[21] which is located first and originally in the rise of the *scientific spirit* and then its consequences in the spheres of *technology*, rationally organized *politics* and *economics*, and, finally, aspects of a global *everyday life culture* (clothing, information, consumption, etc.).[22] On Ricœur's reading, the fact that the industrialized nations have been a steady source of this putative "universal civilization" does not mean that Western culture really is universal civilization. One may have preferred to see Ricœur explore the hegemonic rise of this global civilization, however, the significant point he is making is a different one: whereas this universal *civilization unifies and homogenizes* humanity,[23] the new condition of globalization consists of leaving the *plurality* of human *cultures juxtaposed* on the same level: without any normative priority, without any higher order for arbitration. And all peoples face the same tension between the progress of universal civilization and their own cultural heritage.

On the one hand, Ricœur appreciates in universal civilization the unheard-of progress in the form of a self-awareness of humanity, (the possibility of) access to basic goods, and rights and education on a scale previously unknown. On the other hand, he is concerned about the destruction of the cultural treasures of humanity's diverse traditions. Why? Because these traditions represent the creative core of humanity (elsewhere he refers to them as the "raison d'être" of a people), the destruction of which signals the flooding in of a pervasive nihilism.[24] However, the affirmation of the cultural treasures of humanity is not without its own difficulties, exactly because globalization leaves us with no hierarchy and only the juxtaposition of "others"; *we*, whoever that may be, are only one other among all the others.

In a nutshell, the current predicament is twofold: first, the plurality of cultures is not yet negotiated and, second, the articulation of the relation between an expanding universal civilization and the kaleidoscope of cultural heritages

---

[21] Ricœur, "Civilisation universelle…," 322 / "Universal Civilization…," 271.
[22] There are reasons to question the order of originality in Ricœur's presentation, but even if one does not follow him in this schematic chronology of the formation of "universal civilization", this does not affect the core of the problem that he articulates in this essay.
[23] Likewise, one could question how homogenized and unified modern global culture is, but Ricœur's point is simply that it is so sufficiently to contrast to national cultures, as he subsequently does. Cf. Krishan Kumar, *From Post-industrial to Post-modern Society. New Theories of the Contemporary World.* 2nd ed. (Malden, MA, Oxford, and Carlton: Blackwell, 2005).
[24] In an uncommonly apocalyptic tone, Ricœur claims that, taken to its severest extremes, this nihilism would be as destructive for humanity as an atomic war, cf. Ricœur, "Civilisation universelle…," 331 / "Universal Civilization…," 278.

has not yet been figured out. Ricœur points in the direction where solutions might be found:
- *for industrialized/Western countries*, openness to unfamiliar cultural spheres[25]
- *for developing nations*, the difficult negotiation between progress and tradition,[26] and
- *for both*, a dialogue of cultures.

Now, before one makes of this a facile "happy ending", listen to how Ricœur senses the magnitude of the task ahead:

> No one can say what will become of our civilization when it will have truly met other civilizations other than through the shock of conquest and domination [that is, colonization and war – EW]. But we must admit that this encounter has not yet taken place at the level of a real dialogue. That is why we are in a kind of interlude, an interregnum, where we can no longer practice the dogmatism of the one and only truth and where we are not yet capable of overcoming the scepticism into which we have entered: we are in a tunnel, at the twilight of dogmatism, at the threshold of true dialogues."[27]

I would say, we are historically at an "edge".

One can hardly overestimate the importance of these conclusions: they articulate Ricœur's *cultural critical assessment of the world* at that time, and as far as I

---

25 Ricœur, "Civilisation universelle...," 337 / "Universal Civilization...," 283.

26 Cf. Ricœur, "Civilisation universelle...," 329 / "Universal Civilization...," 277: "Thus we come to the crucial problem confronting nations just rising from underdevelopment. In order to get onto the road toward modernization, is it necessary to jettison the old cultural past which has been the *raison d'être* of a nation? The problem often comes up in the form of a dilemma or a vicious circle. The fight against colonial powers and the struggles for liberation were, to be sure, only carried through by laying claim to a separate personality; for these struggles were not only incited by economic exploitation but more fundamentally by the substitution of personality that the colonial era had given rise to. Hence, it was first necessary to unearth a country's profound personality and to replant it in its past in order to nurture national revendication. Whence the paradox: on the one hand, it has to root itself in the soil of its past, forge a national spirit, and unfurl this spiritual and cultural revendication before the colonialist's personality. But in order to take part in modern civilization, it is necessary at the same time to take part in scientific, technical, and political rationality, something which very often requires the pure and simple abandon of a whole cultural past. It is a fact: every culture cannot sustain and absorb the shock of modern civilization. There is the paradox: how to become modern and to return to sources; how to revive an old, dormant civilization and take part in universal civilization."

27 Ricœur, "Civilisation universelle...," 338 / "Universal Civilization...," 283–84.

can see, *this is the question that his hermeneutics is tasked to respond*. This is a major – if not the primary – motivation for Ricœur's hermeneutics.

To support this claim, let us turn to Ricœur's *Symbolism of Evil*, which appeared only one year earlier in 1960. This is usually held to be Ricœur's first important work in hermeneutics. The conclusion of this book famously outlines Ricœur's hermeneutics of symbols. However, to measure how enormous this task is, we have to turn to the introduction of the same book. There Ricœur argues that the hermeneuticist – in this case, the Western inheritor of the Greek philosophical tradition – is, like everybody else, surrounded by a sea of symbols. But, again like everybody else, our hermeneuticist is oriented. "Orientation" accords a *de facto* privilege to certain cultures; in Ricœur's case the Greek and Hebraic traditions. But this means equally that in the hermeneutic view, *de jure*, symbols from all cultural spheres are matters for study. But how can one practically affirm *both* the significance of all "other" cultures (not just pay lip-service to their importance) *and* the orientation of hermeneutics (without implicitly adopting a view from nowhere)? Ricœur makes two suggestions:

1. The Western hermeneuticist may
   - elucidate the sedimentation of our cultural memory [by using] documents relating to civilizations that do not belong to this [Greco-Hebraic] memory – African, Australian, Asian, etc. – and that are very often [our] contemporary civilizations ; [but] the objective similarity that ethnology discovers between them and our own past allows us to use the knowledge of these civilizations to diagnose our own abolished or forgotten past.[28]
   - This seems to indicate that something could be gained by comparing a genealogy of our self-understanding with even the remotest cultural traditions.
2. Or again, one could acknowledge that the Western orientation in hermeneutics does not correspond with the concrete universal. It cannot in fact do so, since it lacks the required input from other cultures. This implies that although the contingency of thinking from a specific history cannot be over-

---

28 Paul Ricœur, *La symbolique du mal* [1960] in *Philosophie de la volonté 2. Finitude et culpabilité* (Paris: Editions Points, 2009), 224 (own translation, modification to fit main text) / *The Symbolism of Evil*, trans. Emerson Buchanan (Boston, MA: Beacon, 1969), 21.

Is there a hierarchy implied in this passage between the cultures from Africa, Australia and (the rest of) Asia vs India and China? The letter of the text contradicts this, and the impression may be due simply to the selectiveness of the examples given. However, Ricœur passes over the question of contemporary comparisons – this is addressed in the following point.

come, progressively more views can be incorporated and thus the Western view can be broadened.²⁹

It has to be conceded that such a confrontation and/or negotiation between cultures has thus far remained the passion of isolated researchers. To change our memory – the tradition of our thought and culture – great works are needed that will re-create our memory by incorporating the (thereafter former) other into it.

Just as in "Universal Civilization…", Ricœur acknowledges that such a massive encounter between cultures has not yet taken place. However, when such encounters will take place, it is sure to be a world historical moment – Ricœur calls it a moment of "foundation" and "re-creation"³⁰ – in the Western framework, comparable only with the encounter of the Greek and Hebraic traditions. What Ricœur does not say in *Symbolism of Evil*, but in "Universal Civilization…" is that decolonization has pushed us to the point, to the edge, where we can no longer avoid this confrontation with the cultural other (other than by new forms of violence). Allow me to exaggerate my conclusion to make this point clear: *"Ricœur" is the name for hermeneutics as motivated by the question: how are we to prepare ourselves for the encounter with others, now that the end of the colonies has revealed the modern world to be a relativistic juxtaposition of cultures?*

5.1 Interim Conclusion: Disillusioned Modernity and the Task of Hermeneutics

I would like to make a few concluding remarks to round off this reconstruction of Ricœur's motivation for hermeneutics.

First, if we were to project Ricœur's later insights on the post-colonial dispensation back onto his initial critique of the colonies, we may conclude that the colonial project was a *double* catastrophe. On the one hand, it was a unilateral act of violence perpetrated against colonized peoples; on the other hand, it was catastrophic as a futile gesture by which the people in whose midst modernity emerged attempted to hide (from themselves, as from others) the real condition of modernity, namely globalized cultural plurality. Liberating the Western mind of this colonial mind-set is thus a logical extension of the initial task of bringing an end to the colonial project. We may call this the *negative task* of hermeneutics.

---

29 Cf. Ricœur, *La symbolique du mal*, 226–27 / *The Symbolism of Evil*, 22–23.
30 Ricœur, *La symbolique du mal*, 226 / *The Symbolism of Evil*, 23.

Second, Ricœur's understanding of hermeneutics opens the door to increasing inclusion of the cultural other. This is part of the *positive task* of hermeneutics. Therefore, looking back at these texts of the first two post-World War II decades and these two conclusions, one has to infer that Ricœur's return to cultural traditions could be construed as a conservative dream of a revival only at the expense of considerable violence to his political concerns and his diagnosis of the contemporary era. Ricœur's point is not to flee the present by withdrawing to our respective paradises of cultural particularism. It is rather a plea to face the tremendous challenge – partially created by modernity, then revealed in the events of decolonization – of one humanity facing a number of problems under a regime lacking any *a priori* hierarchy between traditions. Summarised in a simple formula: post-coloniality as an essential trait of modernity is the frame from which Ricœur's hermeneutics develops. Or again: *"Ricœur" is the name for a hermeneutics of cultural traditions under the conditions of disillusioned modernity.*

However, third, in *Symbolism of Evil* at least, the confrontation with the cultural other takes place while the other is implicitly being represented by the Western hermeneuticist in an attempt to work through and appropriate this otherness. As a model of appropriation, this is probably inevitable, but it still raises the question of how far this openness to the cultural other can be taken by a single hermeneuticist. In response to this question, I need to refer to two components of Ricœur's work, to demonstrate that he was aware of this problem and worked on it. We could cite, on the one hand, his contribution to the work of non-Western philosophers, for example, in the numerous prefaces written to books.[31] On the other hand we should note his published contributions to intercultural philosophy in the framework of his involvement in UNESCO.[32]

---

[31] In Frans Vansina (and Pieter Vandecasteele), *Paul Ricœur. Bibliographie primaire et secondaire. Primary and secondary bibliography. 1935–2008* (Leuven: Peeters, 2008) see references to René Habachi, Nabil Mouannes, Kha Sae-Yang, Bechara Sargi, Beatriz Couch and Humberto Giannini. See also the tribute to Ricœur in the volume *Présence de Paul Ricœur* (Tunis: Beït al-Hikma, 2003) prepared by the Académie Tunisienne de sciences, des lettres et des arts. However, given the strong Western philosophical nature of these books, this point should not be exaggerated.

[32] Among these, the most important are his introductions to *Cultures and Time* (Paris: UNESCO, 1976), 13–33 and to *Time and the Philosophies* (Paris: UNESCO, 1977), 13–30. Also noteworthy are his "Introduction" to *Philosophical Foundations of Human Rights* (Paris: UNESCO, 1986), 9–29, and "Projet universel et multiplicités des héritages," in *Où vont les valeurs? Entretiens de XXIe siècle II* [2001], ed. Jérôme Bindé (Paris: Unesco – Albin Michel, 2004), 75–80. My point is not to hail these works as blueprints for intercultural philosophy (the precise nature of the

These two points amount at least to the suggestion that Ricœur concedes that his own project of hermeneutics requires completion by the cultural other. The very constitution of the postcolonial predicament to which hermeneutics is a response would require that the others' response to the same disillusioned modernity has to be faced by Westerners.

Let me unpack the implications of this point. The postcolonial predicament is that the very cultural life-force from which people act threatens us with nihilism and/or geopolitical conflict. In response to this ambiguity of cultural plurality, hermeneutics is charged with understanding ourselves in this situation. We, whoever we may be, come from a cultural background. However, we are also people living with others in this plurality. More generally, we may claim that if we want to understand ourselves (as people of postcolonial modernity) we can do so only if we also listen to others trying to understand themselves (and they listen to us doing that too). Such engagement with the other does not suspend our contingency, but helps in dealing with the relativism. Hence, if we ask how others deal with Ricœur's question of the postcolonial predicament or disillusioned modernity, this is not a simple nicety, a flight of exoticism, or a fad called "post-colonial studies" – it is essential to confronting the stated predicament. In this regard, it is not trivial to name (as a first step) the significant reception of Ricœur in post-independence Africa.[33] The cumulative message is clear: there is something in Ricœur that helps us, as Africans, to understand our situation even if we are situated quite differently in the global order. *"Ricœur" is the name for something that is also our concern.*

But even this point remains insufficient as long as we have not listened to these authors, making their claims on their own terms. Let us explore this avenue, by turning to at least one example.

---

strengths and weaknesses of these works needs to be studied carefully), but simply to cite the massive evidence of Ricœur's openness towards the philosophies of the whole world.

33 Cf. especially Theophilus Okere, *African Philosophy: A Historico-Hermeneutical Investigation of the Conditions of its Possibility* (Lanham, MD: University Press of America, 1983), Nkombe Oleko, *Métaphore et métonymie dans les symboles parémiologiques. L'intersubjectivité dans les "Proverbes Tetela"* (Kinshasa, Faculté de théologie catholique, [1975] 1979) and Okolo Okonda, *Tradition et destin. Essai sur la philosophie herméneutique de P. Ricœur, M. Heidegger, et H. G. Gadamer* (Lubumbashi: Université Nationale du Zaïre: 1978–1979). More recently, Raphael Okechukwu Madu, *African Symbols, Proverbs and Myths. The Hermeneutics of Destiny* (New York, NY: Peter Lang, 1992) and Vincent Davy Kacou oi Kacou's trilogy: *Penser l'Afrique avec Ricœur* (Paris: L'Harmattan, 2013), *Paul Ricœur. Le cogito blessé et sa réception africaine* (Paris: L'Harmattan, 2014), and *L'herméneutique du soi chez Paul Ricœur. Prolégomènes à une éthique de la reconstruction de l'Afrique* (Paris: Mon Petit Éditeur, 2014).

6 Okolo – "Praxis Triggers the Hermeneutical Process and Gives it an Orientation"

In the remainder of this chapter I engage with the difficult question of how such a dialogue may be constituted. To be precise, we are not thinking of just any exchange between any two random people. *If* Ricœur's own project of hermeneutics requires completion from the cultural other, *and if* studying how others deal with disillusioned modernity is essential to our own dealing with this predicament, *then* we have to show how a dialogue on these terms and with a view to this problem could possibly be set out. My concern here is not the outcome of such a debate, but the structure of it (in as far as it can take place in philosophical practice). I attempt to clarify this issue with the help of Okolo Okonda,[34] one of the younger, major role-players of what Tshiamalenga Ntumba and others have named "the Kinshasa school".[35] Let us look for an entry to Okolo's thought via the theme with which he chose to open his book *Pour une philosophie de la culture et du développement* [*Towards a Philosophy of Culture and Development*] (1986)[36], namely *proverbs*. What could fit better with Ricœur's hermeneutics than an examination of another kind of linguistic expression, alongside symbols, metaphors, and narratives? The transition from Ricœur to Okolo seems to be a natural one. Yet, by this choice of theme, Okolo implicitly identifies his situation in world cultures, a situation that can hardly be further away from that of Ricœur. Let us have a look at this.

Ricœur famously liked to think of philosophical work as having a continuous dialogue with the authors of the past and the present through their books, lying open on his desk;[37] this is how Ricœur thought and wrote. Now, imagine a world where you can enter only if you close all those books; imagine a world where human intelligence circulates independently from books, because...

---

34 Following Zairian/Congolese patronymic practice, the philosopher is called Okolo.
35 Tshiamalenga Ntumba, "Die Philosophie in der aktuellen Situation Afrikas," *Zeitschrift für philosophische Forschung* 33, no. 3 (July – September, 1979): 428–43, here 433. For a historical perspective on the position of Okolo's early work in the panorama of African philosophies, see A. J. Smet, *Histoire de la philosophie africaine contemporaine. Courants et problèmes* (Kinshasa: Limete, 1980), 232–33.

 I am currently finalizing a volume on African philosophical hermeneutics in which a whole chapter will be devoted to Okolo. The very thin slice of his work presented here is motivated by the specific problem stated in this paragraph.
36 Okolo Okonda, *Pour une philosophie de la culture et du développement. Recherches d'herméneutique et de praxis africaines* (Kinshasa: Presses Universitaire du Zaïre, 1986).
37 "Paul Ricœur: un parcours philosophique." Interview with F. Ewald, *Magazine littéraire* 390 (2000): 20–26.

there are none: no ancient philosophical texts, no Holy Scripture, no published poetry, no volumes of historiography, no printed constitution, no handbook of linguistics. Imagine an oral culture. In such a world, the extraordinary philosophical capability of Ricœur is reduced to nothing, because it simply does not belong there.[38] We are in the world of the mnemosphere, the importance of which I insisted on in Chapter 1 (especially §3.2).

There was a time when many people looked upon this contrast between oral culture and the mountains of published thought in the West as suggesting that intelligence cannot circulate in such a world. Yet this is precisely the paradigmatic situation from which so many of the first post-independence African philosophers thought and, indeed, many contemporary African philosophers think. The beginnings of contemporary *written* African philosophy do not start with ancient documentation of the autonomous affirmation of philosophical reason – as with Greek philosophy[39], but with the very existence of such a rationality being questioned by others.

A very simplified and schematic history of the emergence of written philosophy in Africa since World War II can help us to appreciate the significance of proverbs in respect of the core concern of this tradition. A "first generation" of authors strongly affirmed both that Africans were quite as gifted with reason as all other humans, and that they were *philosophising* long before the tragic advent of their "civilizers". These ethno-philosophers claimed to have pin-pointed African philosophy by studying the languages and oral literature of African peoples and by synthesizing their underlying metaphysical, ethical, and anthropological insights. With their languages and oral literatures, Africans safeguarded and transmitted the thought – indeed, the philosophy – of the ancestors through the troubled colonial era to our day. Therefore, when Okolo later focuses on proverbs, he is not merely investigating a kind of linguistic utterance – he is returning to the *locus of debate* on
- the conditions for the possibility of African philosophy,
- the defence of the rationality and thus the human dignity of African peoples, and

---

38 This does not mean that Ricœur was ignorant of the question of orality. See Paul Ricœur, "Philosophy," in *Main Trends of Research in the Social and the Human Sciences*, Part 2/2. Legal Science. Philosophy, ed. J. Havet (The Hague, Paris, New York, NY: Mouton-Unesco, 1978), 1071–1567, here 1367.
39 In the framework of this schematic presentation I do not consider the place of ancient Egyptian thought in African philosophy. On this question, see Théophile Obenga, *La philosophie africaine de la période pharaonique, 2780–330 avant notre ère* (Paris: L'Harmattan, 1990).

– the attempt to subvert a presumed basis of European chauvinism (the claim of intellectual superiority), and thus continue to dismantle the heritage of colonialism, which is a major point of orientation in African politics.

So, when speaking about proverbs with Okolo, we are ideally situated for the kind of debate to which Ricœur's thought opens, but that he cannot complete by himself. It is ideal because the proverb as oral literature, depending as it does on an oral socio-cultural world,[40] represents an important *other* vis-à-vis Ricœur's writing-dominated world; at the same time, as a significant cultural fact of many divergent peoples, proverbs are a theme around which philosophers from different traditions may *gather*.

But these introductory remarks are still insufficient to appreciate what an intercultural hermeneutics of linguistic utterances would mean. To appreciate the complexity of setting up such a debate in a meaningful way, we have to consider two dilemmas faced by Okolo due to his situation *in* African philosophy.

As a "third generation" African philosopher, he cannot simply participate in the celebration of the intelligence of traditional African culture, because the "second generation" has spoiled the party. They did so by critiquing the "first generation's" very ethnographic attribution of a "philosophy" to all Africans, without qualification, thus attributing to traditional African societies a set of universally and unanimously held ideas. Paulin Hountondji,[41] a key second generation philosopher, claims that there is actually no philosophy underlying the cultures studied by first generation ethnophilosophers; the ideas they formulate are projected onto African tradition, but are in reality the invention of the philosopher. According to him, there is indeed such a thing as African philosophy, but it is to be found not directly within African traditions, but rather in the books of ethnophilosophers. This is a great *and* disturbing conclusion: great, because he still affirms the reality of an African philosophy; disturbing, because it amounts to making European philosophy the measure for philosophy in Africa after all (European particularity just happens to be universal). And thus the question of pre-colonial African philosophy independent of the European mind is raised again. Therefore, if Okolo wants to philosophise about proverbs as an *African* philosopher, he has to work his way through this critique.

His second problem is related to his philosophical practice itself. For an African philosopher, as an *African* philosopher, the questions of culture, heritage,

---

40 Cf. Chinua Achebe, *Things Fall Apart* (London: Penguin, [1958] 2006), 7: "Among the Igbo, the art of conversation is regarded very highly, and proverbs are the palm-oil with which words are eaten."

41 Cf. Paulin Hountondji, *Sur la "philosophie africaine"* (Paris: Maspéro, 1976).

history, origin and therefore situation are of defining importance. Yet, as a person who also participates in modernity and "global civilization", Okolo practises a philosophy that is shaped by his doctoral research at a more or less western styled university, developing debates in writing (publishing in journals and books), with a view to exchanging ideas with colleagues elsewhere in the world.[42] Thus, on the one hand, he should be careful not to take his own practice for granted, in such a way that he inadvertently declares the European mode of philosophising, the European agenda and concerns, to be the standard. On the other hand, he cannot pretend to be a pre-colonial African, for instance, as if his own culture is purely oral.

In short, Okolo is *part of the same globalizing, homogenizing universal culture – even if he is situated quite differently in it – and he knows this to be the case.* Now, how will he deal with these dilemmas? By choosing proverbs as the focal point, he can deal with all these issues at once.

What qualifies them as theme for debate? Proverbs exist first of all as a component of oral exchange. Second, they are exchanged and thus spread over space and transmitted over time. Third, proverbs have a recognizable stability. Fourth, proverbs contain ideas about a variety of aspects of life. Fifth, the second, third and fourth traits conjoin to make of proverbs a form of literature. In fact, based on these latter traits we may claim that proverbs, though oral, form text-like entities.[43]

Their text-likeness has made it possible for scholars to catalogue and systematise proverbs, thus allowing Okolo and his colleagues a synoptic view, in printed version, from which to launch his study. Okolo captures his own conclusions in three claims:

Claim 1: Proverbs don't think. The wisdom of proverbs cannot be systematized into a systematic whole. At least three facts can be cited in support of this claim. First, different proverbs reflect different life situations (family, profession, etc), different stages of life (youth, old age, etc.), different socio-economic conditions (poverty, wealth, etc). Second, proverbs contradict each other. Third, tradition transmits only an ideologically biased selection of proverbs, so the collection of proverbs partially reflects the interests of the powerful.[44] The iconoclastic con-

---

[42] This is what Valentin-Yves Mudimbe calls the "epistemological filiation", cf. *The Invention of Africa. Gnosis, Philosophy and the Order of Knowledge* (Bloomington, IN and Indianapolis, IN: Indianapolis University Press, 1988), 19, 185.
[43] These five points are cited from (and is argued in more detail) in my forthcoming chapter on Okolo referred to above.
[44] On this point see historian Jeffrey Peires's observation: "In oral societies even more than in literate ones, it is the victors who record the history, particularly if the losers become reconciled

clusion that Okolo draws is that the ethnophilosophers are mistaken in considering proverbs as embodying African philosophy. Between the proverbs, there is no eloquent philosophy; there is only silence.[45]

Claim 2: Proverbs provoke thinking. However, Okolo finds no reason to believe that people would transmit these proverbs for ages without the corresponding contradictions striking them and stimulating their thought. Quite the contrary – and the advances in historiography of oral culture[46] support him: the transformation and variations in transmission, the creation of new proverbs, the creative application of proverbs – all of these testify to proverbs' *provoking* thought.[47] In fact, the history of oral traditions teaches us not to remain fixated on the particular proverbs, but to include them in a circuit of *proverb use*. Two components are inherently part of the use of proverbs: reading and "re-taking" (*reprise*). The more "stock-taking" part, which Okolo calls *"reading"*, includes understanding proverbs and using them. The more creative part, Okolo which calls *"re-taking"*, refers to all appropriations of proverbs, ranging from returning to them and resuming their use, to repairing and correcting them.[48] The core of Okolo's hermeneutics consists of describing how people *read* and *re-take* proverbs with a view to their specific context of praxis.

Claim 3: Thinking from the proverb is a paradigm for all African thought. The catalogues of proverbs, amplified by the action-restoring historiography, suffice to conclude not only that the contemporary philosopher could still think from and via proverbs, but also that the colonial and precolonial ancestors already did so. Whether that thinking is to be called "philosophy" or not does not seem to concern Okolo any longer. But why would anybody return to such prov-

---

to their defeat." Peires, *The House of Phalo: A History of the Xhosa People in the Days of their Independence* (Berkeley, CA and Los Angeles, CA: California University Press, 1981), 30.

45 Following Njoh Mouelle, "wisdom is not to be sought in what each of these proverbs expresses, but rather in the interval between them; and this interval is unfortunately made of silence" (cited in Okolo, *Pour une philosophie*, 14).

46 Cf. Jan Vansina's pioneering work, *Oral Tradition. A Study in Historical Methodology*, trans. H. M. Wright (London: Routledge and Kegan Paul, [1961] 1965). But recently also Okolo Okonda and Jacques Ngangala Balade Tongamba, *Introduction à l'histoire des idées dans le contexte de l'oralité. Théorie et méthode avec application sur l'Afrique traditionnelle* (Louvain-la-neuve: Academia-L'Harmattan, 2018).

47 This point is made in critical debate with Nkombe, *Métaphore et métonymie*.

48 In other words, the creative work on tradition that Houtondji attributed to the ethnophilosphers was already part of the work of oral tradition. At the same time, ethnophilosophy missed its own point, as it were, by assuming that African philosophy was to be sought in a putative set of common convictions, and in this way missed the rational ability to engage with social contradictions (cf. Okolo, *Pour une philosophie*, 66).

erbs, or rather proverb use? Certainly for the insights gained in an oral tradition, but also because proverb use serves as the paradigm for African tradition in general, in other words, as a model for thinking about reading and re-taking *any* aspect of tradition. Such "thinking from the tradition" is motivated in two ways. To begin with, the crisis of life in many parts of Africa requires reflection on the culture to be saved and also on all the intellectual means available to do so (for example, to unmask ideologies of development). Next, there is a need to mobilise people to confront the demands of development, and this can be done much better if engagement with these demands from the tradition allows people a culturally specific self-identification, as agents of this process.[49] In Okolo's words:

> The interest in going to the past is sparked by the current situation: a hermeneutical situation that is at the same time a practical situation. For us it is a question of spiritual and material survival. We feel invaded by a culture that disposes of powerful means to expand and to dominate. We are also among those who are starving and suffering from material deprivation. This situation has been going on for a long time and is still going on. [...] Praxis triggers the hermeneutical process and gives it an orientation. Hermeneutics, in turn, offers praxis a cultural self-identification, required for the ideological struggle.[50]

One could rephrase in Ricœurian parlance this forceful affirmation of "thinking from the tradition" motivated by current praxis: Okolo is the name for *a critique of the current socio-political conditions of life in Zaïre (the DRC), conditions shaped to a great extent by global modernity; this critique is practised knowing what the positive potential of modernity is too.* But it is also the name for *continued engagement with the local traditions* by which people may find for themselves the terms in which they want to struggle for their freedom in this world.[51]

---

49 This affirmation of the feedback loop between hermeneutics and praxis is not meant exclusively as a general ideal for (African) hermeneutics, but reflects also Okolo's motivation for his work in hermeneutics, already in his thesis of 1979: "our hermeneutical situation is that of a reader who is searching for the identity of his/her tradition in a context of almost total dependence, who knows that our individual, national or continental struggle must join the planetary struggle for more equality and justice. This hermeneutical situation directs our present research in a particular way." Okolo, Tradition et destin, 6.
50 Okolo, Pour une philosophie, 28, 46. This echoes significantly Ricœur: "In order to confront a self other than one's own self, one must first have a self." Ricœur, "Civilisation universelle...," 337 / "Universal Civilization...," 283, but for that matter his entire hermeneutics of the capable human.
51 Since the critique of modernity does not amount to a one-sided demonization of foreign influence, and insofar as the work on tradition is (a) guided by the struggle for freedom of all citizens and (b) based on tradition as a place of debate rather than as dogma, I do not see this position echoing a Mobutuist ideology of authenticity. On this subject see the dossier "Université

6.1 Taking Stock: Engagement without Promises

Let us now specify the precise nature and limits of the conclusions to be drawn from this brief excursion into Okolo's thought. Nothing more has been offered than a table set for dialogue. Nothing has been said about the outcomes of a possible debate between Ricœur and Okolo, no indication has been given of any problem solved. In fact, nothing of what has been said allows us to take for granted that such a dialogue would result in a constructive outcome.[52] Rather, it has demonstrated that Ricœur's idea of completing his project with the help of the cultural other – an other thinking on his/her own terms about disillusioned modernity – is not vain.

In principle, such dialogue could – and should – be set up between a thousand other authors, but not with just anybody. There can be a meaningful exchange for the purposes outlined here, only on three *conditions* that are met in the debate I have set up:
1. Both authors must be aware of the mutually relativising juxtaposition of world cultures. Accepting the relativity of their own cultural background, they need to understand the difficulties of coordinating one's local culture-specific views with the increasingly globalized "universal civilization". However, referring repeatedly to people's cultural background, it was never supposed that African or Western intellectual expression necessarily thematized one's cultural background in a central way.[53] Nor should one

---

national du Zaïre: débat sur l'authenticité revisitée" in Isidore Ndaywel è Nsiem, ed., *Les années UNAZA (Université Nationale du Zaïre). Contribution à l'histoire de l'Université Africaine*. Tome II (Paris: L'Harmattan, 2018), 9–84.

In this way, I think, Okolo escapes the bitter judgement of Hountondji: "At a time when the gap between oppressor and oppressed is widening throughout our continent and political differences are becoming more radical, the ethnophilosopher claims that we have always been, still are and always will be unanimous. On every side we see terror tightening its stranglehold on us [...]; every word spoken spells danger and exposes us to untold brutality and may even cost us our lives; insolent neocolonial state apparatuses parade in triumph, leaving a trail of intimidation, arbitrary arrest, torture and legal assassination and poisoning genuine thought at its source. And the official ideologue smiles, content, and declares: 'Alleluia, our ancestors have thought!'" *African Philosophy: Myth and Reality* (Bloomington, IN: Indiana University Press, [1976] 1983), 170.

52 My review of Jörn Rüsen and Henner Laass, eds., *Humanism in Intercultural Perspective: Experiences and Expectations* (Bielefeld: Transcript, 2009) in *Geschichte transnational / History Transnational*, http://geschichte-transnational.clio-online.net/rezensionen/, published May 2012, last accessed 5 February 2021 contains an example of how dialogue can be undermined.
53 Compare for instance (on the African side), David Oyedola, "The Culture-oriented Bias of African Philosophical Inquiry," *Filosofia Theoretica* 3, no. 2 (2014): 62–80 with Bekele Gutema,

at any stage assume that the awareness of culturally specific perspectives takes for granted something like pure cultures – I have demonstrated how Okolo speaks from a position of mixture; Ricœur's *Symbolism of Evil* is a long genealogy of his own cultural heterogeneity. By extension one has to assume that "culture" here includes any form of transmitted symbolism and practice (and not just mainstream tradition).

2. Therefore, initially, at least, neither may speak *for* the other – each gets the opportunity to advance and develop problems on his/her own terms, on an equal footing. The African philosopher is not summoned merely to respond to the initiative of a Western philosopher, and nor is he/she required to contribute while representing the Western epistemic or political concerns. My paper started from Ricœur, but there is no substantial reason why I could not have started with Okolo, since the need for debate is generated independently from both settings.

3. While recognizing that each thinks from a dissimilar position, we should also note that the similarities due to the globalisation of modernities are not wished away in this debate. Rather, the socio-political conditions of globalisation and the diversified ways that "universal civilization" spreads through different localities[54] are both at stake in this exchange. These conditions explain why both discussants are able to identify the subjects of discussion in which they are versed; subjects that are relevant to cultural diversity in the absence of hierarchy. At the same time, the table is set for reciprocal critique.

In short, the point of discussing Okolo in the framework of this study on Ricœur was to thematize these conditions for the kind of intercultural confrontation *required by disillusioned modernity* by means "other than the shock of conquest and domination".[55] The motivation for participation in such a dialogue arises from an awareness (a *prise de conscience*, perhaps) that modernisation has globalised a diverse humanity and the artificial cover-up for this situation by means of colonization has fallen away. We have seen Ricœur's picture of this predicament, but Okolo's is not substantially different – he describes this crisis as the "choice between tradition and modernity; conflict between two cultures, African and European; growth crisis of young countries; struggle between the nascent bourgeoisie, backed by capitalist imperialism and exploited proletarians;

"The Intercultural Dimension of African Philosophy," *African Study Monographs* 36, no. 3 (2015): 139–54.
54 Cf. Kumar, *From Post-industrial to Post-modern Society*, 7–16.
55 Ricœur, "Civilisation universelle…," 337 / "Universal Civilization…," 282.

etc.".⁵⁶ Whatever the conditions may have been and still are that ignite this crisis, according to Okolo, this is the motivation for a hermeneutics in response to modernity *mode africano demonstrata*.

But before we get swept away by this beautiful picture, we have to consider what *dialogue* means here. When it is applied to personified entities such as "cultures", "dialogue" may refer to any form of exchange that does not, in a lasting way, consist of mere force. In other words, "dialogue" between cultures does not exclude the power dynamics that may include episodic and strategic deployment of forceful means (a fact that I examine in Chapter 2, §4). I say this to emphasise that I do not subscribe to the dream that intercultural conflict can be solved in seminars. At the same time, this is no vision of the inevitable "clash of civilizations" either. I support Mohammed Arkoun's idea that there is no clash between civilizations, only a clash between institutionalized forms of ignorance.⁵⁷ Cultural diversity is not only a threat – quite the contrary: I concur with the spirit of Ricœur's claim when he says: "I am convinced that a progressive Islamic or Hindu world in which old ways of thinking would inspire a new history, would have with our European culture and civilization that specific affinity that all creative people share."⁵⁸ Of this wide, realistic understanding of dialogue, the reconstructed exchange between two philosophers is only one very particular manifestation.⁵⁹ In Chapters 7 and 8 of this book I will attempt to demonstrate some of the broader complexities of the conflict of interpretation in action, as I understand it.

7 Conclusion: Philosophising at the Edge

In this chapter I strove to fan the conflict of interpretations over the meaning of the name "Ricœur". Taking his early anti-colonial tract as my point of departure, I traced two lines of development in his thought: first, his geopolitics for the

---

56 Okolo, *Pour une philosophie*, 40.
57 E.g. in Mohammed Arkoun, "Clarifier le passé pour construire le futur," *Confluences. Méditerranée* 16 (1995–1996): 17–30, here 19.
58 Ricœur, "Civilisation universelle...," 337 / "Universal Civilization...," 283 (citation modified).
59 There are also other kinds of intercultural dialogue possible and are taking place; to give one example: the centuries-old exchanges between mystics. As far as I can see, mystics share with hermeneuticists a willingness to self-relativise, and a refusal of dogmatism and contextualisation. However, I think (like Okolo) that there is an intimate link between hermeneutics, and modernity considered as a crisis. This makes of the point of departure of hermeneutic dialogues something different from mystic exchanges.

post-independence world and, second, his cultural critical view on modernity, as revealed by decolonization. I highlighted the significance of these two lines of thought for understanding Ricœur's hermeneutics as a response to disillusioned modernity. A major implication of this view on Ricœur's work is that it requires completion by the cultural and geopolitical other. Finally, I reflected on the conditions of such "inter-continental" philosophical debate by taking Okolo Okonda as an exemplary partner. The necessity and feasibility of such a debate both point to the importance of *feeding* it *back* into a broader philosophical practice, notably in working on issues such as those of *geopolitics* and *social critique*, which I have touched on here.

Altogether, this chapter results in a view on "Ricœur" as the name for a philosophical *ethos* of letting the fate and views of the others resonate in our own mind, under global conditions of increasing uncertainty and perplexity. Whether this ethos finds expression in intercultural philosophy or just as a commitment to allow others' concerns to bear on our reflection, it nevertheless still requires us to exert maximum critical vigilance (as I have argued in Chapter 1). This is indispensable in the kind of general anthropological exploration of action that I attempt in this book. Accordingly, Chapters 7 and 8 aim, amongst other things, to advance our understanding of the technicity of action from sources other than Western ones.

Given the extremely complex nature of all possible interactions (artistic, commercial, political, military, etc.) between individuals and groups from different backgrounds in general, and the fragility of planned debate aimed at mutual understanding in particular, it would be injudicious to assume that such exchanges tend to lead to mutual understanding and appreciation, or to practically sustainable compromises (on this, see Chapter 2). There are no guarantees, and there are many risks. As far as I can see, the only unquestionable motivation to pursue such a treacherous enterprise and the clearest vanishing point for directing discussions is the constant stream of miserable hordes huddling at the edges of our social life. The ultimate orientation of our scholarly and political endeavours can only be the almost uncountable people who, like the waste of the modern word, are pushed beyond the edge of a meaningful existence into social death. Only an awareness of their fate can generate responses to the sceptical question of nihilism.[60]

---

60 Coda: *"we have adopted their language in turn"* ("nous avons tour à tour adopté leurs langages" Okolo, *Tradition et destin*, 268)

It is on the question of intercultural philosophical dialogue that my discussion ended. But this was still a position taken by a single philosopher – hence, a single contingent perspective. What then is the status of my *monologue*?

Is it not fundamental to the intelligibility of my whole chapter to respond to the question of where I stand when I construct this debate? Am I Ricœur's advocate and thereby a campaigner for a Western-dominated stance; is this chapter a slanted exercise of assimilation in the name of Western thought? Or was the whole chapter, from the beginning, arranged to assert a set of African concerns, marked by the figure of Okolo, whose spokesperson I have made myself? Is this nothing but a masked exercise in the revenge of African thought?

This question should at least be mentioned in order to signal its significance. However, since I have no intention of writing an autobiography here, a schematic response will have to suffice. What I have been doing is neither merely exposing myself to the cultural other (Ricœur? Okolo?), nor merely reconstructing a debate between two partners. I am assuming a third possibility, taking on a third position. In this way, I was engaging in a hermeneutics of my situation in this world, by setting up in debate two authors from different contexts from mine, to learn from them both. And through my agreements and disagreements with them, I continued a life of intellectual bastardizing, which is a fate and a chance (cf. Ernst Wolff, "Adam Small's Shade of Black Consciousness," in *Philosophy on the Border. Decoloniality and the Shudder of the Origin*, ed. Leonard Praeg (Pietermaritzburg: UKZN Press, 2019), 112–47).

Chapter 7:
Acts of Violence as Political Competence? From Ricœur to Mandela and Back

1 Introduction

"The people shall govern!"[1] These words encapsulate the principle of popular sovereignty and the essence of all democratic constitutions. They state what the people have by right; they do not describe a state of fact. If the people shall govern, they shall have the right to participate in the political life of society and to enjoy a reasonable share of its goods. And if these rights are not upheld, the people shall struggle to set this right: the people shall engage in public debate, they shall elect other representatives, they shall form new political parties, they shall strike, they shall expose abuses of power, etc. This is what democracy should be.

However, in so many nominally democratic countries, this ideal is undermined from all sides: how can the people engage in public debate if the system of education does little to equip them with the means to formulate their views in public fora? How are the people to struggle if joblessness relegates them to the margins of irrelevance to social disputes, or when their normal living conditions are so precarious that the only struggle possible is that for their survival? Under such limiting situations, where democracy remains little more than a promise, to what kind of action may people justifiably take recourse?

In this chapter, I entertain the question of acts of violence as a form of political competence. I do so with the intention of thinking about democracy with realism, not as a starry-eyed visionary. But I feel some trepidation at doing so. If philosophising is more than merely toying with ideas, one has to recognize immediately the double enormity of this question. It is intellectually enormous in the sense that one cannot cover here the entire range of manifestations of violence[2] (not even if we include the extension of the discussion in Chapter 8). It

---

[1] This is the rallying call which captures the principles and demands of the 1955 Freedom Charter. The full text is available from https://www.sahistory.org.za/archive/freedom-charter-original-document-scan, last accessed 5 February 2021. For a historical perspective, see Raymond Suttner and Jeremy Cronin, *50 Years of the Freedom Charter* (Pretoria: UNISA Press, 2006), and for a contemporary assessment, see Raymond Suttner, "The Freedom Charter @ 60: Rethinking its democratic qualities," *Historia* 60, no. 2 (2015): 1–23.

[2] Violence is a notoriously slippery term. Over the course of this chapter, it will become clear why I cannot avoid using it, even when concentrating on only some forms of violence. A mas-

is also normatively enormous, since I do not intend to discard the possibility that certain acts of violence may be normatively legitimate or at least may have a measure of legitimacy. While I make an appeal for this discussion to be accepted in the safe space of open academic exploration and debate, it has to be understood that these socio-political perplexities in turn generate difficult questions around the nature of social scientific and philosophical work, which I touch on again in the concluding paragraph of this chapter.

Following the same approach as throughout this book, I start by gaining insights from Paul Ricœur. There is a thought-provoking perspective on some forms of violent action tucked away in his later work and that he apparently overlooked. Once this perspective has been brought to light (amongst others with some insights drawn from Luc Boltanski), I develop it into a contribution to an understanding of the possibility of some forms of violence as a legitimate response to institutionalized forms of injustice. Nelson Mandela is my guide on this road. The overall aim of this course of exploration is to study the perplexities that arise from the mutual impact that the technical and the ethical dimensions of action have on each other. This chapter serves as a provisional presentation of the question and the argument is deepened in the next chapter.

2 Three Categories of Competence in Socio-political Action

The place where my exploration starts is probably unexpected: Ricœur's study of "states of peace" or "radical love [*agapé*]" in *The Course of Recognition*, Ricœur's last monograph. This is a book of great erudition and remarkable suggestive force, but it also contains many half-developed ideas and unfinished debates. Ricœur's "surprising take" on recognition (as Laitinen[3] called it) consists of three studies on three different philosophical meanings of the term "recognition". This well-ordered polysemy guides the reader through a course or a trail from the epistemological question of "recognition as identification", through "recognition as attestation of one's capabilities to act", to the ethico-political theme of "mutual recognition". My focus falls on an aspect of the third study of this book – the

---

terly orientation to the concept is found in Peter Imbusch, "The concept of violence," in *The International Handbook of Violence Research*, eds. John Hagan and Wilhelm Heitmeyer (Dordrecht: Kluwer, 2003), 13–39.
3 Arto Laitinen, "Paul Ricœur's Surprising Take on Recognition," *Études Ricœuriennes / Ricœur Studies* 2, no. 1 (2011): 35–50.

one that has drawn the most scholarly attention, namely Ricœur's debate with Axel Honneth's *Struggle for Recognition*[4] on mutual socio-political recognition.[5]

2.1 Ricœur with and against Honneth

The easiest way to introduce Ricœur's argument in this section is to present his non-exhaustive ideal typology of socio-political action. Social and political interaction consists either of struggles for recognition, or acts of radical love, or compromises between them. Let us have a closer look at what this entails.

In his depiction of the ideal-types of struggle for recognition, Ricœur simply follows Honneth: people suffer experiences of personal, social and political misrecognition; in response to these experiences of misrecognition, people struggle for recognition in relations of affection, rights and solidarity. Ricœur gives his own twist to Honneth's theory of recognition by means of a social theoretical extension, borrowed from Boltanski and Thévenot:[6] he emphasises the logic by which people *justify* their struggles – political struggles are struggles by means of claims about failing equivalence between people, ideal *equivalence* between people, but in any case claims about commensurability. We struggle, for instance, for equal rights for women, reasonable conditions of employment, fair accommodation of the disabled, etc. In order to dispute the justness of existing social categories, laws, etc., one has to accord to relevant people, artefacts, events, procedures, measures, laws, etc. a measure of appropriateness or inappropriateness as contributions to a just order. In other words, denouncing injustice consists in pointing out an insufficient degree of equivalence, for instance,

---

4 Axel Honneth, *Kampf um Anerkennung. Zur moralischen Grammatik sozialer Konflikte* (Frankfurt am Main: Suhrkamp, [1992] 1994) / Axel Honneth, *The Struggle for Recognition: The Moral Grammar of Social Conflicts* (Cambridge: Polity Press, 1995).
5 For a fuller reconstruction of this debate, situating it in Ricœur's political philosophy, see Ernst Wolff, "Responsibility to Struggle – Responsibility for Peace: Course of Recognition and a Recurrent Pattern in Ricœur's Political Thought," *Philosophy & Social Criticism* 41, no. 8 (2015): 771–90.
6 Luc Boltanski and Laurent Thévenot, *De la justification: Les économies de la grandeur* (Paris: Gallimard, 1991) / Luc Boltanski and Laurent Thévenot, *On Justification: Economies of Worth* (Princeton, NJ: Princeton University Press, 2006). A short version is given by Luc Boltanski and Laurent Thévenot, "The Sociology of Critical Capacity," *European Journal of Social Theory* 2, no. 3 (1999): 358–77. See also Peter Wagner, "Soziologie der kritischen Urteilskraft und der Rechtfertigung: Die Politik- und Moralsoziologie um Luc Boltanski und Laurent Thévenot," in *Französische Soziologie der Gegenwart*, eds. Stephan Moebius and Lothar Peter (Konstanz: UVK, 2004), 417–48.

between a category of social actors and their share of social goods, and in advocating a better way to establish that equivalence. In short, socio-political struggles strive to promote claims related to a recognition or misrecognition of the appropriate equivalence between elements in social reality.

In *The Course of Recognition*, nothing is said about the *form* that such struggles may take. Nevertheless, two things need to be made clear here. First, struggles for recognition are responses to experiences of misrecognition. Misrecognition is Honneth's preferred term to re-activate the mobilising force of what Hegel called "crime" [*Verbrechen*].[7] In other words, violence in a broad, often institutionalized sense already forms part of considerations of struggles for recognition, in the form of the *problem(s)* to which the struggles are responses. Second, if Ricœur does not seem interested in the forms that struggles for recognition may take in practice, Honneth's book, surprisingly, does not give us much more; in fact, he leaves the question undecided – following his approach

> there is no theoretical pre-commitment in favour of either non-violent [*gewaltlos*] or violent [*gewaltsam*] resistance. Instead, at the level of description, it is left entirely open whether social groups employ material, symbolic or passive force [*Gewalt*] to publicly articulate and demand restitution for the disrespect and violation that they experience as being typical.[8]

This undecidedness is not a trivial matter, since for Honneth and Ricœur struggles for recognition are forms of conflict that are structured by a *moral* grammar; they are explicitly not seen simply as forms of the struggle for self-preservation or the maximisation of interests.[9] Hence, they emphasise the symbolic dimension of interaction in struggles, but shift aside the question of strategy or *efficacy* in the transmission of these meanings. In continuity with my exploration of the efficacy of symbols in Chapter 1, I rather argue that the capabilities and means

---

7 Crime interpreted in terms of social disrespect (*Missachtung*) – Honneth, *Kampf um Anerkennung*, 88 / *Struggle for Recognition*, 53.
8 Honneth, *Kampf um Anerkennung*, 261–62 / *Struggle for Recognition*, 163. For a development of Honneth's theory on the point of violence, see Jean-Philippe Deranty, "Injustice, Violence and Social Struggle. The Critical Potential of Axel Honneth's Theory of Recognition," *Critical Horizons* 5, no. 1 (2004): 297–322, here 309–12. Also, Shane O'Neill, "Struggles Against Injustice: Contemporary Critical Theory and Political Violence," *Journal of Global Ethics* 6, no. 2 (2010): 127–39 develops criteria for violent political action in response to the tendency in Critical Theory to avoid it. His definition of political violence largely sidesteps the peculiarity of sabotage, to which I will turn, but in broad strokes his argument is compatible with mine.
9 Honneth's own theorizing of social conflict, motivated by utilitarian considerations, need not concern us here (cf. Honneth, *Kampf um Anerkennung*, 163–66 / *Struggle for Recognition*, 261–66).

by which people struggle for recognition cannot be suspended forever. In the remainder of this and the following chapter, I aim to clarify this point.

If in *The Course of Recognition* there is a debate between Ricœur and Honneth, it has to be sought elsewhere. Ricœur is willing to yield all initiative on social struggles to Honneth, in order to focus on his own concern: do these struggles exhaust the forms of action relevant to people's socio-political aspirations? Ricœur argues that there is another, entirely different, kind of experience which he calls "states of peace". States of peace are truces in, or interruptions of, the continuous struggles. States of peace are not the continuation of struggles by other means, in fact, they emerge from an entirely different logic, namely a logic of generosity, incommensurability or *non-equivalence*. This logic of action is designated *agape* or radical love, the ideal-typical description of which we will examine in a moment. Ricœur claims that the struggles for recognition draw their strength, amongst others, from the real experience of recognition, brought about in fleeting "states of peace".[10]

Since it takes some convincing to accept that there is something like radical love at all, or states of peace that interrupt the struggles for socio-political recognition, let us consider Ricœur's favourite example: German Chancellor Willi Brandt's kneeling at the memorial for the victims of the Warsaw ghetto, the famous "Kniefall" of 7 December 1970. By means of this symbolic act Brandt gave recognition to the fate of the Warsaw victims, and by extension to all the victims of Nazi massacres. The continued political power relations in which he played his role as the head of state was in this way momentarily suspended to draw attention to the kind of normative concern that should somehow infuse current political relations, without becoming itself a political programme.

Having now established this conceptual, ideal-typical distinction between struggles and states of peace, one may well ask if the purity of the distinction lasts in practice. As much as Ricœur wants to remind us of the reality of a logic other than one of struggle, he is fully cognisant of the fact that very often we encounter that logic in real-life action only as already taken up in a *compromise* with its opposite. Ricœur's long exposition on gift-giving in *The*

---

[10] The structure of Ricœur's response to Honneth is quite similar to the response he offered to Merleau-Ponty on the coordination of "progressive" violence and efficient peaceful action – see the paper I discussed in the Introduction: Paul Ricœur, "L'homme non-violent et sa présence à l'histoire" [1949], *Histoire et vérité* (Paris: Seuil, 1964), 265–77 / "Non-violent Man and his Presence to History," in *History and Truth*, transl. Charles A. Kelbley (Evanston, IL: Northwestern University Press, 1965), 223–33. For detail on this earlier debate, see my *Lire Ricœur depuis la périphérie. Décolonisation, modernité, herméneutique* (forthcoming).

Course of Recognition serves as a paradigm for the "bridge" between these two logics of action, in real-life action.

To summarise, if we want to follow Ricœur's political thought in *The Course of Recognition*, we have to take into account *three* categories of action and competence: pure struggles for equivalence or justice, pure interruptions of struggles or states of peace, and the realization of such categories of action in reality in mixed forms or compromises.

2.2 A Missed Opportunity. Boltanski's Two Forms of Non-equivalence

Having thus established the general frame of the debate, allow me to hone in on radical love, the exquisite manifestation of a state of peace. To do justice to Ricœur's thought, one needs to do two things: situate the question about love in the right disciplinary debate, and then undertake some exegetical work.

It may help to rid oneself of false anticipation regarding the thrust of Ricœur's argument if one keeps in mind that the discussion in *The Course of Recognition* of *agapé* or radical love as a form of competence in action is *not*, in the first place, informed by New Testament theology,[11] but by the work of French sociologist Luc Boltanski, specifically his book *Love and Justice as Competences*, in particular Section 2, "*Agape:* an introduction to states of peace".[12]

The book in question is presented by Boltanski as a kind of addendum to the work he did with Laurent Thévenot on the ways by which social actors dispute the evaluation of events, persons and things by taking recourse to a series of different grammars of justification. I have pointed out earlier that Ricœur explicitly uses Boltanski and Thévenot's *On Justification* in *The Course of Recognition* and that he equates the disputes about justification with struggles for recognition. But why would a sociologist of action take an interest in *agapé?* It is because radical love would represent a response to disputes about justification, but a re-

---

[11] This is not to deny that Ricœur reflected on *agapé* as part of New Testament ethics. There is an interesting antecedent of Ricœur's coordination of love and recognition in his 1956 article "Sympathie et respect," in Paul Ricœur, *A l'école de la phénoménologie* (Paris: Vrin, 1986), 266–83, here 282–83, but it is presented only as an after-thought to the article. For a more theologically informed elaboration see Paul Ricœur, "Amour et justice," in *Amour et justice* (Paris: Editions Points, 2008), pp. 13–42 / "Love and Justice," in *Paul Ricœur: The Hermeneutics of Action*, ed. Richard Kearney (London: Sage Publications, 1996), 23–39 and the commentary on it by Fred Dallmayr, "Love and Justice: A Memorial Tribute to Paul Ricœur," in *Paul Ricœur: Honoring and Continuing the Work*, ed. Farhang Erfani (Lanham, MD: Lexington Books, 2011), 5–20.
[12] Luc Boltanski, *Love and Justice as Competences. Three Essays on the Sociology of Action*, trans. Catherine Porter (Cambridge: Polity Press, 2012).

sponse of a different nature from justification: loving action simply lets the entire game of justification go.[13] The sociologist who is interested in mapping the entire field of actions related to the social conflict of evaluations would need to give an account of *agapé*.

Boltanski maps four kinds of social action. Two of these are based on a *logic of equivalence:* justice, which is involved in human-human relations, and appropriateness or rightness (*justesse*), which applies to human-object relations. The two other kinds of interaction are based on a *logic of non-equivalence* – extreme love and violence. What Ricœur takes up in *The Course of Recognition*[14] is radical love understood within *this* action typology. Here we are interested in what Ricœur does with it in *The Course of Recognition*. According to him, what are the characteristics of radical love that qualify it as competence to interrupt struggles for recognition?

Ricœur offers three types of specification. *In general*, states of peace represent an interruption of dispute; they are therefore still critical of current practices, but remain non-institutionalized and ephemeral. *In its ideal-typical form*, radical love is based on a logic of non-equivalence. It therefore abolishes a practice of giving counter-gifts, and it does not retort. It is unilateral, and it is carefree in the sense of letting go of some interests and being practised with neither regret nor expectation. It calls for an appropriate form of expression: praise or imperative. *In connection or compromise with acts of equivalence*, acts of love take on a ceremonial or symbolic form, by which an optative is articulated.

To this list has to be added two additional traits, captured in a key summarising passage:[15]

> Experiences of peaceful recognition cannot take the place of a resolution of the perplexities raised by the very concept of a struggle, still less of a resolution of the conflicts in question. The certitude that accompanies states of peace offers instead a confirmation that the moral motivation for struggles for recognition is not illusory. This is why they [experiences of peaceful recognition – EW] can only be truces [*trêves*], clear days [*éclaircies*] that we

---

[13] Reaffirmed in Luc Boltanski, *De la critique. Précis de sociologie de l'émancipation* (Paris: Gallimard, 2009), 105–106.
[14] I need to emphasise that my speaking about action types is motivated by my effort to get into Ricœur's and Boltanski's thought. In general, I maintain my suspicion of typological approaches to action (as throughout Ernst Wolff, "'Technology' as the Critical Social Theory of Human Technicity," *Journal of Philosophical Research* 41 (2016): 333–69), as indeed the necessity to take into account the compromises between types confirms.
[15] On this passage, see Wolff, "Responsibility to Struggle," 778–79 and the corresponding end notes.

might call 'clearings' [*clairières*], where the meaning of action emerges from the fog of doubt bearing the mark [*estampille*] of *fitting action* [*action qui convient*].[16]

The last two traits of states of peace are present here in the form of indirect citations. First, states of peace are *clearings*. In *Being and Time*, Heidegger presents human existence, or *Dasein*, as open to the world. It is as if human existence is a clearing (*Lichtung*)[17] in a forest – an openness in the forest from where one gains a view on the forest. Human existence is marked by this openness by which this existence can become, to itself, understandable and questionable. For Heidegger, the central fact of this openness is care, in other words, my openness is rooted in the fact that my existence is a matter of concern for me. When Ricœur, then, opts to call states of peace "clearings", he suggests that the openness to our political world[18] – that which makes our vision of it as a valid normative project possible – is its rootedness in experiences of real recognition, that is, ephemeral experiences of states of peace. Just as care structures the entire existence of *Dasein*, so the experience of politically caring or receiving care – that is, experiences of recognition in states of peace – (can) structure our entire political existence.

Second, states of peace *accredit* subsequent struggles as fitting. Laurent Thévenot, in his article "L'action qui convient" ["*Fitting action*"][19], gives an outline

---

[16] Paul Ricœur, *Parcours de la reconnaissance* (Paris: Stock, 2004), 339 / *The Course of Recognition*, trans. David Pellauer (Cambridge, MA: Harvard University Press, 2005), 218, translation modified.

[17] Cf. "In the analysis of understanding and the disclosedness of the there in general, we referred to the *lumen naturale* and called the disclosedness of being-in the *clearing* [*Lichtung*] of Dasein in which something like sight first becomes possible. [...] The being that bears the name Dasein is 'cleared' ["*gelichtet*"]. The light that constitutes this clearedness [*Gelichtetheit*] of Da-sein is not a power or source, objectively present ontically, for a radiant brightness sometimes occurring in this being. What essentially clears this being, that is, makes it 'open' as well as 'bright' for itself, was defined as care [*Sorge*], before any 'temporal' interpretation. The full disclosedness of the There is grounded in care" (Martin Heidegger, *Being and Time: A Translation of Sein und Zeit*, trans. Joan Stambaugh (Albany, NY: State University of New York Press, 1996), 157, 321 / Martin Heidegger, *Sein und Zeit* (Tübingen: Max Niemeyer Verlag, [1927] 1993), 170, 350.

[18] Already in Paul Ricœur, *Temps et récit 3. Le temps raconté* (Paris: Seuil, 1985), 422, 458 / *Time and Narrative*. Volume 3, trans. Kathleen Blarney and David Pellauer (Chicago, IL and London: University of Chicago Press, 1988), 235, 256, Ricœur offered a political reinterpretation of Heidegger's "care" as a central component in his (Ricœur's) understanding of political initiative.

[19] Laurent Thévenot, "L'action qui convient," in *Les formes de l'action*, eds. Patrick Pharo and Louis Quéré (Raisons pratiques 1), (Paris: Éditions de l'EHESS, 1990), 39–69, cf. "The idea of fitting action sheds light on the articulation of the two terms 'to act' and 'to fit'. It calls for a change in the division of roles assigned respectively to a notion of action that encloses all open-

2 Three Categories of Competence in Socio-political Action — 199

of the prudent[20] coordination of action and convention, of individual and society, through divergent types of context-sensitive fit (namely in self-object relations, project relations and relations of justification). According to Ricœur, action infused with the meaning of states of peace fit the socio-political world to which they respond.

Taken together, these two traits of states of peace serve to name the points of orientation by which agents may come out of the "forest of perplexities" about political struggles with the moral motivation that these struggles are not in vain, that their competence in struggling can help them approximate a good fit between people and society.

The characteristics enumerated as the "ideal-typical form" of states of peace express the essential logic of acts of radical love. They develop the central point of non-equivalence. However, in practice, this non-equivalence is visible to different degrees, since very often the logic of radical love finds expression in actions in which this non-equivalence has already had to be traded off against considerations of equivalence. Ricœur argues that this logic "irrigates" or nourishes the actions in which it functions. In *The Course of Recognition*, Ricœur unpacks the problems associated with the compromise of these two opposing logics of action – their "practical everyday entanglement" (*enchevêtrés dans la pratique quotidienne*)[21] – with reference to the perplexities involved in gift-giving.[22] The "general" and "compromise" characteristics of states of peace (presented above) are necessary conditions of radical love to function as a state of peace, as a truce, in the struggles for recognition.

By this time the reader may wonder if I have not lost the theme of my chapter altogether. But I have really just arrived at the core of it. The question that I would like to raise is the following: suppose we accept Ricœur's argument that there are indeed such ephemeral experiences of truces in the struggles for recognition, is there not another family of actions and competences that conform sufficiently to the basic characteristics of acts of radical love to count as manifestations of the logic of non-equivalence, at least in the compromise form? I am

---

ness to individual initiative, and to a notion of convention that carries the burden of all the requirements of agreement," Thévenot, "L'action qui convient," 50.

A seminar in which this text is subject to extensive commentary is available at https://www.canal-u.tv/video/fmsh/retour_sur_l_action_qui_convient_raisons_pratiques_n_1_1990.28351, last accessed 22 March 2020.

20 The specific sense of the term "prudence" used here, is discussed in Chapter 8, §1.
21 My translation. Ricœur, *Parcours de la reconnaissance*, 367 / *Course of Recognition*, 238.
22 For this Ricœur draws from the work of historian Natalie Zemon Davis, *The Gift in Sixteenth-Century France* (Madison, WI: University of Wisconsin Press, 2000).

thinking of some acts of violence. I do not have in mind the entire range of individual, collective, institutional and state violence, nor the physical, symbolic, moral and ritual[23] forms thereof, and I do not intend to discuss them all. What I set out to explore is one kind of violent action, namely violent resistance to institutionalized injustice. And even here, I want to focus not on the attempt to defeat unjust power, but on the use of violence as a symbolic means.

It is with a view to make this case that I turn to a specific episode in South African history.

3 Mandela on Sabotage and the Gradient of Violent Strategies

It is the year 1963. The security machinery of the apartheid state has struck at the young movement of armed black resistance: the leadership of the movement has been arrested on charges of sabotage and conspiracy to overthrow the government. To those who have been arrested is added Nelson Mandela, who is already serving a prison sentence at that time.

The accused were members of the African National Congress (ANC), a movement with a history of peaceful resistance, but which had formed an armed wing two years earlier under the name Umkhonto we Sizwe (MK).[24] On 20 April 1964, Mandela opened the defence case at the Rivonia trial with his famous "statement from the dock".[25] In this speech, he explains and justifies the movement's turn to violent means. It is on this text that I draw to advance my argument.

Integrating this text into the argument of my chapter requires dealing with at least three interrelated difficulties. First, one has to get to the historical Mandela, the man behind the "Mandela" icon. At the same time, it is true that in turning to his early political activism, I draw on the widespread acceptance of the legitimacy of his long walk to freedom, a legitimacy which is in part amplified by his iconic aura. Second, while drawing on Mandela's arguments as a historical instance of a justification of taking recourse to violence, one has to take into ac-

---

[23] The whole range of forms of violence are already mapped by Ricœur in Ricœur, "L'homme non-violent," 267–71 / "Non-violent Man and his Presence to History," 225–28.
[24] This sentence aims only at introducing major references in Mandela's speech, which we will now study. I do not deal with the historical complexities regarding the relation between the ANC and the South African Communist Party, or their members.
[25] Nelson Mandela, "The Rivonia Trial," in *No Easy Walk to Freedom* (Harlow: Heinemann, [1965] 1990), 162–89.

count that strategic self-representation may have trumped factual accuracy.[26] Third, it has to be borne in mind that the chosen text was prepared for a self-defence in a court of law and not for the current context of philosophical, social theoretic reflection. This is not the place to detail the ways in which I work through these difficulties. Suffice it to say that I read the speech in a text-immanent manner,[27] as an argument on the legitimacy of taking recourse to violent strategies, not only in the specific circumstances for which the speech was written, but in circumstances that could be argued to be similar.

Early on in the speech, Mandela declares the need to "deal immediately and at some length with the question of violence".[28] In essence, he makes seven points justifying his and his collaborators' decision to turn to violence:

- The situation for black people in South Africa was intolerable and unjust; it was maintained by institutionalized forms of violence (courts of law, the police force, etc).[29]
- The most appropriate way to oppose such injustice is through peaceful means.
- The ANC tried for a long time to bring about change in a peaceful way, but to no avail.
- Only against the backdrop of failed non-violence could the strategy of taking recourse to violent means be adopted.

---

26 For instance, on the question of Mandela's relation to the Communist Party, the reasons for adopting violent means, or his portrayal of the relation between MK and the ANC's pacifist politics. A useful historian's overview of points of contention is given by Thula Simpson, "Nelson Mandela and the Genesis of the ANC's Armed Struggle: Notes on Method," *Journal of Southern African Studies* 44, no. 1 (2018): 133–48.

27 For the complex history leading up to the decision to turn to violent means, and in particular sabotage, see Simon Stevens, "The Turn to Sabotage by the Congress Movement in South Africa," *Past & Present* 245, no. 1 (2019): 221–55.

28 Mandela, "Rivonia Trial," 163. An insightful positioning for Mandela as "un-Gandhian" and "un-Fanonian", examining his strategic thought and complex attitudes toward militarism against the backdrop of Cold War politics, is Jonathan Hyslop's "Mandela on War," in *The Cambridge Companion to Nelson Mandela*, ed. Rita Barnard (New York, NY: Cambridge University Press, 2014), 162–81.

29 One could of course also study the "technologies of oppression", as discussed by Mahmood Mamdani, see, for instance, "Making Sense of Political Violence in Postcolonial Africa," *Identity, Culture and Politics* 3, no. 2 (2002):1–24 (here 10–11), or Mahmood Mamdani, *Define and Rule. Native as Political Identity* (Cambridge, MA, and London: Harvard University Press, 2012). The place for an exploration of these has been indicated by the political paradox.

- Violent means were adopted according to a plan of a gradual increase of severity: from the "soft violence" of "unlawful" defiance[30] (if you want to include it) to the scale of direct use of violence: "Four forms of violence were possible. There is sabotage, there is guerrilla warfare, there is terrorism, and there is open revolution. We chose to adopt the first method and to exhaust it before taking any other decision."[31] In this way each new step implies a possible exit from the course of violent action.[32]
- The exit from violent confrontation would ideally open up to peaceful negotiation or confrontation, although the more severe the chosen course of violence, the less realistic this ideal would become.
- The programme of violent action planned and executed by Umkhonto we Sizwe remained under the political supervision of the ANC, which would maintain its politics of non-violence.

With this general outline of Mandela's argument in mind, I would like to hone in on a number of aspects of his argument, in order to get a more nuanced picture of how he understood the strategy of violence. At the same time, I use Ricœur's criteria for states of peace as a heuristic key to examine the speech in search for the logic of non-equivalence. Certainly, not all of Mandela's points fit into this perspective. But just as Ricœur knows how to find the traces of non-equivalence in the "practical everyday entanglement"[33] with equivalence (as in the practices of gift-giving described by historian Natalie Zemon Davis),[34] so I will trace the logic of non-equivalence in the broader development of Mandela's thought on violence in real-life engagement in action.

---

[30] Mandela would obviously not have been ignorant about the "weapons of the weak", but they are neither directed at national politics, nor always violent. They warrant a study on their own terms as relevant to the technicity of action. Cf. James Scott, *The Weapons of the Weak. Everyday Forms of Peasant Resistance* (New Haven, CT, and London: Yale University Press, 1985).

[31] Mandela, "Rivonia Trial," 171.

[32] Hence, despite formal overlap, Mandela's point of view on the increasing scale of violence is clearly that of strategic (and normative) planning, not a theoretical bird's-eye view on the taxonomy of violence in politics, as for instance, in Edward Crenshaw and Kristopher Robison, "Political Violence as an Object of Study: The Need for Taxonomic Clarity," in *Handbook of Politics: State and Society in Global Perspective*, eds. Kevin T. Leicht and J. Craig Jenkins (New York, NY: Springer, 2010), 235–46 or in Stathis N. Kalyvas, "The Landscape of Political Violence," in *The Oxford Handbook of Terrorism*, eds. Erica Chenoweth, Richard English, Andreas Gofas, and Stathis N. Kalyvas (Oxford: Oxford University Press, 2019), 11–33.

[33] Ricœur, *Parcours de la reconnaissance*, 367 / *Course of Recognition*, 238.

[34] As referenced above.

First, Mandela recognized the strategic limits of peaceful resistance. These limits are historically contingent, which means that it is the particular make-up of a given situation and the way leading to it that determines whether one has to ask the question of a turning away from peaceful means.

– This is clear when Mandela cites MK's Manifesto: "The time comes in the life of any nation when there remain only two choices – submit or fight. That time has now come to South Africa. We shall not submit and we have no choice but to hit back by all means in our power in defence of our people, our future, and our freedom."[35] Quite clearly the refusal to submit is implied to be morally justified.

– At the same time this turn to violence is understood as a *response* (namely to violence suffered), rather than as a pro-active or pre-emptive strategy. This is true also for the most violent action that Mandela was willing to plan. Thus, he and his collaborators would "*use force in order to defend [them]selves against force.* If war were inevitable, we wanted the fight to be conducted on terms most favourable to our people. The fight which held out prospects best for us and the least risk of life to both sides was guerrilla warfare."[36] Here we move in the arena of equivalence which requires justification (named in the previous point). This is ultimately the sphere of the principles of a just war.

Second, as has been hinted in the previous citation, the turn to violent action cannot be detached from the requirements of *strategic* thinking. This is not a trivial point, since if the recourse to violent means is to remain subject to moral questioning, the precise detail of the kind of violence and the manner in which it is implemented – the strategic qualities of that action – are of decisive importance. Thus, even if there were to be a logic of non-equivalence informing Mandela's reasoning, this would take nothing away from the strategic thrust dominant in it.

– In general, Mandela presents violence as an improvement on the insufficiency (the strategic inefficacy) of previous non-violent political struggles: "…we felt that without violence there would be no way open to the African people to succeed in their struggle."[37] But more specifically, strategic reflection is required to deal with the conflicting demands of the urgent need to take initiative and the desire to limit damage – as is witnessed in the following ci-

---

35 Mandela, "Rivonia Trial," 169.
36 Mandela, "Rivonia Trial," 173–174, my emphasis.
37 Mandela, "Rivonia Trial," 164.

tation: "...violence by the African people had become inevitable, and that unless responsible leadership was given to canalize and control the feelings of our people, there would be outbreaks of terrorism which would produce an intensity of bitterness and hostility between the various races of this country which is not produced even by war."[38] Note here how the strategic deployment of violence necessarily elicits the question of strategic compromises, and how the question of the legitimacy of this course of action is thereby amplified.

Third, the first two points present the turn to violence as a response, and specifically as a strategic response. One can identify the logic captured in these two points to be a logic of equivalence. On what basis do I then still insist that there is in Mandela's understanding of violent action also a logic other than to "use force in order to defend ourselves against force" (as in the citation above) – a logic of non-equivalence? In describing the transition from non-violent forms of contestation to the adoption of violent means, Mandela says the following:

> We first broke the law in a way which avoided any recourse to violence; when this form was legislated against, and then the Government resorted to a show of force to crush opposition to its policies, only then did we decide to *answer violence with violence*. ¶ But the violence which we chose to adopt was not terrorism.[39]

I propose that "answering violence with violence", at the bottom end of the scale of violent action (sabotage), does not have the same meaning as the phrase "use force in order to defend ourselves against force" (cited above). The two *uses* of the word "violence" in "answering violence with violence" are not equivalent. Let us study this citation carefully to see why.

- As explained above, according to Mandela, diverging from the normal course of political contestation provided for by the institutionalized framework of justice (as it existed at that time), was to be done through step-by-step intensification of violent strategies. The form of action with which the turn to violence starts may well be presented as the first step into the whole range of increasing violence, but it is also explicitly demarcated from the more violent forms.
- Violence at the bottom end of the scale does not have the objective of defeating institutionalized violence, but to point out its futility. Its objective could

---

38 Mandela, "Rivonia Trial," 164.
39 Mandela, "Rivonia Trial," 164, my emphasis.

be construed as the creation of a clearing from where to obtain a better view on current political disputes.[40] It is not, at least not for Mandela, a form of attrition warfare.
- The acts of sabotage may have been strategically chosen, but they are symbolic and explicitly exclude the idea of eliminating the enemy.[41] Ideally, acts of sabotage are spent on objects, never on people.[42]
- Never are the acts of sabotage presented as acts of vengeance (an impression that the formula "answer violence with violence" may otherwise create).[43]
- Mandela suggests that violent action can be "properly controlled" only if it is "properly institutionalized". How such institutionalization has to be done probably depends on the demands of the particular context. In his case, the group responsible for the violent initiative is set up in a *contradictory* relation to a mother organization with an avowed commitment to non-violence,[44] in a relation of "properly controlled violence". The only way of accepting that this is not simply nonsensical would be to concede that this arrangement serves as a kind of subordination in a "separation of powers."[45] This subordination would serve to preempt episodic, creative initiatives by individuals or small groups and violent extremes.

---

[40] Compare the expression of intention: "We hope that we will bring the Government and its supporters to their senses before it is too late, so that both the Government and its policies can be changed before matters reach the desperate state of civil war" (Mandela, "Rivonia Trial," 171) with the provisional outcome that "the response of the Africans was one of encouragement. Suddenly there was hope again" (Mandela, "Rivonia Trial," 173).

[41] Cf. "sabotage on Government buildings and other symbols of apartheid" (171). Unfortunately, the specificity of a strategy of sabotage is lost in Crenshaw's and Robison's taxonomy, in "Political Violence as an Object of Study", where, in the absence of direct treatment of sabotage, one is led to interpret it as a symbolic act of terrorism. Likewise, Kalyvas, "The Landscape of Political Violence" gives too broad a view on the landscape to zoom in on the specific strategy of sabotage.

[42] Mandela, "Rivonia Trial," cf. 171.

[43] Following Scott's famous study, *Weapons of the weak*, acts of sabotage are considered at the more assertive or violent end of the repertoire of peasant resistance. However, "sabotage" in this context is not meant as a symbolic confrontation (Scott, *Weapons of the weak*, xvi), does not have an "author" (Scott, *Weapons of the weak*, 282), and is part of a strategy of attrition (Scott, *Weapons of the weak*, 248) – quite unlike the sabotage Mandela had in mind.

[44] "I say 'properly controlled violence' because I made it clear that if I formed the organization I would at all times subject it to the political guidance of the ANC and would not undertake any different form of activity from that contemplated without the consent of the ANC" (Mandela, "Rivonia Trial," 170).

[45] A principle to which Mandela explicitly subscribes in the speech, see Mandela, "Rivonia Trial," 183.

- Embarking on sabotage is never severed from a broader political struggle – it remains a restricted, distinguishable moment, in the service of a larger project.
- Each of the points above serves to explain the strategy of violence, but as "properly controlled violence" avoids a logic of equivalence. At this point "answering violence with violence" is not a formula of equivalence and could, given the context of gross institutionalized injustice and the strategic inefficacy of non-violence, be considered to be a fitting action for the specific context, in other words, an element of a "repertoire of contentious politics" that normatively and strategically fits the particular form of "regime" (to use Charles Tilly's terminology[46]). Sabotage, devoid of this logic of non-equivalence, is nothing more than the beginning of acts of terror or guerrilla war. How one judges these two other actional possibilities is beside the point; the issue is the difference in the underlying logic.

Fourth, if my reading is correct, if Mandela's understanding of violent action contains a logic of equivalence *and* a logic of non-equivalence, what is the relation between actions stemming from the two forms of logic? It seems plausible to infer that the two may be equally present at the bottom end of the entry into violence (into sabotage as Mandela conceives of it), but that non-equivalent violence slowly recedes and perhaps even disappears as one progresses up the scale of increasing violence. That the "irrigating force" of non-equivalence diminishes as the scale of violence increases does not seem to me to contradict the presence of non-equivalence, but rather to contribute to the phenomenology of its possible manifestations.[47]

With these insights from Mandela, I conclude that the case for the possibility of violent courses of action based on a logic of non-equivalence has been made. Now we can resume our reflection on political struggles by a reflection on their implications.

4 Elaboration: Mutual Implication of Strategy and Value

If all action has a technical dimension – the thesis which informs this whole book – then this should hold also for political action. The technical dimension

---

46 Charles Tilly, *Regimes and Repertoires* (Chicago, IL: University of Chicago Press, 2006).
47 Approaching the highest point of violent conflict, another form of non-equivalence increasingly becomes a reality, as is witnessed in indiscriminate massacres in mob violence and war.

of the most peaceful verbal strategies in politics has already been touched on (in Chapters 1, 2 and 6). The current chapter shifts the focus to the more violent side of the scale of political action, and started with the question of whether (or when) acts of violence can be understood as *political competence* (in a sense other than the brutal pursuit of self-interest by the powerful). Throughout, I assumed that such a competence was indeed to be found in Mandela's (and his allies') turn to violent means in their struggle. What I set out to determine was what this competence consisted of. I did so in the hope that this specific case would also instruct us about features of the technical dimension of action more generally in politics, and in social interaction.

I would now like to pinpoint two insights which this case helps to foreground. On the one hand, it opened another perspective on the technicity (capabilities and means) of action as a dimension of political action. In political action, the planned deployment of the technical dimension of action may also be called strategy. On the other hand, this case serves as a first approach to the entanglement of normative and strategic concerns in action. Next, I give a provisional discussion of both points, starting with the second. These themes are taken up again in the next chapter, in view of a more complex discussion.

4.1 Entanglement with Ethics

If we accept Mandela's account, then his and his allies' entire course of action, the process of deciding, and even the path of gradual implementation, was normatively informed. At the same time, since I could assume that the basic, underlying normative issue was not subject to debate, the question of the validity of his struggle could simply be bracketed (of course, often action is much more subject to normative uncertainty and/or dispute, as we will see in the next chapter). Together these two points help us to introduce the weight of ethical consideration in action, while we are relieved, for the moment, of the question of justification. In other words, I could proceed with the work of description and interpretation that is compatible with the position of simple exteriority that I described in the "Intermediary reflection", §§ 2 and 3. Thus, the chosen case has provided a relatively simple entry to an examination of the coordination of ethical and strategic considerations, a coordination which one may assume is active in almost all action. Granted, often the difficulty of finding any coordination is solved by habitual repetition, or remains much less acute, informing everyday action in the form of almost unconscious "monitoring" (as discussed in Chapter 5). The extreme case – and even more so its retrospective justification in Mandela's speech – helps us to see more clearly how capabilities (speaking, doing, narrating) are always telescoped into (implicit) normative imputation, as has been unpacked in Ricœur's hermeneutics of action.[48]

From this conclusion one could glance back at the interpretative examination of the technicity of action in the previous chapters and identify numerous places where this impact of ethical considerations on the capabilities and means of action has been touched on, for instance, the efficacy of symbols (Chapter 1), the interrelation of understanding through means and other forms of relating understandingly with the world (Chapter 2), the (in)capabilities of individuals and of organization of action (Chapters 3 and 4) and the equal or unequal distribution of resources by institutions (Chapter 5). All of these are presupposed in the current chapter. The specificity of the current exploration is the focus on politically motivated action, the normative infiltration of action and the action typologies involved in an attempt to clarify this.

Ethics weighs on strategy and a descriptive clarification of action has to account for the ways in which it does so, even if we stop short of questioning the legitimacy of those commitments.

4.2 Combining Strategy and Value

Once we recognize the entanglement of ethical concerns with action, it helps us to understand better that, and how, the technicity of action takes shape in relation to this "other than technical" dimension, namely the ethical dimension of action. It is the specific way in which Mandela trades off strategy and ethical concerns that allows me to describe his turn to violence as political competence. The question is relative to initiatives that are acted out with a view to (re)instating or rehabilitating the political community, not to vengeance or to neutralising the enemy in war. With Mandela, we explored the possibility that struggles for recognition could be interrupted by acts of violence which may do similar work to that which Ricœur attributes to states of peace. This obviously does not hold for all acts of violence – it does so as little as Ricœur's claim is relevant to all acts of selfless love. Likewise, as little as peaceful abstention from violence is for Ricœur a good in itself, so little can acts of violence be approved of categorically. The investigation carried out in this chapter suggests the phenomenol-

---

[48] See especially Ricœur, *Soi-même comme un autre* (Paris: Seuil, 1990), 337–44 / *Oneself as Another* (Chicago, IL: University of Chicago Press, 1992), 291–96 and also Chapter 3, §1, Figure 1 (above).

ogy of a particular kind of recourse to violence in politics that may be claimed to be a political competence. Such actions
- are initiated when non-violent strategies have been exhausted;
- imply a gradual entry into the sphere of violent alternatives;
- involve violent action which has as its goal the return to non-violent forms of dispute and contestation; and
- involve actions where turning to violence stands under the supervision of an independent instance with a non-violent mission.

Acts of violence that correspond to these traits would comply with the spirit of what Ricœur calls an "ethic of limited violence" or what Mandela calls "properly controlled violence".

Moreover, if such a symbolic function is granted to specific acts of sabotage, then one has to concede that the non-equivalence at work in such acts can be symbolically effective only as part of a broader politics (of ideological struggle, soliciting international pressure,[49] etc.) for which it serves as point of orientation. After all, acts of sabotage on their own are not a serious political strategy. In other words, sabotage only makes sense as a "claims-making performance"[50] and only as part of a broader strategy with which it is interwoven in compromise forms. Accordingly, only in as far as the act of sabotage is a political symbol and aims at effectiveness can it be considered an act of political competence. And the competence and means of such symbolic acts point back to the competence and means required for political action in general.

The practical consequences of this conclusion may not be so foreign to Ricœur as one might perhaps expect. Consider his meditation on violence, "Non-violent man and his presence to history" (1949), which I have presented in the Introduction. As a first step Ricœur categorically contrasts non-violence with "progressive violence" or revolution. Progressive violence participates in the "harsh law of history",[51] which refers to repeated use of violent means. But what remains then of non-violence? Non-violence transcends history thus viewed as the progression of violence, first, by its awareness and judgement of violence, second, through seemingly untimely or misplaced actions which break the spell of the violent *status quo*. When such "gestures" gain social support and become movements, they may gain historical efficiency. It is the coordination of a "spirituality" and a "technology" (of Gandhi, for instance) to which

---

[49] This issue is curiously undertheorized in Tilly's study on violence in South African anti-apartheid politics, *Regimes and Repertoires*, Chapter 5.
[50] Again Tilly, *Regimes and Repertoires*, 2006.
[51] Ricœur, "L'homme non-violent," 276 ("dure loi de l'histoire") / "Non-violent Man," 232.

this historical efficiency is due. However, non-violent action does not become a programme of its own either. It has to enter into a "dramatic relation" (*The Course of Recognition* would say "compromise") with progressive violence. Surprisingly, then, Ricœur's idea of non-violent political action can, through a fitting combination of spirituality/symbolics and technology/strategy, function as an inspiration for violent acts,[52] like the struggles of the proletariat or the colonized.[53] Hence, Ricœur concedes that non-violent resistance is inherently limited and often needs to be completed by fitting, competent political action, which requires an even wider repertoire of capabilities and means.

And this is the point Mandela helps us to see and appreciate. Under conditions of severe "exclusion, alienation, oppression",[54] under conditions where symbolic gestures of states of peace and the quest for mutual recognition they point to have been fruitless, these peaceful initiatives may make place for indignation and urgency – not necessarily the struggle for equivalence by other means, but an interruption of a violent socio-political order by violent means ("answer violence with violence" in the non-retaliating sense discussed above). The temporary deceleration of political struggles through states of peace makes place for an acceleration of struggle through violence. The one is as revealing, as much a clearing, of the true nature of the "normal" capability of political struggles as the other. And nothing says that this has to be a one-way street. [55]

The heaviness of the example – the reticence one rightly feels to embrace this turn to violence – speaks to the fact that *strategy* (political capability and means) *weighs on ethics* – as we saw above, ethics also weighs on strategy.

4.3 Maintaining the Perplexity

In the previous two points, I have tried to shed some light on the relation of mutual implication between ethical (or normative) and strategic (or technical) concerns in action. But this effort of theoretical clarification cannot dispel the perplexity generated by this very need to combine ethics and technics. The extreme

---

[52] What is described as "irrigation" in Ricœur, *Parcours de la reconnaissance*, 377 / *Course of Recognition*, 245.
[53] Evoked in Chapter 6, §3, and see Ricœur, "L'homme non-violent, 275 / "Non-violent Man," 232.
[54] Ricœur, *Parcours de la reconnaissance*, 314 / *Course of Recognition*, 201.
[55] The complex switching from one regime to another need not detain us here. This has already been examined by Boltanski, *Love and justice as competences*, 153–59.

case of the turn to violent contestation demonstrates this graphically. Let me identify a number of points.[56]

Recourse to violence at the bottom of the hierarchy of violent options attempts to achieve symbolic efficacy. But the moment the capacity to emit and transmit symbols is augmented, the risk involved translates into an augmentation of the *unintended consequences*. In the short term, it is difficult in practice to perform acts of sabotage without collateral damage.[57] In the longer term, one may think of the spread of a culture of militarisation, the celebration of the soldier-hero in the public space,[58] etc. One may, of course, try to reduce the technical force of sabotage to its minimum, but only at the expense of symbolic efficacy – it may become a laughable gesture, revert to a form of peaceful protest, or remain simply invisible. On the other hand, as one amplifies the force of the act – the more sting it has – the more difficult it becomes to maintain it in the spirit of the act of sabotage and the closer it comes to a real act of violent resistance (for which, I repeat, under certain circumstances there may be justification, but that would require a separate discussion). At the same time, let it not pass unmentioned that these arguments do not amount to a conclusive case for peaceful resistance, since the patience of non-violence equally has unintended consequences: the tolerance of injustice, the internalization of defeat, etc.[59]

Second, this very push for *efficacy* of the symbol also generates increasing *ambiguity* of the symbol: the means of transmission, that by which the message is amplified, lends itself to divergent interpretations. The act of power turns out to have a fragile flip side, since the ambiguity gives opponents something to turn against the initiators of the act, from two opposing sides. First, those who support the status quo can take advantage of this ambiguity. Mandela evoked this problem implicitly when he spoke about the way in which the acts of sabotage elicited a violent response.[60] Why should the oppressor interpret the act of sabotage as an invitation for the peaceful settlement of dispute, rather than as a

---

[56] Historiography remains an indispensable help to grasp the untidiness of compromise seeking action. For the examined case, see again Stevens, "The Turn to Sabotage".
[57] Cf. *Truth and Reconciliation Commission of South Africa Report*, volume 3 (1998), 51, https://www.justice.gov.za/trc/report/finalreport/Volume%203.pdf, last accessed 7 April 2020.
[58] An excellent example of these perplexities is the short-lived political life of Thomas Sankara – cf. Bruno Jaffré, *Biographie de Thomas Sankara. La patrie ou la mort...* édition revue et augmentée (Paris: L'Harmattan, 2007).
[59] One of the points that inform Kenneth Kaunda's reflections in *Kaunda on Violence* (London: William Collins, 1980).
[60] "But we in Umkhonto weighed up the white response with anxiety. The lines were being drawn. The whites and blacks were moving into separate camps, and the prospects of avoiding a civil war were made less" (Mandela, "Rivonia Trial," 173).

confirmation that the suppression of a perceived violent enemy is a legitimate goal? From the side of the oppressed, the ambiguity allows for an opposite suspicion. Why should one follow Mandela in presenting sabotage "positively" as an entry into violent action? Should the historical context of oppression and institutionalized violence not rather favour a "negative" understanding of sabotage as an all too generous gift of restraint, of withholding the violence, of deferring civil war?

Third, the attempt to coordinate a violent initiative and a longer-term view of peaceful settlement may just as well generate scepticism. While one may accept the gesture of restraint that is represented by the *division of powers* (between an armed movement of resistance and a pacifist institution of supervision), what qualifies the supervisors to execute their function and what constrains the armed movement to heed the supervisor's restriction, when both are called on to compromise? Moreover, the idea that violent action could be gifted with a prophetic heart of peace (the formula is derived from Ricœur, but captures the spirit of Mandela's idea about sabotage), is this not finally all too close to the legitimation of acts of violent strategies everywhere, and even up to the most world-foreign form of rage of which Max Weber speaks of in "Politics as a Vocation," namely brotherly love, which, through indignation, turns into chiliastic violence, that is, the utopia of committing the last act of violence that will make an end to all violence?[61]

4.4 Responsibility in Politics and Science

That such perplexities should arise from the technicity of action should not come as a surprise. The difficult trade-off between strategic and normative concerns is clearly an instance of the (in)capabilities that arise from the coordination of different actional specifications (see Chapters 3 and 4) and the inevitable generation of unintended consequences in action that was highlighted in Chapter 5, §3.2(2). And since (in)capabilities and the generation of unintended consequences stretch as far as the human ability to act, one may take this as an indication of the fact that such perplexity has the potential of creeping into all forms of action.

---

[61] There is a possible hint of this in Mandela's speech: "It has taken more than fifty years for the scars of the South African War to disappear. How much longer would it take to eradicate the scars of inter-racial civil war, which could not be fought without a great loss of life on both sides?" (Mandela, "Rivonia Trial," 170).

It is true that sometimes in life the demands of technical efficacy and of ethical excellence point in the same direction. But nothing guards human beings from the tragic possibilities of outcomes that contradict the spirit in which action is undertaken. This is indeed an age-old insight, as Max Weber has already pointed out.[62] And I agree with him that this dilemma can be responded to fittingly only in an attitude of responsibility. But what are we to understand by "responsibility"? At this stage, I only venture the thesis that a good understanding of responsibility, at least for most contemporary contexts of action, requires a long detour through the interpretation of the capabilities and means of action. More is said about this in the Conclusion (§3) of the book.

In the meantime, let me just point out that the social scientist and the philosopher are not spared these dilemmas. I started Part 2 of this book with a reflection on the fact that academic practice is also a set of actions. It too has to coordinate strategy and norm. Scholarly practice is not only an effort to stand outside of practice (exteriority evoked in the "Intermediate Reflection", §§2 and 3), but always remains part of social reality. Therefore, its meaning is to be understood, also in relation to those other social contexts, where people do not always have the luxury of standing away a bit from the "edge" of action (as mentioned in the Chapter 6, §1). This fact certainly intensifies the demand for academics to be responsible made by their social context. Would one be willing to accept accountability for the justification of acts of violence, however qualified it may be, if there are innocent victims? Or conversely, if there is never any possibility of such implications in one's work, if there is no risk, how would one justify assuming such a free-standing position in a world of institutional injustice? Or how could one justify writing as if the victims of institutional violence have to exercise infinite patience?

---

62 Cf. Max Weber, "Politics as a Vocation," in *From Max Weber: Essays in Sociology*, trans. Hans Heinrich Gerth and Charles Wright Mills (London: Routledge, 1991), 77–128, and echoed by Maurice Merleau-Ponty in the preface to *Humanism and Terror: The Communist Problem* (New Brunswick, NJ: Transaction, [1947] 2000).

Chapter 8:
Justice Despite Institutions. Struggling for a Good Life from the Destitute Edge of Society

> [S]trengthened by analysis and description, we must stand ready for unprecedented forms of action that will alternate in a complex strategy the phases of negotiation and consultation and the phases of disruption and open conflict; this very difficult game requires that we have overcome the old schematizations crystallized around the words reform and revolution.
>
> Paul Ricœur, "Le conflit: signe de contradiction ou d'unité?"[1]

Ricœur's hermeneutics stands in solidarity with practical philosophy. It is not meant as an ideal theory to be applied to reality, but as a constant exchange between existing traditions of thought and the demands of practice. This is certainly true for his reflection on justice. The aspiration to live the good life may find its expression in a general, abstract formula – life with and for others in just institutions[2] – but this aspiration can only be correctly understood as an *optative:* may it come about that I live with and for others in just institutions! And the optative expresses the aspiration of particular people, to be actualised in specific places, in particular times in history. In other words, justice is not merely theorized *a priori*, or declared to be in place *de facto* – justice is still *at stake* (*en jeu*) in the complex unfolding of events. Allow me to develop two examples from Ricœur's thought to illustrate this point.

First example: striving for justice, Ricœur tells us, is a striving for justice mediated or facilitated by just institutions. However, those people who strive for such justice are, as socialized and interacting beings, already situated in institutions. Now, the institutional context in which people strive for justice is not simply just or unjust, but is just to this or that extent (and it may improve or degenerate over time). The more just current institutions are perceived to be, the more people will count on those institutions in their efforts to improve justice; the less just the intuitions are perceived to be, the more people have to take re-

---

[1] In Paul Ricœur, "Le conflit: signe de contradiction ou d'unité?" in *Contributions et conflits: naissance d'une société*, (Lyon: Chronique sociale de France, 1971), 189–204, here 204: "fort de l'analyse et de la description, nous devons nous tenir prêts pour des formes d'action inédites faisant alterner dans une stratégie complexe les phases de négociation et de concertation et les phases de rupture et de conflit ouvert; ce jeu très difficile demande qu'on ait dépassé les schématisations anciennes cristallisées autour des mots réforme et révolution." (my translation).
[2] Repeatedly used throughout. Paul Ricœur, *Soi-même comme un autre* (Paris: Seuil, 1990) / *Oneself as Another*, trans. Kathleen Blamey (Chicago, IL: University of Chicago Press, 1992).

course to other means to find justice, while existing institutions become obstructions to their pursuit of a just life. At this end of the spectrum of institutions, the question that arises is then not merely how to improve the justice of the institutions in which one lives, but *how to aspire for justice despite unjust institutions*. Moreover, the further institutions fall short of people's aspiration to live in justice, the more urgent the question of how to aspire to justice without just institutions (of the economy, of the state, etc.) becomes. Perhaps we can *get a clearer look at what is at stake in the optative for justice if we focus on the destitute "edge"* ³ *of social co-existence* far removed from the institutions of justice that function relatively well.

Second example: whereas Ricœur typically speaks of institutions in the plural, in most cases, the state remains the encompassing institutional frame. The state is therefore regularly presented as the prime institution within which one can aspire to live a just life. This does not mean that Ricœur takes a rosy view of the state. For him, the state is a site of conflict (even under democratic constitutions), and it is always marked by a "violent residue".⁴ Furthermore, states are diverse: they may differ in respect of their constitutional forms and of the quality of justice they can guarantee their citizens. The less just a state is, the more one can expect the state to be contested and the more its violent residue may come to the fore, for instance, to oppose that contestation. Nevertheless, democratic states – perhaps especially democratic states – are made for contestation.⁵ Ricœur identifies different levels of contestation, corresponding to different levels of perceived injustice. However, the different levels of contestation in democratic states all depend on an institution – namely the democratic ethos – which allows us to engage in disputes in and against the state through discourse. But what happens when we move beyond the sphere of practice of this democratic ethos to the destitute edge of society where people may be *excluded from public discourse* or where *the effect of their participation is strategically neutralized?*⁶ Perhaps we can get the best glimpse of what it means to use democrat-

---

3 The polysemic term "edge", of which I deploy only one aspect in this chapter (as in Chapter 6), is inspired by Johan Snyman, "Filosofie op die rand," *Koers* 62, no. 3 (1997): 277–306.
4 See discussion under Point 1. of in §1, below.
5 On this point Ricœur follows Claude Lefort, cf. *Soi-même comme un autre*, 303 / *Oneself as another*, 260. The same point is made in Ricœur, "Langage politique et rhétorique" [1990], in *Lectures 1. Autour du politique* (Paris: Seuil, 1991), 161–75, here 166–67, 174 / "The fragility of political language," *Philosophy Today*, 31, no. 1 (Spring 1987): 35–44, here 38–39, 43.
6 Axel Honneth's formulation of this problem is still valuable: "Moralbewuβtsein und soziale Klassenherrschaft. Einige Schwierigkeiten in der Analyse normativer Handlungspotentiale" [1981], in *Die zerrissene Welt des Sozialen* (Frankfurt am Main: Suhrkamp, 1990), 182–200, especially 191–93.

ic forms of contestation when we can no longer count on their efficacy and when we are therefore compelled to think about taking *recourse to other means*, means for which the state makes no institutional provisions, and which may well have to be deployed to advance justice despite the institutions safeguarded by the state.

These two examples show us how Ricœur's (later) political philosophy and his hermeneutic anthropology are always moved by the practical stakes of the questions concerning the realization of justice. In this chapter, I remain very close to Ricœur on this point. However, I interrogate his thoughts on justice with the question of the optative for the good life in just institutions under conditions where such institutions are failing badly and therefore obstruct the aspiration for justice. I approach this question from the position of those who are most tragically on the receiving end of these failures – those who have to cope at the brink of social life. Staying true to a major trend in Critical Theory, I weave insights from the social sciences into my exploration, since this is a fruitful way to keep in play the difficulties of prudence in practice.

In the first section of the chapter, I explore the place of conflict and violence in Ricœur's work. The focus is on his political philosophy as framed by his later hermeneutic anthropology. I argue that Ricœur assigns a major role to conflict in his political thought. But conflict does not always imply violence, and it is important to see exactly how he demarcates the place of violence in "the political". In the second and third sections, I pursue my line of enquiry with a detour through studies in labour sociology written in Johannesburg in the last decade or so. These studies are included in my conversation with Ricœur for two reasons: these empirical studies can help us to retain the practical philosophical thrust that Ricœur's hermeneutics calls for; and they help to counterbalance Ricœur's unwarranted limitation of his reflection on conflict (in the context of a general hermeneutic anthropology) to Western modern democracies (more on this demarcation in §1). I reject the tacit assumption, which still prevails in political theory, that one can think through something such as democracy sufficiently by focusing on Western examples alone. A gain of my other-than-Western orientation is that it gives me a much better vantage on the miserable edges of social co-existence (which, as I have shown in my two examples above, promises to help us understand Ricœur's practical concern with justice better). The second section is devoted to a reflection on "violent democracy". This background then allows me to explore the distinction between violence closer to the centres of privilege and violence closer to the precipice of social destitution. In the third section, I explore two ways of pursuing the aim of justice from this "edge": first, responding to injustice by means of violent action; second, responding by means of contestation, closer to the peaceful possibilities of democracy. In violent democracies, it is impossible to understand one without the other. They are both ambiguous attempts at practically astute strategies to improve justice where institutions are failing the people. Each is defined in relation to the other, and for each, the other remains a viable alternative. Finally, in the fourth section, a number of conclusions are drawn regarding the value of this detour for the attestation by capable and suffering humans of their ability to act and to pursue justice. This also has implications for those whose profession requires thinking about this quest for justice in the second order of theory or philosophy.

1 Conflict and Violence in View of Justice

Conflict is a major concept throughout Ricœur's political thought. The salient place of conflict in his thought may be profiled by considering a recurring pattern in his political thought.[7] First, with due regard for the factual constitution of politics, he considers political action firmly from an ethical point of view. Second, this ethical view is split into a positive or constructive side, the aspiration for a good life (the good), and a negative or critical side, which limits what people can rightfully aspire toward (the right). Third, since there is no theoretical way of resolving the tension between these two ethical dimensions, the conflict has to be arbitrated in practice. Accordingly, by the 1990s, Ricœur's political philosophy is constructed within three relations of tension: between the good and the right, between "fundamental" ethics and "applied" ethics, and between the various social spheres and the political.[8] These three tensions confirm that struggle and conflict are an integral part of Ricœur's vision of political interaction. Furthermore, Ricœur never succumbs to a simple opposition between presumably unethical conflict and conflict-free ethics – ethics is always at stake through the wide range of possible forms of political action of which different kinds of conflict are a part.

---

[7] In a previous study, I have presented this pattern by covering examples from the 1940s until the end of his life. Cf. Ernst Wolff, "Responsibility to Struggle – Responsibility for Peace. *Course of Recognition* and a recurrent pattern in Ricœur's political thought," in *Philosophy & Social Criticism* 41, no. 8 (2015): 771–90, especially 776.

[8] Apart from the texts discussed here, these tensions can be found, for instance, in Paul Ricœur, "De la morale à l'éthique et aux éthiques," in *Le juste 2* (Paris: Esprit, 2001), 55–68 / "From the Moral to the Ethical and to Ethics," in *Reflections on the Just*, trans. David Pellauer (Chicago, IL: University of Chicago Press, 2007), 45–57 and Ricœur, "La pluralité des instances de justice," in *Le juste 1* (Paris: Esprit, 1995), 121–42 / "The Plurality of Instances of Justice," in *The Just*, trans. David Pellauer (Chicago, IL: University of Chicago Press, 2000), 76–93.

The three named tensions remain irresolvable on the *theoretical* level and have to be dealt with by *practical* arbitration. Ricœur calls the ability to arbitrate in practice "prudence" and it is exclusively in this sense that I use the words "prudence" and "prudent" in this book. But Ricœur also attempts reflectively to support even this passage from the theoretical tensions to their compromise in practice. Arguably, the best example of this reflective accompaniment of the question of practice in politics is found in the study on prudence in *Oneself as Another* and a parallel re-articulation in the essay "The Fragility of Political Language".[9] Focusing on the question of prudence (or phronetic judgement) in politics, Ricœur offers his readers a three-tiered schema of increasing depth of conflict. These conflicts range from day-to-day political debate, to debate related to the ultimate ends of government and, finally, to contestations of the legitimacy of the democratic state itself. This typology reflects Ricœur's view on political conflict during the last two decades of his work in philosophy.

My reflections in this chapter challenge Ricœur (and also a certain orthodoxy in Ricœur scholarship[10]) in respect of two dimensions of this typology of conflict. First, Ricœur confines his whole discussion of politics in Study 9 of *Oneself as Another* to modern, Western, liberal democracies (A).[11] Second, on all three levels of conflict, his exposition covers only conflict in the form of *debate* at the expense of *other strategies of contestation* (B). One is led to understand that prudence in matters of political conflict can be sufficiently (and perhaps, exhaustively) exercised in debate. This impression is reinforced when one reads how the levels of prudent contestation are rethought from the perspective of "the fragility of political language".[12]

Both these constraints are problematic. Concerning the first constraint, (A), one may simply acknowledge that nothing in the broader set-up of a hermeneutics of the self or anthropology of the acting and suffering human necessitates or

---

9 Ricœur, *Soi-même comme un autre*, 298–305 / *Oneself as Another*, 256–62 and Ricœur, "Langage politique et rhétorique" / "The Fragility of Political Language".
10 My point is not to engage with any of his commentators in particular, but to debate with Ricœur and to attempt a reactivation of neglected potential in his thought.
11 Ricœur, *Soi-même comme un autre*, 299, 300, 335 / *Oneself as Another*, 257, 258, 289. Ricœur has pre-modern societies in mind when, in a footnote, he states: "One would have to consider in this connection sociological studies on the existence of a political bond without a state, found in certain societies still in existence". (*Soi-même comme un autre*, 299n2 / *Oneself as Another*, 257n28).
12 As in Ricœur, "Langage politique et rhétorique" / "The Fragility of Political Language".

justifies this limitation.¹³ Concerning the one-sided exposition of conflict in the form of debate (B), one might mention the myriads of contestations of the legitimacy of the state or of parts of it through violent means.¹⁴ These two points overlap in the question of the *means* of political action that are both strategically effective and prudently commendable.¹⁵ Both the perspective from the destitute edge of social life in a non-Western context and the possibility of taking recourse to violent action help us to thematize this point.

This requires some clarification on *violence as a concern in Ricœur's thought*. Let us note that there are many possible forms of conflict, of which violent conflict is only one set. Since conflict is not necessarily violent, it is possible to write about conflict in politics by side-stepping the question of violence. However, this bracketing is not the rule in Ricœur's work, and he certainly was not blind to the continued presence of violence in politics. What better illustration of this fact than the typology of forms of socio-political violence on all scales and in all dimensions of social life, in the pages devoted to an anatomy of war and a physiology of violence in "Non-violent Man and his Presence to History", discussed-mentioned in my Introduction?¹⁶ Violence retains a place in Ricœur's later political thought, up to the last decades of his life. However, his tendency then is to adopt two specific views on violence: the violent residue inherent in all states and the fragility of people exposed to violence.

1. *The violent residue of the state.* The first place Ricœur explicitly accords to violence is in politics and the institution of the state. This place can simply be read from one of his later articulations of the "political paradox",¹⁷ where

---

13 In the §4 of this chapter, I argue that this demarcation narrows both the political scope of Ricœur's later thought and the value that conflict has for the context I refer to here, namely attestation of one's abilities through acts of prudential conflict.
14 In §2 and 3 of this chapter, I demonstrate that thinking through politics, even democratic politics, requires reflection on violence.
15 In politics, a course of action can be prudentially commendable only when it reflects a reasonable trade-off between ethical and moral considerations *and* if it meets either of two further conditions: (1) either it has to be *strategically or instrumentally effective*, or (2) it has to be *symbolically meaningful*. Having explored the question of the articulation between political prudence and symbolics in the Chapter 7, in this chapter I focus only on the articulation of prudence and strategic efficacy.
16 Paul Ricœur, "L'homme non-violent" [1949], *Histoire et vérité* (Paris: Seuil, 1964), 265–77, especially 267–70 / "Non-violent Man and his Presence to History," *History and Truth,* trans. Charles A. Kelbley (Evanston, IL: Northwestern University Press, 1965), 223–33, especially 225–27.
17 The initial version is Ricœur's essay of 1957, "Le paradoxe politique," *Histoire et vérité,* 294–321 / "The Political Paradox," *History and Truth,* 247–70. I have discussed that essay briefly in the Introduction and, from another angle, in "Ricœur's contribution to a notion of political re-

Ricœur attempts to affirm two apparently contradictory approaches to politics, as articulated by theories of power and by theories of decision respectively: "...a reflection on *force* leads directly to the enigma constituted by the phenomenon of power, whereas a reflection on *form*, better suited to the concrete rational function of the State, leads to an emphasis on the constitutional aspect characteristic of a State of law".[18] What defines the state, Ricœur would repeatedly claim (following Eric Weil), is that it is an organisation of collective decision-making and, as a rational form, the act by which to reduce the arbitrariness of violence.[19] Which violence? The violence of the "grabbers or consolidators of land" and the violence which "in traditional societies, educated people in the ways of modern labour" from which states emerged.[20] The residue of this violence remains part of the functioning of the state. In fact, following Max Weber[21], Ricœur considers the state to be the institution that holds a monopoly on the legitimate recourse to physical force within a given territory.[22] This legitimate recourse to violence testifies to the fact that the institution of the state is not the termination of violence, but the shaping of violence – all states retain a residue of their non-founded violence and authority,[23] as can be seen in a variety of phenomena, ranging

---

sponsibility for a globalised world," in Ernst Wolff, *Political Responsibility for a Globalised World. After Levinas' Humanism* (Bielefeld: Transcript, 2011), 221–66, especially 222–33. The evolution of the "political paradox" in Ricœur's work has been studied in detail by Pierre-Olivier Monteil, in *Ricœur politique* (Rennes: Presses Universitaires de Rennes, 2013).

18 Paul Ricœur, "Ethique et politique" [1985], *Du texte à l'action* (Paris: Seuil, 1986), 433–48, here 440 / "Ethics and Politics," *From Text to Action. Essays in Hermeneutics II*, trans. Kathleen Blamey and John Thompson (London: Athlone Press, 1991), 325–338, here 331 (my emphasis).
19 See already "La 'philosophie politique' d'Eric Weil" [1957], *Lectures 1*, 95–114, citation 106.
20 The original reads: "Tous les États modernes sont issus de la violence des rassembleurs de terres; c'est la même violence qui, dans les sociétés traditionnelles, a éduqué l'homme au travail moderne." Ricœur, "Ethique et politique," 441–42 (education to labour is meant ironically) / Ricœur, "Ethics and politics," 332 (translation modified).
21 E. g. Paul Ricœur, *Lectures on Ideology and Utopia*, ed. George H. Taylor (New York, NY and London: Columbia University Press, 1986), 199; Paul Ricœur, "Herméneutique et critique des idéologies," in *Du texte à l'action*, 367–416, here 378–79 / "Hermeneutics and the Critique of Ideology," in *From Text to Action*, 270–303, here 278; Ricœur, *Le juste 2*, 259–60 / *Reflections on the Just*, 225–26.
22 Cf. Max Weber, "Politics as a Vocation," in *From Max Weber: Essays in Sociology*, trans. Hans Heinrich Gerth and Charles Wright Mills (London: Routledge, 1991), 77–128, here 78.
23 Paul Ricœur, *La critique et la conviction* (Paris: Calmann-Lévy, 1995), 151 / *Critique and Conviction*. Conversations with François Azouvi and Marc de Launay (New York, NY: Columbia University Press, 1998), 98.

from the police force to the power to grant amnesty.²⁴

Therefore, when Ricœur affirms for decades the paradoxical nature of politics, he argues that (arbitrary) power is "consubstantial to the 'form' of the state"²⁵ and that the political is "an advanced form of rationality" *and* "an archaic form of irrationality".²⁶ Certainly "violence is not the whole of the political [or the state – EW], but its dark side. It implies a constant threat of resurgence, but it is not, in my opinion, constitutive of the state".²⁷ Note that this is violence *committed* by the state, despite the rational formation of the state. Correspondingly, already in his first exposition of the political paradox, Ricœur calls for something like an ethics of limited violence: "the morality of force, of methodological violence, of calculated culpability"²⁸ (as Ricœur concludes). This is an ethics of the citizens (for example, in their capacity as labourers and as voters) and of institutions (such as the media, or the courts of law) to limit the violence of the *state*. Hence the designation of this efficient ethical action as "techniques or technologies for controlling the State".²⁹ However, in his later philosophy, Ricœur would rearticulate the same principle in a much more placid way as "placing domination under the control of the power-in-common".³⁰

My question is what the political significance is of acts of violence committed by *citizens* in protest against deficiencies of the state or of other institutions, particularly the economy.

2. *Suffering under violence.* A second place which Ricœur accords violence in his later philosophy is in his discussions of suffering and fragility, in other words, the harm inflicted by violence. An example of this perspective

---

24 Cf. Paul Ricœur, "Avant la justice non violente, la justice violente," *Vérité, réconciliation, réparation. Le genre humain* 43 (April 2004): 157–71.
25 Ricœur, "La 'philosophie politique' d'Eric Weil," 106.
26 Ricœur, *La critique et la conviction*, 152 / Ricœur, *Critique and Conviction*, 98.
27 Ricœur, *La critique et la conviction*, 161 / *Critique and conviction*, 105. The same idea is formulated by means of Weber's understanding of the state's possible recourse to violence: "…for Weber the coercion of the state is finally sustained not by its physical power but by our response of belief to its claim of legitimacy", Ricœur, *Lectures on Ideology and Utopia*, 195.
28 Paul Ricœur, "Tâches de l'éducateur politique," *Lectures 1*, 241–57, here 253 / "The tasks of the political educator," in *Political and Social Essays*, eds. David Steward and Joseph Bien (Athens, OH: Ohio University Press, 1974), 271–93, citation 288.
29 "[T]echniques de contrôle de l'Etat", Ricœur, "Le paradoxe politique," 321 / Ricœur, "The Political Paradox," 270.
30 Ricœur, *Soi-même comme un autre*, 299 / *Oneself as Another*, 257.

is the 1995 essay, "Autonomy and Fragility"[31]. Here, the capable human is argued to be fragile and vulnerable, not only because of his/her finitude,[32] but because interaction with others holds the possibility of succumbing to the effects of others' force.[33] This negative impact of some people's actions on that of others is as multifaceted as the human capabilities of saying, doing, narrating and imputing, on which violence infringes. And all of these forms of violence at the hands of others may occur both in face-to-face interaction and by means of institutional mediations.[34] This wide phenomenology of fragility cautions one not to think too quickly of violence simply in terms of isolated acts of physical violence, but to remain attentive to ways in which such violent actions are interwoven into institutional, historical, symbolic and other forms of violence (which are the echoes of Ricœur's physiology of violence in "Non-violent Man and His Presence to History" in his later work). However, from this perspective on the vulnerability of human capabilities, violence is implicitly presented as part of a problem: the deprivation of autonomy. Surely a hermeneutics of the capable and suffering human requires reflection on the intricate lines of capability and incapability that weave the net of a tragedy of action, this tragedy which some consider to compel them to go over to violence?[35]

It is thus out of the question simply to attribute naivety to Ricœur regarding the reality of political violence. However, the combined effect of these two predominant places accorded to violence in his later work amounts to *discarding the question of legitimate recourse to violent acts by citizens in democratic politics.* This is partially understandable if one thinks about the violence of the 20th century and the fate of its victims, and considers in comparison the advantages of the high degree of social stability in contemporary Western democracies. Moreover, major contemporary political philosophers – for example, Arendt, Haber-

---

31 Ricœur, *Le juste 2*, 85–106 / *Reflections on the Just*, 72–90 with some parallels of argumentation, for instance, in Paul Ricœur, "Fragilité et responsabilité," in *Eros and Eris. Contributions to a Hermeneutical Phenomenology.* Ed. Paul van Tongeren et al. (Dordrecht: Kluwer, 1992) 295–304.
32 On finitude in relation to Ricœur's understanding of the capable human see Chapters 3, §2.3 and 4, §4.
33 Eg. Ricœur, *Soi-même comme un autre*, 172, 370 / *Oneself as Aanother*, 144–45, 320.
34 See again Chapter 3, §1 (above).
35 This is a question not unfamiliar to Ricœur shortly after World War II: "…comment la violence et l'oppression n'appellerait-elle pas la violence de la révolte ?" Ricœur, "L'homme non-violent," 269 / "would not the violence of oppression call forth the violence of revolt?", Ricœur, "Non-violent Man and his Presence to history," 226.

mas or Rawls – tend to support such abstinence. However, sometimes, although quite rarely and primarily in his earlier work, Ricœur does concede that recourse to violent means of opposition to the state (not in cases of wars between countries) may be the only viable option left (as in the citation chosen as epigraph for my chapter). This does not fit in well with the decidedly Weberian understanding of legitimate violence as monopolised by the state prevalent in Ricœur's later philosophy. My question in this chapter is then about the legitimacy or rather the ethical justifiability of taking recourse to any means of contestation where the state is the adversary, or is complicit with people's (perceived) adversaries at least to the extent that it is not protecting its citizens against powerful people and institutions. In other words: how can we conceive of the quest for the good life in just institutions where such institutions are absent or failing, and when the presumed measure of democratic contestation, Ricœur's three levels of dispute, have been exhausted?[36]

By reflecting on taking recourse to violent means in the argument of this chapter, I have three objectives. Celebrating intimidation, sabotage, injury and murder is not one of them. First, I argue that due attention to the real possibility of people's taking recourse to violent forms of contestation opens up a larger view on the real range of possibilities of action that exist (or that may not exist) before going over to the final recourse of adopting violence. The political dimension of a hermeneutics of the capable human cannot avoid examining this range of possibilities. Second, one needs to understand why people with ethically laudable motives might want to engage in acts of violence, notably where the institutional means of furthering their desire for justice are lacking. A hermeneutic understanding of the quest for justice cannot do without this. Third, under some circumstances, an understanding of the violent option may help us to understand those options that avoid this avenue better. Understanding prudent compromises in practice requires a view on both alternatives.

2 Violent Democracy and the Violence of the Vulnerable

In the preceding discussion, two assumptions regarding political conflicts in Ricœur's later philosophy came to light. The first is the assumption of efficacy, the notion that in a democracy all differences can be settled through verbal conflict. The second is the assumption of legitimacy: even at the deepest level of dispute, attempts to deal practically with such disputes can draw on wide consensus re-

---

[36] I am thus not thinking of mere retaliation or revenge.

garding the legitimacy of debate as the appropriate means for conflict settlement. One of Ricœur's most important convictions can be read from these assumptions: the power by which to contest the *status quo* and to limit domination arises from acting in common,[37] but this "commonality" is first of all a matter of language, acting *in concert* (as Ricœur affirms, following Arendt).[38] This is not to deny that language can succumb to violence (a point Ricœur affirms repeatedly).[39] It means that only through acting in concert can those institutions be instituted which would facilitate the citizenry's aspiration to live together in justice. In other words, instituting institutions capable of facilitating a life of justice for those who participate in them is the *aim* of people acting in concert, and those institutions depend on the power in common of those who participate in them. The point I am working towards in this section is to identify a different stance towards institutions. This stance consists, first, of opposing the "justice" that is claimed to be institutionalized, when such claims are extremely exaggerated or are demonstrably false (hence the title of this chapter – "justice despite institutions"). The second aspect of this alternative stance consists of creating ephemeral institutions, which means that they do not serve as a lasting structure for living together or participating in a justly organized collective (following Ricœur's definition[40]), but that they are merely a *means*[41] by which to oppose injustice. By focusing on these different stances to institutions, I hope to foreground the kind of aspirations for justice that can be grasped only once we abandon Ricœur's two assumptions (as reflected in the subtitle of this chapter – "struggling for a good life from the destitute edge of society").

The best way to achieve this aim is to turn to sociological studies that could widen our scope on people's political actions and on the kinds of institution in

---

37 Ricœur, *Soi-même comme un autre*, 299 / *Oneself as Another*, 257.
38 Ricœur, *Soi-même comme un autre*, 228n2 / *Oneself as Another*, 195n36.
39 Cf. Paul Ricœur, "Violence et langage" [1967], in *Lectures 1*, 131–40.
40 Ricœur's definition of institution: "By 'institution', we are to understand here the structure of *living together* as this belongs to a historical community – people, nation, region, and so forth – a structure irreducible to interpersonal relations and yet bound up with these in a remarkable sense which the notion of distribution will permit us [...] to clarify. What fundamentally characterises the idea of institution is the bond of common mores and not that of constraining rules. In this, we are carried back to the *éthos* from which ethics takes its name." Ricœur, *Soi-même comme un autre*, 227 / *Oneself as Another*, 194. In Chapter 4, §2.1 I have already commented on the tendency in Ricœur, when thinking about institutions, to take as paradigmatic those that have the same scope as a society or a country.
41 I have elaborated on the instrumental character of institutions in debate with Ricœur in Chapters 3, 4 and 5. The proximity of such ephemeral institutions and organized action (discussed in Chapter 4) should be evident.

which they have to act. For the purposes of this chapter I draw on studies on violent democracy, notably in South Africa, which I present from the perspective of work done by Karl von Holdt (and colleagues), from which I discuss only some key points.

This vantage point is not even that far from Ricœur's in his later political philosophy: I do not consider politics outside of democracies or politics in what are sometimes called "democratorships".[42] Presenting another reality of democracy[43] places us sufficiently far away from Ricœur to show how arbitrary and limiting his focus on Western liberal democracies is. Von Holdt's studies present violent democracy not as something from science fiction, but as a descriptively and analytically valid category. The *first* gain of examining his work is to demonstrate that, even remaining within the theory of democracy, one cannot necessarily count on verbal disputation alone, and therefore one cannot simply assume Weber's idea of a monopoly on legitimate violence in thinking about democratic states. I assume that here too Ricœur's motto will hold: explaining more improves understanding.[44] My use of sociological studies aims at improving the hermeneutic quality of my reflection on the capable human's prudent striving for the good life. The *second* gain from Van Holdt's theory is that it helps us to make significant distinctions between two forms of violence that fall outside of the violence demarcated by Weber's idea of the state's monopoly on legitimate recourse to violence in a demarcated territory. These two forms are intra-elite violence and subaltern violence. I am critical of the phenomenon of intra-elite violence, but this point cannot be thematized here. However, the development of my argument requires the introduction of intra-elite violence and institutional violence as a background against which to interpret the phenomenon of subaltern violence. Doing so will help me to reflect on the aspiration to justice from the destitute edge of social life.

---

42 As for instance, in Max Liniger-Goumaz's study on Equatorial Guinea, *La démocrature. Dictature camouflée, démocratie truquée* (Paris: L'Harmattan, 1992).
43 Whether or not we consider these other forms of democracy legitimate, is not important for the current argument, since in either case the question of legitimate recourse to violent contestation may be raised.
44 "[E]xpliquer plus, c'est comprendre mieux", Ricœur, *Du texte à l'action*, 25 [missing from English translation].

2.1 Violent Democracy – Von Holdt's Challenge

So let us now travel with Von Holdt[45] to South Africa, a choice of case study which, I may remind the reader, is no more arbitrary than the choice to visit France or Great Britain, for instance. In fact, the new democratic state of South Africa at its inception in 1994 was hailed the world over as an exemplary constitutional democracy. In some respects, for example, regarding gay rights and certain social rights, its constitution was at that time seen as more progressive than that of many Western democracies. It also fits in very well with Ricœur's schematic understanding of the institution of states: based on a history of violent confrontation, it enjoyed a pacifying transition; now, its constitution, with its separation of powers and Bill of Human Rights institutes a balance of form and force as described by Ricœur's understanding of the "political paradox"[46] (discussed above).

In the first decade after democratization, socio-political conflict in South Africa tended to correspond quite well with the spirit, if not the letter, of Ricœur's three levels of democratic conflict: "The period saw a shift towards engagement in electoral politics, parliamentary debate and legislation, and in the institutions of collective-bargaining, land claims, black economic empowerment, and constitutional law".[47] By contrast, recent history has seen an increase in violence of all sorts: violence committed by institutions of the state (the police), inter-elite violence and subaltern-elite violence.[48] The question Von Holdt asks as a sociologist is how to understand the "relation between such violent practices and the constitutional democratic order".[49] I follow him in rejecting the ready-made response, of categorically declaring that democracy is the opposite of violent contestation or that taking recourse to violence is merely a symptom of the failure of

---

[45] Karl von Holdt, "Overview. Insurgent Citizenship and Collective Violence: Analysis of Case Studies," in *The Smoke That Calls. Insurgent Citizenship, Collective Violence and the Struggle for a Place in the New South Africa. Eight Case Studies of Community Protest and Xenophobic Violence*, eds. Karl von Holdt et al. (Centre for the Study of Violence and Reconciliation, Society, Work and Development Institute, 2011), 5–32. Karl von Holdt, "South Africa: The Transition to Violent Democracy," *Review of African Political Economy*, 40, no. 138 (2013): 589–604. Karl von Holdt, "On Violent Democracy," *The Sociological Review* 62, no. S2 (2014): 129–51.
[46] Ricœur, *Soi-même comme un autre*, 299 / *Oneself as Another*, 257.
[47] Von Holdt, "South Africa: The Transition to Violent Democracy," 590.
[48] Von Holdt, "South Africa: The Transition to Violent Democracy," 590. Of course, one has to keep in mind the long history of pre-democratic violence – for a historical overview of the complex foundation of the South African democracy, see Von Holdt, "South Africa: The Transition to Violent Democracy," 592–93.
[49] Von Holdt, "South Africa: The Transition to Violent Democracy," 590.

democracy.[50] To find an alternative understanding of the relation between democracy and violence, let us consider the contemporary situation in South Africa.

Two decades after the dramatic institutional changes, this society is marked by enormous inequalities, high levels of joblessness, widespread poverty, failing medical services, dismally performing schools and high crime rates.[51] In so far as these tendencies reflect a trap from which the largest portion of society will never be able to escape, one may call this massive *institutional violence*. However, this is only half of the picture. The tragedy of unequal distribution and of social participation stabilised by malfunctioning institutions provokes people to respond.

Under such circumstances, relations of *patronage* form – it becomes the very fibre of democratic institutions.[52] This means that economic opportunities and political power and influence become objects of dispute in intra-elite conflict. Since the stakes are extremely high (sometimes the difference is as simple as either holding onto political power and an income or returning to a life of poverty), intra-elite conflict boils over into violence (disruption of political meetings, assassinations, abuse of public office, etc.[53]), which may be spent inside or outside of the institutions of the state. Associated with this development is the co-option of clients for the interests of the elite in the circuit of violence. All this happens in a context where the *Constitution* (but also the realities of global trade) imposes

---

50 An overview of such theories of democracy is provided by Von Holdt, "South Africa: The Transition," 591 and Von Holdt, "On Violent Democracy," 131–32.
51 I have given an overview of this situation in "Decolonizing Philosophy. On the Protests in South African Universities," *Books and Ideas*, 15 May 2017. http://www.booksandideas.net/Decolonizing-Philosophy.html, French original in *La Vie des idées*, 28 octobre 2016, last accessed 5 February 2021.
52 Such a development is of course not restricted to African states. An excellent case of comparison would be patronage or "sottogoverno" in post-World War II Italian society and politics. Cf. Martin Clark, *Modern Italy 1871–1995*. 2nd ed. (London, and New York, NY: Longman, 1996), especially 334–37. Here, the point of moral ambiguity of this form of patronage is captured succinctly as "a curious mixture of faction networks and a quest for efficiency, of financing party politics and a genuine concern for welfare, of jobs for supporters and moral crusade," 335.
53 "Intra-elite conflict thus takes several forms. The first is the struggle for factional control over the coercive instruments of the state. These practices subvert the rule of law from within state institutions. The second is the use of direct violence in the form of assassinations. The third is the mobilisation of collective violence" – Von Holdt, "South Africa: The Transition," 599.

significant constraints on the influence that the state can exercise on the *economy*.⁵⁴

A detailed examination of these developments brings Von Holdt to the conclusion that in South Africa (and *mutatis mutandis* in many other countries) violence is not a contingent accident in respect of the institution of a constitutional democracy. Rather, democracy and violence condition each other mutually. Hence, he claims that the term "violent democracy" is descriptively and analytically appropriate.⁵⁵

2.2 Violence close to the Centres of Privilege and Violence at the "Edge"

One may deplore the constitutive role that violence plays in this society – I certainly do so. However, this is the kind of social setting in which many people aspire for the good life, with and for others in just institutions. It is no use simply to assert that violence has to be stopped, since this requires setting the social fibre of action aside, an intellectual procedure for which one cannot expect any support from Ricœur. In order to engage philosophically with this situation, then, we have to work through the terms in which the problem confronts us. Any aspiration to see violence diminish must first deal with it as a reality of social reproduction and of the fibre of some democratic states.

In what follows, I emphasise Von Holdt's distinction between intra-elite violence and subaltern violence. In order to visualise the social dynamics and the personal stakes of these two forms of violence better, I refer to them as *violence closer to the centres of privilege* and *violence at the "edge"* (in other words, not as two absolute categories, but as the two extremes on a continuum). Although systemic factors contribute to the formation of both of these dimensions of violence

---

54 This is the non-spectacular violence, "la violence du droit et de l'ordre" of which Ricœur wrote in an early essay: Ricœur, "L'homme non-violent," 269 / "violence of law and order", Ricœur, "Non-violent Man," 226.

55 Von Holdt, "On Violent Democracy". See also Von Holdt, "South Africa: The Transition," 590: "In this article I avoid such assumptions, exploring instead how the interaction between democratic institutions and power relations within the elite and between the elite and subalterns produces particular forms of violence. Rather than democracy and violence being mutually exclusive, democracy may configure power relations in such a way that violent practices are integral to them – producing a social system we may call *violent democracy*. It may be objected that a violent democracy is not a democracy at all. This is not a helpful stance if we want to understand the dynamics of the kind of actually existing democracy emerging in South Africa, which resembles many other democracies in the developing world. It is all too clear that democratic systems can continuously produce violence without systemic breakdown."

in violent democracies, it is safe to assume that those who engage in violence from positions closer to the centres of privilege have greater room to manoeuvre than those who are closer to the edge of society. The latter almost constantly *risk, as it were, falling from the edge of social co-existence* into that abject, incapacitating and total suffering for which I reserve the name "social death",[56] *but have not just yet done so.*[57] It is violence at this "edge" that is of interest to me here.

Let me stress again that by turning the discussion to violent action I do not intend to compromise the interweaving of political action and the imputation of normativity. Quite the contrary: I am exploring a part of the quest for the good life in just institutions, in the ways in which this quest is practically expressed through complex combinations of abilities to act and the prudent calculation of *strategy and ethics*. My exploration of violent action is therefore motivated neither by a facile theoretical excitement about revolution (although some allies for my argument may come from revolutionary practice), nor by a belief in the purifying or humanizing effect of violence (although I do subscribe to one aspect of this Fanonian idea in §4.2). I argue that one can only take recourse to violence seriously, and appropriately respect people who do so, if one considers taking this recourse as being *not* inevitable, in the sense of being the outcome of the *work* of prudence and the *exertion* of capabilities, in short, as one option of practice alongside other options.

3 Two Ambiguous Strategies to Further the Good Life in Violent Democracies

There is no better way to confront the intensity and complexity – the uncertainty – of life at the edge of violent democracies than to begin with case studies.

---

56 This term is obviously taken from Orlando Patterson and is not my own invention – cf. *Slavery and Social Death. A Comparative Study* (Cambridge, MA, and London: Harvard University Press, 1982). However, I define it here in terms of my typology of different social situations of human capabilities, namely as the most acute and pervasive socially inflicted decay of capabilities.

57 By acknowledging the factors that reduce people's range of initiative, I have thus not simply hypostasised groups (a socio-theoretic problem energetically opposed by Ricœur in "Hegel et Husserl sur l'intersubjectivité" [1977], in *Du texte à l'action*, 311–34, here 334 / "Hegel and Husserl on Intersubjectivity," *From Text to Action*, 227–45, here 244–45).

Here we are not concerned with people who act out of revenge or vindictiveness, but with people who strive for justice from the edge of society. Where just institutions are failing most, the optative for justice may be very strong and the question of improving the conditions for justice may be the most pressing.

When, in *The Course of Recognition*, Ricœur wanted to demonstrate how the clearly distinguishable categories of exchanging gifts and exchanging merchandise may be enmeshed in everyday practice, he turned to historiography (that of Natalie Zemon Davis[58]). What I attempt to do with the two chosen cases is no different: viewing the extremely complex practical situations of violent democracy will help us gain insight into the distressful decision – which is a distressful indecision[59] – of adopting a course of action. In this, I follow Ricœur partially in claiming that "[t]his limit-situation [*situation-limite*], by which ethics splits into two ethics of distress, is undoubtedly not a constant situation, nor even a lasting or frequent one. But like all extreme things, it throws light on the average, normal situations".[60] However, unlike Ricœur, I do not speak about the ethics of conviction and the ethics of principle as two forms of an ethics of distress. And in the two cases that I present, violent democracy and the background of neo-liberal politics – the context of distress – are not only enduring, but have become normalised. At the edge of violent democracy, an ethics of distress is often the only form of ethical option left.

3.1 The Ambiguities of Violence at the "Edge"

Labour sociologist David Dickinson studied the following case.[61] In the year 2000, the state-owned postal service, the South African Post Office, embarked on a new strategic organisation of its labour force, in particular its mode of employment. Up to that date, all employees were directly in the service of the Post Office, received their salary from the Post Office, could bargain for wage increases with the Post Office and, if need be, could engage in labour action against the Post Office. Then, all positions on the lower levels were frozen and they were henceforth occupied by labourers provided by so-called labour brokers. These

---

58 See Paul Ricœur, *Parcours de la reconnaissance* (Paris: Gallimard, 2004), 369–372 / *The Course of Recognition*, trans. David Pellauer (Cambridge, MA: Harvard University Press, 2005), 238–43.
59 Following the happy choice of words of Jacques Derrida, *Adieu à Emmanuel Lévinas* (Paris: Galilée, 1997), 199–200. This insistence on *indecision* has nothing to do with claiming the luxury of endless contemplation which academics often enjoy, but which those acting under the often unbearable pressures and demands of practice can usually not afford. Insisting on agents' indecision is a way of taking them seriously in their claim to be acting strategically and ethically.
60 Ricœur, "Etat et violence" [1957], in *Histoire et vérité*, 278–93, here 292–93 / "State and Violence" [1957], in *History and Truth*, 234–246, here 246 (translation modified).
61 David Dickenson, *Fighting Their Own Battles. The Mabarete and the End of Labour Broking in the South African Post Office*, SWOP working paper 2, February 2015.

placement agencies were less subject to the constraints of labour rights, and consequently turned out to be more than able to provide the Post Office with a sufficient number of labourers, while reducing the income of these labourers. A decade of this practice proved the outrageous injustice of this system when it was revealed labour-broker labourers received a 50% smaller wage than their Post Office colleagues for exactly the same work; at the same time it was practically impossible to oppose this system without being summarily laid off.

But now, is South Africa not a constitutional democracy, with labour rights and institutions charged with protecting and fighting for these rights? It turned out that the labour-broker labourers tried every possible means to further their legitimate cause: labour action (where possible), labour courts, political parties, etc. To no avail. And this is the point: people who were systematically subjected to the violence of exploitation explored all peaceful means and exhausted all institutional possibilities, ultimately all in vain.

In the five months running up to April 2012, a group of these workers, the Mabarete, embarked on a number of protest initiatives, which continued even after they were laid off. Their initiatives included mobilisations of former colleagues, intimidation and harassment of postal workers who did deliveries (typically in townships and not in richer suburbs) and finally "home visits" which included threats to incumbents or relatives of incumbents of the labour broker, the trade unions or the Post Office. It was this combination of active obstruction of the work of the Post Office and drawing the personal life of incumbents into labour disputes that finally moved the Post Office to reconsider its labour practices.

In my view, Dickenson captures the nexus of strategic and normative considerations involved in this case when he explains:

> these tactics involved the *use or threat of violence*. This *did not* sit comfortably with the Mabarete leadership, but they *saw no other option* and this form of pressure was only applied after exhausting available legal channels. Given this context, blanket condemnation of violence as an instrument of struggle is likely to cut little ice.[62]

If we now resume our role as political philosophers and hermeneuticists of the capable human, after having read Dickenson's report against the backdrop of Von Holdt's exposition on violent democracy, how are we to think about recourse to violence at the edge of violent democracies?

---

[62] Dickenson, *Fighting their own battles*, 33 (my emphasis).

First, studies such as Dickenson's show that strategies that resort to violence may really be *effective*.[63] However, it seems fair to speculate that they are not necessarily always so; they might also be ineffective. Likewise, where this violence was limited, it could also have been increased with the hope of being more efficient sooner.

Second, although I emphasise the recourse to violent means and strategies in order to engage Ricœur, it would be an error to think of such strategies as devoid of *discursive* reason. In fact, in some cases, such strategies are similar to the community protest movements described elsewhere by Von Holdt, of which he says that they "are not inchoate mobs, but are characterised by an explicit *discourse about human and democratic rights* and constitute an insurgent citizenship struggle against the differentiation of citizenship rights".[64] In Ricœurian parlance, they are attempts to realize people's aspiration to live in just institutions. Therefore, they *cannot be reduced to the violent means of action*. Yet, this point should not be exaggerated, because of the recurrent use of intimidation by protesters to mobilise others to collaborate in their protests. The extremes of mob-violence and mob-justice therefore fall outside of the difficult combination of prudence and forceful means, since it leaves no, or hardly any, room for the discursive moment.[65] On the other hand, such recourse to violent strategies *cannot be reduced to discursive reason* either, in fact, they constitute many ways to *combine* discursive claims to legitimacy with ultimate recourse to violence. As such, these movements represent a fragmentation and pluralization of legitimately taking recourse to violence within the state – against the Weberian idea of a monopoly of such legitimacy[66] (this point is developed further in §4.3).

---

[63] Here I refer to violent acts as an integral part of the strategy of contestation – not primarily as symbols. This possibility was explored in Chapter 7.

[64] Von Holdt, "Overview. Insurgent citizenship...," 25 (my emphasis).

[65] Mob justice falls outside of my reflection on the turn to violent means for justice. Interpreting mob psychology and action requires an entirely different set of conceptual and analytical tools.

[66] Von Holdt's conclusion on intra-elite violence in terms of Weber's thesis holds equally for the implications of subaltern violence: "The rule of law is a foundational institution of democratic regimes, designed to ensure that all citizens are equal before the law and that the coercive agencies of the state are bound by and accountable to the law. The examples above indicate a drift away from the rule of law. But violent democracy is not only marked by the kind of extra-legal violence deployed by protesters or police discussed so far – it is marked as well by institutional struggles for control over the instruments of law, that is to say, the instruments of institutionalized coercion over which the Weberian state is supposed to hold a monopoly. This is precisely to avert the equal application of the law to all citizens and the accountability of the state's coercive agencies". Von Holdt, "On Violent Democracy," 145.

3 Two Ambiguous Strategies to Further the Good Life in Violent Democracies — 233

Third, affirming the penetrability of violent initiatives by discursive, normative considerations does not cancel its tragic *ambiguity*. Again I follow Von Holdt's caution:

> these insurgencies do not constitute an unproblematic notion of expanded citizenship. They have a darker side too, reproducing patriarchal prejudices, xenophobic exclusion, and the use of violence in political and social disputes and to buttress local power – practices which corrode, undermine and restrict the basis of citizenship. Community protests, collective violence and the associational practices that underlie them are ambiguous and contradictory in their implications for citizenship and democracy.[67]

Furthermore, some such forms of social contestation are also systemically bound up with violence closer to the centres of social privilege. There can thus be no question of investing messianic hope in courses of violent action initiated under the extremely demanding conditions of life close to the precipice of destitution. Ricœur's warning applies: "a freedom that does not become institutionalized is *potentially* terrorist",[68] provided that we concede that this potential for "terrorism" does not reside primarily in taking recourse to violent means, but in the attempt to impose one's understanding of justice on society despite of, or at the expense of, institutional means of finding justice.[69] That is, by the way, why "terrorism" is such an ambiguous phenomenon.[70]

However, fourth, one should not draw overly simplistic conclusions about the non-institutional character of such contestations. On the one hand, the fact that some social movements of labour protest bind people together for a limited time, around a limited set of objectives, based on only a few shared values, does not mean that there is no institution. *Small, ephemeral institutions* are still institutions.[71] On the other hand, one should be careful to distinguish between

---

[67] Von Holdt "Overview," 7, similarly Von Holdt, "South Africa: The Transition to violent democracy," 599.
[68] "[U]ne liberté qui n'entre pas en institution est *potentiellement* terroriste". Ricœur, "Le conflit: signe de contradiction ou d'unité?" 200 (my emphasis).
[69] This is the problem of one-sidedness and lack of perspective on the internal contradictions in one's own position that Ricœur identifies in his reading of Antigone and Creon in Sophocles' play.
[70] On the problem of ethics leading to "terrorism", see my critique of Levinas in *De l'éthique à la justice. Langage et politique dans la philosophie de Lévinas* (Dordrecht: Springer, 2007), Chapter 9. A similar critique of excessive morality in politics is presented in Axel Honneth, *Freedom's Right. The Social Foundations of Democratic Life*, trans. Joseph Ganahl (Cambridge: Polity, [2011] 2014), section B.II. (3).
[71] In Chapter 1, §3, I laid a basis for this claim. On the minimalist institutionalization of moral freedom, see Honneth, *Freedom's Right*, 173–205.

the institutions one may aspire to live in because they facilitate one's striving for justice (and in that sense are provisional *ends* of our action) and institutions that are instituted as a *means* by which to achieve the former ones.

Five, whatever the kinds of institution under consideration, one does well to view institutions too as *ambiguous* phenomena, because they are constituted in a paradoxical way: whereas institutions are essential to enable individuals to live out their human abilities, they can have this augmenting effect on action only by sometimes obstructing some forms of action or even by being perpetuated at some expense to people.[72] This is of great importance for my argument: institutions are the outcome of collective action and they in turn condition action (even if these are the actions of a relatively small group of people and only for a short time), but they are always the outcome of *action compositions.* Whenever we consider an institution in a personified way, its actions have to be considered as a (more or less failed or successful) combination of *strategic* objectives (means) and *normative* aspirations (ethics and morality). The valid distinction between the two dimensions of means and ethics/morality should not seduce us to separate them – in prudent action, instrumental and normative dimensions are interwoven and mutually conditioning.[73] No theory of social protest, political contestation or civil disobedience can circumvent this point.

Now that we have established these points, we can move to the second case study.

3.2 The Ambiguities of Refraining from Violence at the "Edge"

In *Grounding Globalization. Labour in the Age of Insecurity,* Edward Webster, Rob Lambert and Andries Bezuidenhout[74] studied the effects of increasing global neo-liberal pressures of competition for share-holder value and decreasing employment security on the work and private lives of people in three very different localities: South Korea, Australia and South Africa. They carefully document the devastating fragilization of people's financial position, the undermining of their social agency and the heavy burden on household life. Especially in the South

---

[72] This "institutional paradox" has been detailed in Chapters 3, §5 and 5, §2.1d.
[73] See Wolff, "'Technology' as the Critical Social Theory of Human Technicity," *Journal of Philosophical Research* 41 (2016): 333–69; Wolff, "Towards a Post-Levinasian Understanding of Responsibility: The Weberian Contribution of Apel," in *Political Responsibility for a Globalised World. After Levinas' Humanism* (Bielefeld: Transcript, 2011), 205–19.
[74] Edward Webster, Rob Lambert and Andries Bezuidenhout, *Grounding Globalization. Labour in the Age of Insecurity* (Malden, MA, Oxford, and Carlton: Blackwell, 2008).

African case (on which I focus), the situation is comparable to the life-world realities of the labourers studied by Dickenson in the previous section. The interest of their study for my argument is the wide variety of responses from the people involved and the divergent outcomes they document.

On the one hand they report on varieties of *defeat:* adaptation to market pressures, retreat into the household, fatalism, migration, etc.[75] Although each of these requires new action initiatives, they all represent some sort of defeat, since they represent instances of an unwilling acceptance of a decrease in the good life. These findings can also be translated into a register of the hermeneutics of the capable and suffering human by extensions to *Oneself as Another* such as "Autonomy and Fragility" (discussed in §1.2, above).

On the other hand, the authors also document how, in all three cases, some people have embarked on *experiments in mobilisation* against the new tendencies in labour management. These experiments vary between imposing new conditions for their support of old political parties, creating community-based support organizations, activism to open local government's budget for public debate, forming international labour alliances, forming coalitions with NGO's or protest groups from civil society, etc.[76] The authors identify the "emergence of transnational activism" as especially promising, demonstrating

> how labour has begun to work space through engaging scale from the local to the nation-state to the global level. We identify the emergence of new sources of workers' bargaining power – what we call moral or symbolic power – where unions and community activists have begun to mobilize around the discourse of global justice, fair trade, fair employment and, in the case of South Africa, access to anti-retroviral drugs in the treatment of the AIDS pandemic. Various new initiatives are currently underway in which logistical power is being carefully and strategically evaluated.[77]

Yet a lot of what they are excited about remain an extension of current experiments.[78] The initiatives they document have resulted in some alleviation of people's fate, but without radical change.

What instruction can the hermeneuticist of the capable human draw from these varied findings? First, the strategies of coping with trying circumstances are – as elsewhere in human life – the outcome of *prudent* trade-offs of conflict-

---

75 Webster et al., *Grounding Globalization*, 106, 157–58.
76 Cf. the summarising table in Webster et al., *Grounding Globalization*, 215.
77 Webster et al., *Grounding Globalization*, 159–60 (the citation applies to Chapter 9 of their book)
78 Cf. Webster et al., *Grounding Globalization*, 185.

ing demands on practice. Correspondingly, each of these actions remains open to our assessment as to its *strategic* and *normative* appropriateness.

Second, since this is the case, one cannot declare the avoidance of violent means good without some qualification. As commendable as it is for not generating more injuries and deaths, it comes at a price: a sacrifice of family life, internalization of systemic violence, inability to oppose an unjust *status quo* – in short, considerable sacrifice of the desire for the good life. Ricœur's caution from another context may therefore apply here: "Everything happens as if mutual tolerance between people of the word [*gens de parole*] were surreptitiously transformed into tolerance towards *states* of violence, intolerance towards *acts* of violence".[79] The rejection of violence does not settle the question of ethics; it represents only one kind of response to injustice and requires assessment as much as violent strategies do. However, one has to be very careful here, since internalization and defeatism are also marks of life beyond the "edge", where desperation has done its work of reducing agency to almost nothing. Under such circumstances, moral assessment from the outside is, at best, inappropriate, at worst, a continuation of structural violence by other means. This fate of social death lies beyond the scope of this chapter.

Third, on the positive side, in as far as the alternative strategies result in positive outcomes, they point to the avoidability of violence without loss of effectiveness. As oppressive and desperate as circumstances may become, they do not thereby automatically make the recourse to violence inevitable. Declaring that "there was no other option", very often expresses the hopelessness of the situation, but it should *not* be taken as *a claim about real determinism*. And in as far as the recourse to violence is avoidable, one may conclude that when it occurs, it is the outcome of a decision, hence strategically and normatively assessable. This decisive point has to be nuanced: it does not mean that there is always an effective, workable alternative to violence; it means that when people embark on a course of violent initiative, their action cannot simply be said to be somehow determined by socio-political pressures. To relinquish or retreat are as much options as outright, ruthless violence. Decision and assessment are what make it human action – and what continues to call for judgement even at the brink of social reality. However, where people are pushed beyond the edge of destitution into social death, such assessment may well be obscene.

Fourth, the study of the three sociologists demonstrates that institutionalization, even when provisional and fluid, tends to increase the efficiency of contestation. Hence the instrumental view of such institutions is affirmed. At the same

---

79 Ricœur, "Le conflit: signe de contradiction ou d'unité?" 199 (my emphasis).

time, the less effective the non-violent means of contestation are, the greater the need for experimentation with new strategies. The three authors' enthusiasm for "moral or symbolic power" speaks to this point. However, on the road of further experimentation, one discovers that the less violent strategies are not necessarily the exact opposite of the violent options: for instance, the recourse to "logistic power" (as in the citation above) which means obstructing the manufacturing process at a factory or blocking public roads,[80] is only one step away from intimidation or sabotage.

Fifth, I have spent more time exploring the violent option than its non-violent counterpart. This is because the less violent one corresponds more closely with the forms of discursive contestation already theorized by Ricœur (as discussed above, §1). However, the similarity between discursive contestation in the Ricœurian sense and forms of non-violent protest and local politics described by Webster et al. should not be exaggerated. Indeed, the kinds of non-violent protest and local politics Webster et al. have in mind can only be understood as potentially viable or commendable ways of pursuing the good life when the backdrop of a violent democracy is borne in mind, since the meaning of such strategies depends on this specific context. Furthermore, such non-violent options may still lead on to violent options in the future, or may for strategic ends be combined with violent strategies. Whatever the case may be, it is decisive to see that these non-violent options (and I think here only about the strategically successful ones) are always non-violent options *in relation to* violent ones. In other words, they are non-violent not because violent options have been eliminated *a priori* by definition or demarcation, but because violent options remain actional alternatives.

This is my point: *the violent and non-violent options of composing strategic and normative requirements of social contestation remain horizons of the intelligibility of each other within a context of violent democracy.*

This is not really a happy ending. In fact, it is not an ending at all, but rather a beginning: the point of departure of all (in)decision about ethical dilemmas in politics, at least in states similar to South Africa. And here, everything depends on people's attestation to their degree of capability under varying depths of tragic circumstances.

---

80 Discussed by these three authors, cf. Webster et al., *Grounding Globalization*, 207.

4 Conclusion: Attestation of Prudence at the "Edge"[81]

When Adorno declared that "there is no right life in false life",[82] he articulated the desperation of those who would like to do what is right or good, but know their action to be decisively bound up by unjust societal conditions that co-determine the meaning of even their best-intentioned initiatives. In this chapter, I have contemplated this problem by means of Ricœur's hermeneutics of the capable human, a philosophy that considers ethical decision-making to be a context-bound act. I have looked closely at a dramatic current case: acting from the "edge" of violent democracies where people are not yet socially dead, but where the optative for the good life has to be pursued *despite* the pressures of political and economic institutions. In as far as we consider the political dimension of this situation, the capable and suffering human's ability to take prudent action – action which is both effective and a fair compromise between ethics and morality – is tested to the extreme. Can one effectively and ethically oppose a structurally violent social order from the edge?

4.1 Conflictual Ethics: Composing Action as Prudent "Relative to us"

Early in this chapter, I presented Ricœur's view on ethics as essentially conflictual. For him, ethics is not the avoidance of conflict, tension, struggle or compromise for the sake of peace or principle. Ethics is about striving for a good life with and for others in just institutions by prudently working one's way through these tensions in practice. Understandably, therefore, Ricœur opens the chapter on prudence in *Oneself as Another* with a meditation on tragedy. Sophocles taught Ricœur to consider Antigone and Creon as tragic agents *because* they aspire to do good. They enact the extreme possibilities of tragedy that often befall people in their everyday life circumstances. Antigone and Creon are tragic in their attempts to avoid the prudent negotiation, the compromise, between *conflicting valid* normative claims. Their first imprudence consists in absolutizing their respective position (morality and ethics) and thus not even seeing the

---

[81] It is of decisive importance that I use the terms "attestation" and "prudence" the specific sense Ricœur gives them – see Chapter 3, §1 (on attestation) and §1, above (on prudence).
[82] Theodor Adorno, *Minima Moralia. Reflexionen aus dem beschädigten Leben*, Gesammelte Schriften 4. (Frankfurt am Main: Suhrkamp, [1951] 1997), §18, 43: "Es gibt kein richtiges Leben im falschen."

valid side of the other's point of view. Their second imprudence resides in not being aware of the contradictions in their own view.[83]

When, in the framework of a general hermeneutic anthropology, Ricœur limited his view on prudence in politics to Western liberal democracies, he exposed himself unwittingly to such a one-sidedness. This is evidenced most strikingly by his omission of violence as a means by which prudently to pursue the good life under certain circumstances. It is no use to say that this is merely circumscribing his argument, as justified by his objective of a hermeneutics of attestation,[84] since it is precisely by revoking this unjustifiable limitation to the easiest case of a political constitution (Western democracy) and the least dramatic of prudential possibilities (those where recourse to violence is evidently out of the question), that we gain a more sophisticated view on prudent action under tragic circumstances. I have opposed this tendency in Ricœur's later work, one could say, by doing something similar to what he did with Antigone and Creon: drawing from the work of Johannesburg labour sociologists, I offered two views on the pursuit of the good life from the brink of social desolation.[85] Both have their merits, but neither can lay claim to being the solution to all similar situations. It is the tension between the two that guides us right into the intricacies of prudent (in)decision. In these two cases, the tension of prudence between ethics and morality is at stake, but they represent something more: they stand for two divergent positions on a continuum of ways to articulate the actional requirements of *strategic efficacy* and *prudent excellence*. In short, when unjust circumstances confront people at the "edge" with a practical doubt (*soupçon*) of their ability to act, only the context-bound, practical compromise between different requirements can serve as an attestation of the ability to act – we are at the core of Ricœur's concern in *Oneself as Another*.

I have concluded above that the two approaches to initiatives from the "edge" each forms a horizon of intelligibility for the other. Those who hesitate about the course of action may well contemplate (a) the problems when one of these is absolutized (violent escalation, or defeatist adaptation or interiorization), but also (b) the internal contradictions of each strategy (visible each time in the divergent outcomes). This is the work of prudence. It has to find the difficult compromises that would maximally avoid these extremes, in ways depend-

---

83 Cf. Ricœur, *Soi-même comme un autre*, 284 / *Oneself as Another*, 243.
84 Cf. especially Ricœur, *Soi-même comme un autre*, 295 / *Oneself as Another*, 253.
85 Elsewhere, Ricœur adopts a more ideal typical schematization by opposing an "ideology of dialogue" and an "ideology of conflict at all costs" – cf. Paul Ricœur, "Le conflit: signe de contradiction ou d'unité?" 193.

ing on the contingencies of the context. The optative for the good life requires compromises, and compromises mean rejecting the logic of yes/no, all/nothing, to embrace the conflicting valid claims to varying *degrees*.[86] The degree of ethics or morality, of effectiveness or prudence, of violence committed against others or self-sacrifice, all depend on people's assessment of the degree of injustice suffered and the degree of their own capabilities. By developing this point, I have highlighted a major Aristotelian thrust inherent in Ricœur's ethics, namely that the practice of virtue is always "relative to us" (*pros hémas*):[87] it is a matter of practical hermeneutics.[88] The tensions involved in this ethical dilemma remain unresolvable in *theory*; the ultimate response to the question "what then shall we do?" has to be given in *practice*. Even under extremely trying *circumstances* both the strategic and normative dimensions of action composition are open to incremental variation: a little bit more peace, a little more force, a bit more patience – but each time with its own difficulties. The point remains attestation of the ability to be responsible: to act and to impute.[89]

4.2 Attestation, Action, Self-confidence

The self-attestation that occurs when agents impute actions to themselves in difficult cases of prudential decision-making goes to the heart of a hermeneutic anthropology, and therefore it is also important for sociology and political theory, in particular for protest theory. Nowhere is this more patent than in the urgent affirmation of the practical ability to deal with dilemmas by making an impact on events to this or that degree, by deploying these or those means and by engaging in this or that prudent compromise. The dramatic intensity of recognizing oneself as able or unable to act can be felt on one's own body; the consequences of both good and rash decision-making are inscribed in the proximate social environment. Each time the fact of acting, and of acting ethically, serves as attestation to one's being more than a suffering being, to one's ability to act. But this attestation is always a weak epistemic confirmation of the *degree* to which one can recognize oneself as able to act, because the affirmation is always *mixed*

---

[86] Cf. Wolff, "'Technology' as the Critical Social Theory of Human Technicity," 344–60; Wolff, "Towards a Post-Levinasian Understanding of Responsibility: the Weberian Contribution of Apel," 205–19.
[87] Aristotle, *Nicomachean Ethics*, 1106b36.
[88] This relativism is not absolute as long as it is constituted by the tension between mutually contradicting requirements that are constitutive of Ricœur's ethics (as explained in §1).
[89] "Impute" in the specific Ricœurian sense – see Chapter 3, §1.

with doubt (to a degree inverse to the strength of affirmation in the attestation). This is why successful action is so significant in augmenting people's self-confidence to intervene in their own fate – as has been theorized for the political context by Fanon[90] and many others, including Von Holdt[91] and arguably Ricœur.[92]

In such contexts where compromise is called for, there are only "not-nice" solutions;[93] however, we have seen that the agents in question do not therefore consider it a matter of indifference what course of action they choose. Often those who are the closest to the "edge", those who live under the severest constraints, have the most difficult questions of "dirty hands" to answer – issues about which life in the middle class, despite its own concerns and worries, could remain unaware or at least respond to with less urgency. Therefore, the mere perspective of "putting one's hand on the wheel of history",[94] of the possible outcomes of one's action, like causing or tolerating the other's suffering, may generate a doubt that would undermine the self-confidence in one's ability to intervene in social reality. On the other hand, what more dramatic instance of attestation and imputation than the realization that even as a victim of structural violence one can engage in a legitimate contestation while turning others into victims of one's own initiative?

Approaching the question of taking recourse to violence from the perspective of attestation in a context of structural violence thus helps us to avoid two opposing pitfalls. On the one hand, we *avoid demonizing the agents*. If we do not accord violence due attention, we may miss the desperation and hopelessness of people's situation and require the exceptional from people who are already tried to the utmost. This applies equally to those who finally decide against vio-

---

90 This is the (demythologized) point I accept from Frantz Fanon, *The Wretched of the Earth* (London: Penguin, 1965), 51–52.
91 Cf. "Collective violence in community protests constitutes a symbolic disruption of the dominant symbolic order, underpinned by a subaltern symbolic order (or local moral order), through which the subaltern classes are enabled to assert an insurgent citizenship". Von Holdt, "Overview. Insurgent citizenship…," 31. Within the scope of the current project, I cannot do full justice to the complexities of Von Holdt argument on this point.
92 This may be demonstrated, for instance, with reference to "Capacities and Social Practices," in Paul Ricœur, *Parcours de la reconnaissance* (Paris: Gallimard, 2004), 215–236 / *The Course of Recognition*. trans. David Pellauer (Cambridge, MA: Harvard University Press, 2005), 135–49 and Ricœur's reading of Honneth and symbolic political actions in the same book (see Chapter 7, §2.1, above).
93 See also Wolff, "For a 'Good Enough' Justice," in *Political Responsibility*, 267–72.
94 Literally: "um seine Hand in die Speichen des Rades der Geschichte legen zu dürfen", Max Weber, "Politik als Beruf" [1919], in *Gesammelte politische Schriften*. Potsdamer Internet-Ausgabe (1999), 396–450, here 435, http://www.uni-potsdam.de/verlagsarchivweb/html/494/html/PS.pdf, last accessed 5 February 2021. / "Politics as a Vocation," 115.

lent action. On the other hand, we *avoid an exonerating determinism*. Living at the "edge" is not yet social death. The people concerned understand themselves not only as able to make ethical decisions and see dilemmas, but as concerned by the practical and ethical dilemmas even when they know what their own interests are. The hermeneutics of their fragile abilities help to describe the position of agents at the edge, but without de-humanizing such people, and to recognize their exceptional efforts and initiatives when we encounter them.

4.3 Justice despite Institutions

By contemplating taking recourse to violent means, we have not abandoned the theme of democracy or of the broader quest for justice, in favour of some vague turn to irrational, erratic or capricious human action. Quite the contrary: we are concerned here with the continued attempt to pursue justice, but under circumstances of greatly reduced capability and extremely advanced tragedy, typical of life at the edge of social co-existence. Here the optative for a life of justice has to be realized, despite the failure of institutions to which people might otherwise appeal or which they might otherwise attempt to reform by the means typically attributed to democratic interaction, namely debate. Three important findings result from this.

First, while thinking about justice for which the state (if not the global order) is the ultimate frame, we get a view on the formation of (sometimes) short-lived, micro institutions that are instituted as means by which to further justice, not as institutions through which to live out justice. My point is not the dream of "liberty without institutions",[95] but the dream of liberty as it has to be pursued under conditions where the institutions do not facilitate but rather obstruct the exercise of liberty. Under such circumstances, at best, this optative can be supported by temporary institutions of protest. There is a definite risk involved in side-stepping the existing institutions of justice, namely the illusion of righteousness without the need to think about the means of action or the illusion of equating the interests of a small group with justice for the whole of society (what I have referred to above as "terrorism").

Second, Max Weber obviously knew about intermediary institutions – a large part of his "Politics as a Vocation" describes the social mechanisms by

---

[95] Ricœur, "Le conflit: signe de contradiction ou d'unité?" 200.

which people attempt to gain access to the power of the state.[96] However, the ultimate horizon of his understanding of politics in journalism, political parties, trade unions, etc. is the question of getting a share in the power of the state defined as the entity which can successfully claim a monopoly on the legitimate recourse to violence. By contrast, in violent democracies the institutionalization of inequalities and a system of patronage undermines the legitimacy of the state's coercive power; at the same time, the violent action of protests from the "edge" *fragments the monopoly on this legitimate claim*, due to the *de facto* consent such protests draw from sections of the society. Consequently, even following Weber's understanding of the embeddedness of responsibility in sociopolitical reality, responsibility becomes contingent on the realities of intersecting forms of violence and their contradictory claims to legality or legitimacy. In this sense, as we have seen, Von Holdt claims, violence and democracy condition each other.

Third, perhaps unexpectedly, but precisely because one cannot deny the ethical fibre of these violent initiatives from the "edge", and despite the fact that such initiatives may draw our sympathy, we cannot abandon the question of how to evaluate such initiatives, strategically and normatively. Even at the brink of social desolation there is no unconditional or *a priori* legitimacy. Legitimacy is always qualified: something can only be legitimate with regard to the reasonableness of its means, context, amount, extent, etc. In short, legitimacy is determined through prudent judgement. Without some form of prudent consent, legitimation is *in fact* arbitrary. Taking recourse to violence seriously as a moral initiative implies keeping open the strategic and normative assessment of it.[97] Thus, even when we as academics agree with the concerns of those who take recourse to violence at the "edge", we cannot therefore abolish the question of assessment. This question only becomes more complex.[98] Respecting precarious and destitute agents as agents of ethics does not exempt them from responding (even in principle) to concerns. What they have to answer for sometimes includes their compromises that strengthen ties of elite violence, excesses of xenophobia or harassment, and the incalculable consequences of their action

---

96 Weber, "Politics as a Vocation," 81–115. On Weber's philosophy or responsibility see Etienne de Villiers, *Revisiting Max Weber's Ethic of Responsibility* (Tübingen: Mohr Siebeck, 2018).
97 Above, I have already alluded to the significance of coordinating strategic and normative assessments; see again Wolff, "'Technology' as the Critical Social Theory of Human Technicity," 344–60.
98 Boltanski reached similar conclusions from a different perspective, cf. Luc Boltanski, "Critical Sociology and Pragmatic Sociology of Critique," in *On Critique. A Sociology of Emancipation* (Cambridge, and Malden, MA: Polity, [2009] 2011), 18–49.

(as presented in §2 and see also Chapter 5, §3.2, point 2). One therefore has to assume a real *ethics of turning to violence* (and *mutatis mutandis* resisting doing so or postponing doing so). Of such an ethics of progressive entry into violence – which is also an ethic of postponing the total adoption of maximal violence – the young Mandela gave us a viable sense in his Rivonia trial speech.[99]

4.4 Epilogue

Two general observations may be added in conclusion to point out two further possibilities of future work.

Although I have adopted a geo-politically de-centred view on attestation compared to the versions bequeathed to us by Ricœur, my point is not to establish a new centre. Again I follow Von Holdt in claiming that the questions of violent democracy are, and may increasingly become, part of the West, where progressive undermining of the institutionalized social support network may stimulate people's thoughts on the array of means available for understanding their situation and for understanding themselves as agents of justice.

What I have not developed in this essay, but have acknowledged all along, is the significance of Ricœur's earlier socio-political thought, that part of his work where he contemplated more openly the ethics of limited violence, "the morality of force, of methodological violence, of calculated culpability".[100] I would suggest that if Ricœur's later hermeneutic anthropology can serve as a social scientific framework by which to interpret many of the issues involved, it can do so much better if many of the insights of his earlier socio-political thought are integrated into his later hermeneutics.

---

99 Nelson Mandela, "The Rivonia Trial," in *No Easy Walk to Freedom* (Harlow: Heinemann, [1965] 1990), 162-89 and see the discussion of this speech in Chapter 7.
100 Paul Ricœur, "Tâches de l'éducateur politique" / "The Tasks of the Political Educator," cited above.

Conclusion

An Integrated View of the Technicity of Action and the Question of Responsibility

What is wisdom in practice (*phronesis*)? What does it mean to act responsibly? These questions concern us practically as we seek the best courses of action, but also as onlookers at what others do, or even as theoreticians. Often these questions accompany people silently throughout their lives; sometimes they boil up, precipitating an existential crisis. To varying degrees these questions are part of the constitutive ambiguities of action. Action is one with of the flow of life, but can, to some degree, be planned. Capabilities enable us to do things, but they confront us in a series of incapabilities. Instruments augment our ability to intervene in the world, but also increase the impact of unintended consequences. Ethical considerations inform our action, but acting in accordance with these values generates secondary effects that may contradict the initial values. Hence, efficacy is bound to ambiguity, and this does not leave us indifferent.

In this book, I have not tried to dispel these perplexities of action – instead, I have attempted to grapple with them as part of the meaning of human action. Hermeneutics, in combination with insights from the social sciences, has helped me to do so, as I restricted my view to one dimension of action: its technicity. If there is something like prudent or responsible action, the preceding chapters have gone some way toward clarifying what constitutes the practical pursuit of it, while still leaving aside the question of the ethical values that should rightfully inform our action.

Proceeding in this way, I have remained true to two significant lessons that can be learned from Paul Ricœur. The first is that the moment of *distantiation* from action allows us to examine it as meaningful, while assuming a spectator's perspective. Thus, the more interpretative means of hermeneutics and the explanatory means of social theory[1] enhance our understanding of action – explaining more helps us to understand better, according to Ricœur's formula. But this is the case only because of what the second lesson teaches us: people

---

[1] My point is not to reduce social theory to the function of explanation, but to accord both interpretation and explanation their place in the effort of clarification in this book. See, for example, Paul Ricœur, "La fonction herméneutique de la distanciation," in *Du texte à l'action. Essais d'herméneutique II* (Paris: Seuil, 1986), 113–32 / "The Hermeneutical Function of Distanciation," in *From Text to Action: Essays in Hermeneutics II*, trans. Kathleen Blamey and John Thompson (London: Athlone, 1991), 75–88 and "Expliquer et comprendre," in *Du texte à l'action*, 179–204 / "Explanation and Understanding," in *From Text to Action*, 125–43, respectively.

get to know and understand themselves as agents when they *attest* to the actions of which they were capable.² One could say that attestation does at a practical level what distantiation does at a theoretical level. It is by trying to speak, do, narrate and impute action to oneself, and by attesting to the varying degrees to which this succeeds that one increasingly gains a practical understanding of one's action. The two lessons belong together in a double hermeneutics: the scholarly reflection on action as meaningful is possible when and because action has already been practically meaningful for agents.

I would like to use this Conclusion in three ways. First, I reflect on the coherence of the entire enterprise as an outline of a theory of the technicity of action. Second, I trace the fact that the hermeneutic-descriptive aspect and the ethico-political aspects of action are integrated in relations of mutual implication. Third, I trace one of the outer limits of the current project. This limitation, which concerns the philosophy of responsibility, will have to be dealt with in subsequent research. However, I would like to offer an outline of the technical nature of responsibility and the dependence of responsibility on a normative supplement, as a final conclusion of this book.

1 The Technicity of Action – a Short Synthesis

The main thesis that that I have defended and elaborated on in this book is that
- practically all human action has a technical aspect, which provides a partial, but fundamental, perspective on human action in general;
- the technicity of action consists of the combination of acquired capabilities and the use of means; and
- the meaning of action as technical is integrated (but not fused) with the normative meaning that the ethical aspect of action is adjudged to have.

I willingly assume the general anthropological stretch of these theses. At the same time, I counted on my hermeneutic approach to maintain the historicity of all forms of human existence and to safeguard the project from essentialisation. In such a hermeneutic action theory, both stable and historical components can be identified.

In turning my attention to "technicity", I do not start with technical artefacts, but define everything to be called "technical" in relation to the technicity

---

2 Cf. Paul Ricœur, *Soi-même comme un autre* (Paris: Seuil, 1990), 33–35 / *Oneself as Another*, trans. Kathleen Blamey (Chicago, IL: University of Chicago Press, 1992), 21–23.

of human agency and action. Correspondingly, I devote fairly little attention to the nature of technical artefacts in this study. However, I constantly bore in mind their rich variety, and I broached the question of the mode of existence of technical objects by discussing the "autonomy" of means, relative to their producers and users (see Chapter 1, §4 and Chapter 2, §3,2 [point 1]).

In the tradition of philosophy and social theory, there are numerous typologies of technical forms of action (for example, instrumental or goal-rational forms of action) and of the forms of reason guiding such action (as is the case in utilitarianism or rational action theory). However, in this study, my approach was *first* of all resolutely *non-typological*.[3] In this, I follow Hans Joas in his work on the creativity of action.[4] For Joas, creativity is not a category of social action that has to be added to complete existing typologies of rational or normative action,[5] a dimension of action that requires an alternative approach to the typological approaches to human action and their residual categories. "Creativity", in Joas's work, refers to an aspect of all action. In a similar vein, I aim to clarify the technical aspect of action.

Second, the flux of everyday action is identified as the primary point of orientation in this theory of action. This insight from pragmatism is confirmed with reference to Anthony Giddens (see Chapter 5, §3.1). Establishing the primacy of the flux of action allows us to draw on pragmatist and phenomenological philosophies of action in which we can then analyse the relation between continual living-forth (*Hinleben*) and the myriad of hindrances to a simple flow of action.[6]

---

3 See Chapter 2, §3.1.
4 Hans Joas, *Die Kreativität des Handelns* (Frankfurt am Main: Suhrkamp, 1992), in particular Chapters 3 and 4 as well as Ernst Wolff, "'Technology' as the Critical Social Theory of Human Technicity," *Journal of Philosophical Research* 41 (2016): 333–69.
5 Joas, *Die Kreativität des Handelns*, 15f, 213f.
6 The phenomenological and hermeneutic approach I have followed in this book shows a clear family resemblance with the main traits of pragmatist thought: anti-foundationalism, fallibilism, the social character of the self, the importance of research and metaphysical pluralism (paraphrased by Joas in Antje Grimmler, Hans Joas and Richard Sennet, "Creativity, Pragmatism and the Social Sciences," *Distinktion* 13 (2006): 5–31, here 24–25, explicitly derived from Richard Bernstein, "The resurgence of pragmatism," *Social Research* 59, no. 4 (Winter 1992): 813–40. This does not mean that this proximity has always been appreciated by scholarship – as is documented by Patrick L. Bourgeois, "Phenomenology and Pragmatism: A Recent Encounter," in *Phenomenology World-Wide*, ed. Anna-Teresa Tymieniecka (Dordrecht: Springer, 2002), 568–70. Closer to the theme of the technicity of action, the proximity of pragmatism and phenomenology is confirmed by Jens Kertscher, "Was heißt eigentlich Primat der Praxis? – Wie Heidegger und Dewey eine erkenntnistheoretische Dichotomie überwinden," *Journal Phaenomenologie* 32 (2009 – Phänomenologie und Pragmatismus): 59–70; and Robert Innes, "Dewey's Aesthetic Theory and the Critique of Technology," in *Studien zum Problem der Technik* (Phäno-

In the order of phenomenological constitution, the technicity of action depends on a non-technical, mainly biological thrust (equivalent to Aristotle's "*orexis*") that lies at the centre of the flux of action (see Chapter 2, §1 and Chapter 3, §2.1 [point 2]). This implies that our consciousness of action is constitutively secondary to the flux of action; to be precise, it results from disruptions of simple acting.[7] My examination of five forms of incapability that impact on capability (in Chapter 3, §2.1) clarifies the interplay between flow and disruption. Disruptions of the flow of action vary in intensity. Often they are quite subtle and barely enough to arouse a light monitoring of action (another term borrowed from Giddens, see Chapter 5, §3.1). Even at the level of the flow, action is executed as something meaningful, which accounts for the foothold that hermeneutics can subsequently gain in the very fibre of action.

Third, the primacy of the flux of action and the pragmatic approach to action that derives from it require us to rethink "technicity". Instead of resorting immediately to the means-end teleological schema traditionally associated with technical action, I argued in Chapter 3 (§§3.1 and 3.2) for a distinction between primary and secondary technicity of action.[8]

Primary technicity is an attribute of the flux of action, and it results from the acquisition of relatively stable bodily skills, which are exercised in response to the requirements and opportunities of each practical context. There is very little action that does not depend on such technicity (some exceptions are reflexes such as suckling, or states such as being drunk). The fact that these skills are exercised in coordination with means of action does not imply that agents necessarily consciously plan the use of these means. Rather, primary technicity is based on the tacit understanding that agents have of their context and their spontaneous or habitual response to it. At this level, the technicity of action includes minimal monitoring of action and interpretation of the practical environ-

---

menologische Forschungen 15), ed. Ernst Wolfgang Orth (Freiburg, and Munich: Verlag Karl Alber, 1985), 7–42.

[7] It follows from the pragmatist orientation of my study that when I refer to "phenomenology", it already implies a critique of the consciousness-centredness prevalent in early phenomenology, and incorporates the pragmatic inflexion. Relevant to this point, see Carl Friedrich Gethmann's commentary on Heidegger's "pragmatism" in "Heideggers Konzeption des Handelns in *Sein und Zeit*," in *Heidegger und die praktische Philosophie*, eds. Annemarie Gethmann-Siefert and Otto Pöggeler (Frankfurt am Main: Suhrkamp, 1988), 140–76. Also see Mark Okrent, "Heidegger's Pragmatism Redux," in *The Cambridge Companion to Pragmatism*, ed. Alan Malachowski. Cambridge Companions to Philosophy (Cambridge: Cambridge University Press, 2013), 124–58.

[8] The notions of primary and secondary technicity are discussed further in Wolff, "'Technology' as the Critical Social Theory," 345–47.

ment. It is not teleologically structured. However, it lends itself to transformation in response to disturbances in the expected course of action, and this in turn intensifies tacit monitoring to conscious observation, and to interpretation, questioning and calculation.

This opens the way to *secondary technicity of action*. In response to the new situation, agents can now plan action. This implies deliberation on the ends that these agents want to achieve and on the capabilities and means by which they are to be achieved. Thus primary technicity acquires a teleological structure. Quite often, of course, this teleological structure is already inscribed in the "rules" of the practices we engage in. However, the whole range of people's actions remains subject to adjustment, both of the "top-down specification" between different levels of intermediary ends and our life plans, and between such more teleologically structured action and aspects of people's life that are not framed in this way (as discussed in Chapter 5, §4 [Task 2]).

Fourth, the skill component of the technicity of action is thus much more complex than "traditional and effective action".[9] Numerous factors contribute to an individualization of bodily skills: transmission is not perfect; there are differences between bodies, differences between levels of talent, changes in the contexts of deployment, different skills are combined in ever new ways, etc.[10] This means that even under the most familiar of circumstances, the deployment of skilful dispositions entails judgment or interpretation[11] (see Chapter 2, §3.3).

---

9 According to the famous formula of Marcel Mauss in "Les techniques du corps" (1934), in *Sociologie et anthropologie* (Paris: PUF, 1950), 365–86, here, 371.

10 I have argued for such a "hermeneutic" understanding of the technical disposition of the human body, by enforcing the phenomenological moments in Bourdieu's theory of the relation between the habitus and the field, cf. Ernst Wolff, "Technicity of the Body as part of the sociotechnical System: The Contributions of Mauss and Bourdieu," *Theoria* 76 (2010): 167–87, here 181–84) and by other means in Wolff, "'Technology' as the Critical Social Theory," 345–47. An obvious result of this procedure is the diminishing of the determinist penchant in Bourdieu's theory of social reproduction. Working methodologically in an opposite direction – from the particular to its generalizations – is Laurent Thévenot's essay "Le régime de la familiarité. Les choses en personne," *Genèse* 17 (1994): 72–101. See also a more recent articulation of this part of his work in Laurent Thévenot, "Grand résumé de *L'Action au pluriel. Sociologie des régimes d'engagement*," *SociologieS*, http://journals.openedition.org/sociologies/3572, online publication 6 July 2011, last accessed 4 May 2019. His and my two approaches converge on the significance of particular judgments in technical action.

11 The classical text in this regard is Heidegger's elaboration on the "hermeneutic as" (*hermeneutische Als*), in Martin Heidegger, *Sein und Zeit* (Tübingen: Max Niemeyer Verlag, [1927] 1993), especially §§32 and 33. On Ricœur's hermeneutic elaboration on it, cf. Andris Breitling, "Paul Ricœur und das hermeneutische Als," in *Vor dem Text: Hermeneutik und Phänomenologie im*

The interpretative demands on action increase as the normal flow of familiar actions is repeatedly put to the test by changes in the bodily condition and/or context. This demonstrates that the activation of stable skills in relatively stable circumstances (what we call following rules) involve a "phronetic moment",[12] a hermeneutic moment, a fact which can be accounted for only if one assumes some form of pre-reflexive monitoring. Moreover, rule-following behaviour is enforced by relatively standardised technical means and dispositives or infrastructure (such as post-offices, school, traffic, etc.).[13] This enforcement is one of the sources of rule-following behaviour in individuals, but the dispositives also generate the context which solicits the phronetic moment to arise from rule-following. On the whole, most of the time, agents have to deploy different skills in different combinations in order to make their way through different social and technical contexts (which is the background from which one could recognize the painful experience of absolute repetition in an unchanging environment). The effort of composing action into a meaningful course depends on the meaningful nature of action and interaction, but also on the mediation of action by the internal, usage and symbolic references of the means deployed (as we saw in Chapter 2, §3.3).

However, *fifth*, this insistence on understanding and interpretation as constitutive of action should not be construed as an intellectualistic reduction of action. Due attention to the technicity of action guards us against this fallacy. Let us consider again the skilful body in interaction with means. On the one hand, it disposes the agent to act in certain ways when confronted with certain contexts; on the other hand, the absence of other skills makes it harder to do other things and disposes agents by default not to act in such ways. Both the acquired dispositions and the context in which they are activated thus exert *enabling and constraining* effects on action. Understanding the technicity of action from this bodily, non-consciousness-centred perspective is made possible by the non-teleological character of primary technicity that I have described.

Sixth, since a non-typological approach to action allows for an exploration of the technicity of action of the primary flux of action, and from there of all

---

Denken Paul Ricœurs, eds. Stephan Orth and Andris Breitling (Berlin: Technische Universität Berlin, 2002), 79–97.
12 Cf. Charles Taylor, "To follow a rule…," in *Bourdieu. A Critical Reader*, ed. Richard Shusterman (Oxford and Malden, MA: Blackwell, 1999), 29–44, here 41.
13 See Bruno Latour and Shirley Strum, "Human social origins. Please tell us another origin story!" *Journal of Biological and Social Structures* 9 (1996): 169–87 and Bruno Latour, "On Interobjectivity," *Mind, Culture, and Activity* 3, no. 4 (1996): 228–45, where the framing of human action by technical dispositives is developed by contrasting it to an "ethnography" of primates.

its modifications into secondary technicity, it allows us to trace the double effect of enabling and constraining, spread over the wide range of human actions. How widely this double effect stretches has been demonstrated by studying the technical dimension of language (Chapter 1), of all cultural acquisition and change (Chapter 2), collective agency (Chapter 4), and ethico-political interaction (Chapters 7 and 8). In all these domains, agents can attest to being capable of acting under the limitations imposed by constraints. Five patterns of enabling/constraining in individual and collective action were identified in Chapters 3 and 4, in the form of capability/incapability. First, the biological body and the organization of agents lend themselves to the acquisition of capabilities, but that these capabilities can never be completely mastered. Second, that which agents learn to do makes doing other things more difficult. Third, action requires combining actions, but not all combinations of actions or combinations of qualities of actions are feasible. Forth, very often, action is interaction, which imposes a limitation on what can be done and how it can be done if this action is to be meaningful as interaction. Fifth, the means of action can amplify the capability to act in some ways, and reduce it in other ways. On the whole, the relation between capability and incapability is almost never a phenomenon of "all or nothing". Rather, the myriad of ways in which the differentiation between degrees of capability and incapability are made in action become visible as the adverbial increments of action (where, when, how, to which degree, etc. something is done).[14] After action, agents can attest to the actions performed according to their adverbial specifications.

Seventh, in organized action, as much as in individual action, incapability accompanies the exercise of capabilities as a constitutive moment of action. I have demonstrated that unrealized or unrealizable actions or qualities of action function like a practical horizon for the intelligibility of the actions performed. The point of differentiation between capability and incapability is a major factor determining the precise adverbial increment of actions. And although experience prepares us for the probable outcome of many actions, there remains a varying

---

14 The term "adverbial increments" is derived from Michael Pakaluk's excellent exposition on the choice in Aristotle's virtue theory in *Aristotle's Nicomachean Ethics. An Introduction* (Cambridge: Cambridge University Press, 2005), 110 ff. The appropriate mid-way between two vices is, according to Aristotle, always relative to the particular agents and their specific contexts. This requires discernment regarding the adverbial increments of action (i.e. agent, object, instrument, manner, time, place, duration, reason, purpose). I have explained this term in Chapter 3, §2.2

degree of *uncertainty* associated with all action.[15] Only at the moment when an action is performed does this uncertainty give way to the fact of a specific degree of capability which a specific action allows the agent to attest to. One therefore has to conclude that the ability to attest to one's capability to act comes about only (a) through dealing with uncertainty and (b) through attesting at the same time to incapability to act otherwise. I would claim that the continuous vacillation between expectation/uncertainty and attestation of specific (in)capabilities is the matrix from which practical understanding of action derives. This in turn serves as a key point of orientation for a hermeneutic theorizing of action.

Eighth, in all the steps followed thus far, capability can be demonstrated to be real only after it has been *activated* in relation to others. Reaffirming a Schützian insight somewhat schematically simplified by Ricœur, I have insisted that encounters with these others form a continuum of degrees of anonymity ranging from the most intimate face-to-face interaction to the most impersonal institutional mediation. Both the exploration of organized action in Chapter 4 and the insights of space-time distantiation and transmission (from Giddens, in Chapter 5, §3.2 [point 6] and Debray in Chapter 1, §3) provided perspectives on this range of mediations of action. This is not a social reduction of all action – the individuation of skill marks the place for an unsocial dimension of action – however, it does indicate the very large extent to which our actions are socially shaped and informed. Due attention to the presence of technical means and institutions in action does not change this fact (see again the technical dimension of language, Chapter 1). In short, the combination of social and technical mediation forms the milieu in which capabilities can be activated into real action.

Ninth, the actions thus acted out by many agents in turn shape the context of the future action of those agents, and of other agents. To some degree, outcomes can be planned, but action always results in domino effects of unintended consequences which also feed into the context from which people act. And thus intended and unintended consequences together exercise enabling and constraining effects on agents. Another way to refer to this is to evoke the unequal distribution of roles, functions and goods, and hence the unequal possibilities for participation in social relations and infrastructural dispositives.

Tenth, deploying an appropriate course of action in a given context requires a combination of disparate actional elements, similar to the way story-telling consists of composing disparate elements (time, place, character, etc.). In Chap-

---

15 And disturbances of the expected action are each a moment of disruption of the flow of action (referred to above), but one could expect that the intensity of the disturbance would be proportionate to the significance of the divergence from the expected outcome of action.

ter 2 (§2), I demonstrated how significant this similarity is by arguing that "the process of the acquisition and use of technical objects and technical know-how brings about an intervention or mediation analogous to that of stories in our ideas and lived experience of what it is to be human". Narrative and technical self-understanding both follow the pattern of prefiguration-configuration-refiguration: just as people exist in a narratable way, express their understanding(s) of their lives through narrated accounts and rethink their lives in the light of stories and histories, so people act from a complex habitus, which is deployed in interaction with means, which action in turn feeds back into their self-understanding of themselves as capable agents in a meaningful relation to their world. Furthermore, these two patterns of prefiguration-configuration-refiguration are interdependent as two dimensions of the understanding and interpreting existence of agents. This intertwinement of narrative with technicity is one of the facts that make the technicity of action susceptible to hermeneutic theorizing.

2 Ambiguity

Since the technical aspect of action is associated with all human action, technicity and the forms of reason associated with it cannot be characterised *a priori* as good/beneficial or bad/undesirable. The study of the technicity of action can therefore claim to *logically precede* the value judgements of all theories that could, for the sake of simplification, be presented as techno-optimist and techno-pessimist.[16] Coordination of the technical and normative dimensions of action has to be dealt with in another way, namely via an examination of the ambiguity of the technicity of action.

The hermeneutic and social theoretic study of the technicity of action has to remain resolutely descriptive and interpretative – practising what I identified in the "Intermediary reflection" as "simple exteriority". However, as explained there, this does not amount to perfect indifference in respect of critical judgement of people's living conditions. Rigorous description and interpretation include due attention to the practical experience of (in)capability. This experience entails the following components:

---

[16] I have voiced my critique of such simplifications in Wolff, "'Technology' as the Critical Social Theory," 334–35. This all too simple schematization of attitudes (philosophical, theoretical, scientific, religious or other), refers to the millennia of traditions of attempts by human beings to orient themselves in respect of matters technical. There is, to my knowledge, no better overview on this subject than the two volumes of Johan Hendrik van der Pot's *Encyclopedia of Technological Progress. A Systematic Overview of Theories and Opinions* (Delft: Eburon, 2004).

- As evoked above, *interpretation and judgement* are already part of action. They are situated in the context-dependent exercise of capabilities in relation to means and other agents, and are augmented by the tension between the expectation of action outcomes and the incapability to realize these expectations perfectly.
- When one is exploring action as something meaningful to agents, one cannot fail to notice that in action something is *at stake* – it is not a mere succession of events. This also applies to the delimited view on the technical dimension of action.
- If it is good to be able to act, as Ricœur claims,[17] then the experience of any limitation to action, and even more of the attestation to a decreased capability to act, must be experienced as a *crisis*.

The hermeneutics of the acting and suffering human adopted in this book can be a helpful guide in interpreting the stakes and crises of action. This hermeneutics plots the activation of the series of capabilities (speaking, doing, narrating, imputing[18]) against interaction with others (I – you) and the mediation of institutions (I/you – it). But one could with equal validity map the interpretation of stakes and crises of action on this grid (see Chapter 3, §1, Figure 1) to give an account of the frustration of initiative and the deterioration of that of which people are capable. This mapping could either render people's testimony of their own suffering, or could document what can be learned about what others are (in)capable of. In this sense, both personal attestation (as a practical registration of (in)capabilities) and the interpretation of accounts about others (testimonies, news reports, scholarly studies and other transmissions of that to which people testify) are located on the borderline between description and normative judgement. Both direct and transmitted attestation are key moments in what, early on, Ricœur called an awareness (*prise de conscience*) of what is going on, and which he considered a springboard for critique. Let me demonstrate what a wealth of experiences attestation and the documentation of attestation can account for with a few illustrative examples:

- On the level of the capabilities of the agent (or *I*), the de-capabilisations inflicted on the whole gamut of actions may be mapped: speaking (e.g. by being relatively deprived of education in the means by which to articulate one's grievances in specific contexts), doing (e.g. by not having at one's dis-

---

[17] This is the implication of his claim that it is the capabilities of people that ultimately provoke our respect, see Paul Ricœur, *Lectures 1: Autour du politique* (Paris: Seuil, 1991), 164.
[18] I repeat that the four capabilities, which are logically telescoped into each other, represent the whole range of human actions and, therefore, the list is in principle open.

posal sufficient means, relative to others, to be able to exercise significant choices of one's life in a meaningful way), narrating (e.g. by being the subject of socially dominant, discriminatory narratives) and imputation (e.g. by not being able to develop the self-esteem required to participate in meaningful assessments of social events). Numerous other examples could be given. The point is the socially inflicted (relative) decapabilisation or maintenance of inequalities of capability.
– Likewise the *you* (or rather, the activation or de-activation of capabilities in relation to people in their direct presence) covers the entire range of actions provisionally represented by the four verbs: speaking (e.g. by being reduced to silence or being subject to verbal abuse), doing (e.g. by a reduction of capabilities through neglect or physical violence), narrating (e.g. by being unrightfully omitted from accounts of praise), and imputing (e.g. by being the victim of unfair judgement, hearings and sentencing, as in biased legal systems). These examples show that very often the relation to others takes the passive or suffering form of undergoing the actions of others, in the four forms of interaction.
– Finally, the institutional mediation (the *it*) could be subjected to hermeneutic scrutiny for its effects on people's capabilities. Accordingly one could interpret the effect on people's speaking (e.g. through the marginalization of forms of discourse and expression in public fora), doing (e.g. through systematic exploitation of categories of labour and maintaining a large section of certain societies in joblessness), narrating (e.g. through symbolic violence by essentialising role attribution), imputation (e.g. by overburdening some people with responsibility for the social fate they suffer).

In this illustration, I have mostly taken individual agents as examples for decapabilisation, but, the whole exercise could be repeated for organized action. And just as one could trace the increasing inability of people to defend themselves against the loss of capability, so one could use the grid to document successful deployment of the individual or organized capabilities of violence, exploitation, repression and humiliation. In all these cases, such an interpretation of the vicissitudes of (in)capability could draw its information from sources ranging from individuals' testimony to large-scale scientific studies of social tendencies. In both individual accounts and scientific studies, one would also find the intersectional and mutual reinforcement of different forms of social suffering (experienced or caused). But even when my study of such experiences remains committed to the simple exteriority assumed in the "Intermediate Reflection", this does not prevent us from accepting Okolo's thesis that "praxis triggers the hermeneutical process and gives it an orientation"[19] (introduced in Chapter 6, §6).

Accordingly, numerous aspects of a hermeneutics of social relations of capabilisation and decapabilisation have been explored in the chapters of this book. The first chapter ended with a short evocation of the common vocation of mediology and hermeneutics, namely political vigilance. The grid of (in)capabilities (above) now gives us a better idea of what this vigilance would have to be able to identify. At the same time, this vigilance has also to be applied reflexively to the interpreter of individual and collective (in)capabilities – Chapters 2 and 6 insisted on the situatedness of the whole hermeneutic undertaking. I have repeatedly pointed out how the technicity of action produces ambiguous effects. This is true for the use of technical means, but more generally, for the exercise of capabilities (Chapters 2, 3 and 4). Most strikingly, it was possible to identify three paradoxes arising from the technicity of action. I named these the technical, the organizational and the institutional paradoxes. Each time, that which is indispensable for human action to come to full flourishing (and is in this sense indispensable) retains the possibility of turning against human beings and undermining their agency. Ambiguity and paradox refer to stable anthropological structures which generate divergent effects in different historical contexts. Therefore neither superb facilitation nor tragic undermining of human initiative can capture the nature of technicity; it is the paradox that captures the nature of technicity. The mutual adherence of technicity and ethics – explored in Chapters 7 and 8 – is a consequence of the ambiguity and paradox of technicity, for if the same anthropological structure can produce divergent outcomes, and if therefore something is at stake for agents in their actions, somehow, they decide what is preferable.

Without at least some inkling of what is preferable, the ambiguity of technicity can only be stated, not confronted. Since people always know (tacitly or consciously) that something is at stake in action, their action takes shape under the influence of normative considerations. At the same time, for such considerations to be efficient, they need to be pursued by efficacious means. Whatever the normative concerns are, from a descriptive point of view, we have every reason to think that they do not simply point in the same direction, for two reasons. On the one hand, cultural differences in the largest sense (differences between linguistic, national, ethnic, professional or sub-cultural values) generate a strange mixture of mutual agreement and disagreement (see Chapter 6, §§5 and 6). On

---

19 Okolo Okonda, *Pour une philosophie de la culture et du développement. Recherches d'herméneutique et de praxis africaines* (Kinshasa: Presses Universitaire du Zaïre, 1986), 46.

the other hand, even within a relatively homogenous cultural setting, conflicting claims need to be arbitrated. Ricœur's opposition of ethics and deontology is the most general formulation of this conflict. All action, in one way or another, represents a practical solution to the conflicting concerns that feed into the execution of action. This compromise is what Ricœur refers to as practical wisdom or prudence[20], which I have invoked in the first sentence of this conclusion.

That said, we still remain merely on the verge of critique, as I claimed in the "Intermediary Reflection". This is the case because, while we do have the means to interpret states of and changes in people's relative (in)capabilities, we do not have the normative orientation by which to assess and relatively hierarchize people's "claims-making behaviour" and, indeed, their general conduct in specific socio-historical contexts. This implies that, using the means by which I want to give account of the technicity of action, I can know that there is a game of normative concerns afoot, but must acknowledge that one cannot participate in the struggle between ethics and deontology and one cannot offer guidance on prudent judgment and action.

Still, it is too early to end this conclusion. One thing remains, namely to demonstrate that when this suspension of ethical commitment is lifted, it will turn out that this commitment itself has its own technical dimension. This may at first glance appear counter-intuitive: the technicity of ethics. To make this case, I now need to reflect on responsibility.

3 Responsibility – On the Technicity of Ethico-political Action

At the start of this concluding chapter, I suggested that philosophical reflection on the place of ethics in action could take the desire for practical wisdom (prudence, or *phronesis* in Ricœur's reinterpretation) as its starting point and could work out a phenomenological genealogy of such action. I willingly assume three consequences from this approach. First, I accept that if there is something like wisdom in action, then it is the outcome of a more or less severe tug-of-war between two contradictory normative logics: the teleological logic of the pursuit of the good life (ethics) and the deontological logic of the prohibition of that which cannot be generalised (morality).[21] Second, as I re-affirmed at the end of the pre-

---

[20] I repeat that the term "prudence" is used in the very specific sense discussed in Chapter 8, §1.
[21] In the present context I have to conjecture that this opposition is at least approximately something of a general anthropological fact. For the time being I simply assume that this can

vious section, normative considerations are part of the very fibre of (in)capable action. Third, since this is the case, the technicity of action has an impact on what prudent action can and should be, and *vice versa*.

However, from this point on, I steer the reflection in quite a different direction to that taken by Ricœur, by introducing a terminological distinction between practical wisdom (prudence) and responsibility. For Ricœur, these terms are often synonymous, to the point that one may read "responsibility" as an appropriate term to encapsulate Ricœur's entire ethico-political philosophy.[22] When, in the framework of his hermeneutics of human capabilities, Ricœur develops his ethico-political thought as his response to the fourth of his anthropological questions, namely, "who is the subject of imputation?", he simply renders this question in many places as "who is responsible?". Thus he subsumes the entire ethico-political development of this hermeneutics under responsibility and claims equivalence between the agent to whom prudent action can be imputed and the agent of responsible action.

By contrast, I would like to emphasise that for prudent action to be acceptable as practically wise, an idea of normative *validity* is required. Yet, as I have made plain since the "Intermediate Reflection", normative validity is not part of the *technical* dimension of action. For this reason, the examination of the technicity of action simply cannot settle this issue and has to proceed while suspending the question of validity. This means that I may continue to study the full breadth of human action, even to the extent of taking into account the fact that people *de facto* consider normative claims to be valid (or invalid), but have to practise a methodological agnosticism with regard to the validity of the norms involved. What remains of practical wisdom when all questions of validity are suspended? To this rest, I give the name "responsibility". I define *responsibility* as *the technical dimension of ethico-political action*. Since this diverges not only from Ricœur's understanding of responsibility but also from all scholarship on responsibility known to me, this definition requires some justification.

---

be demonstrated, even while I am aware of the scholarly claims to the historicity, particularly, of deontology.

22 The issue is somewhat more complex than I can demonstrate here, because Ricœur does not use the notion of "responsibility" consistently – see Ernst Wolff, *Political Responsibility for a Globalised World. After Levinas' Humanism* (Bielefeld: Transcript Verlag, 2011), 245–48.

3.1 Technicity of Ethico-political Action and the Need for Normative Orientation

Classical philosophies of responsibility tend to take two forms: some promote responsibility as the essence of ethics itself, while others theorize the structure of ethical conduct in relation to other forms of normative thought. Let us consider these in turn:

- The first tendency equates responsibility with ethicity itself. The stronger ethics is equated with ethicity, the more responsibility becomes *normatively void* or purely formal. This is the case in Husserl, Weischedel, Levinas and perhaps also Weber.[23] Arguably, the most significant objections against such views of responsibility are related to this indeterminacy in practice. In the case of Levinas, for instance, responsibility without content opens itself up to the threat of anarchic violence.[24] On the other hand, as in the case of Weber, one can cite those among his readers who align him with boundless decisionism and the concomitant cult of the leader.[25]
- The second tendency makes responsibility *dependent on other forms of ethical or normative thinking*. This can be seen in authors such as Jonas, Apel

---

23 Cf. Edmund Husserl, "Meditation über die Idee eines individuellen und Gemeinschaftslebens in absoluter Selbstverantwortung," in *Erste Philosophie (1923/1924)*, Zweiter Teil: *Theorie der phänomenologischen Reduktion*, Husserl Gesammelte Werke Band VIII, ed. Rudolf Boehm (Den Haag: Martinus Nijhoff, 1959), 193–202; Wilhelm Weischedel, *Das Wesen der Verantwortung. Ein Versuch* (Frankfurt am Main: Klostermann, [1932] 1972); Emmanuel Lévinas, *Totalité et infini. Essai sur l'extériorité* (La Haye: Martinus Nijhoff, [1961] 1998) and Max Weber, "Politik als Beruf" (1919), in *Gesammelte politische Schriften*, Postdamer Internet-Ausgabe (following the "Marianne-Ausgabe"), (1999), 396–450, https://www.uni-potsdam.de/verlagsarchivweb/html/494/html/PS.pdf, last accessed 5 February 2021.

Levinas's recurrent use of the imperative "Thou shalt not kill!" is an excessive verbalisation of what – if one follows his own presentation – is nothing more than the merely formal imperative of responsibility for the other.

My uncertainty in the case of Weber is based on the fact that at the beginning of his "Politics as a Vocation," he seems to present the collapse of the state into anarchy as a negative normative point of reference of political responsibility.

24 This objection is developed in Ernst Wolff, *De l'éthique à la justice. Langage et politique dans la philosophie de Lévinas* (Dordrecht: Springer, 2007), 383–99 and Ernst Wolff, "The Quest for Justice Versus the Rights of the Other?" in *In Levinas' Trace*, ed. Maria Dimitrova (Newcastle upon Tyne: Cambridge Scholars Publishing, 2011), 101–11.

25 On these readings, see for instance, Sylvie Mesure, "Rationalisme et faillibilisme," in *Histoire de la philosophie politique. Tome V, Les philosophies politiques contemporaines*, ed. Alain Renaut (Paris: Calmann-Lévy, 1999), 149–84, especially 151–53.

and, of course, Ricœur.²⁶ Here responsibility is always understood in terms of another meta-ethical commitment, the validity of which is separately established. Often scholars working in applied fields of ethics have opted for a deontological supplementation of the theory of responsibility, since this fits in snugly with the practice of professional codes. However, there are also more classical philosophical approaches that advocate supplementation from deontology (Apel, Jonas), and again such thinkers include other supplements (Ricœur uses both teleological and deontological moments in a genealogical reconstruction of the capability of responsible decision-making).

Both these tendencies seem to concur that a theory of responsibility cannot, by its own devices, provide the normative reference according to which judgements and actions are to be qualified as "responsible": either it side-steps the question of responsible *action* by focusing on ethicity, or it focuses on responsible action while out-sourcing the question of validity to other modes of philosophising. Instead of identifying this as a weakness of either or both of the two tendencies, I conclude that they rather point to something important about responsibility, and that I explicitly affirm. Responsibility shares an essential feature of all technicity of action: *it is unable to generate from and for itself the ultimate criteria of its excellence*. And one has to add that the reason for this is that responsibility is best understood as the technicity of ethico-political action.

Yet, as I have argued in Chapters 7 and 8, there is no excellence of action which is not materialised by the capability of agents and their deployment of means. If responsibility is the technicity of ethico-political action, then studying responsibility amounts to studying efforts to actualise excellence in action. The reason for this is *not* that technicity and responsibility represent merely the means to ends, but that *excellence exists only as an attribute of action* (of which technicity is an essential component) – excellence as recognized by agents or onlookers.

Having demarcated the place of responsibility in relation to the technicity of action and a fully validated ethical theory, we now have to examine more closely the character of responsibility that would fit in this space. Which qualities of responsibility make it a suitable fit for the technicity of action examined in this book? And how does our understanding of responsibility affect what we may expect of ethico-political action?

---

26 Cf. Hans Jonas, *Das Prinzip Verantwortung. Versuch einer Ethik für die technologische Zivilisation* (Frankfurt am Main: Suhrkamp, [1979] 1984); Karl-Otto Apel, *Diskurs und Verantwortung. Das Problem des Übergangs zur postkonventionellen Moral* (Frankfurt am Main: Suhrkamp, 1988) and Ricœur, *Soi-même comme un autre / Oneself as Another*.

3.2 Responsibility as a Key to Thinking Action in an Era of Uncertainty

What then are the general features of responsibility which would commend it as a component of the technicity of ethico-political action?
- Reflection on responsibility in the widest sense has a very long history. Its antecedents stretch as far back as the traditions of reflection on guilt (for retrospective responsibility) and obligation (for prospective responsibility).[27] However, apart from very few exceptions,[28] reflection about responsibility in the strict sense starts after the First World War with Weber's speech on "Politics as a vocation".[29] It would require a study on its own to trace the genealogy of this term in philosophy and social theory. For my current purposes, I merely conjecture that in some form all human societies attribute responsibility to human action, but that it emerges with particular salience as a dilemma due to the normative challenges and uncertainties of social life under the conditions of late modernity. At least two of these conditions should be called to mind: (1) the increasing *uncertainty, complexity and risk* involved in decision-making – induced by rapid and unpredictable social and technical change[30] – and (2) the increasing loss of effectiveness and credibility of foundationalist approaches to normative decision-making, accompanied by an increase in conflicting claims of validity (Weber's "*polytheism*").[31] Both these conditions are at work as much in the Global South[32] as

---

27 Cf. the lemma "Verantwortung" in *Handbuch Ethik*, eds. Marcus Düwell and Micha Werner (Stuttgart: Metzler, 2011), 541–48.
28 Cf. Benjamin Constant, *De la responsabilité des ministres* (Paris: H. Nicolle, 1815) and Lucien Lévy-Bruhl, *L'idée de la responsabilité* (Paris: Hachette, 1884).
29 Etienne de Villiers, *Revisiting Max Weber's Ethic of Responsibility* (Tübingen: Mohr Siebeck, 2018).
30 The fact that the philosophy of responsibility has proven to be very productive in the subdiscipline of the *philosophy of technology* speaks to this point. This is particularly visible in the philosophy of technology in Germany. See Hans Lenk and Matthias Maring, "Verantwortung in Technik und Wissenschaft," in *Handbuch Verantwortung*, eds. Ludger Heidbrink, Claus Langbehn and Janina Loh (Wiesbaden: Springer VS, 2017), 715–31 and some of the important milestones: Hans Sachsse, *Technik und Verantwortung. Probleme der Ethik im technischen Zeitalter* (Freiburg: Verlag Rombach, 1972); Hans Lenk, *Konkrete Humanität. Vorlesungen über Verantwortung und Menschlichkeit* (Frankfurt am Main: Suhrkamp, 1998), Hans Lenk and Matthias Maring, eds., *Technikverantwortung: Güterabwägung – Risikobewertung – Verhaltenskodizes* (Frankfurt am Main: Campus Verlag, 1991); Günther Ropohl, "Das Risiko im Prinzip Verantwortung," *Ethik und Sozialwissenschaften* 5 (1994): 109–20; and Armin Grunwald, "Verantwortungsbegriff und Verantwortungsethik," in his *Rationale Technikfolgenbeurteilung. Konzeption und methodische Grundlagen* (Berlin: Springer, 1999), 175–94.
31 Read, for instance, Weber's "Politics as a Vocation" together with his "Science as Vocation".

in the Global North, albeit in different manifestations (as reflected in Chapter 6, §6).
- Generally, theories of responsibility tend to take the *situatedness of ethical or political judgement and action* seriously.[33] Again Weber can be taken as paradigmatic: one can only understand what it means to have a vocation for (responsible) politics once one has carefully taken account of the specificities of the social phenomenon of politics in which an individual politician has to act and interact. In a similar vein, a number of philosophers have worked on establishing a phenomenology of the *types and dimensions* of responsibility. They have mapped the distinguishable aspects of responsibility: temporality (prospective, retrospective), subjectivity (individual responsibility or co-responsibility), conditionality (formal, informal, legal, contractual), and modality (responsibility for action, for failing to act or preventing someone from acting).[34] Sometimes, the dimensions of responsibility are summarised in a formula, for instance: X takes responsibility for Y, in X's capacity as X^1 before instance A and with appeal to a set of criteria M.[35] This is of no small

---

This is not to deny that philosophers of responsibility have also engaged in an attempt to construct a philosophy of responsibility as the very foundation of ethics. Hans Jonas's efforts in this regard are telling: after having attempted to present a metaphysics of ethics (responsibility as the foundation of all ethics), he later questions the validity of his own attempts. Compare Hans Jonas, *Das Prinzip Verantwortung*, with Hans Jonas, *Philosophische Untersuchungen und metaphysische Vermutungen* (Frankfurt am Main, and Leipzig: Insel: 1992). See my commentaries Ernst Wolff, "Responsibility in an Era of Modern Technology and Nihilism, Part 1. A Non-Foundational Rereading of Jonas," *Dialogue* 48, no. 3 (2009): 577–99 and "Responsibility in an Era of Modern Technology and Nihilism, Part 2. Inter-connection and Implications of the Two Notions of Responsibility in Jonas," *Dialogue* 48, no. 4 (2009): 841–66.

32 Cf. Olúfẹ́mi Taiwò, *How Colonialism Pre-Empted Modernity in Africa* (Bloomington, IN, and Indianapolis, IN: Indiana University Press, 2010); Elísio Macamo, ed., *Negotiating Modernity: Africa's Ambivalent Experience* (Dakar, and London, Pretoria: Codesria Books and others, 2005); Manuel Castells, "'The Rise of the Fourth World': Informational Capitalism, Poverty, and Social Exclusion," in *End of Millennium* (Oxford: Blackwell, 1998); Chapter 2 and region-specific chapters in *Handbuch Moderneforschung*, eds. Friedrich Jaeger, Wolfgang Knöbl and Ute Schneider (Stuttgart: J. B. Metzler, 2015).

33 Obviously, the simplest reductions of responsibility to obedience of the stipulations of ethical codes cannot do justice to this point.

34 Hans Lenk, "Typen und Dimensionen der Verantwortlichkeit," in *Konkrete Humanität. Vorlesungen über Verantwortung und Menschlichkeit* (Frankfurt am Main: Suhrkamp, 1998), 261–84 and in Heidbrink et al., *Handbuch Verantwortung*, especially the chapters by Janina Loh, "Strukturen und Relata der Verantwortung," 35–56, and by Hans Lenk, "Verantwortlichkeit und Verantwortungstypen: Arten und Polaritäten," 57–84.

35 Roughly similar to Hans Lenk and Matthias Maring, "Deskriptive und normative Zuschreibung von Verantwortung," in Hans Lenk, *Zwischen Wissenschaft und Ethik* (Frankfurt am

interest for my point. The types and dimensions of responsibility reflect *both* the complexity of the socio-historical context of decision-making and acting *and* the adverbial qualifications of the prospective actions under evaluation: who? when? where? how? by which means? by what strategy? through which trade-offs? etc.[36] The combination of the dimensions of responsibility and the adverbial qualifications of responsible action describe the capabilities activated, as well as the ways in which means are deployed in the act of responsible action, i.e. the technicity of ethico-political action. Moreover, this helps us to see that the situatedness of action and of decision-making is not a secondary aspect of responsible action, but has an impact on the very content of the notion of responsibility. Finally, the dimensions of responsibility allow one to appreciate the fact that claiming responsibility to be the technicity of ethical and political action is *not* the same as claiming that the technical aspects of action exhaust the meaning of ethico-political action. I defend the thesis that ethics and politics *cannot do without* due consideration for the technicity of action.

– The situatedness of responsibility and its dimensions implies tacit or calculated judgement of the appropriateness of action for a particular context. This judgement points to a markedly *hermeneutic concept of responsibility.* This fact is in accord with the general hermeneutic nature attributed to action throughout this study. Only as part of the hermeneutic and technical nature of ethico-political action under contextual demands can a concept of responsible action meet the four criteria which I have identified for it elsewhere.[37] (i) Responsible decision-making has to be able to coordinate ethical considerations with strategic ones. This inevitably brings the question of mutual sacrifice of these considerations into the ambit of responsible action. The cases examined in Chapter 8 illustrate this point vividly. (ii) Responsible action has to be undertaken from the complex anatomy of the forms and dimensions of responsibility (as discussed above, following

---

Main: Suhrkamp, 1991), 76–100, here 81; and Günther Ropohl, "Das Risiko im Prinzip Verantwortung," 111. See also the commentary by Micha Werner, "Die Zuschreibung von Verantwortung. Versuch einer Annäherung von Handlungstheorie und Ethik," in *Zukunftsverantwortung in der Marktwirtschaft*, eds. Thomas Bausch, et al. (Münster: LIT, 2000), 85–109.

36 Here I follow again Michael Pakaluk's reading of Aristotle's understanding of the discernment regarding the adverbial increments of action (i.e. agent, instrument, manner, place, duration, purpose, etc.), as discussed in Chapter 3, §2.2. Aristotle's virtue theory presents us with a precursor of responsible decision-making – not only through his notion of *phronésis*, which Ricœur redefines, but in providing a rudimentary phenomenology of the nature of the phronetic judgment.

37 Wolff, *Political Responsibility*, 213–19.

Lenk). (iii) Reflection on responsibility needs to accord the context of action sufficient attention. This context consists not only of the social and normative expectations of interactional partners (see Chapter 6), but also of the means of action, broadly understood – bodily skills, chemical substances, artefacts, instruments (physical or intellectual), media of communication, organizations, institutions, etc. (see Chapters 1 and 2). (iv) Responsible judgment cannot simply be oriented to conformity with established principles or values of action; it has to be able to take into account the problematisation of the very norms which can be justified under unproblematic circumstances. Responsible action has to be "found" in the horizon of reflection of equity, i.e. the revision of the "letter of the law" by appeal to the "spirit of the law". Mandela's reflections on violence illustrate this point (Chapter 7, §3).

- Sometimes responsible action consists simply of complying with rules or following generally accepted practices. One should not sneer at this fact – those who are acquainted with the personal and social harm inflicted by nepotistic and corrupt innovations on rules in bureaucracies and companies know to appreciate this aspect of responsibility. However, compliance with rules is a rather singular manifestation of responsibility and has to be conducted under vigilant observation from a second-order responsibility which has to test the desirability of compliance. More typically, acting responsibly requires serious effort, since both the course of action and the hope of success are uncertain. Striving to find responsible action steers agents right into the thicket of capability-incapability relations in action, and this holds for individual action as much as for organized action (see Chapters 3 and 4). Every responsible action comes at the price of a compromise, which means that something of what it aspired to had to be relegated to the sphere of the unrealizable (i.e. incapability). Hence, in agreement with our findings on (in)capability, the incapability fully to realize all aspirations of responsible action remains the horizon of intelligibility of the course of action adopted, and this is true even for the most honest attempts to find the best course of action. *Responsibility is the task of confronting the uncertainty, ambiguity and paradox of contexts by composing actional (in)capabilities under the weight of ethical and moral concerns.* Evidently, then, the reflection on responsibility to which my study leads is not that of an applied ethics of technology (but it does not exclude this either). It is a philosophy of responsibility as such.

3.3 The Fragility of Responsibility

In this outline of responsibility, I strove to remain true to its complexity in real-life action, and more particularly as an aspect of the technicity of action. Failure in this respect would easily lead to fatalism (neglect of the potential of agency) or moralism (neglect of any regard for the inevitable use of powerful means in complex situations). My attempt to steer clear of these fallacies can be gauged by the relation I assume to two other thinkers on responsibility.

On the one hand, I have been guided by Weber's insight that responsible decision-making and action are worthy of this label only if they take into consideration the means for its realization – in the case of politics, this is the means particular to politics, namely "power backed up by *violence*",[38] and the uncertainty of outcomes associated with the deployment of such means. However, whereas Weber delved into the sociological constitution of politics, I adopted a different perspective on "means", in the form of an exploration of the technicity of action. My intention is not to downplay the sociological perspective – my recourse to the work of social scientists in this book vouch for this sufficiently – but simply to benefit from a hermeneutic view on action to account for the complexity of the technicity of ethico-political action. In this, my book complements Weber's ground-breaking study on responsibility. However, unlike Weber, (a) I do not focus on the highest tiers of decision-makers; (b) I do not accept the distinction between unreserved role obedience (in the form of bureaucratic responsibility) and charismatic decision-making (in political responsibility), and (c) I have allowed for a much broader view on the legitimate recourse to violence in modern states than the one which informs his view on responsibility.[39] I enquire into the responsibility of all people, as potentially penetrating all action in all social contexts. Whoever speaks about human capabilities and the means by which actions are mediated has to think about responsibility.[40]

---

38 Max Weber, "Politics as a Vocation," in *From Max Weber: Essays in Sociology*, transl. Hans Heinrich Gerth and Charles Wright Mills (London: Routledge, 1991), 77–128, here 119.
39 See Karl von Holdt's idea of violent democracy, discussed in Chapter 8, §2.1.
40 One can gauge the contemporary potential of the notion of "responsibility" in socio-political matters by consulting, for instance, Heidbrink et al., *Handbuch Verantwortung*, and the three volumes of Ludger Heidbrink and Alfred Hirsch, eds., *Verantwortung in der Zivilgesellschaft. Zur Konjunktur eines widersprüchlichen Prinzips* (Frankfurt am Main: Campus Verlag, 2006), *Staat ohne Verantwortung? Zum Wandel der Aufgaben von Staat und Politik* (Frankfurt am Main: Campus Verlag, 2007) and *Verantwortung als Marktwirtschaftliches Prinzip. Zum Verhältnis von Moral und Ökonomie* (Frankfurt am Main: Campus Verlag, 2008).

But I also situate myself in relation to another key thinker about responsibility: Emmanuel Levinas.[41] Levinas was absolutely right in claiming that "[e]veryone will readily agree that it is of the highest importance to know whether we are not duped by morality".[42] Although I have not confronted this question in this book, I have indicated its significance (see Chapter 6, §5). However, the reason for the daring originality of Levinas's philosophy is at the same time the source of its failure to present us with a viable notion of responsibility: it attempts to construct a notion of responsibility (as the essence of ethics itself) outside of the demands of practical philosophy. The result is a philosophy of responsibility coupled with the pathos of an appeal to the urgency of responsible action, but which is simply not convincing, since it fails to work through the difficulties associated with the capability of the ethico-political agent to respond to this task and this appeal, in other words, it neglects an examination of the nature of ethical agency. In sum, his ethical and political thought *lacks an accompanying reflection on the inevitable mediation* of the plurality of mutually conflicting responsibilities of the ethical agent for the plurality of others and thus *lacks reflection on the competence and means* of the agent of responsibility who has to act in a particular context.[43] I hope this book has gone some way toward clarifying the technicity of action and toward demonstrating why reflection on ethics and politics cannot do without it.

The degree to which an agent is able to exercise responsibility could be attested to retrospectively, as part of the composite of the adverbial increments of a course of action, or prospectively as the anticipation in reflection of the responsibility that an agent will later be able to attest to. At least three fragilities affect both of these forms of responsibility.

3.3a Fragility of Responsibility as Mediated, Practical Relation to Self

The first fragility of responsibility arises from the finitude of agents. In Chapter 3, §2.3, I described finitude as the point of differentiation between capability and incapability in practice. It is not possible to overcome the contextuality, perspectivism or limitations of one's view on a context of context. Admittedly, by acquiring more information, engaging in careful reasoning and through consultation

---

41 My critique of Levinas on this point is summarised in Wolff, *Political Responsibility*, 167–68.
42 "On conviendra aisément qu'il importe au plus haut point de savoir si l'on n'est pas dupe de la morale." Lévinas, *Totalité et infini*, here 5 / *Totality and Infinity: An Essay on Exteriority* (Dordrecht: Kluwer, 1991), 21. On the context of this citation cf. Wolff, *De l'éthique à la justice*, 52–60.
43 Cf. Wolff, *Political Responsibility*, 166.

with others, the boundaries set by these limitations can be shifted. And that is good. But they can never be fully overcome.

Moreover, our ability to take responsibility for that which we deem worthy of doing so could be augmented by the invention of new means (technologies, forms of organization, institutions, etc.) and by the initiative to new interactions. However, as the means of our action become more powerful, and the organization of our interaction becomes more varied, the consequences of these initiatives also become more extensive and the ambiguities and paradoxes of the technicity become more acute. Consequently, the demands made on our responsibility become more complex, while our ability to calculate the outcomes of actions cannot keep up with these developments.

A hermeneutics of responsibility thus has to conclude that taking responsibility depends on the features of the actional possibilities of agents in every specific context, that is, the variety of their capabilities and the degrees to which these could be activated through the intermediary of their means. Responsibility as a complex feature of human capability is, as Aristotle already said of the practice of virtues, always relative to us.[44] Agents attesting to their ability to take responsibility for something (retrospectively or prospectively), do so exactly in proportion to the increments of capability they are able to activate (or anticipate being able to activate) and relative to specific actional contexts.

3.3b Fragility in Holding Responsible

I have defined responsibility as an aspect of action. But action itself is an ambiguous phenomenon: part initiative, part consequence of enabling and constraining social and material circumstances. One should thus be careful not to overlook the fact that responsibility is *both* something assumed by agents for themselves *and* something imposed on them by others. Moreover, like all acquisition of capabilities, learning responsible action is characterised by the ambiguity of augmented ability and internalized constraint, captured in terms such as "habitus" or "discipline" (discussed in Chapter 2, §§1 and 3.1). The extent to which responsibility is *exercised by agents* in a socio-institutional milieu, or rather *imposed on them by this milieu*, has to be a matter of dispute. It is therefore not possible to declare the social fact of responsibility categorically positive. It is

---

[44] Because of the hermeneutic constitution of agency, coupled with the understanding of responsibility as the technicity of ethico-political action, there can be no question of secretly promoting a sovereignist view of subjectivity. I therefore think that Frieder Vogelmann's critique of philosophical responsibility discourse, in *Im Bann der Verantwortung* (Frankfurt am Main: Campus Verlag, 2014), does not apply to what I present here.

rather one of the tasks of a hermeneutic study of the technicity of ethico-political action to give an account of the ways in which organized action and the institutional mediation of action assign people to positions of responsibility for which the (in)capabilities available to them may be insufficient (in other words, to give an account of overtaxing of people by holding them responsible).[45]

At the same time, one has to refrain from simply equating responsibility with a social imposition. After all, since all agency requires institutional mediation to be acquired and practised, it would be problematic to expect that responsibility can be assumed only in a kind of free-floating social vacuum. Responsibility exists only through and for its social context. In Chapters 7 and 8, we examine the fact that even living under conditions of severe injustice or socio-economic precarity does not make people ethically indifferent. Those living at the edge would consider attributing their norm-sensitivity to nothing more than the interiorization of social pressures as dehumanizing.[46] Besides, this would attribute *a priori* to them a lack of agential initiative which is not matched by their exercise of choices and acting according to strategies in practice.

The ambiguity and even sometimes the undecidability between the passive and active side of responsibility is the second fragilization of responsibility.

3.3.c Fragility of Justification

A particular fragility infiltrates responsibility because of its dependency on something non-technical: its justification in terms of norms, values or ethics. Even a view on action, which is restricted to the technicity of ethico-political action, has to give account of this fragility, since agents sensitive to the call of responsibility are affected by it. The reason for this fragility has to do with the loss of certainty about normative orientations in general, due to the undermining of tradition and religion by science, social changes that have resulted in a loss of

---

[45] The negative side of responsibility attribution has been studied in social science and philosophy. It is quite closely related to the issue of risk management, as presented with reference to Elísio Macamo in Chapter 4, §4.2. See also Vogelmann, *Im Bann der Verantwortung*. ; Jean-Louis Genard and Fabrizio Cantelli, "Êtres capables et compétents: lecture anthropologique et pistes pragmatiques,"*SociologieS* [Online], Theory and research, Online since 27 April 2008, http://journals.openedition.org/sociologies/1943, last accessed 28 April 2019; and Jean-Louis Genard and Fabrizio Cantelli, "Pour une sociologie politique des compétences," *Les Politiques Sociales* 70, nos. 1–2 (2010): 103–20. Since I have given incapability its due place, also in relation to responsibility, this critique does not apply to me. Quite the contrary, I have provided at least some of the means by which to describe the undue imposition of responsibility.
[46] This does not mean that I have overlooked the tragedy of an interiorization of victimhood – cf. Chapter 8, §3.2.

the authority of institutions, the declining credibility of philosophies of history and the plurality of contradicting normative claims in and between societies. These phenomena, which have been known and studied for many years,[47] have been partially dealt with in Chapter 6. On the one hand, one may recall that responsibility represents exactly those modes of action that are supposed to confront this uncertainty head on (see §3.2, above), but, on the other hand, it has to be underscored that uncertainty undermines justification and thus accords responsibility an *essential* fragility.

This fact has implications for all action, since responsibility could in principle apply to all action. However, it comes most clearly to the fore in such actions that connect directly with justification. Here one has to think about claims-making practices to which I have mentioned in this book – with reference to authors such as Charles Tilly or Boltanski and Thévenot – or about theorizing and philosophising which are reflexive actions (as I have emphasised in Chapter 6). All these actions are subject to the same ambiguities and paradoxes, due to the technicity of action in general, but also due to the fragility of responsibility. Finally, if critique requires the supplementation of simple exteriority with a normative justification that would enable one to assume complex exteriority,[48] it has to be expected that such a critique will also be marked by this fragility.

---

[47] The historical development on modernity discourses is rendered well in Jaeger et al., *Handbuch Moderneforschung*, especially the chapters by Gerald Hartung, "Philosophie," 204–15, and Wolfgang Knöbl, "Soziologie," 261–74.
[48] See discussion in "Intermediate Reflection," §§2 and 3.

Bibliography

Abrutyn, Seth, ed. 2016. *Handbook of Contemporary Sociological Theory*. Cham: Springer.
Académie Tunisienne de sciences, des lettres et des arts. 2003. *Présence de Paul Ricœur*. Tunis: Beït al-Hikma.
Achebe, Chinua. [1958] 2006. *Things Fall Apart*. London: Penguin.
Adler, Paul S. 2010. *The Oxford Handbook of Sociology and Organization Studies: Classical Foundations*. Oxford: Oxford University Press.
Adler, Paul S., Paul Du Gay, Glenn Morgan, and Michael I. Reed. 2014. *The Oxford Handbook of Sociology, Social Theory, and Organization Studies: Contemporary Currents*. Oxford: Oxford University Press.
Adorno, Theodor. [1951] 1997. *Minima Moralia. Reflexionen aus dem beschädigten Leben*, Gesammelte Schriften 4. Frankfurt am Main: Suhrkamp.
Apel, Karl-Otto. 1988. *Diskurs und Verantwortung. Das Problem des Übergangs zur postkonventionellen Moral*. Frankfurt am Main: Suhrkamp.
Arendt, Hannah. 1972. *Crises of the Republic: Lying in Politics, Civil Disobedience, on Violence, Thoughts on Politics and Revolution*. San Diego, CA: Harvest/Harcourt Brace Jovanovich.
Arendt, Hannah. 1958. *The Human Condition*. Chicago, IL: University of Chicago Press.
Arkoun, Mohammed. 1995–1996. "Clarifier le passé pour construire le futur." *Confluences. Méditerranée* 16: 17–30.
Austin, J. L. 1962. *How to Do Things with Words*. The William James Lectures Delivered at Harvard University 1955. Oxford: Clarendon.
Badie, Bertrand. 2018. *Quand le Sud réinvente le monde. Essai sur la puissance de la faiblesse*. Paris: Découverte.
Badie, Bertrand. 2019a. "L'acte II de la mondialisation a commencé", interview with Marc Semo, *Le monde*, 8 November 2019. https://www.lemonde.fr/idees/article/2019/11/08/bertrand-badie-l-acte-ii-de-la-mondialisation-a-commence_6018418_3232.html, last accessed 5 February 2021.
Badie, Bertrand. 2019b. *L'hégémonie contestée. Les nouvelles formes de domination internationale*. Paris: Odile Jacob.
Badiou, Alain. 2007. *De quoi Sarkozy est-il le nom?* Paris: Éditions Lignes.
Baert, Patrick, and Filipe Carreira Da Silva. 2010. *Social Theory in the Twentieth Century and Beyond*, 2nd ed., Cambridge: Polity Press.
Beck, Ulrich. 1992. *Risk Society: Towards a New Modernity*. London: Sage.
Benjamin, Walter. 1974. "Das Kunstwerk im Zeitalter seiner technischen Reproduzierbarkeit" [Zweite Fassung]. In *Walter Benjamin, Gesammelte Schriften*, Band I, 2, edited by Rolf Tiedemann and Hermann Schweppenhäuser, 471–508. Frankfurt am Main: Suhrkamp.
Benzecry, Claudio E., Monika Krause and Isaac Reed, eds. 2017. *Social Theory Now*. Chicago, IL, and London: University of Chicago Press.
Bernet, Rudolf. 1994. *La vie du sujet. Recherches sur l'interprétation de Husserl dans la phénoménologie*. Paris: PUF.
Bernstein, Richard. 1992. "The resurgence of pragmatism," *Social Research* 59, no. 4, Winter: 813–40.

Bollenbeck, Georg. 2005. "Zivilisation." In *Historisches Wörterbuch der Philosophie*, Band 12 (W-Z), edited by Joachim Ritter, Karlfried Grunder and Gottfried Gabriel, 1365 – 79. Basel: Schwabe.
Bolouri, Maryam. 2019. *Medial Transformations: Theorising the Intelligent Mediation Sphere*. Tübingen: Eberhard Karls-Universität Tübingen.
Boltanski, Luc. 1990. *L'amour et la justice comme compétences. Trois essais de sociologie de l'action*. Paris: Métaillé.
Boltanski, Luc. 2009. *De la critique. Précis de sociologie de l'émancipation*. Paris: Gallimard.
Boltanski, Luc. 2011. *On Critique: A Sociology of Emancipation*, trans. by Gregory Elliot. Cambridge: Polity.
Boltanski, Luc. 2012. *Love and Justice as Competences. Three Essays on the Sociology of Action*, trans. by Catherine Porter. Cambridge: Polity Press.
Boltanski, Luc, and Laurent Thévenot. 1991. *De la justification: Les économies de la grandeur*. Paris: Gallimard.
Boltanski, Luc, and Laurent Thévenot. 1999. "The Sociology of Critical Capacity." *European Journal of Social Theory* 2, no. 3: 358 – 77.
Boltanski, Luc, and Laurent Thévenot. [1991] 2006. *On Justification: Economies of Worth*. Princeton, NJ: Princeton University Press.
Borradori, Giovanna, ed. 2003. *Philosophy in a Time of Terror: Dialogues with Jürgen Habermas and Jacques Derrida*. Chicago, IL: University of Chicago Press.
Bouamama, Saïd. 2017. *Figures de la révolution africaine. De Kenyatta à Sankara*. Paris: Découverte.
Bourdieu, Pierre. 1980. *Le sens pratique*. Paris: Editions de Minuit.
Bourdieu, Pierre. 1990. *The Logic of Practice*. Stanford: Stanford University Press.
Bourgeois, Patrick L. 2002. "Phenomenology and Pragmatism: A Recent Encounter." In *Phenomenology World-Wide: Foundations – Expanding Dynamics – Life-Engagements. A Guide for Research and Study*, edited by Anna-Teresa Tymieniecka, 568 – 70. Dordrecht: Springer.
Breitling, Andris. 2002. "Paul Ricœur und das hermeneutische Als." In *Vor dem Text: Hermeneutik und Phänomenologie im Denken Paul Ricœurs*, edited by Stephan Orth and Andris Breitling, 79 – 97. Berlin: Technische Universität Berlin.
Breviglieri, Marc. 2006. "Le fond ténébreux de la routine. À propos des morales du geste technique au travail." In *L'ordinaire et le politique*, eds. Sandra Laugier and Claude Gautier, 189 – 217. Paris: PUF/Curapp.
Breviglieri, Marc. 2012. "L'espace habité que réclame l'assurance intime de pouvoir. Un essai d'approfondissement sociologique de l'anthropologie capacitaire de Paul Ricœur Ricœur, Paul." *Études Ricœuriennes / Ricœur Studies* 3, no. 1: 34 – 52.
Breyer, Thiemo. 2013. "Handlung, Text, Kultur. Überlegungen zur Hermeneutischen Anthropologie Zwischen Clifford Geertz und Paul Ricœur." *Meta: Research in Hermeneutics, Phenomenology and Practical Philosophy* 5, no. 1: 107 – 29.
Bryant, Christopher, and David Jary, eds. 1997. *Anthony Giddens: Critical Assessments*. New York, NY: Routledge.
Bryant, Christopher, and David Jary. 2011. "Anthony Giddens." In *The Wiley-Blackwell Companion to Major Social Theorists*, volume 2, edited by George Ritzer and Jeffrey Stepnisky, 432 – 63. Malden, MA, Oxford: Wiley-Blackwell.

Bucholc, Marta, and Daniel Witte. 2018. "Transformationen eines Klassikers: Norbert Elias Zwischen Kanonpflege und Kanonverschiebung." *Soziologische Revue* 41, no. 3: 384–99.
Calhoun, Craig, Joseph Gerteis, James Moody, Steven Pfaff and Indermohan Virk, eds. 2012. *Contemporary Sociological Theory*, 3th ed. Malden, MA: Blackwell.
Caron, François. 1997. *Les deux révolutions industrielles du XXe siècle.* Paris: Albin Michel.
Caron, François. 2010. *La dynamique de l'innovation. Changement de technique et changement social (xvi-xxe siècle).* Paris: Gallimard.
Carstens, Jana Alvara. 2019. *Complacency: An Action Theoretical Approach via Paul Ricœur and Anthony Giddens.* PhD diss., University of Pretoria, November.
Castells, Manuel. 1998. *End of Millennium.* Oxford: Blackwell.
Castonguay, Simon. 2010. "Michel Foucault et Paul Ricœur, vers un dialogue possible." *Études Ricœuriennes/Ricœur Studies* 1, no. 1: 68–86.
Castoriadis, Cornelius. 1978. *Les carrefours du labyrinthe.* Paris: Seuil.
Clark, Martin. 1996. *Modern Italy 1871–1995.* 2nd ed. London, and New York, NY: Longman.
Constant, Benjamin. 1815. *De la responsabilité des ministres.* Paris: H. Nicolle.
Corcuff, Philippe. 2019. *Théories sociologiques contemporaines: France, 1980–2020.* Malakoff: Armand Colin.
Crenshaw, Edward, and Kristopher Robison. 2010. "Political Violence as an Object of Study: The Need for Taxonomic Clarity." In *Handbook of Politics: State and Society in Global Perspective*, edited by Kevin T. Leicht and J. Craig Jenkins, 235–46. New York, NY: Springer.
Crozier, Michel, and Erhard Friedberg. 1995. "Organizations and collective action." In *Studies of Organization in the European tradition*, edited by Samuel B. Bacharach, Pasquale Gagliardi and Bryan Mundell, 71–93. Greenwich: Jai Press.
Dale-Ferguson, Darryl Scott. 2019. *Capable Agents and Just Institutions. A Reconstruction of Paul Ricœur's "Ethical Aim" Using Anthony Giddens' Theory of Structuration.* PhD diss., University of Chicago.
Dallmayr, Fred. 2011. "Love and Justice: A Memorial Tribute to Paul Ricœur." In *Paul Ricœur: Honoring and Continuing the Work*, edited by Farhang Erfani, 5–20. Lanham, MD: Lexington Books.
Davidson, Scott A., ed. 2018. *A Companion to Ricœur's Freedom and Nature.* Lanham, MD: Lexington Books.
Davis, Natalie Zemon. 2000. *The Gift in Sixteenth-Century France.* Madison, WI: University of Wisconsin Press.
Debray, Régis. 1992. *Vie et mort de l'image. Une histoire du regard en Occident.* Paris: Gallimard.
Debray, Régis. 1998. "Histoire des quatre M." *Cahiers de Médiologie* 6: 7–24.
Debray, Régis. 2000a. *Introduction à la médiologie.* Paris: PUF.
Debray, Régis. 2000b. *Transmitting culture*, trans. by Eric Rauth. New York, NY: Columbia University Press.
Debray, Régis. [1991] 2001. *Cours de médiologie générale.* Paris: Gallimard.
Debray, Régis. 2005a. "Technique." *Médium* 3: 162–69.
Debray, Régis. 2005b. "Un dialogue manqué." *Médium* 5: 116–31.
Debray, Régis. 2007. *Un mythe contemporain: le dialogue des civilisations.* Paris: CNRS Editions.

Delanty, Gerard. 2006. *Handbook of Contemporary European Social Theory.* London: Routledge.
Delmotte, Florence, and Christophe Majastre. 2017. "Violence and *Civilité:* The Ambivalences of the State." In *Norbert Elias and Violence,* edited by Tatiana Savoia Landini and François Dépelteau, 55–80. New York, NY: Palgrave Macmillan.
Deranty, Jean-Philippe. 2004. "Injustice, Violence and Social Struggle. The Critical Potential of Axel Honneth's Theory of Recognition." *Critical Horizons* 5, no. 1: 297–322.
Derrida, Jacques. *Adieu à Emmanuel Lévinas.* Paris: Galilée, 1997.
Derrida, Jacques, and Giovanna Borradori. 2003. "Autoimmunity: Real and Symbolic Suicides – A Dialogue with Jacques Derrida." In *Philosophy in a Time of Terror: Dialogues with Jürgen Habermas and Jacques Derrida,* edited by Giovanna Borradori, 85–136. Chicago, IL: University of Chicago Press.
de Villiers, Etienne. 2018. *Revisiting Max Weber's Ethic of Responsibility.* Tübingen: Mohr Siebeck.
Dickenson, David. 2015. *Fighting Their Own Battles. The Mabarete and the End of Labour Broking in the South African Post Office,* edited by, University of the Witwatersrand, Society, Work and Politics Institute (SWOP Institute), working paper 2, February. http://www.ee.co.za/wp-content/uploads/2015/07/Post-Office-Labour-Unrest-Strikes-2009–2014-Prof-Dickinson.pdf, last accessed 11 February 2021.
Dosse, François. 1995. *L'empire du sens. L'humanisation des sciences humaines.* Paris: La Découverte.
Dosse, François. 2018. *Paul Ricœur. Les sens d'une vie (1913–2005).* Edition revue et augmentée. Paris: La Découverte.
Dubet, François. 2009. *Le travail des sociétés.* Paris: Seuil.
Dunning, Michael. 2016. "'Established and Outsiders': Brutalisation Processes and the Development of 'Jihadist Terrorists'." *Historical Social Research / Historische Sozialforschung* 41, no. 3 (157), Special Issue: Established-Outsider Relations and Figurational Analysis: 31–53.
Düwell, Marcus, and Micha Werner, eds. 2011. *Handbuch Ethik.* Stuttgart: Metzler.
Elias, Norbert. 1986. "Zivilisation." In *Grundbegriffe der Soziologie,* edited by Bernard Schäfers, 382–87. Leverkusen: Leske & Budrich.
Elias, Norbert. 2008. *Essays II. On Civilising Processes, State Formation and National Identity.* The collected works of Norbert Elias, volume 15, edited by Richard Kilminster and Stephen Mennell. Dublin: University College Dublin Press.
Elias. Norbert. 2009. *Essays III. On Sociology and the Humanities.* The Collected Works of Norbert Elias, volume 16, edited by Richard Kilminster and Stephen Mennell. Dublin: University College Dublin Press.
Elias, Norbert. 2010. *The Society of Individuals.* [1987] The Collected Works of Norbert Elias, volume 10, edited by Robert van Krieken. Dublin: University College Dublin Press.
Elias, Norbert. 2012. *On the Process of Civilisation. Sociogenetic and Psychogenetic Investigations.* [1939] The collected works of Norbert Elias, volume 3, edited by Stephen Mennell, Eric Dunning, Johan Goudsblom and Richard Kilminster. Dublin: University College Dublin Press.
Elias, Norbert. 2013. *Studies on the Germans. Power struggles and the development of habitus in the nineteenth and twentieth centuries.* [1989] The Collected Works of Norbert

Elias, volume, 11, edited by Stephen Mennell and Eric Dunning. Dublin: University College Dublin Press.

Elias, Norbert, and John Scotson. 2008. *The Established and the Outsiders*. [1965] The Collected Works of Norbert Elias, volume 4, edited by Cas Wouters. Dublin: University College Dublin Press.

Fanon, Franz. 1965. *The Wretched of the Earth*. London: Penguin.

Fletcher, Jonathan. 1997. *Violence and Civilization: An Introduction to the Work of Norbert Elias*. Cambridge: Polity Press.

Foucault, Michel. 1977. *Discipline and Punish: The Birth of the Prison*. New York, NY: Pantheon.

Franssen, Maarten. 2014. "The Good, the Bad, the Ugly… and the Poor: Instrumental and Non-instrumental Value of Artefacts." In *The Moral Status of Technical Artefacts*, edited by Peter Kroes and Peter-Paul Verbeek, 213–34. Dordrecht: Springer.

Friedberg, Erhard. 1992. "Les quatre dimensions de l'action organisée." *Revue française de sociologie* 33, no. 4: 531–57.

Friedland, William, and Carl Rosberg. 1967. *African Socialism*. Stanford, CA: Stanford University.

Geertz, Clifford. [1973] 2000. *The Interpretation of Cultures: Selected Essays*. New York, NY: Basic Books.

Genard, Jean-Louis, and Fabrizio Cantelli. 2008. "Êtres capables et compétents: lecture anthropologique et pistes pragmatiques." *SociologieS* [Online], Théories et recherches, online on 27 April 2008. http://sociologies.revues.org/1943, last accessed 29 February 2020.

Genard, Jean-Louis, and Fabrizio Cantelli. 2010. "Pour une sociologie politique des compétences." *Les Politiques Sociales* 70, nos. 1–2: 103–20.

Gethmann, Carl Friedrich. 1988. "Heideggers Konzeption des Handelns in *Sein und Zeit*." In *Heidegger und die praktische Philosophie*, edited by Annemarie Gethmann-Siefert and Otto Pöggeler, 140–76. Frankfurt am Main: Suhrkamp.

Giddens, Anthony. 1979. *Central Problems in Social Theory: Action, Structure and Contradiction in Social Analysis*. London: Macmillan.

Giddens, Anthony. 1984. *The Constitution of Society. Outline of the Theory of Structuration*. Berkeley and Los Angeles, CA: University of California Press.

Giddens, Anthony. 1985. *The Nation-state and Violence*. Volume 2 of *A Contemporary Critique of Historical Materialism*. Cambridge: Polity.

Giddens, Anthony. [1976] 1993. *New Rules of Sociological Method: A Positive Critique of Interpretative Sociologies*, 2nd ed. Stanford, CT: Stanford University Press.

Greisch, Jean. 2015. *L'herméneutique comme sagesse de l'incertitude*. Paris: Le cercle herméneutique éditeur.

Grimmler, Antje, Hans Joas and Richard Sennet. 2006. "Creativity, Pragmatism and the Social Sciences." *Distinktion* 13: 5–31.

Grondin, Jean. 2003. *Le tournant herméneutique de la phénoménologie*. Paris: PUF.

Grunwald, Armin. 1999. *Rationale Technikfolgenbeurteilung. Konzeption und methodische Grundlagen*. Berlin: Springer.

Gutema, Bekele. 2015. "The Intercultural Dimension of African Philosophy." *African Study Monographs* 36, no. 3: 139–54.

Habermas, Jürgen. 1969. *Technik und Wissenschaft als "Ideologie"*. Frankfurt am Main: Suhrkamp.
Habermas, Jürgen. 1972. *Toward a Rational Society: Student Protest, Science, and Politics*. London: Heinemann.
Habermas, Jürgen, and Giovanna Borradori. 2003. "Fundamentalism and Terror – A Dialogue with Jürgen Habermas." In *Philosophy in a Time of Terror: Dialogues with Jürgen Habermas and Jacques Derrida*, edited by Giovanna Borradori, 25–43. Chicago, IL: University of Chicago Press.
Hann, Chris, and Keith Hart. 2011. *Economic Anthropology. History, Ethnography, Critique*. Cambridge, and Malden, MA: Polity.
Hartung, Gerald. 2015. "Philosophie." In *Handbuch Moderneforschung*, edited by Friedrich Jaeger, Wolfgang Knöbl and Ute Schneider, 204–15. Stuttgart: J. B. Metzler.
Haudricourt, André-George. 1987. *La technologie science humaine. Recherches d'histoire et d'ethnologie des techniques*. Paris: Editions de la maison des sciences de l'homme.
Heidbrink, Ludger, and Alfred Hirsch, eds. 2006. *Verantwortung in der Zivilgesellschaft. Zur Konjunktur eines widersprüchlichen Prinzips*. Frankfurt am Main: Campus Verlag.
Heidbrink, Ludger, and Alfred Hirsch, eds. 2007. *Staat ohne Verantwortung? Zum Wandel der Aufgaben von Staat und Politik*. Frankfurt am Main: Campus Verlag.
Heidbrink, Ludger, and Alfred Hirsch, eds. 2008. *Verantwortung als Marktwirtschaftliches Prinzip. Zum Verhältnis von Moral und Ökonomie*. Frankfurt am Main: Campus Verlag.
Heidegger, Martin. [1927] 1993. *Sein und Zeit*. Tübingen: Max Niemeyer Verlag.
Heidegger, Martin. 1996. *Being and Time: A Translation of Sein und Zeit*, trans. by Joan Stambaugh. Albany, NY: State University of New York Press.
Hick, Rod, and Tania Burchardt. 2016. "Capability Deprivation." In *The Oxford Handbook of the Social Science of Poverty*, edited by David Brady and Linda M. Burto. Oxford: Oxford University Press. https://doi.org/10.1093/oxfordhb/9780199914050.013.5, last accessed 5 February 2021.
Honneth, Axel. 1990. *Die zerrissene Welt des Sozialen*. Frankfurt am Main: Suhrkamp.
Honneth, Axel. [1992] 1994. *Kampf um Anerkennung: Zur moralischen Grammatik sozialer Konflikte*. Frankfurt am Main: Suhrkamp.
Honneth, Axel. 1995. *The Struggle for Recognition: The Moral Grammar of Social Conflicts*. Cambridge: Polity Press.
Honneth, Axel. 2001. *Leiden an Unbestimmtheit*. Stuttgart: Reclam.
Honneth, Axel. 2011. *Das Recht der Freiheit. Grundriß einer demokratischen Sittlichkeit*. Berlin: Suhrkamp.
Honneth, Axel. 2014. *Freedom's Right: The Social Foundations of Democratic Life*, trans. by Joseph Ganahl. Cambridge: Polity.
Hountondji, Paulin. 1976. *Sur la "philosophie africaine"*. Paris: Maspéro.
Hountondji, Paulin. 1983. *African Philosophy: Myth and Reality*. Bloomington, IN: Indiana University Press.
Hubig, Christoph. 2006. *Die Kunst des Möglichen I. Technikphilosophie als Reflexion der Medialität*. Bielefeld: Transcript.
Hubig, Christoph. 2007. *Die Kunst des Möglichen II. Ethik der Technik als provisorische Moral*. Bielefeld: Transcript.
Hubig, Christoph. 2015. *Die Kunst des Möglichen III. Macht der Technik*. Bielefeld: Transcript.

Husserl, Edmund. 1959. "Meditation über die Idee eines individuellen und Gemeinschaftslebens in absoluter Selbstverantwortung." In *Erste Philosophie (1923/1924), Zweiter Teil: Theorie der phänomenologischen Reduktion*, Husserl Gesammelte Werke Band VIII, edited by Rudolf Boehm, 193–202. Den Haag: Martinus Nijhoff.

Ihde, Don. 1979. *Technics and Praxis*. Dordrecht, Boston, MA, and London: Reidel.

Ihde, Don. 1990. *Technology and the Lifeworld. From Garden to Earth*. Bloomington, and Indianapolis, IN: Indiana University Press.

Imbusch, Peter. 2003. "The concept of violence." In *The International Handbook of Violence Research*, edited by John Hagan and Wilhelm Heitmeyer, 13–39. Dordrecht: Kluwer.

Innes, Robert. 1985. "Dewey's Aesthetic Theory and the Critique of Technology." In *Studien zum Problem der Technik*, Phänomenologische Forschungen 15, edited by Ernst Wolfgang Orth, 7–42. Freiburg, and Munich: Verlag Karl Alber.

Jaeger, Friedrich, Wolfgang Knöbl and Ute Schneider, eds. 2015. *Handbuch Moderneforschung*. Stuttgart: J. B. Metzler.

Jaffré, Bruno. 2007. *Biographie de Thomas Sankara. La patrie ou la mort…*. Paris: L'Harmattan.

Joas, Hans. 1992. *Die Kreativität des Handelns*. Frankfurt am Main: Suhrkamp.

Joas, Hans. 2000. *The Genesis of Values*. Cambridge: Polity Press.

Joas, Hans. 2015. *Sind die Menschenrechte westlich?*. Munich: Kössel Verlag.

Joas, Hans, and Wolfgang Knöbl. 2004. *Sozialtheorie. Zwanzig einführende Vorlesungen*. Suhrkamp: Frankfurt am Main.

Joas, Hans, and Wolfgang Knöbl. 2009. *Social Theory: Twenty Introductory Lectures*. Cambridge: Cambridge University Press.

Jonas, Hans. 1979. *Das Prinzip Verantwortung. Versuch einer Ethik für die technologische Zivilisation*. Frankfurt am Main: Suhrkamp.

Jonas, Hans. 1992. *Philosophische Untersuchungen und metaphysische Vermutungen*. Frankfurt am Main, and Leipzig: Insel.

Kacou oi Kacou, Vincent Davy. 2013. *Penser l'Afrique avec Ricœur*. Paris: L'Harmattan.

Kacou oi Kacou, Vincent Davy. 2014a. *Paul Ricœur. Le cogito blessé et sa réception africaine*. Paris: L'Harmattan.

Kacou oi Kacou, Vincent Davy. 2014b. *L'herméneutique du soi chez Paul Ricœur. Prolégomènes à une éthique de la reconstruction de l'Afrique*. Paris: Mon Petit Éditeur.

Kalyvas, Stathis N. 2019. "The Landscape of Political Violence." In *The Oxford Handbook of Terrorism*, edited by Erica Chenoweth, Richard English, Andreas Gofas, and Stathis N. Kalyvas, 11–33. Oxford: Oxford University Press.

Kaspersen, Lars Bo. 2000. *Anthony Giddens: An Introduction to a Social Theorist*. Oxford: Blackwell.

Kertscher, Jens. 2009. "Was heißt eigentlich Primat der Praxis? – Wie Heidegger und Dewey eine erkenntnistheoretische Dichotomie überwinden." *Journal Phaenomenologie* 32: 59–70.

Kieser, Alfred, and Mark Ebers, eds. 2019. *Organisationstheorien*, 8th ed. Stuttgart: Kohlhammer, 2019.

Kneer, Georg, and Markus Schroer, eds. 2009. *Handbuch Soziologische Theorien*. Wiesbaden: Springer VS.

Knöbl, Wolfgang. 2007. *Die Kontingenz der Moderne. Wege in Europa, Asien und Amerika*. Frankfurt am Main: Campus Verlag.

Knöbl, Wolfgang. 2015. "Soziologie." In *Handbuch Moderneforschung*, edited by Friedrich Jaeger, Wolfgang Knöbl and Ute Schneider, 261–74. Stuttgart: J. B. Metzler.

Kolarz, Peter. 2016. *Giddens and Politics Beyond the Third Way*. London: Palgrave Macmillan.

Koloma Beck, Teresa. 2018. "Mehr als der Mythos vom Zivilisationsprozess. Warum es sich lohnt, Norbert Elias' bekanntestes Werk neu zu lesen." *Zeithistorische Forschungen* 15, no. 2: 383–90.

Korte, Hermann. 2017. *On Norbert Elias – Becoming a Human Scientist*, edited by Stefanie Ernst. Wiesbaden: Springer VS.

Krämer, Sybille. 2015. *Medium, Messenger, Transmission: An Approach to Media Philosophy*. Amsterdam: Amsterdam University Press.

Kumar, Krishan. 2005. *From Post-industrial to Post-modern Society. New Theories of the Contemporary World*. 2nd ed. Malden, MA, Oxford, and Carlton: Blackwell.

Laitinen, Arto. 2011. "Paul Ricœur's Surprising Take on Recognition." *Études Ricœuriennes / Ricœur Studies* 2, no. 1: 35–50.

Latour, Bruno. 1996. "On Interobjectivity." *Mind, Culture, and Activity* 3, no. 4: 228–45.

Latour, Bruno, and Shirley Strum. 1996. "Human social origins. Please tell us another origin story!" *Journal of Biological and Social Structures* 9: 169–87.

Lenk, Hans. 1982. *Zur Sozialphilosophie der Technik*. Frankfurt am Main: Suhrkamp.

Lenk, Hans. 1998. *Konkrete Humanität. Vorlesungen über Verantwortung und Menschlichkeit*. Frankfurt am Main: Suhrkamp.

Lenk, Hans. 2017. "Verantwortlichkeit und Verantwortungstypen: Arten und Polaritäten." In *Handbuch Verantwortung*, edited by Ludger Heidbrink, Claus Langbehn and Janina Loh, 57–84. Wiesbaden: Springer VS.

Lenk, Hans, and Matthias Maring. 1991a. "Deskriptive und normative Zuschreibung von Verantwortung." In *Zwischen Wissenschaft und Ethik*, edited by Hans Lenk, 76–100. Frankfurt am Main: Suhrkamp.

Lenk, Hans, and Matthias Maring, eds., 1991b. *Technikverantwortung: Güterabwägung – Risikobewertung – Verhaltenskodizes*. Frankfurt am Main: Campus Verlag.

Lenk, Hans, and Matthias Maring. 2017. "Verantwortung in Technik und Wissenschaft." In *Handbuch Verantwortung*, edited by Ludger Heidbrink, Claus Langbehn and Janina Loh, 715–31. Wiesbaden: Springer VS.

Leroi-Gourhan, André. 1943. *Evolution et techniques*, Tome 1: *L'homme et la matière*. Paris: Albin Michel.

Leroi-Gourhan, André. 1964–1965. *Le geste et la parole*. Paris: Albin Michel.

Lévinas, Emmanuel. 1991. *Totality and Infinity: An Essay on Exteriority*. Dordrecht: Kluwer.

Lévinas, Emmanuel. [1961] 1998. *Totalité et infini. Essai sur l'extériorité*. La Haye: Martinus Nijhoff.

Lévy, Pierre. 1998. "La place de la médiologie dans le trivium." *Cahiers de Médiologie* 6: 43–58.

Lévy-Bruhl, Lucien. 1884. *L'idée de la responsabilité*. Paris: Hachette.

Liniger-Goumaz, Max. 1992. *La démocrature. Dictature camouflée, démocratie truquée*. Paris: L'Harmattan.

Loh, Janina. 2017. "Strukturen und Relata der Verantwortung." In *Handbuch Verantwortung*, edited by Ludger Heidbrink, Claus Langbehn and Janina Loh, 35–56. Wiesbaden: Springer VS.

Loyal, Steven. 2003. *The Sociology of Anthony Giddens*. London, Sterling: Pluto Press.

Luhmann, Niklas. 1993. "Die Moral des Risikos und das Risiko der Moral." In *Risiko und Gesellschaft. Grundlagen und Ergebnisse interdisziplinärer Risikoforschung*, edited by Gotthard Bechmann, 327–38. Opladen: Westdeutscher Verlag.

Macamo, Elísio, ed. 2005. *Negotiating Modernity: Africa's Ambivalent Experience*. Dakar, and London, Pretoria: Codesria Books and others.

Macamo, Elísio. 2012. "Conclusion." In *Risk and Africa*, edited by Lena Bloemertz, Martin Doevenspeck, Elísio Macamo and Detlef Müller-Mahn, 265–72. Vienna, Berlin: LIT Verlag.

Machalek, Richard, and Michael W. Martin. 2016. "Social Evolution." In *Handbook of Contemporary Sociological Theory*, edited by Seth Abrutyn, 503–26. Cham: Springer.

Madu, Raphael Okechukwu. 1992. *African Symbols, Proverbs and Myths. The Hermeneutics of Destiny*. New York, NY: Peter Lang.

Mandela, Nelson. [1965] 1990. *No Easy Walk to Freedom*. Harlow: Heinemann.

Martucelli, Danilo. 1999. *Sociologies de la modernité*. Paris: Gallimard.

Mauss, Marcel. 1950. *Sociologie et anthropologie*. Paris: PUF.

Mennell, Stephen. 1989. *Norbert Elias. Civilization and the Human Self-image*. Oxford, and New York, NY: Blackwell.

Merleau-Ponty, Maurice. 1945. *Phénoménologie de la perception*. Paris: Gallimard.

Merleau-Ponty, Maurice. 1947. *Humanisme et terreur: Essai sur le problème communiste*. Paris: Gallimard.

Merleau-Ponty, Maurice. 2000. *Humanism and Terror: The Communist Problem*, trans. by John O'Neill. New Brunswick, NJ: Transaction.

Merzeau, Louise. 1998. "Ceci ne tuera pas cela." *Cahiers de Médiologie* 6: 27–39.

Merzeau, Louise, and Régis Debray. 2005. "Médiasphère," *Médium* 4: 146–52.

Mesure, Sylvie. 1999. "Rationalisme et faillibilisme." In *Histoire de la philosophie politique. Tome V, Les philosophies politiques contemporaines*, edited by Alain Renaut, 149–84. Paris: Calmann-Lévy.

Micheelsen, Arun. 2002. "'I Don't Do Systems': An Interview with Clifford Geertz." *Method and Theory in the Study of Religion* 14, no. 1: 2–20.

Michel, Johann. 2006. *Paul Ricœur. Une philosophie de l'agir*. Paris: Cerf.

Michel, Johann. 2012a. "Le sens des institutions." *Il Protagora* 39: 105–17.

Michel, Johann. 2012b. *Sociologie du soi. Essai d'herméneutique appliquée*. Rennes: Presses Universitaires de Rennes.

Michel, Johann. 2013. "Crise de soi et substitution narrative." *Archivio di filosofia* 1: 281–90.

Michel, Johann. 2013. *Ricœur et ses contemporains: Bourdieu, Derrida, Deleuze, Foucault, Castoriadis*. Paris: PUF.

Miconi, Andrea, and Marcello Serra. 2019. "On the Concept of Medium: An Empirical Study." *International Journal of Communication* 13: 3444–61.

Monteil, Pierre-Olivier. 2013. *Ricœur politique*. Rennes: Presses Universitaires de Rennes.

Mouzelis, Nicos. 1997. "Social and System Integration: Lockwood, Habermas, Giddens." *Sociology* 31, no. 1: 111–19.

Mudimbe, Valentin Yves. 1988. *The Invention of Africa: Gnosis, Philosophy, and the Order of Knowledge*. African Systems of Thought. Bloomington, IN: Indiana University Press.

Murray, Montagu, and Ernst Wolff. 2015. "A Hermeneutic Framework for Responsible Technical Interventions in Low-income Households. Mobile Phones for Improved

Managed Health Care as Test Case." *The Journal for Transdisciplinary Research in Southern Africa* 11, no. 3: 171–85.
Ndaywel è Nsiem, Isidore, ed. 2018. *Les années UNAZA (Université Nationale du Zaïre). Contribution à l'histoire de l'Université Africaine*. Tome II. Paris: L'Harmattan.
Nizet, Jean. 2007. *La sociologie de Anthony Giddens*. Paris: La Découverte.
Nkombe Oleko. [1975] 1979. *Métaphore et métonymie dans les symboles parémiologiques. L'intersubjectivité dans les "Proverbes Tetela"*. Kinshasa, Faculté de théologie catholique.
Ntumba, Tshiamalenga. 1979. "Die Philosophie in der aktuellen Situation Afrikas." *Zeitschrift für philosophische Forschung* 33, no. 3, July – September: 428–43.
Obenga, Théophile. 1990. *La philosophie africaine de la période pharaonique, 2780–330 avant notre ère*. Paris: L'Harmattan.
Okere, Theophilus. 1983. *African Philosophy: A Historico-Hermeneutical Investigation of the Conditions of its Possibility*. Lanham, MD: University Press of America.
Okolo Okonda. 1978–1979. *Tradition et destin. Essai sur la philosophie herméneutique de P. Ricœur, M. Heidegger, et H. G. Gadamer*. Lubumbashi: Université Nationale du Zaïre.
Okolo Okonda. 1986. *Pour une philosophie de la culture et du développement. Recherches d'herméneutique et de praxis africaines*. Kinshasa: Presses Universitaire du Zaïre.
Okolo Okonda, and Jacques Ngangala Balade Tongamba. 2018. *Introduction à l'histoire des idées dans le contexte de l'oralité: théorie et méthode avec application sur l'Afrique traditionnelle*. Louvain-la-Neuve: Academia-L'Harmattan.
Okrent, Mark. 2013. "Heidegger's Pragmatism Redux." In *The Cambridge Companion to Pragmatism*, edited by Alan Malachowski, 124–58. Cambridge: Cambridge University Press.
O'Neill, Shane. 2010. "Struggles Against Injustice: Contemporary Critical Theory and Political Violence." *Journal of Global Ethics* 6, no. 2: 127–39.
Oyedola, David. 2014. "The Culture-oriented Bias of African Philosophical Inquiry." *Filosofia Theoretica* 3, no. 2: 62–80.
Pakaluk, Michael. 2005. *Aristotle's Nicomachean Ethics. An Introduction*. Cambridge: Cambridge University Press.
Panayotova, Plamena, ed. 2019. *The History of Sociology in Britain: New Research and Revaluation*. Cham: Palgrave Macmillan.
Papoulias, Constantina. 2004. "Of Tools and Angels: Régis Debray's Mediology." *Theory, Culture and Society* 21, 3: 165–70.
Patterson, Orlando. 1982. *Slavery and Social Death. A Comparative Study*. Cambridge, MA, and London: Harvard University Press.
Peires, Jeffrey. 1981. *The House of Phalo: A History of the Xhosa People in the Days of their Independence*. Berkeley, CA, and Los Angeles, CA: California University Press.
Powell, Walter W., and Christof Brandtner. 2016. "Organizations as Sites and Drivers of Social Action." In *Handbook of Contemporary Sociological Theory*, edited by Seth Abrutyn, 269–92. Cham: Springer.
Preisendörfer, Peter. 2016. *Organisationssoziologie. Grundlagen, Theorien und Problemstellungen*, 4th ed. Wiesbaden: Springer VS.
Rabinbach, Anson. 1992. *The Human Motor. Energy, Fatigue, and the Origins of Modernity*. Berkeley, CA: University of California Press.

Rabinbach, Anson. 2018. *The Eclipse of the Utopias of Labor. Forms of Living.* New York, NY: Fordham University Press.
Rammert, Werner. 2016. *Technik – Handeln – Wissen: Zu einer pragmatistischen Technik- und Sozialtheorie,* 2nd ed. Wiesbaden: Springer VS.
Raub, Werner, and Thomas Voss. 2017. "Micro-macro models in sociology. Antecedents of Coleman's diagram." In *Social Dilemmas, Institutions, and the Evolution of Cooperation,* edited by Ben Jann and Wojtek Przepiorka, 11–36. Berlin, and Boston, MA: Walter de Gruyter.
Rawls, John. [1971] 1999. *A Theory of Justice.* Rev. ed. Cambridge, MA: Harvard University Press.
Reader, Keith. 1995. *Régis Debray: A Critical Introduction.* London: Pluto.
Ricœur, Paul. 1947. "La question coloniale." *Réforme* 3, no. 131, 20 September: re-edited by Ernst Wolff. https://bibnum.explore.psl.eu/s/psl/ark:/18469/1z0z0#?c=&m=&s=&cv=, last accessed 5 February 2021.
Ricœur, Paul. 1964. *Histoire et vérité.* Paris: Seuil.
Ricœur, Paul. 1965a. *De l'interprétation. Essai sur Freud.* Paris: Seuil.
Ricœur, Paul. 1965b. *History and Truth,* trans. by Charles A. Kelbley. Evanston, IL: Northwestern University Press.
Ricœur, Paul. 1967. *Histoire et vérité.* Paris: Seuil.
Ricœur, Paul. 1969. *The Symbolism of Evil,* trans. Emerson Buchanan. Boston, MA: Beacon.
Ricœur, Paul. 1970. *Freud and Philosophy. An Essay on Interpretation,* trans. by Denis Savage. New Haven, CT, and London: Yale University Press.
Ricœur, Paul. 1971. "Le conflit: signe de contradiction ou d'unité?" In *Contributions et conflits: naissance d'une société,* 189–204. Lyon: Chronique sociale de France.
Ricœur, Paul. 1974a. *The Conflict of Interpretations. Essays in Hermeneutics,* trans. by Don Ihde et al. Evanston, IL: Northwestern University Press.
Ricœur, Paul. 1974b. "The tasks of the political educator." In *Political and Social Essays,* edited by David Steward and Joseph Bien, 271–93. Athens, OH: Ohio University Press.
Ricœur, Paul, et al. 1976. *Cultures and Time.* Paris: UNESCO.
Ricœur, Paul, et al. 1977. *Time and the Philosophies.* Paris: UNESCO.
Ricœur, Paul. 1978. "Philosophy." In *Main Trends of Research in the Social and the Human Sciences,* Part 2/2. Legal Science. Philosophy, edited by J. Havet, 1071–1567. The Hague, Paris, New York, NY: Mouton-Unesco.
Ricœur, Paul. 1979. *Freedom and Nature: The Voluntary and the Involuntary,* trans. by Erazim Kohák. Evanston, IL: Northwestern University Press.
Ricœur, Paul. 1983. *Temps et récit 1. L'intrigue et le récit historique.* Paris: Seuil.
Ricœur, Paul. 1984. *Time and Narrative.* Volume 1, trans. by Kathleen Blamey and David Pellauer. Chicago, IL: University of Chicago Press.
Ricœur, Paul. 1985. *Temps et récit 3. Le temps raconté.* Paris: Seuil.
Ricœur, Paul. 1986a. *A l'école de la phénoménologie.* Paris: Vrin.
Ricœur, Paul. 1986b. *Du texte à l'action. Essais d'herméneutique II.* Paris: Seuil.
Ricœur, Paul. [1965] 1986c. *Fallible Man,* trans. by Charles A. Kelbley. New York, NY: Fordham University Press.
Ricœur, Paul. 1986d. "Introduction." In *Philosophical Foundations of Human Rights,* edited by Alwin Diemer, 9–29. Paris: UNESCO.

Ricœur, Paul. 1986e. *Lectures on Ideology and Utopia*, edited by George H. Taylor. New York, NY: Columbia University Press.
Ricœur, Paul. 1987. "The fragility of political language." *Philosophy Today*, 31, no. 1, Spring: 35–44.
Ricœur, Paul. 1988. *Time and Narrative*. Volume 3, trans. by Kathleen Blamey and David Pellauer. Chicago, IL, and London: University of Chicago Press.
Ricœur, Paul. 1990a. "Préface." In Maurizio Chiodi, *Il cammino della libertà. Fenomenologia, ermeneutica, ontologia della libertà nella ricerca filosofica di Paul Ricœur*, ix-xix. Brescia: Morcelliana.
Ricœur, Paul. 1990b. *Soi-même comme un autre*. Paris: Seuil.
Ricœur, Paul. 1991a. *From Text to Action: Essays in Hermeneutics II*, trans. by Kathleen Blamey and John Thompson. London: Athlone.
Ricœur, Paul. 1991b. *Lectures 1: Autour du politique*. Paris: Seuil.
Ricœur, Paul. 1992a. "Fragilité et responsabilité." In *Eros and Eris. Contributions to a hermeneutical phenomenology*, edited by Paul van Tongeren et al., 295–304. Dordrecht: Kluwer.
Ricœur, Paul. 1992b. *Oneself as Another*, trans. by Kathleen Blamey. Chicago, IL: University of Chicago Press.
Ricœur, Paul. 1994. "La souffrance n'est pas la douleur." *Autrement* "Souffrances" 142, February: 58–69.
Ricœur, Paul. 1995a. "Fragility and Responsibility." *Philosophy and Social Criticism* 21, nos. 5–6: 15–22.
Ricœur, Paul. 1995b. *Hermeneutics and the Human Sciences: Essays on Language, Action and Interpretation*, edited, trans., and introduced by John B. Thompson. Cambridge: Cambridge University Press.
Ricœur, Paul. 1995c. *La critique et la conviction. Entretien avec François Azouvi et Marc De Launay*. Paris: Calmann-Lévy.
Ricœur, Paul. 1995d. *Le juste 1*. Paris: Esprit.
Ricœur, Paul. 1996. "Love and Justice." In *Paul Ricœur: The Hermeneutics of Action*, edited by Richard Kearney, 23–39. London: Sage Publications.
Ricœur, Paul. [1986] 1997. *L'idéologie et l'utopie*. Paris: Seuil.
Ricœur, Paul. 1998a. "Architecture et narrativité." *Urbanisme* 303, Nov/Dec: 44–53.
Ricœur, Paul. 1998b. *Critique and Conviction: Conversations with François Azouvi and Marc De Launay*. European Perspectives. New York, NY: Columbia University Press.
Ricœur, Paul. 2000a. *The Just*. Chicago, IL: University of Chicago Press.
Ricœur, Paul. 2000b. *La mémoire, l'histoire, l'oubli*. Paris: Seuil.
Ricœur, Paul. 2000c. "Paul Ricœur: un parcours philosophique." Interview with F. Ewald, *Magazine littéraire* 390: 20–26.
Ricœur, Paul. 2000d. "Proménade au fil d'un chemin." In Fabrizio Turold, *Verità del metodo. Indagini su Paul Ricœur*, 13–20. Padua: Il Poligrafo.
Ricœur, Paul. 2001. *Le juste 2*. Paris: Esprit.
Ricœur, Paul. [1946] 2003a. "Le chrétien et la civilisation occidentale." *Autres Temps* 76–77: 23–36.
Ricœur, Paul. [1955] 2003b. "Vraie et fausse paix." *Autres Temps* 76–77: 51–65.
Ricœur, Paul. 2004a. "Avant la justice non violente, la justice violente." *Vérité, réconciliation, réparation. Le genre humain* 43: 157–71.

Ricœur, Paul. 2004b. *Memory, History, Forgetting.* Chicago, IL: University of Chicago Press.
Ricœur, Paul. 2004c. *Parcours de la reconnaissance.* Paris: Gallimard.
Ricœur, Paul. 2004d. "Projet universel et multiplicités des héritages." In *Où vont les valeurs? Entretiens de XXIe siècle II* [2001], edited by Jérôme Bindé, 75–80. Paris: Unesco – Albin Michel.
Ricœur, Paul. 2005. *The Course of Recognition*, trans. by David Pellauer. Cambridge, MA: Harvard University Press.
Ricœur, Paul. 2006. "Architecture and Narrativity." *Études Ricœuriennes / Ricœur Studies* 7, no. 2: 31–42.
Ricœur, Paul. 2007. *Reflections on the Just,* trans. by David Pellauer. Chicago, IL: University of Chicago Press.
Ricœur, Paul. 2008. *Amour et justice.* Paris: Editions Points.
Ricœur, Paul. [1950] 2009a. *Philosophie de la volonté 1. Le volontaire et l'involontaire.* Paris: Point.
Ricœur, Paul. [1960] 2009b. *Philosophie de la volonté 2. Finitude et culpabilité.* Paris: Edition Points.
Ricœur, Paul. 2010. "Power and Violence." trans. by Lisa Jones, *Theory, Culture and Society* 27, 5: 18–36.
Ricœur, Paul. [1969] 2013. *Le conflit des interprétations. Essais d'herméneutique I.* Paris: Seuil.
Ritzer, George, and Jeffrey Stepnisky. 2018. *Modern Sociological Theory,* 8th ed. Los Angeles, CA: Sage.
Robeck, Johannes. 1993. *Technologische Urteilskraft. Zu einer Ethik technischen Handelns.* Frankfurt am Main: Suhrkamp.
Robbins, Stephen P., and Timothy A. Judge. 2017. *Essentials of Organizational Behavior,* Global 17th ed. Upper Saddle River, NJ: Pearson Prentice Hall.
Roman, Sébastien. 2015. "Hétérotopie et utopie pratique: comparaison entre Foucault et Ricœur." *Le Philosophoire* 44, no. 2: 69–86.
Ropohl, Günther. 1994. "Das Risiko im Prinzip Verantwortung." *Ethik und Sozialwissenschaften* 5: 109–20
Ropohl, Günther. 2009. *Allgemeine Technologie. Eine Systemtheorie der Technik,* 3rd ed. Karlsruhe: Universitätsverlag Karlsruhe.
Sacchetti, Francesca. 2012. *Alfred Schütz e Paul Ricœur. Percorsi della soggettività tra fenomenologia ed ermeneutica.* Acireale-Roma: Bonanno Editore.
Sachsse, Hans. 1972. *Technik und Verantwortung. Probleme der Ethik im technischen Zeitalter.* Freiburg: Verlag Rombach.
Schatzki, Theodore. 1997. "Practices and Actions. A Wittgensteinian Critique of Bourdieu and Giddens." *Philosophy of the Social Sciences* 27, no. 3: 283–308.
Schwinn, Thomas. 2015. "Interaktion, Organisation, Gesellschaft. Eine Alternative zu Mikro-Makro?" In *Interaktion – Organisation – Gesellschaft* revisited. *Anwendungen, Erweiterungen, Alternativen.* Sonderheft der Zeitschrift für Soziologie, edited by Bettina Heintz and Hartmann Tyrell, 43–64. Stuttgart: Lucius & Lucius.
Scott, James. 1985. *The Weapons of the Weak. Everyday Forms of Peasant Resistance.* New Haven, CT, and London: Yale University Press.
Scott, Richard W., and Gerald F. Davis. 2007. *Organizations and Organizing: Rational, Natural, and Open System Perspectives.* Upper Saddle River, NJ: Pearson.

Séris, Jean-Pièrre. 1994. *La technique.* Paris: PUF.
Shicha, Luo. 2018. "Media as Mediation: Régis Debray's Medium Theory and Its Implications as a Perspective." *Empedocles: European Journal for the Philosophy of Communication* 9, no. 2: 121–38.
Sigaut, François. 2013. *Comment Homo devient faber. Comment l'outil fit l'homme.* Paris: CNRS Éditions.
Simpson, Thula. 2018. "Nelson Mandela and the Genesis of the ANC's Armed Struggle: Notes on Method." *Journal of Southern African Studies* 44, no. 1: 133–48.
Smet, A. J. 1980. *Histoire de la philosophie africaine contemporaine. Courants et problems.* Kinshasa: Limete.
Snyman, Johan. 1997. "Filosofie op die rand." *Koers* 62, no. 3: 277–306.
Stahl, Titus. 2017. "The Metaethics of Critical Theories." In *The Palgrave Handbook of Critical Theory,* edited by Michael J. Thompson, 505–23. New York, NY: Palgrave Macmillan US.
Stevens, Simon. 2019. "The Turn to Sabotage by the Congress Movement in South Africa." *Past and Present* 245, no. 1: 221–55.
Stones, Rob. 2005. *Structuration Theory.* New York, NY: Palgrave MacMillan.
Suttner, Raymond, and Jeremy Cronin. 2006. *50 Years of the Freedom Charter.* Pretoria: UNISA Press.
Suttner, Raymond. 2015. "The Freedom Charter @ 60: Rethinking its democratic qualities." *Historia* 60, no. 2: 1–23.
Taiwò, Olúfémi. 2010. *How Colonialism Pre-Empted Modernity in Africa.* Bloomington, IN, and Indianapolis, IN: Indiana University Press.
Taylor, Charles. 1999. "To follow a rule…" In *Bourdieu. A Critical Reader,* edited by Richard Shusterman, 29–44. Oxford, and Malden, MA: Blackwell.
Tellez, Jean. 2010. *L'âme et le corps des idées. Introduction à la pensée de Régis Debray.* Meaux: Germina.
Thévenot, Laurent. 1990. "L'action qui convient." In *Les formes de l'action,* edited by Patrick Pharo and Louis Quéré (Raisons pratiques 1), 39–69. Paris: Éditions de l'EHESS.
Thévenot, Laurent. 1994. "Le régime de la familiarité. Les choses en personne." *Genèse* 17: 72–101.
Thévenot, Laurent. 2006. *L'action au pluriel. Sociologie des régimes d'engagement.* Paris: La Découverte.
Thévenot, Laurent. 2011. "Grand résumé de *L'Action au pluriel. Sociologie des régimes d'engagement.*" *SociologieS:* online publication 6 July 2011. http://journals.openedition.org/sociologies/3572, last accessed 4 May 2019.
Thévenot, Laurent. 2012. "Des institutions en personne. Une sociologie pragmatique en dialogue avec Paul Ricœur." *Études Ricœuriennes/Ricœur Studies* 3, no. 1: 11–33.
Thompson, John. 1981. *Critical Hermeneutics. A Study in the Thought of Paul Ricœur and Jürgen Habermas.* Cambridge: Cambridge University Press.
Tilly, Charles. 2006. *Regimes and Repertoires.* Chicago, IL: University of Chicago Press.
Truc, Gérôme. 2005. "Une désillusion narrative? De Bourdieu à Ricœur." *Tracés* 8: 47–67.
Truth and Reconciliation Commission. 1998. *Truth and Reconciliation Commission of South Africa Report*, volume 3. https://www.justice.gov.za/trc/report/finalreport/Volume%203.pdf, last accessed 7 April 2020, 51.
Turnley, Melinda. 2011. "Towards a Mediological Method: A Framework for Critically Engaging Dimensions of a Medium." *Computers and Composition* 28, no. 2: 126–44.

van Binsbergen, Wim. 2001. "Ubuntu and the Globalization of Southern African Thought and Society." *Quest. An African Journal of Philosophy* 15, no. 1–2: 53–90. https://www.quest-journal.net/Quest_2001_PDF/binsbergen.pdf, last accessed 23 February 2020.

Vandenberghe, Frédéric. 2007. "Régis Debray and Mediation Studies, or How Does an Idea Become a Material Force?" *Thesis Eleven* 89, no. 1: 23–42.

van de Poel, Ibo, and Peter Kroes. 2006. "Introduction: Technology and Normativity." *Techné: Research in Philosophy and Technology* 10, no. 1: 1–9.

van der Pot, Johan Hendrik. 2004. *Encyclopedia of Technological Progress. A Systematic Overview of Theories and Opinions*. Delft: Eburon.

van Krieken, Robert. 1998. *Norbert Elias*. London, and New York, NY: Routledge.

Vansina, Jan. [1961] 1965. *Oral Tradition. A Study in Historical Methodology*, trans. by H. M. Wright. London: Routledge and Kegan Paul.

Vansina, Frans D. 2008. *Paul Ricœur. Bibliographie primaire et secondaire. Primary and secondary bibliography. 1935–2008*. Leuven: Peeters.

Verbeek, Peter-Paul. 2005. *What Things Do: Philosophical Reflections on Technology, Agency, and Design*. University Park, PA: Pennsylvania State University Press.

Vogelmann, Frieder. 2014. *Im Bann der Verantwortung*. Frankfurt am Main: Campus Verlag.

von Holdt, Karl. 2001. "Overview. Insurgent Citizenship and Collective Violence: Analysis of Case Studies." In *The Smoke That Calls. Insurgent Citizenship, Collective Violence and the Struggle for a Place in the New South Africa. Eight Case Studies of Community Protest and Xenophobic Violence*, edited by Karl von Holdt, Malose Langa, Sepetla Molapo, Nomfundo Mogapi, Kindiza Ngubeni, Jacob Dlamini and Adele Kirsten, 5–32. Centre for the Study of Violence and Reconciliation, Society, Work and Development Institute.

von Holdt, Karl. 2013. "South Africa: The Transition to Violent Democracy." *Review of African Political Economy*, 40, no. 138: 589–604.

von Holdt, Karl. 2014. "On Violent Democracy." *The Sociological Review* 62, no. S2: 129–51.

Wagner, Peter. 2004. "Soziologie der kritischen Urteilskraft und der Rechtfertigung: Die Politik- und Moralsoziologie um Luc Boltanski und Laurent Thévenot." In *Französische Soziologie der Gegenwart*, edited by Stephan Moebius and Lothar Peter, 417–48. Konstanz: UVK.

Weber, Max. 1991. "Politics as a Vocation." In *From Max Weber: Essays in Sociology*, trans. by Hans Heinrich Gerth and Charles Wright Mills, 77–128. London: Routledge.

Weber, Max. [1919] 1999. "Politik als Beruf." In *Gesammelte politische Schriften*. Potsdamer Internet-Ausgabe, 1999. http://www.uni-potsdam.de/verlagsarchivweb/html/494/html/PS.pdf, last accessed 5 February 2021, 396–450.

Webster, Edward, Rob Lambert and Andries Bezuidenhout. 2008. *Grounding Globalization. Labour in the Age of Insecurity*. Malden, MA, Oxford, and Carlton: Blackwell.

Weischedel, Wilhelm. [1932] 1972. *Das Wesen der Verantwortung. Ein Versuch*. Frankfurt am Main: Klostermann.

Werner, Micha. 2000. "Die Zuschreibung von Verantwortung. Versuch einer Annäherung von Handlungstheorie und Ethik." In *Zukunftsverantwortung in der Marktwirtschaft*, edited by Thomas Bausch, et al., 85–109. Münster: LIT.

Winnicott, Donald. [1971] 1996. *Playing and Reality*. London, and New York, NY: Routledge.

Wolff, Ernst. 2006. "Transmettre et interpreter." *Médium* 6, January-March: 30–47.

Wolff, Ernst. 2007. *De l'éthique à la justice. Langage et politique dans la philosophie de Lévinas*. Dordrecht: Springer.
Wolff, Ernst. 2008. "Aspects of technicity in Heidegger's early philosophy: rereading Aristotle's *techné* and *hexis*." *Research in Phenomenology* 38, no. 3: 317–57.
Wolff, Ernst. 2009. "Responsibility in an Era of Modern Technology and Nihilism, Part 1. A Non-Foundational Rereading of Jonas." *Dialogue* 48, no. 3: 577–99.
Wolff, Ernst. 2009. "Responsibility in an Era of Modern Technology and Nihilism, Part 2. Inter-connection and Implications of the Two Notions of Responsibility in Jonas." *Dialogue* 48, no. 4: 841–66.
Wolff, Ernst. 2010. "Technicity of the Body as Part of the Socio-technical System: The Contributions of Mauss and Bourdieu." *Theoria* 76, no. 2: 167–87.
Wolff, Ernst. 2011a. *Political Responsibility for a Globalised World. After Levinas' Humanism*. Bielefeld: Transcript Verlag.
Wolff, Ernst. 2011b. "The Quest for Justice Versus the Rights of the Other?" In *In Levinas' Trace*, edited by Maria Dimitrova, 101–11. Newcastle upon Tyne: Cambridge Scholars Publishing.
Wolff, Ernst. 2012. Review of "Rüsen, Jörn, and Henner Laass, eds. 2009. *Humanism in Intercultural Perspective: Experiences and Expectations*. Bielefeld: Transcript." in *Geschichte transnational / History Transnational*, published May 2012. http://geschichte-transnational.clio-online.net/rezensionen/, last accessed 5 February 2021.
Wolff, Ernst. 2014. "Hermeneutics and the capabilities approach. A thick heuristic tool for a thin normative standard of well-being. Practices of spatial arrangement as example." *South African Journal of Philosophy* 33, no. 4: 487–500.
Wolff, Ernst. 2015. "Responsibility to Struggle – Responsibility for Peace: Course of Recognition and a Recurrent Pattern in Ricœur's Political Thought." *Philosophy and Social Criticism* 41, no. 8: 771–90.
Wolff, Ernst. 2016. "'Technology' as the Critical Social Theory of Human Technicity." *Journal of Philosophical Research* 41: 333–69.
Wolff, Ernst. 2017. "Decolonizing Philosophy. On the Protests in South African Universities." *Books and Ideas*, 15 May 2017, French original in *La Vie des idées*, 28 octobre 2016. ISSN: 2105–3030. http://www.booksandideas.net/Decolonizing-Philosophy.html, last accessed 5 February 2021.
Wolff, Ernst. 2019. "Adam Small's Shade of Black Consciousness." In *Philosophy on the Border. Decoloniality and the Shudder of the Origin*, edited by Leonard Praeg, 112–47. Pietermaritzburg: UKZN Press.
Wolff, Ernst. 2020. *Mongameli Mabona. His life and work*. Leuven: Leuven University Press.
Wolff, Ernst. Forthcoming 2021. *Lire Ricœur depuis la périphérie. Décolonisation, modernité, herméneutique*. Bruxelles: Éditions de l'Université de Bruxelles.
Wolff, Ernst. Forthcoming 2021. "Ricœur's Polysemy of Technology and its Reception." In *Interpreting Technology. Ricœur on Questions Concerning Ethics and Philosophy of Technology*, edited by Mark Coeckelbergh, Wessel Reijers and Alberto Romele. Lanham: Rowman and Littlefield.

Author Index

Abrutyn, Seth 4, 58, 105
Académie Tunisienne de sciences, des lettres et des arts 178
Achebe, Chinua 182
Adler, Paul S. 105
Adorno, Theodor 238
Apel, Karl-Otto 234, 240, 261 f.
Arendt, Hannah 22, 74, 109, 133–137, 222, 224
Aristotle 12, 88 f., 92, 113, 140 f., 143, 240, 250, 253, 265, 269
Arkoun, Mohammed 188
Austin, J. L. 46 f.

Badie, Bertrand 21, 25, 172
Badiou, Alain 167
Baert, Patrick 4
Beck, Ulrich 126 f.
Benjamin, Walter 66
Benzecry, Claudio E. 4
Bernet, Rudolf 96
Bernstein, Richard 249
Bezuidenhout, Andries 234 f., 237
Bollenbeck, Georg 60
Bolouri, Maryam 34, 39
Boltanski, Luc 5–7, 17, 25, 90, 108, 130, 160, 162, 192 f., 196 f., 210, 243, 271
Borradori, Giovanna 22 f.
Bouamama, Saïd 172
Bourdieu, Pierre 40, 61, 67, 69, 92, 129, 143, 251 f.
Bourgeois, Patrick 249
Boy, Stalin 40
Brandt, Willy 25, 195
Brandtner, Christof 105, 111, 116
Breitling, Andris 251
Breviglieri, Marc 89, 96, 98, 156
Breyer, Thiemo 129
Bryant, Christopher 129, 131
Bucholc, Marta 59, 63
Burchardt, Tania 101

Calhoun, Craig 129

Cantelli, Fabrizio 84, 270
Caron, François 76
Carreira Da Silva, Filipe 4
Carstens, Alvara 130
Castells, Manuel 264
Castonguay, Simon 129
Castoriadis, Cornelius 5, 55
Clark, Martin 227
Coleman, James 106
Constant, Benjamin 263
Corcuff, Philippe 4, 129
Crenshaw, Edward 202, 205
Cronin, Jeremy 191
Crozier, Michel 103

Dale-Ferguson, Darryl Scott 130
Dallmayr, Fred 196
Danto, Arthur 140 f.
Davidson, Scott 7, 16
Davis, Gerald 105, 117
Davis, Natalie Zemon 199, 202, 230
de Villiers, Etienne 11, 243, 263
Debray, Régis 5, 17 f., 33–43, 45–50, 53–56, 80–82, 123, 151, 254
Delanty, Gerard 4
Delmotte, Florence 62 f.
Deranty, Jean-Philippe 194
Derrida, Jacques 22–24, 230
Dickinson, David 230
Dosse, François 7, 98, 172
Drèze, Jean 115
Dubet, François 156
Dunning, Michael 59, 63
Düwell, Marcus 263

Ebers, Mark 105
Elias, Norbert 5 f., 18, 58–63, 78, 148

Fanon, Frantz 201, 229, 241
Fletcher, Jonathan 63
Foucault, Michel 54, 76, 124, 129, 149
Franssen, Maarten 73

Friedberg, Erhard 103, 110
Friedland, William 172

Gandhi, Mahatma 10 f., 49, 201, 209
Geertz, Clifford 6 f., 67, 128 f.
Genard, Jean-Louis 84, 270
Gethmann, Carl Friedrich 250
Giddens, Anthony 5, 20, 58, 92, 96, 98 f., 123, 128–131, 144–158, 249 f., 254
Greisch, Jean 8, 16
Grimmler, Antje 249
Grondin, Jean 55
Grunwald, Armin 263
Gutema, Bekele 186

Habermas, Jürgen 22–24, 33, 67, 130, 151, 222
Hann, Chris 103
Hart, Keith 103
Hartung, Gerald 271
Haudricourt, André-George 69
Hegel, G.F.W. 12, 67, 135, 194
Heidbrink, Ludger 264, 267
Heidegger, Martin 68, 76, 88, 96, 137, 143, 198, 249–251
Hick, Rod 101
Hirsch, Alfred 267
Honneth, Axel 24, 130, 135, 142, 193–195, 215, 233, 241
Hountondji, Paulin 182, 184, 186
Hubig, Christoph 4
Husserl, Edmund 96, 111, 131, 134, 261

Ihde, Don 73, 90, 99
Imbusch, Peter 192
Innes, Robert 249

Jaeger, Friedrich 264, 271
Jaffré, Bruno 211
Jary, David 129, 131
Joas, Hans 5, 15 f., 22, 86, 129, 131, 141, 162, 249
Jonas, Hans 58, 78, 261 f., 264
Judge, Timothy 105, 117, 121–123

Kacou oi Kacou, Vincent Davy 179
Kalyvas, Stathis 202, 205

Kaspersen, Lars Bo 131
Kertscher, Jens 249
Kieser, Alfred 105
Kneer, Georg 4
Knöbl, Wolfgang 5, 15 f., 129, 131, 264, 271
Koestler, Arthur 10
Kolarz, Peter 129
Koloma Beck, Teresa 58
Korte, Hermann 58, 60
Krämer, Sybille 37, 42, 50
Kroes, Peter 73
Kumar, Krishan 174, 187

Laitinen, Arto 192
Lambert, Rob 234 f., 237
Latour, Bruno 71, 252
Lenin, Vladimir 13
Lenk, Hans 65 f., 263 f., 266
Leroi-Gourhan, André 69, 91
Lévi-Strauss, Claude 6
Lévinas, Emmanuel 137, 233, 261, 268
Lévy, Pierre 35
Lévy-Bruhl, Lucien 263
Liniger-Goumaz, Max 225
Lockwood, David 116, 151
Loh, Janina 263 f.
Loyal, Steven 149
Luhmann, Niklas 127, 141
Lyotard, Jean-François 137

Macamo, Elísio 127, 264, 270
Machalek, Richard 58
MacIntyre, Alasdair 19, 105, 140–142, 144, 158
Madu, Raphael Okechukwu 179
Majastre Christophe 62 f.
Mandela, Nelson 5, 24 f., 191 f., 200–212, 244, 266
Mannheim, Karl 6
Maring, Matthias 263 f.
Martin, Michael 58
Martucelli, Danilo 60, 62
Marx, Karl 13, 22, 54 f., 149
Mauss, Marcel 40, 69, 87 f., 251
McLuhan, Marshall 41
Mennell, Stephen 59 f., 63

Merleau-Ponty, Maurice   9–11, 44, 69, 77, 91, 146, 195, 213
Merzeau, Louise   35, 38 f.
Mesure, Sylvie   261
Micheelsen, Arun   7
Michel, Johann   8, 16, 54, 93, 98, 129, 140, 143
Miconi, Andrea   36
Monteil, Pierre-Olivier   8, 13, 100, 220
Mouzelis, Nicos   131, 151
Mudimbe, Valentin Yves   7, 24, 183
Murray, Montagu   66, 77

Ndaywel è Nsiem, Isidore   186
Ngangala, Jacques Balade Tongamba   40, 184
Nkombe Oleko   179, 184
Nizet, Jean   131
Nussbaum, Martha   101

Obenga, Théophile   181
Okere, Theophilus   179
Okolo Okonda   5, 27, 40, 164, 179–190, 258
Okrent, Mark   250
O'Neill, Shane   194
Oyedola, David   186

Pakaluk, Michael   92, 253, 265
Panayotova, Plamena   129
Papoulias, Constantina   50
Peires, Jeffrey   183 f.
Powell, Walter W.   105, 111, 116
Preisendörfer, Peter   105, 119, 122

Rabinbach, Anson   79
Rammert, Werner   4
Raub, Werner   106
Rawls, John   109, 135 f., 154, 223
Reader, Keith   34
Ricœur, Paul.   4–20, 24–28, 33, 36, 42 f., 45–57, 61, 63 f., 66–68, 70–72, 75, 83–87, 89 f., 93 f., 97–101, 104–118, 121 f., 125 f., 128–144, 146 f., 151 f., 154–158, 167–182, 185–200, 202, 208–210, 212, 214–226, 228–230, 232 f., 236–242, 244, 247 f., 251 f., 254, 256, 259 f., 262, 265
Ritzer, George   129, 131

Robbins, Stephen   105, 117, 121–123
Robeck, Johannes   4
Robison, Kristopher   202, 205
Roman, Sébastien   129
Ropohl, Günther   72, 263, 265
Rosberg, Carl   172

Sacchetti, Francesca   129
Sachsse, Hans   263
Schatzki, Theodore   92, 144
Schneider, Ute   264
Schroer, Markus   4
Schütz, Alfred   108 f., 113, 128 f., 131, 151
Schwinn, Thomas   111
Scott, James   202, 205
Scott, Richard   105, 117
Sen, Amartya   101, 115, 118, 130
Sennet, Richard   249
Séris, Jean-Pierre   41, 73
Serra, Marcello   36
Shicha, Luo   36, 39, 41
Sigaut, François   91
Simpson, Thula   201
Smet, A. J.   180
Snyman, Johan   167, 215
Sophocles   233, 238
Stahl, Titus   163
Stepnisky, Jeffrey   129, 131
Stevens, Simon   201, 211
Stones, Rob   131, 149, 153, 157
Strum, Shirley   252
Suttner, Raymond   191

Taiwò, Olúfémi   264
Taylor, Charles   54, 67, 252
Tellez, Jean   34 f.
Thévenot, Laurent   6 f., 88, 90, 110, 130, 156, 193, 196, 198 f., 251, 271
Thompson, John   6, 43, 130,
Tilly, Charles   206, 209, 271
Truc, Gérôme   143
Truth and Reconciliation Commission   211
Tshiamalenga Ntumba   180
Turnley, Melinda   39

van Binsbergen, Wim   81
van de Poel, Ibo   73

van der Pot, Johan Hendrik   255
van Krieken, Robert   59–61
Vandenberghe, Frédéric   34, 37, 39, 49
Vansina, Frans   178
Vansina, Jan   184
Verbeek, Peter-Paul   73
Vogelmann, Frieder   269 f.
Von Holdt, Karl   5, 225–228, 231–233, 241, 243 f., 267
Voss, Thomas   106

Wagner, Peter   193

Weber, Max   6, 11–13, 29, 111, 130, 132, 212 f., 220 f., 223, 225, 232, 240–243, 261, 263 f., 267
Webster, Edward   234 f., 237
Weil, Eric   12 f., 220 f.
Weischedel, Wilhelm   261
Werner, Micha   263, 265
Winnicott, Donald   141
Witte, Daniel   59, 63
Wolff, Ernst   9, 11, 22, 27, 40, 56, 62, 65 f., 68, 77–79, 86–88, 95, 155, 168, 190, 193, 197, 217, 220, 234, 240 f., 243, 249–251, 255, 260 f., 264 f., 268

Subject Index

action   3f., 6, 9f., 11, 13–26, 28f., 33–35, 43f., 46–49, 51–57, 62–64, 67–74, 77f., 83f., 86–93, 95–101, 103–107, 109–128, 130, 132, 134f., 137–164, 168, 170, 184, 188f., 191–199, 202–204, 206–214, 217, 219–225, 228–232, 234–236, 238–243, 247–271
– actor, agent   3, 9, 15, 19f., 23–25, 33, 36, 65, 67–70, 73, 75–78, 83, 87–100, 104–106, 108, 110, 112121, 123–125, 127, 130, 132f., 134–142, 143–151, 153, 154f., 157–159, 161, 185, 194, 196, 199, 230, 238, 240–244, 248, 250–258, 260, 262, 265f., 268–270
– agency   19f., 71, 73, 103–105, 112, 116, 118f., 121–124, 144, 146, 148f., 159f., 234, 236, 249, 258, 267–270
– collective agency   110, 114, 116, 118f., 124, 253
adverbial increments   90, 92, 111, 122, 159, 253, 265, 268
advisory bodies   106, 112, 114
African philosophy   179–184, 186f.
ambiguity   9, 17, 20, 25f., 55, 62, 125, 137, 140, 150, 154, 161, 179, 211f., 217, 227, 229f., 233f., 247, 255, 258, 266, 269–271.
anthropology   6–8, 16, 18, 20, 24, 26, 57, 60, 62, 66f., 70, 79, 91, 103, 134, 163f., 181, 189, 216, 218, 239f., 244, 248, 258–260
anti-colonialism   169f., 173
appropriation   18, 36, 44–46, 48, 50–53, 71, 74, 80, 106, 178, 184
attestation   26, 87, 92, 94–96, 113–116, 120, 124, 167, 192, 217, 219, 237–241, 244, 248, 253f., 256, 268f.
augmentation   21, 61, 90f., 99f., 121, 123, 137, 153, 178, 211, 234, 247, 269
authority   5, 40, 117, 133, 136–140, 149, 153, 157, 220, 271

autonomy   18, 36, 40, 45–49, 51–53, 56, 61, 71–75, 80, 85, 158, 171, 222, 235, 249
awareness   10f., 29, 97, 127, 144, 168, 170f., 187, 189, 209, 256

Bandung Afro-Asian conference   171–173
bodily technics   39–41, 44, 68f., 72, 87–89, 95, 250f.
body   40f., 44, 69, 78, 87–89, 96f., 19f., 147–149, 157, 159, 240, 251–253

capabilities   3–5, 8, 12, 15–21, 26–28, 33f., 54f., 57, 65, 67, 70, 77, 83–105, 110–126, 128–131, 134f., 137, 146f., 153–161, 176, 181, 185, 188f., 192, 194, 207f., 210, 212f., 219, 222f., 225, 229, 231, 234f., 237f., 240, 242, 247f., 250f., 253–260, 262, 265–270
– capability deprivation   101, 160
– social capabilities   20, 106, 114f., 118
civilizing processes   18, 58f., 61, 63
clothes   40–43, 52, 174
colonization   59, 63, 168–171, 175, 177, 182, 187, 210, 264
communication   17f., 34–42, 45f., 48f., 56f., 72, 85, 99, 150f., 158, 266
competence   24f., 57, 71, 94f., 97, 101, 114, 120, 122, 145, 147, 158, 161, 168, 191f., 196f., 199, 207–210, 268
compromise   15, 20, 24, 29, 90, 122, 125, 164, 189, 193, 195–197, 199, 204, 209–212, 218, 223, 229, 238–241, 243, 259, 266
configuration   18, 66, 70, 72–77, 80, 107, 112f., 255
consequences (unintended, unexpected)   91, 96, 111, 122, 125, 133f.,148f., 154, 211f., 247, 254
constraint   20, 61, 115f., 132f., 135, 143, 149–151, 153f., 156–158, 212, 218, 224, 228, 231, 241, 252–254, 269
conveyor   36–39, 43f., 49, 51–53, 80

Subject Index — **293**

critique   5 10, 12, 17, 23, 28, 74, 84, 127, 159–164, 170, 175, 177, 182, 185, 187, 189, 217, 255f., 259, 271
culture   4, 18f., 23f., 27, 41f., 44, 48, 57f., 60, 63, 65–67, 69, 74f., 78–82, 118, 121, 159, 170–190, 211, 253, 258f.

decolonization   16, 27, 170–173, 177–179, 189
democracy   14, 25f., 125, 191, 215–219, 222f., 225–228, 231–233, 239, 242f.
– violent democracy   26, 216f., 222f., 225–233, 237f., 243f., 267
dialogue   22f., 27, 35, 38, 40, 46, 48, 56, 76, 79–82, 175, 180, 186–189, 239
discipline   5, 7, 14, 23, 34–36, 54, 57, 76, 88, 149, 263, 269
discourse   46–50, 71, 79f., 87, 215, 232, 235, 257
distantiation   45f., 150, 152, 158, 247f., 254

edge   25–27, 153, 167f., 175, 177, 188f., 213–216, 219, 224f., 228–231, 234, 236, 238f., 241–243, 270
efficacy   8–11, 13–15, 28f., 35, 41, 49–51, 53, 56, 62, 69, 79f., 83, 88, 126, 140, 150, 159f., 194, 208–211, 213, 216, 219, 223, 227, 236, 239f., 247, 263
– symbolic efficacy   17–19, 33, 47, 49–51, 53f., 57, 80, 159, 161, 164, 211
enablement   61, 140, 149–151, 153, 158, 161, 234, 241, 247, 252–254, 269
equivalence   193f., 196f., 199, 202–204, 206, 210, 260
ethics   3f., 8–11, 14f., 17, 20f., 28f., 54, 78f., 84, 88, 92, 106, 114, 130, 142f., 155f., 161–164, 181, 192, 194, 196, 207f., 210, 213, 217, 219–221, 223f., 229f., 233f., 236–240, 242–244, 247f., 253, 258f., 261f., 264–266, 268, 270
– ethics of conviction   11, 29, 230
eurocentrism   27, 173
explanation   52f., 106, 163, 247
exteriority   160, 213, 268
– complex exteriority   17, 161f., 271
– simple exteriority   17, 160–162, 207, 255, 257, 271

facilitation   71, 73–76, 111, 117, 121, 149, 157, 214, 224, 234, 242, 258
familiarity   67, 69f., 251f.
figuration   60–62, 148
finitude   19, 84, 92–94, 96, 124, 176, 222, 268
flux   65, 89, 95–97, 144f., 147, 154f., 247, 249f., 252, 254
forgetting   64, 86, 121, 123, 127f., 133, 136–139, 141
fragility   63, 87, 94, 120, 127, 135, 164, 189, 211, 218f., 221f., 234f., 242, 267–271

globalization   21, 27, 173f., 177, 183, 186f.

habitus   8, 18f., 40, 58, 61, 63, 65, 68–70, 74–78, 87f., 117, 120, 129, 143, 251f., 255, 269
hermeneutics   4, 6, 8, 16–20, 26f., 33–35, 37, 42–47, 49–57, 63f., 66–68, 71, 75, 77, 79f., 83–86, 89, 95, 97–99, 101, 104, 106f., 114, 117, 128–132, 135, 146, 154–158, 161–164, 167, 176–180, 182, 184f., 188–190, 196, 208, 214, 216, 218, 220, 222f., 235, 238–240, 242, 244, 247, 250, 256, 258, 260, 269
– double hermeneutics   147, 154, 248
hominization   18, 58, 62, 79, 82, 91
– anthropogenetic factors   18, 62, 70
horizon   70, 75f., 91f., 96f., 142, 194, 237, 239, 243, 266
– practical horizon   19, 91f., 95, 124, 253

imputation   83f., 86, 89, 97, 100, 121f., 208, 222, 229, 240f., 248, 256f., 260
incapabilities   16, 19f., 43, 65, 83, 86–88, 90–101, 105, 112, 119–127, 130, 148, 159, 191, 222, 241, 247, 250, 253f., 256, 266, 268, 270
innovation   44, 71, 76, 113, 122, 266
institutions   3, 6, 14, 17, 19, 25f., 36, 43, 49, 53, 62f., 73, 75, 80, 83–85, 90f., 97f., 100f., 104, 106f., 109f., 113, 118, 128, 130–140, 147, 149, 152–161, 200,

208, 213–217, 221–229, 231–234, 236, 238, 242, 254, 256 f., 266, 269–271
– institutionalization   113, 138, 205, 233, 236, 243
integration   21, 110, 116, 151, 153
– social integration   98 f., 116, 136, 151, 153, 155
– systemic integration   99, 116, 151, 153
interpretation   3 f., 817, 24, 27, 33, 45, 47, 49–55, 57, 72, 75, 92, 124, 126, 142, 159, 167, 188, 198, 207 f., 211, 213, 247, 250–252, 255–257

justification   3, 15, 17, 29, 90, 114, 171, 193, 196 f., 199 f., 203, 207, 211, 213, 223, 266, 270 f.

life   3, 5 f., 12 f., 21, 25, 50, 62 f., 65–67, 69, 72, 77, 79, 81, 88 f., 96 f., 100, 103, 112 f., 115 f., 118, 135, 137, 139, 141–144, 148, 152, 155 f., 163, 167 f., 171, 174, 179, 183, 185, 189–191, 195 f., 202 f., 211–217, 219, 223–225, 227–229, 231, 233–242, 247, 251, 257, 259, 263, 267
– narrative unity of human life   112 f., 140 f.
logistics   37, 47, 235

means   3, 8–15, 17–22, 26, 28, 43 f., 48–50, 52, 54–58, 60, 63–65, 67–70, 72–86, 90, 97, 99–101, 103–105, 116–121, 123, 125, 128–130, 134, 137, 139, 142, 153, 157–161, 163, 171, 185, 187 f., 194 f., 200–204, 207–211, 213, 215 f., 219, 223 f., 231–234, 236, 240, 242–244, 247–259, 262, 265–270
mediaspheres   38–40, 42, 44 f., 49, 55 f., 181
mediology   17 f., 3357, 80, 161, 258
medium   18, 36 f., 39–46., 48–53, 55 f., 85, 99, 148 f., 152, 221, 266
mnemonics   40, 43, 64
modernisation   171, 175, 187
modernity   6, 27, 126, 131, 170, 173–175, 177–180, 183, 185–189, 218, 220, 263 f., 267, 271
monitoring   75, 96, 145 f., 207, 250–252

morality   15, 54, 73, 163 f., 168, 194, 199 f., 203, 219, 221, 227, 233–241, 243 f., 259, 266, 268

narrative, narrativity   18, 54, 62–64, 66, 68, 71—75, 78, 83 f., 86, 106—110, 112—115, 121, 140 f., 207, 222, 248, 255–257
nationalism   107, 169–172
nihilism   163 f., 174, 179, 189, 264
non-equivalence   25, 195–197, 199, 202–204, 206, 209
non-violence   9–11, 15, 194 f., 200–206, 209–212, 237
– states of peace   24 f., 192 f., 195–199, 202, 208, 210
norm, normativity   8, 12, 14, 22, 28 f., 59, 62, 67 f., 73, 77, 88, 113, 126, 153, 156 f., 159–163, 169 f., 174, 192, 195, 198, 202, 206–208, 210, 212, 215, 229, 231, 233 f., 236–238, 240, 243, 248 f., 255 f., 258–264, 266, 270 f.

organization   13, 20, 37, 47 f., 56, 80, 91, 97, 103–105, 107, 111–114, 116–119, 121–125, 127, 140 f., 158–160, 205, 208, 235, 253, 266, 269
organized action   19, 91, 103–105, 110–114, 116 f., 119, 121–126, 140, 159–161, 224, 253 f., 257, 266, 270

paradox   13–14, 17, 44, 63, 92, 100 f., 124–126, 135, 138 f., 160 f., 169, 171, 175, 201, 219, 221, 258, 266, 269, 271
– institutional paradox   100, 138 f., 158, 160 f., 234, 258
– political paradox   13–15, 100 f., 125, 139, 201, 219–221, 226
– organizational paradox   124—126, 160 f., 258
– technical paradox   44, 92, 100 f., 125, 140, 158, 160 f., 258, 269, 271
participation   45, 51, 60, 109 f., 111, 126, 133, 135–137, 139, 154 f., 215, 224, 227, 254, 259
– participatory belonging   20, 105–107, 111

Subject Index — **295**

plurality   12, 27, 61, 65, 99, 109, 125, 134, 164, 172–174, 177, 179, 217, 232, 258, 268, 271
politics   8, 12–14, 18, 21f., 36, 53f., 109, 123, 127, 129, 136–138, 159, 168, 171f., 174, 182, 198f., 201f., 206f., 209, 212f., 217–222, 225–227, 230, 233, 237, 239, 241–243, 261, 263–265, 267f.
– geopolitics   21, 27, 171, 188f.
– the political   12, 14f., 22, 26f., 84, 100f., 125, 131, 135, 138f., 173, 191, 201f., 205, 208, 216f., 219, 221, 223, 238, 241, 244
power   12–14, 22f., 54, 60–63, 73, 75, 87, 93, 100f., 109, 111, 118, 121–125, 133–139, 146f., 149, 151, 153f., 157, 159f., 169, 172, 175, 188, 191, 195, 198, 200, 203, 205, 211f., 220f., 224, 226–228, 233, 235, 237, 243, 267
– power-in-common   121, 133f., 138f., 158, 221
practices   3, 17, 19, 22, 38, 40, 42, 72, 74, 77f., 88, 92, 98, 105, 112–116, 118, 130, 132, 134, 138, 140–144, 148, 150–152, 155, 157, 163, 197, 202, 226–228, 231, 233, 241, 251, 266, 271
praxis   7, 37, 62, 73, 88, 90, 140, 155, 164, 180, 184f., 249, 258
prefiguration   18, 66–68, 70f., 255
proletarian   10f., 22, 187, 210
prop   8, 36–38, 41–43, 47f., 64, 67, 85, 121, 173
prophet   10f., 212
protest   3, 16, 21f., 24f., 49, 103, 169, 211, 221, 226f., 231–235, 237, 240–243
proverbs   179–185
prudence   15, 26, 78, 83, 114, 199, 216, 218f., 223, 225, 229, 232, 234f., 238–240, 243, 247, 259f.

quasi-characters   106–108, 110–114, 116, 118, 121, 123f., 126f., 132

readability   67
reading   7, 36, 39, 42, 46, 50f., 53–55, 66, 71f., 74f., 80f., 85, 184f.
reception   5f., 34, 37, 43f., 50f., 55f., 58, 67, 80f., 179

recognition, misrecognition   6, 11, 24f., 87–89, 93–96, 101., 108, 115, 126, 169, 192–199, 208, 210, 241f., 252, 262
recursiveness   148f.
reduction   45, 73, 90f., 96, 100, 123, 133, 257
reference   52, 64f., 72, 75f.
– threefold reference   52, 76f.
refiguration   18, 66, 73f., 255
respect   84, 101, 196, 229, 243, 256
responsibility   11, 28f., 83, 97, 100, 112, 168, 204f., 212f., 240, 243, 247f., 257, 259–271
risk   82, 122, 124, 126f., 160, 172, 189, 203, 211, 213, 229, 242, 263, 270
roles   10f., 78, 107, 110, 113f., 117, 136, 159, 171, 195, 198, 254, 257, 267
routine   88, 92, 124, 146–148, 155f.

sabotage   194, 200–202, 204–206, 209, 211f., 223, 237
skill, know-how   19, 38, 64f., 70, 75f., 78, 83f., 88, 90, 96, 98, 100, 144, 157, 250–252, 254f., 266
social death   189, 229, 236, 238, 242
social science   5–7, 10, 18, 22, 28, 55f., 66, 106f., 126, 147, 160, 164, 192, 213, 216, 244, 247, 269f.
social theory   4–9, 15–17, 20, 33, 55, 58, 97f., 128f., 132f., 135, 137, 144, 147f., 154f., 159f., 164, 193, 201, 247, 249, 255, 263
sociology   6, 17f., 25f., 60, 71, 105f., 108, 122, 129, 131, 141, 149, 151, 193, 196, 213, 216, 220, 240, 243, 267
speaking   36, 38, 45, 47f., 84f., 87, 112, 148f., 248, 256f.
– spoken   36, 38, 40f., 45f., 48f., 85
speech acts   46f., 85
stories   63–66, 69, 72, 74f., 89, 255
strategy   4, 11, 18, 22, 25, 29, 37, 47, 56, 80, 82, 117, 122f., 145, 173, 188, 194, 201–210, 212–214, 219, 229–232, 234, 236f., 239f., 243, 265

structuration 20, 58, 98, 128–131, 144, 147, 149 f., 154 f., 157 f.
– duality of structure 20, 99, 130, 147, 149 f., 154 f.
symbolics 16, 67, 80, 187, 210, 219

technicity 3–5, 14–22, 27 f., 40, 57, 62–66, 68–71, 74 f., 78, 80, 83, 86–88, 91, 93–95, 98–100, 103 f., 120, 124 f., 140, 155, 159–162, 164, 189, 197, 202, 207 f., 212, 234, 240, 243, 247–252, 255 f., 258–263, 265, 267–271
– primary technicity 95 f., 155, 250–252
– secondary technicity 95 f., 122, 155, 250 f., 253
techniques 14, 39, 41, 44, 47, 69, 87–91, 125, 221, 251
technology 4, 9, 11 f., 16, 18, 22, 36, 38 f., 49, 53 f., 56 f., 61 f., 64–66, 68, 71–82, 86 f., 90, 95, 100, 117, 155, 174, 197, 209 f., 234, 240, 243, 249–251, 255, 263 f., 266
– technical disposition 18, 251
teleology 141, 143, 146, 155 f., 259, 262
– purposiveness 97, 143, 145
– teleological scheme of action 20, 128, 141 f., 154, 159, 250–252
terrorism 9, 11, 22 f., 63, 186, 202, 204–206, 213, 233, 242
text 6 f., 9, 11, 13, 15–18, 33 f., 37, 40, 43, 45–56, 64, 66, 71–73, 75 f., 85, 89, 107, 110 f., 128–130, 132, 134, 137, 143, 145, 147 f., 157 f., 167, 176, 178, 181, 183, 191, 199–201, 217, 220, 225, 229, 247, 251

transmission 18, 34, 36–51, 55–57, 65 f., 72, 74, 78–83, 123, 138, 151, 159, 161, 183 f., 194, 211, 251, 254, 256
typology 22, 68, 86, 134, 193, 197, 208, 218 f., 229, 249, 252

uncertainty 10–14, 20, 91 f., 124, 126, 142 f., 154–156, 159, 161, 164, 189, 207, 229, 254, 261, 263, 266 f., 271
usability 72 f.

validity 12 f., 41, 57, 90, 161–163, 207, 256, 260, 262–264
vigilance 18, 53, 55, 57 f., 156, 159, 189, 258
violence 3, 9–13, 21–26, 62 f., 99, 109, 136–138, 147, 154, 159, 168 f., 177 f., 191 f., 194 f., 197, 200–213, 215–217, 219–234, 236–244, 257, 261, 266 f.
– ethics of limited violence 12, 14, 125, 209, 221, 244
– violent action 16, 26, 192, 200, 202–206, 209, 212, 216, 219, 222, 229, 233, 242 f.
virtue 12, 18, 78 f., 89, 92, 168 f., 240, 253, 265, 269

world 5 f., 11, 18, 21, 27, 36, 40–45, 51–53, 58, 60, 64 f., 67–70, 74–76, 81 f., 108 f., 122, 127, 129, 131, 146, 148, 156, 159, 168–170, 173–175, 177–183, 185 f., 188–190, 198, 208, 212 f., 220, 222, 226–228, 234 f., 247, 249, 255, 260, 263 f.
worldliness 18 f., 58, 65, 74, 77
writing 10, 36, 39 f., 45–50, 59, 66, 71 f., 74, 85, 135, 141, 182 f., 190, 213

www.ingramcontent.com/pod-product-compliance
Lightning Source LLC
Chambersburg PA
CBHW031309150426
43191CB00005B/139